Post-War Babies

Sputnik Generation

Pepsi Generation

LOVE GENERATION

Now Generation

Protest Generation

Woodstock Generation

New Age

&, in their twenties and thirties,
they've only just begun...

"A POPULARIZED STUDY IN THE VANCE PACKARD TRADITION...Along the way, it makes the science of demography seem like the liveliest read around."

Publishers Weekly

"WITH FLAIR AND SENSITIVITY, Landon Jones has written of the baby boom generation...tracing its profound impact on American life."

Charles Westoff, Director,
Office of Population Research
Princeton University

"TRIVIA FREAKS, NOSTALGIA JUNKIES, CHAUVINIST BABY BOOMERS, this is your finest hour. Finally somebody has recognized who's *really* running the show."

Playboy

GREAT EXPECTATIONS

America and the
Baby Boom Generation

Landon Y. Jones

BALLANTINE BOOKS • NEW YORK

For Sarah

The author is grateful for the permission to quote from the following materials:

"Old Friends" (Paul Simon) © 1968 by Paul Simon. Used by permission.

"My Generation," words and music by Peter Townshend, © 1965 Fabulous Music Ltd., London, England, TRO-Devon Music, Inc., New York, controls all publication rights for the U.S.A. and Canada. Used by permission.

Lines from "Vacillation" are reprinted by permission of Macmillan Publishing Co., Inc., from *Collected Poems* of William Butler Yeats. Copyright © 1933 by Macmillan Publishing Co., Inc., renewed 1961 by Bertha Georgie Yeats.

"Rock Around the Clock" by Jimmy DeKnight and Max C. Freedman, © 1953 by Meyers Music Corp. Used by permission.

"Alice's Restaurant" by Arlo Guthrie, © Copyright 1966, 1967 by Appleseed Music Inc. All Rights Reserved. Used by permission.

Library of Congress Catalog Card Number: 80-14769

ISBN 0-345-29750-4

This edition published by arrangement with Coward, McCann & Geoghegan, Inc.

Manufactured in the United States of America

First Ballantine Books Edition: October 1981

Contents

As is the generation of leaves, so too of men:
At one time the wind shakes the leaves to the ground,
* but then the flourishing woods*
Gives birth, and the reason of spring comes into existence
So it is of the generations of men, which alternately
* come forth and pass away.*

—Homer, *Iliad*

"*. . . and as you leave these tranquil, ivied walls to face
the stern realities of life . . .*"

Drawing by Carl Rose; © 1947, 1975 The New Yorker Magazine, Inc.

Introduction: The Pig and the Python

This book is about the generation of the baby boom. It is the story of the group of Americans who have changed us more than any other. The change began after World War II, when the first boom baby was born, and will continue until sometime after the middle of the next century, when the last survivor of the baby boom will die. No single generation has had more impact on us than the baby boom, and no single person has been untouched. The baby boom is, and will continue to be, the decisive generation in our history.

From the beginning, it was something unique in American life and we did not know what to call it. We tried to cover it with labels. War Babies. Spock Babies. Sputnik Generation. Pepsi Generation. Rock Generation. Now Generation. Love Generation. Vietnam Generation. Protest Generation. Me Generation. But the names did not stick because the baby boom is a moving target. At every age it takes on a different character and presents us with a different set of problems. What the names we have given the boom generation most accurately describe is its continuing dominance in our national life.

It is, above all, the biggest, richest, and best-educated generation America has ever produced. The boom babies were born to be the best and the brightest. They were the first raised in the new suburbs, the first with new televisions, the first in the new high schools. They were twice as likely as their parents to go to college and three times as likely as their grandparents. They forced our economy to regear itself to feed, clothe, educate, and house them. Their collective purchasing power made fads overnight and built entire industries. In the 1980s, the boom children are continuing their imperious ways. They are turning a youth-centered society into an adult-centered one as they make their particular concerns, whether housing

1

prices or tax reform, into national obsessions. They are a generational tyranny.

The boom generation has simultaneously shaped the lives of all of the individuals within it. They were born into the biggest generation in history and have been forever affected—often adversely—by the high drama of that fact. Blessed with the great expectations of affluence and education, the boom children were raised as a generation of idealism and hope. Yet they are now growing into the eighties as a generation of uncertainty, unsure about what their expectations really are, unsure about their role in society, unsure about marriage and family, unsure even about reproducing themselves.

But the fault was not in the stars nor in themselves; it was in their size. We have not found it easy to make room for the baby boom, whether in school or in the workplace. Much of our history over the past thirty years amounts to our generally unsuccessful effort to accommodate and absorb its enormous number. Our failures have undermined the generation's confidence in the older generation, the society, and ultimately its own future. Condemned to achieve its greatness en masse, the boom generation has in the end produced surprisingly few leaders or even genuine individualists. What had once seemed its greatest strength —its overwhelming size—has turned out to be its tragedy.

What *is* the baby boom? Surprisingly, there is not full agreement, even among scholars, about who or what it really is. Let me define this generation in the following way. For two centuries, the birthrate in the United States and the world has steadily declined. It is still declining. There is only one exception: the single, unprecedented aberration we call the postwar baby boom. It was not, as is often thought, a short rise in the birthrate caused by returning GIs making up for lost time. It began that way in 1946, but instead of stopping in the 1950s (as in Europe), the tidal wave of births continued, affecting all races and classes with astonishing uniformity. This national euphoria—what I shall call the "Procreation Ethic"—peaked in 1957, when more than 4.3 million babies were born. At least 4 million babies were born in each of the bumper-crop years from 1954 through 1964, the last real year of the baby binge. All totaled, 76,441,000 babies—one-third of our present population—arrived in the 19 years from 1946 through 1964.

The fertility boom is over, but the boom's babies are

2

still with us. By 1980, the 70 million survivors of the generation had reached the ages of 16 through 34. They were led by a cutting edge of persons born in 1946 who outnumbered the 1945 babies by one million. Because the boom was both preceded and followed by smaller generations, it makes a permanent but moving bulge in the population, a Goliath generation stumbling awkwardly into the future. Demographers use the vaguely discomfiting metaphor of a "pig in a python" to describe the resulting motion of the baby-boom bulge through the decades as it ages. But peristalsis, as that digestive process is called, hardly does justice to the violence and disruption felt along the way—by both pig and python. America has yet to digest its baby boom.

My purpose here is to find out what the baby boom is doing to America and to itself. This is not strictly a social history nor is it demography or psychohistory, though elements of all three are present. I prefer to call it a generational biography. It looks at history through the window of a single generation as it ages. What it reveals is an America since World War II dealing with the growth strains of a single generation. I do not think it overstates the case to say that almost every social and economic issue facing the nation today has a population dimension and that every population dimension has a baby-boom dimension.

This book is *not* the "generation gap," a shopworn idea that should have been retired long ago. But since the argument I am presenting rests on three different notions about generations, I want to say explicitly what they are.

One is that the idea of a "generation" is a useful way of looking at history. This is not the truism it might at first seem. The word is slippery enough that few people can agree on what exactly a generation is, including the people in the generation. The Bible speaks of three generations to a century, and modern demographers often define generations in terms of thirty years, or the approximate time it takes a female to replace herself by giving birth to a daughter. François Mentré and other European intellectuals around the turn of the century thought that generations had a regular rhythm of around three to a century. So did F. Scott Fitzgerald, who spoke of a gen-

3

eration as "that reaction against the fathers that seems to occur about three times in a century."

But that said nothing about *who* was in the generation. The critic Harold Rosenberg saw generations as meaningless journalistic conceits and scoffed that "belonging to a generation is one of the lowest forms of solidarity." As Rosenberg put it, "To be in favor of someone, or to act or think like him, because he was born in the same decade or two is inferior to taking out a membership in the League of Red-Headed Men." Even the "Lost Generation" of the 1920s, Rosenberg wrote, "shared few ideas deeper than raccoon coats, hip flasks, and Stutz Bearcats." At a time when some generations, like Andy Warhol's celebrities, are famous for only fifteen minutes, a generation can seem less like a valid organizing concept in history than what Kurt Vonnegut, Jr. (a favorite baby-boom author) called a *"granfalloon,"* a group of people who think they have something in common but do not. (His examples were "the Communist Party, the Daughters of the American Revolution, the General Electric Company, the International Order of Odd Fellows—and any nation, anytime, anywhere.")

Then what does make a generation? Clearly, a historical generation is not like a family or a political party, in which people are bound by kinship or commonly stated purposes. A generation is something that happens to people; it is like a social class or an ethnic group they are born into; it does not depend on the agreement of its members. Even people who disagree politically can perceive that they share a common self-awareness and a common destiny. A group's collective self-identity can become so powerful, so compelling, that it not only binds together its own members but also draws older and younger generations to its particular *Weltanschauung,* rather like iron filings attracted and held in a magnetic field.

My second assumption is that a generation is the primary agent of social change. Each generation is born in a time it shares with no other and is a product of a life experience it shares with no other. At first, the aggregate values and tastes of a rising generation—what José Ortega y Gasset called its "vital sensibility"—may be dominated by an older and more powerful generation ahead of it. But as the older generation dies off, or is de-

4

feated, the younger generation is able to carry its own world view into adulthood. Reform is thus brought organically into a society. People don't change, generations do.

We have seen this happen in our time. The rural values of nineteenth-century Americans were replaced by the urban values of their twentieth-century offspring. Unschooled parents have been replaced by educated children. European-born parents have been replaced by native-born children. These gaps are too wide to be bridged naturally and a tension develops that is not resolved until the older generation passes on. The credo of the older generation passes with it. In the next decade, for example, the last soldiers who fought "The War to End All Wars" will die and take with them that memory. Soon the living memory of the Great Depression will begin to fade and, with it, the conviction that government can intervene successfully to promote social welfare (an idea that no one who came of age in the 1970s can easily believe).

Throughout most of this century, of course, the word "generation" has meant not the mass of men but a small elite. Usually it is the intellectual and literary class which has best articulated the prevailing *Zeitgeist*. At its most trivial, it is a small band whose music, clothes, and manner can come to represent an entire generation. As Mentré observed, "The majority of men play nonspeaking roles in the great human choir and provide the backdrop for the great dress ball of history." Here I will inevitably use the phrase "boom generation" to refer exclusively to the educated elite of the middle and upper classes. But, as Ortega pointed out, the life of the prominent individuals within a generation cannot stand apart from the generation itself. If they are the fish, the mass is the sea in which they swim. The generational sensibility they share is far more significant than the things that separate them.

My third assumption is that the impact of a generation, whether on the individuals within it or on the larger culture, is directly related to its size.

It remained to demographers to introduce the idea of a generation as a *cohort*. In its original meaning, a cohort was one-tenth of a 5000-man Roman military legion. Now it has come to mean a group of people sharing a common experience over time, usually defined by year of birth (though cohorts can also be defined by year of marriage, year of entry into the labor force, and so forth).

The size of a cohort is the force that shapes its life. If successive generations are of comparable size, there can be an orderly transition of power. But if there is a generational imbalance, the delicate watchworks of a society can be jammed. If an older generation finds itself outnumbered by the "barbarians" of the young, socialization can break down. We know, for instance, that revolutionary movements have erupted after dramatic increases in the proportion of youth in a population. During the French Revolution, 40 percent of the population were between the ages of 20 and 40 and only 20 percent were over 40. Both the Protestant Reformation and the American Revolution were predominantly youthful. Totalitarian movements have traditionally been built on the backs of committed youth. In Mussolini's Italy, "Giovinezza! Giovinezza!" celebrated youth as the official Fascist hymn. What's more, the imbalance can work both ways. The failure of the Weimar Republic in Germany was due to the onslaught of Hitler youth as well as the weakness of the older generation which had been diminished both in numbers and in will by the Great War.

For the baby boomers, locked in their Brobdingnagian cohort, its size defines both their limits and possibilities. Like a proliferating species of microbe, the baby boomers *are* their environment.

These assumptions—that a generation is worth study, that a generation is the carrier of social change, and that the size of a generation is its most crucial characteristic— are the ideas that set this book in motion. If they smack of demographic determinism, it is because I know of no other way to point out what the baby boom is doing to us. But, if only to combat the clear and present danger of oversimplification that arises where I have necessarily painted with a broad brush, I want to post four warnings.

WARNING ONE. The baby boom is not monolithic. Although my argument rests on its commonality, there are distinctions within its population worth noting. The people born from 1946 through the boom's high-water mark in 1957, for example, experienced far more turbulence in their life than those born during the ebbing of the boom from 1958 through 1964. The earlier group, living on the boom's cutting edge, suffered the growing pains of a

6

world constantly straining and expanding to make room for them. Everywhere they went, from maternity wards to law schools, they saw overcrowding and short supplies. At the same time, they have always enjoyed an acute sense of their own power. The later group, however, entered a society already overexpanded by their older brothers and sisters. The biggest battles had already been fought. They had less agony—but also less ecstasy. Events like the assassination of President Kennedy mean something altogether different to them. This difference, I think, is ultimately as important as the better-known differences within the boom generation between men and women or between those who have college degrees and those who don't.

WARNING TWO. The baby boom is not the *sole* cause of everything going on here. Change is not caused by the baby boom; it is carried by it and intensified by it. The baby boomers jolted us in the sixties, but the thirties were a period of turbulence with a *small* younger generation. Of course, we might wonder what would have been the history of the thirties if the younger generation then were as big and boisterous as the generation of the sixties.

WARNING THREE. Demography is not necessarily destiny. I mention this despite the common temptation to project changes in society along with changes in population. We know that the baby-boom generation will greatly increase the proportion of the aged in America. But we cannot similarly say that the behavior we presently attribute to today's elderly will increase in like proportion. What we now think is the parochialism of the elderly may be less a function of aging than the fact that the over-sixty-five segment of our population is the least educated. It also contains the largest number of people born in other countries. In its time, the baby-boom generation will change just as many of our ideas about the old as it already has about the young.

WARNING FOUR. The baby boom is not the *only* generation to register social change today. Few historic movements, after all, are so age-specific that they can be entirely located within one generation. An event like the Vietnam War affected all generations differently, depending upon which point in its life cycle the generations were then entering. Yet every generation insists on its own uniqueness, believing its experience to be more stressful than that of any generation before it. Indeed, the concept of a generation almost requires that there will be this kind of generational chauvinism. It is useful to remember that the basis of a generation's self-image may be less substantial and more prosaic than one might imagine. The "Lost Generation" epithet that Gertrude Stein angrily gave to Hemingway and Fitzgerald and their friends was because of their ill manners. She, moreover, had heard the phrase originally used by a French garage-owner in the Midi to describe his mechanics.

The real question is whether the changes we observe around us are particular to the times or to a generation. The divorce rate for all Americans, for example, has doubled since 1970, but it has increased by 296 percent among baby-boom couples under thirty. The percentage of women working has increased at all ages, but fastest among baby-boom women. The incidence of suicide, drug use, and political cynicism are all highest among baby boomers. The impact of television, which changed the life of every family when it arrived in the early fifties, fell heaviest on the baby boomers. It was not just because the baby boomers were young and vulnerable then. Any other young generation would have been affected the same way. But, the elephantine size of the baby boom redoubled television's effect. Advertisers perceived an enormous market waiting to be tapped and accordingly shaped the medium to do it. For the baby boomers, size is the feedback loop that, more than anything else, separates their experience from all other generations.

None of the warnings I have sounded here should detract from the central proposition of this book: that the baby-boom generation is leaving a unique imprint on American life. Its power grows from its extraordinary size and the extraordinary history of its times. It has strained our institutions and itself has suffered the strains of its growth. It can expect to continue to cause and experience disruption throughout its life cycle. Yet its values will set the national temper and from its ranks will come our next generation of leaders. Because its destiny is to adapt to the changes it has forced on the world, we can expect the boom generation to continue to introduce the innovative and experimental ways of life, work, and family that have already characterized its growth. As Dr. Bergen Evans wrote, "We may be finished with the past, but the past is not finished with us."

PART I

The Army of Babies

And God blessed them, and God said unto
them, Be fruitful, and multiply, and re-
plenish the earth, and subdue it: and have
dominion over the fish of the sea, and over
the fowl of the air, and over every living
thing that moveth upon the earth.

—Genesis 1:28

Chapter 1

THE BIRTH OF THE BOOM

At one second after midnight on Tuesday, January 1, 1946, Kathleen Casey was born to a Navy machinist's wife in Philadelphia. Four seconds later into the New Year, Mark Bejcek, the son of an Army trombone player and his wife, arrived in Chicago. Neither of them was truly the first baby of the postwar era. (They were conceived several months before Japan surrendered on August 16, 1945.) But, statistically at least, Kathleen Casey and Mark Bejcek were the first glimmerings of the most extraordinary population boom in history.

In May of 1946, exactly nine months after V-J Day, births in the United States jumped from February's low of 206,387 to 233,452. In June they swelled to 242,302. In October births had spurted to 339,499 and were running at a record rate. By the end of the year, the cry of the baby was heard across the land. An all-time high of 3.4 million babies had been born in the United States— one every nine seconds—20 percent more than in 1945. Every known measure of fertility had soared dramatically as the overall population made its biggest one-year gain in history to a total of 143 million.

Suddenly pregnancy was patriotic. More than a million Army wives had waited for President Truman to "bring the boys back home" and now they and their husbands were celebrating a massive affirmation of childbearing. Marriages were booming, too, as GIs delivered on their furlough promises to the Girl Back Home. More than 2.2 million couples, twice as many as in any year before the war, said their vows in 1946 and set a nuptial record that was not equaled for 33 years. Divorces were also running at an all-time high, to be sure, as some couples untied hasty wartime unions, but that was not enough to

10

stop the ceaseless production of babies. In the next year, 1947, more than 3.8 million babies arrived, another record. To cartoonists and grandparents, it was a delightfully lusty way to end the war and roar into peacetime. They didn't know it, but these ex-soldiers and their wives were making history at home in bed that would ultimately affect the country into the next century. Before anyone could catch a breath, the baby boom was off and squalling.

Demographers were unimpressed. The rise in births was sudden, they agreed, but surely it was little other than a freakish postwar adjustment, a classic case of satisfying pent-up demand. Americans who had delayed marriage and children during the war were now making up for lost time. Look at the long-term trend, they reasoned. American fertility had declined sharply all during the twenties and early thirties. In fact, not enough women were born during the Depression to replace the women then leaving the childbearing ages. Social scientists were beginning to talk grimly about "incipient decline" and "economic maturity." Ominous wartime speculations about "race suicide" were still taken seriously, and some thinkers believed they were witnessing Oswald Spengler's "decline of the West" unfolding in their bedrooms. *Life* magazine nervously noted that "without exception every country in the Western world is dedicated in varying degrees to the policies of 'more babies'" and guessed that as early as 1970 the Soviet Union would have more men of military age than the United States, Britain, France, and Italy combined. In 1946, the Census Bureau director said that the U.S. population would not reach 163 million until the year 2000.

Academics were worried about the American woman. The eminent sociologist Talcott Parsons of Harvard thought she had discovered that "she must compete for masculine favor and cannot stand on her own feet." Her resulting insecurity produced aggression, which "underlies the widespread ambivalence among women toward the role of motherhood." Five years into the boom, David Riesman in *The Lonely Crowd* based his analysis of the "other-directed" American social character in part on a presumed incipient decline in the population.

We know now that the immediate postwar surge in births was not a blip but a beginning, the nose of the camel under the tent. But in all fairness, at the time the historical record was fully on the side of the "static population" forces (and still is, ironically, given the postboom decline in fertility). We can see this most clearly by looking back for a moment at what has happened to fertility in America over the years.

In Colonial days, America was one of the most prolifically fertile countries in history. Women were averaging eight or so births per family, and the median age in the Colonies was under 17. Children were as necessary to farmers and frontiersmen as plows: the more helping hands they had the better. Benjamin Franklin, one of the first to note his country's extraordinary growth rate, was himself one of fifteen children (by two mothers). Death rates, however, were decreasing, most dramatically among infants. The result was an exploding population that had begun to double every twenty-five years. Samuel Johnson complained that Americans were multiplying like their own rattlesnakes. The astonishing American fertility so struck a thirty-two-year-old English parson named Thomas Robert Malthus, in fact, that he cited it as the clinching proof of the notorious *Essay on the Principle of Population* he first published in 1798. To Malthus, the profligate growth of the American Colonies demonstrated his Dismal Theorem of the inevitability of human misery. The doctrine of "capital dilution" held that the more people there were, the lower their per capita income, all else equal. Adam Smith had already noted that men, like all other animals, tended to multiply in proportion to the means of their subsistence. Malthus took the argument a step further with his battle cry: "Population, when unchecked, increases in geometrical ratio. Subsistence increases only in arithmetical ratio." This meant that famine, epidemics, and war were the inevitable checks on population unless it was otherwise controlled by "moral restraint"—meaning abstinence or delayed marriage—or "vice," as he called "promiscuous intercourse, unnatural passions, violations of the marriage bed, and improper acts to conceal the consequences of irregular connections." (Nowadays we have controlled fertility in part through these "vices," but we call them sexual freedom, homosexuality, adultery, and birth control.) One of eight children, Malthus, a kind and sincere man for all his bleak doctrine, successfully limited himself to three, only one of whom survived to adulthood. (Slanderers cruelly tried to discredit him by

12

spreading the rumor that he had fathered a brood of eleven.)

The Malthusian doctrine became a sensation. Clergymen thought him blasphemous. Men like Lord Byron scoffed at Malthus's "eleventh commandment" ("Thou shalt not marry unless well"), and accused him of "turning marriage into arithmetic." Others feared a catastrophe for humankind. But such a disaster did not befall the world because something entirely different began to happen in the nineteenth century that knocked the gloom out of the Dismal Theorem. In traditional societies, birthrates and death rates remained as high as always. In Western Europe, death rates were continuing to decline. Then, amazingly, birthrates started dropping, too. At a time when contraceptive technology was undreamed of and when family planning was unthinkable—just spreading information about it was enough to bring persecution and imprisonment—millions of families were making decisions to have fewer children and were somehow succeeding.

How did this miracle come about? It was as if some extraordinary force—the demographic equivalent of Adam Smith's "Invisible Hand"—was working in the affairs of men and women. That, according to a theory developed fifty years ago, is just what happened. Here is how it worked. In preindustrial society, population growth was held in check because high birthrates were equaled by high death rates. Then, during the first stages of modernization, society gained some control over mortality. There was more food and better hygiene and medicine. Fewer children died and more people lived longer. But then the death rate was no longer balancing the high birthrate. Mothers were still turning out babies at the same rapid pace as before and the population suddenly boomed (as in Colonial America). This period of rapid population growth was the first stage of what demographers call the Demographic Transition.

Remember that the expansion was caused not because more people were born but rather because fewer were dying (as in underdeveloped countries today). The Demographic Transition was not completed and balance restored until economic development—demography's "Invisible Hand"—came into play. As a traditional, religious, rural society transformed itself into a modern, secularized, urban one, children began to lose economic

13

value. A city family did not need a houseful of twelve children to harvest the crops. In fact, in the city children were liabilities who ate more in food than they could ever produce. Moreover, many families began to realize that because more and more children survived the diseases of infancy, they did not need to produce as many to wind up with the desired total. Accordingly, they reduced their fertility—at first by following Malthus's urging by either delaying marriage or not marrying at all. (In 1890, the median age of marriage for American men was twenty-six, two years higher than it is today.) Later, in more advanced societies, fertility within marriage began to fall as education and birth control took hold. To demographers, then, the Invisible Hand was alive and well and living in European bedrooms.

Let us return now to the American experience. When the administration of President James Monroe first measured the nation's birth-rate in 1820, it was still high: women had seven or eight children apiece, of whom five survived. In 1852, a demographer named Francis Bonygne enthusiastically forecast a U.S. population of 703 million by the year 2000. Instead, the birthrate slipped steadily for almost another century. Among women who married and had children, average family size fell to just over three children by 1940. Though the drop was most precipitous in the cities, it cut across all social classes. Even blacks in the rural South experienced a similar drop in their relatively higher fertility. Yet all the while the population itself steadily increased, helped in part by waves of European immigrants.

The steepest rate of decline occurred during the relatively prosperous twenties—a fact often overlooked by those who blame the Depression for the fertility collapse. The long slide actually bottomed out during the thirties. In 1933, nine months after the economy had also scraped bottom, total births ebbed to the modern low of 2,307,000, a full 700,000 less than back in 1914. During the entire decade, the U.S. population grew by only 9 million, compared to an increase of 17 million in the twenties. It was the smallest percentage increase in American history and the lowest absolute increase since the decade of 1860–70.

Who were the women who so successfully limited their fertility? They were the grandmothers of the baby-boom

14

kids. Born in the cohorts between 1906 and 1910, they had fewer children than any other group of American women, before or since. (The books have yet to close on the current generation of mothers.) Fully 22 percent of all women born in the cohort of 1908 had no children at all, and the average for the entire cohort was only 2.27 children per woman. (As a result, the approximately four million baby-boom grandmothers who are still alive, now in their early seventies, are facing the disturbing prospect of having few children to care for them in their old age.)

What they did prove, convincingly, is that American women *could* limit the number of children they bore. Just how they did it, in an era before modern contraception, remains one of the mysteries of demography. In those days, the leading methods of birth control were either unpopular (withdrawal, abortion) or ineffective (rhythm, douche).

Many of the women were forced not to marry (the 1932 rate was the lowest since 1867) or married late. Two demographers, George Masnick and Joseph McFalls, have argued that the Depression mothers became effective contraceptors *because* they had waited longer to marry. They had delayed their marriages but not their sex lives. The only way to reconcile that conflict, and to remain socially respectable, was to develop effective contraceptive methods. In contraception, as in everything else, practice makes perfect. The contraceptive methods the Depression women learned before and early in marriage helped them prevent unwanted pregnancies all through their marriages. Interviewed now, however, these women deny that they practiced birth control to any great extent. Instead, they maintain that they steeled themselves to practice abstinence within marriage. In any case, the lesson of history seemed to be that if people are desperate enough, if the addition of another mouth to a family is enough of a hardship, if the inhibition is powerful enough, then people *will* find a way not to have children.

This impressive display of marital willpower was not heartening to those who saw in the falling birthrate a metaphor for America's own decline. We seemed to be at a turning point in our history: after closing the Western frontier in the 1890s, we were now closing another frontier of human expansiveness. If the Depression raised doubt about the inherent strength of the system, then the birth decrease seemed to confirm it. Newspapers and magazines were suddenly filled with doomsday predictions. Low fertility was blamed on everything from emancipation of females to the work of the devil. Some direly noted that the lowest birthrates belonged to the "best" classes—the urban middle class whose frugality and Protestant Ethic had built American capitalism—while only the poor and black were busily reproducing. Some sociologists proposed tax and pay incentives to promote parenthood. Others wondered seriously about financing professional "breeder" women to ensure the preservation of the species. Experts were urging, *Fortune* reported, that we "change public opinion so that the large family would be looked upon as socially admirable instead of as a butt for slightly obscene jokes." Why? Because "at least one aim of the population policy of these demographers would be to persuade the 'best' people, of all social classes and economic levels, to produce the generations that are to inherit the U.S."

Europeans took even more seriously the idea that few babies was a sign of national decay. Books appeared with apocalyptic titles like *The Menace of British Depopulation* and *The Twilight of Parenthood*. Frenchmen worried about becoming a nation of *vieillards* and instituted pronatalist policies. Italy levied a tax on bachelors (though the story that Mussolini rang church bells in the middle of the night to remind citizens of their conjugal obligations is probably apocryphal). Germany propagandized its own people about the virtues of Aryan reproduction and, after German births hit a low in 1933, the Nazis outlawed abortions, suppressed methods of birth control and gave marriage loans to couples judged to be politically "right-minded" and free from "hereditary mental or physical defects." Of all the European pronatalist policies, only Germany's had even limited success. But the idea that fertility was associated with national virility and competitive health was planted. The economist Gunnar Myrdal worried aloud in 1938 that "no other factor—not even that of peace or war—is so tremendously fatal for the long-term destinies of democracies as the factor of population. Democracy, not only as a political form but with all its content of civic ideals and human life, must either solve this problem or perish." In the postwar decade, American mothers would put this philosophy into vigorous action.

Demographers, meanwhile, were gloomily marching to what would become their Waterloo. Everywhere they saw evidence of population stagnation and decline. They had already seen an erosion in fertility lasting one hundred years. Mothers were on the verge of no longer replacing themselves. How low could it go? In 1934, Frank Lorimer and Frederick Osborn wrote that U.S. population growth would "presumably cease absolutely somewhere from twenty to forty years from now with a maximum population of some 150 millions or less." Two years later, another eminent demographer, Joseph Spengler, saw an actual decline in population in developed countries within "the next quarter-century." None other than John Maynard Keynes flatly pronounced in 1937 that "we know much more securely than we know almost any other social or economic factor relating to the future that, in the place of the steady and indeed steeply rising level of population . . . we shall be faced in a very short time with a stationary or a declining level." In 1938, the judgment of the social science community was sealed by an influential report of President Franklin Roosevelt's National Resources Committee which, after sorting over eighteen possible scenarios of the population future, came up with an estimate of 158 million in 1980, followed by a steady decline. No longer could anyone doubt this inescapable fact: American parents were not reproducing the way they used to. Our population was heading downward, perhaps sooner than anyone thought.

By the mid-thirties, the evidence seemed irrefutable that America would *never* cross the unthinkable 200 million mark (a barrier that actually fell in 1968). Demographic transition theory, not to mention sound sociological reasoning, backed it up. For one thing, America's urbanization and education seemed to be plainly and irreversibly bringing down birthrates. The more people moved to the cities, and the more they went to college, the fewer children they had. The decline of such traditional forces as religion further made people more receptive to the secular and rationalist idea of limiting their families. Children were a hindrance in the city to an educated, upwardly mobile family. Demographers had already observed that the sharpest declines in fertility

17

were in fact among the pacesetting bourgeois families. Since their middle-class values were spreading inexorably through society, thanks to mass communications, it only stood to reason that the fertility decline had not run its course. Other social changes in America clinched the argument. Contraceptive use was increasing. More and more American women were working—a record of 40 percent in 1940—and were thereby removed from the mothering market. Finally, shifts in the age distribution itself suggested decline was imminent: the number of women in the high-fertility ages of 20–29 would drop by 23 percent in the 1950s, more than enough to drastically limit the number of births.

Then, as World War II broke out, something changed. Spurred by military "good-bye marriages," births rose steadily from 1940 until 1943. The first peak came nine months after the Selective Service bill was introduced, the next was nine months after the bill passed, and another came ten months after Pearl Harbor. In 1941, the Census Bureau proudly announced the highest birthrate in a decade. In 1942, total births crossed three million for the first time.

To some, mothering was an important part of the war effort. After Rosie the Riveter finished her stint on the assembly lines, she was expected to keep up wartime production in bed. *Life* crowed that Americans were gaining in their fertility struggle with Germany's Reichmothers, headlining one story, "They Are Fighting a Birth Rate War with Hitler." As the editors summarized it, "If the trend goes on, next year may see the U.S. winning the baby war against Hitler. . . . The U.S. baby boom is bad news for Hitler." Sure enough, by 1943 American mothers had defeated Germany in the maternity-ward war, posting the highest birthrate since 1924 and delivering a record 3.1 million "furlough" babies.

Yet even in the face of burgeoning fertility, demographers clung stubbornly to their theoretical guns. Rises in births, they pointed out, were frequent during wars. Besides, the birthrate had slumped during 1944 and 1945 as soldiers shipped out overseas. In 1945, the Census Bureau looked ahead to postwar peak population of 163 million in 1965–80, then a slow decline. A month after V-J Day, *Life* had recovered from its wartime euphoria and printed a chart showing an aging U.S. population. "The U.S. will probably suffer an eight percent cut in its youth base between 1940 and 1970," the editors concluded. "Population will be stationary." A year later, Frank Notestein, the dean of American demographers, urged Americans to look beyond the transitory wartime fluctuations in the birthrate and consider instead the long-term decline. In an *Atlantic Monthly* article he confidently called "The Facts of Life," Notestein concluded, "In the next five years . . . the birthrate will almost certainly fall below its wartime level."

Few people could disagree. How was anyone to know, peering into the tunnel of the future, that the baby boom was highballing at them from the other end?

Chapter 2

THE PROCREATION ETHIC

Like most historic changes, the baby boom was either poorly understood or not noticed at all in its earliest stages. After births peaked at the then dizzying high of 3.8 million in 1947, one-third more than in 1945, they dropped back for the next three years. Demographers felt vindicated: American families had made up their wartime postponements in just two years. Now, despite an unanticipated delay, the long-term trend of declining birthrates seemed ready to reassert itself. As the academic journal *Population Index* observed, ". . . there is at least a minimum of agreement among demographers. No one anticipates the restoration of levels of fertility that could be regarded as high in a world setting."

How wrong they were. Even the reduced 1950 total of 3,645,000 births was greater than that in any year before 1945. In the decade of the 1940s, some 32 million babies were born, compared to 24 million in the previous decade. The net increase in the size of the population, 19.5 million, was twice the Census Bureau's original forecast. The rate of growth was twice that before the war and the fastest since the first decade of the century.

Some questions about the previously unassailable demographic estimates began to be heard. *Population Index* wrote uneasily, "Until recently, the course of population development in Western nations was generally believed to be well-charted and understood. This is now a matter of some doubt." One demographer, Joseph Davis of Stanford, jeered at the earlier predictions as "naive" and found demographers guilty of turning their theories into laws. Others like Frank Notestein admitted that "our earlier work may have exaggerated the decline" but held to their theoretical positions based on the Demographic Transition. The Population Reference Bureau in Washington collected statistics proving that college graduates were not doing their share of parenthood. Looking back at the Class of '24, it found in 1949 that Harvard men had only 1.74 children and Vassar girls 1.49 and worried, "Does an A.B. mean 'Abolish Babies'?"

Hardly. In the years afterward, the United States continued to turn itself into a vast maternity ward. The 1951 crop of 3,845,000 babies outran the Census Bureau's predictions by 450,000. Then 1952 topped it with a new all-time record, 3,889,000. By 1953, the population had hit 160 million, adding more people in the past six years than it had in the previous thirty. In 1954, when total births reached 4 million for the first time, the United States was producing more babies each year than the entire population in 1790. American mothers were having babies so rapidly that the Census Bureau not only was unable to predict them accurately, it was unable even to keep up with the month-to-month totals arriving in any given year.

The country was euphoric. *Fortune* announced that "Americans are merrily reproducing themselves at an unprecedented rate" and hooted that "all the prophecies about fewer young people and more old people, in this generation at least, can be thrown out of the window." No one knew why, but mothers just kept on getting pregnant. Births topped 4 million year after year. By the end of the decade, more than 40 million babies had arrived. "It seems to me," reported a thunderstruck British visitor in 1958, "that every other young housewife I see is pregnant."

The fertility boom coincided with the greatest economic expansion this country has ever seen. In June 1946, *Fortune* reported that women were lining up by the hundreds for new nylon stockings and concluded that "this is the dream era, this is what everyone was waiting through the blackouts for . . . The Great American Boom is on." After the war, Fred Vinson, the director of War Mobilization and Reconversion, boasted that "the American people are in the pleasant predicament of having to learn to live fifty percent better than they ever have before." He almost underestimated the problem. In the fifteen years from 1940 until 1955, personal income of Americans soared 293 percent from $78.5 billion to $307.5 billion. The gross national product (GNP) had doubled by the mid-fifties and the 6 percent of the world's people who lived in the United States were creating two-thirds of the world's manufactured goods and consuming one-third of the world's goods and services. Foreign investment had increased from $12 billion to $80 billion, and the budget of General Motors was bigger than Poland's. Families were floating on a sea of easy credit. From 1952 to 1956, the nation's total consumer debt ballooned from $27.4 billion to $42.5 billion, or 55 percent, as Americans went into hock to finance their split-level homes, second cars, and boats for their vacations.

That such an economic boom would come hand in hand with more babies at first seemed incomprehensible. As early as the turn of the century, French statistician Jacques Bertillon had decreed that "Wealth leads to sterility." Falling birthrates during the 1920s just seemed to confirm the folk wisdom that the rich get richer, but the poor get children. Now something new was in the air. "This kind of progress," speculated *Fortune*, "is erasing old class lines and altering desires, ambitions, tastes, and even ideals. Is it also responsible for the American's new urge to reproduce himself?" Yes, one ambitious Harvard senior seemed to be saying for his generation as he explained that his goal of six children was "a minimum production goal." Economists at the time used a similar bottom-line vocabulary, pointing out that children could no longer be considered "producer durables," generating more income through labor than they cost to feed and clothe. Instead, as one argued, "babies are viewed as a consumer durable good." The dollar costs were high, but babies could be "expected to yield a stream of psychic income through time." As Americans acquired more money to spend on this particular "consumer durable," the argument went, they faced less competition between the cost of children and the cost of living. It could only follow therefore that more babies would be born.

No European nation had anything like the American baby boom. In countries like Italy, Spain, Portugal, and Greece, the fertility decline that had begun before the war continued all but uninterrupted after it. Most other countries of Northern and Western Europe saw baby boomlets in 1946 and 1947 that initially appeared similar to the American experience. But, contrary to the United States, the European births were *only* the result of

22

pent-up baby demand. After the postwar catch-up, their birthrates subsided quickly in the late 1940s and early 1950s, only to rise again in the late 1950s, before collapsing almost totally since then.

The most intriguing comparison, however, is not with those nations that did not experience a baby boom but rather with those that did. Only three other countries—Canada, Australia, and New Zealand—experienced the same prolonged and broad-based baby boom as did the United States. All four countries made substantial recoveries from Depression-era troughs in their fertility and, by 1970, had added about one-third more people to their populations than they would have expected without baby booms.

Why? What was it about their national experience or the mood of their people that compelled them to act so differently from other countries after World War II? Some of the connections are obvious—none was invaded or bombed during World War II. But the characteristic they shared that, I think, tells us more than anything else about the psychological forces that shaped the baby boom was their great expectations. These were the countries of hope, new worlds where lives could begin again. Canada, Australia, New Zealand, and the United States were all originally settled by long-distance immigrants, people who had staked their lives on the future. All four countries, further, had both rich natural resources and a frontier open for settlement. All were spacious and were considered underpopulated. All four countries had—and *still* have—the world's highest rates of individual mobility. Fully 20 percent of the American population moves every year. Mobility is, of course, related to such economic factors as industrialization and urban development. But it is also a sign that the population still believes in the future, in the frontier, and in new worlds to conquer. I do not think it is making too much of this point to say that, at a time when the space between generations is shorter than people think (in his life Oliver Wendell Holmes, Jr. knew both John Quincy Adams and Alger Hiss), the frontier spirit was in robust health in the late 1940s.

All these various threads in American life—the flush of military victory, the staggering prosperity, the renewed faith in the future—combined in the postwar years to create what can be called the Procreation Ethic.

Parents everywhere were under marching orders to have children. This was not a new ideal in America—the family of four had always been exalted—but now for the first time it was within reach. For fifteen long years, fertility and dreams alike had been bottled up by the Depression and World War II. Yet all during that time the image of the American family had been held up like a chalice. First Hollywood strove to lift the country's spirits during the Depression and war's grimmest days with the characteristically sentimental movies of the period. Then the GIs carried abroad with them a shining vision of what they were fighting for—Mom, Dad, Sis, the bungalow with a white picket fence, a young family, the American Way. When they returned, the Procreation Ethic was rooted more firmly than ever and preparing for its greatest flowering. Magazines like *Look* spoke for a nation with its rapturous hymn to the American mother:

> The wondrous creature marries younger than ever, bears more babies and looks and acts far more feminine than the "emancipated" girl of the twenties or thirties. If she makes an old-fashioned choice and lovingly tends a garden and a bumper crop of children, she rates louder Hosannas than ever before.

Men, in fact, were the greatest paladins of the Procreation Ethic. Like Huck Finn, who lit out for the territory ahead of the rest, they found a frontier in the maternity ward. Plato had said that the root of man's love for children was his yearning for immortality. In America, an entire society seemed to crave it. The birthrate in women's magazine stories rivaled that of Calcutta. Television soap operas usually prescribed pregnancy as the best way for a woman to get attention and compete with men. And the housewife in one aspirin commercial spoke for a thousand others when she said, "I'm Alice Cook. I have six children, and they come in all shapes and sizes. So do their colds."

If not all women wanted to join the Doris Day generation, there was little they could do about it. In Cynthia Propper Seton's novel, *A Glorious Third*, a mother of five children explains that she and other such women were really cultural casualties. As she tells a friend, "their appointed time to marry fell after the defeat of Hitler when educated women expressed a humanist solidarity with all victims by democratically giving birth as mindlessly as they could manage." She said this was "typical of what they had taken lying down." And in *Class Reunion,* Rona Jaffe describes how Radcliffe women of that era prepared for "perfect" marriages as professors' wives-in-training with weekly exercises in "gracious living" over demitasses and determined chitchat.

This was a new idea in history, one that no other society had ever put forth. It was that the exclusive role of women was to bear and to rear children. But it was powerful enough that even Betty Friedan could later admit its allure:

> To be honest, those years were not all self-delusion. The babies, the bottles, the cooking, the diapering, the burping, the carriage-wheeling, the pressure-cooker, the barbecue, the playground and doing-it-yourself were more comfortable, more safe, secure, and satisfying than that supposedly glamorous "career" in which you somehow didn't feel wanted and knew you weren't going to get anywhere.

The baby boom would never have happened if a marriage boom had not come first. Encouraged by a thriving economy, and backed up by GI Bill veterans' benefits, more Americans married younger and faster than any other people in history. Everyone who could marry, it seemed, did. The change was startlingly rapid. As recently as 1940, as many as 15 percent of all women who reached their early thirties had never been married. But by 1960, only 7 percent were still unmarried. All totaled, some 95 percent of all Americans of marriageable age were getting married—5 percent more than their parents, 7 percent more than the British, and 25 percent more than the Irish. In fact, the total was passing what had hitherto been thought of as the "practical upper limit" of marriage in *any* industrialized society.

Not only were *more* Americans marrying, they were also marrying *younger*. This meant that more and more married people were preparing to have babies during what are physiologically the peak childbearing ages of 20–24. Throughout the first half of this century, for example, about one-half of all women between the ages of 20 and 24 were married. Social scientists guessed that after the war even fewer of them would marry because they were going to school longer and entering the labor force later.

The experts were wrong again. The median age that women married turned sharply *down* after the war, dropping from 21.5 in 1940 to 20.3 in 1950, and then to a historic low of 20.1 in 1956. By 1960, nearly three-quarters of all women between the ages of 20 and 24 were married, an astonishing increase in just two decades. Eventually, one of every two first-time brides in the United States was still in her teens, and more than half of them had babies before they turned 20. Likewise, the percentage of men 20–24 who were married nearly doubled from 27 to 51 percent between 1940 and 1955. All totaled, the median age of marriage for men, as high as 26 in the Massachusetts Plymouth Colony, dropped to a new low, declining from 24.3 to 22.5 between 1940 and 1956.

Why were couples rushing to the altar? Their answer, in effect, was, Why not? The Procreation Ethic was established. The booming economy was providing the necessary jobs and income to make young people feel secure about beginning families. The government was giving an assist of its own with easy credit for mortgages and education. The economic pressures of the Depression had prevented their parents from marrying early and establishing households. But the fifties' generation had a green light: they could afford it, so why not go out on their own and get married? So, they rushed to marry and establish their status as participating adults in America's economic boom. They were ready for it financially—and even physically. Thanks to improved nutrition, both men and women were maturing earlier. And if nothing else, marriage was the best way to resolve the inevitable conflict between sexual maturity on the one hand and the high value society placed on premarital chastity on the other.

To understand how the rush to marriage contributed to the baby boom, we need to look at some of the larger demographic trends operating during this period. There was actually not just one demographic force powering the baby boom but rather three.

1. A postponement of childbearing by a generation of older women who normally might have completed their families during the Depression and World War II.

2. An advancement of about three years in the time younger women began their families.

3. An overall rise in the number of children women actually had during the boom period.

Consider the older women first. Born between 1910 and 1925, they reached their twenties—the main reproductive period of their lives—between 1930 and 1945. But many young couples were delaying both marriage and childbearing because of the depressed economy and, later, the wartime absence of men. There was a massive buildup of women with fewer-than-expected children. But after the war ended, they rushed to catch up on their delayed childbearing (just as demographers had predicted they would). From 1940 until 1950, in fact, the sharpest fertility gains were actually made by women above the age of 35. *What is most important is that they had an abnormally large number of children late in life.*

Now look at the younger mothers. These were the women born from 1925 until 1940. Relatively unaffected by the Depression and war, they arrived in the fifties as the most euphoric and marriageable generation of women ever. Every day was Sadie Hawkins Day. Not only did they marry earlier, they also had more babies in less time than any women in American history. For couples wed between 1955 and 1959, the median interval between marriage and their first birth shrunk to only thirteen months, an all-time record. (Those married during the early years of the Depression waited nearly two years before having their first child.) From 1940 until 1957, the fertility rate for women 20–24 nearly doubled, while the median age at first birth fell from 23 to 21.4. In roughly the same period, the fraction of women who became mothers by the age of 26 rose from one-half to three-fourths. What's more, the younger a woman married, the more children she ultimately was likely to have. The mothers of the fifties went on to have their second and third children at much earlier ages than their own mothers had.

Obviously, the fact that women were having children sooner does not necessarily mean that they would have more children altogether. Lowering the median age of childbearing in itself does not create *more* babies in the long run any more than lowering the draft age creates *more* soldiers in the long run. For the younger babyboom mothers, then, what is important is that *they were having an abnormally large number of children early in life.*

The net result was that in the years immediately after the war, two different age groups were combining their babies into the same period. They had stretched out their years of childbearing—one group having children later, the other having them earlier—like accordions. These births were overlapping in the same years and swelling the birthrate. Interestingly, because of the altered timing, this bulge in births would have showed up even if women were actually having no more total births than ever before. There would have been valleys and peaks on the charts, "booms" and "busts" in maternity wards, but the total number of babies born to mothers would have remained unchanged. In other words, the early part of the baby boom was in part a statistical phenomenon, an "illusion" of expansion (though the additional babies were just as real to their parents—and to the country) caused not by a change in the *total* number of babies that arrived but by a change in the time *when* they arrived.

Consider by analogy a city that sends a different squad of street cleaners to sweep the streets each week of the month. If the first week's team delayed its chores until the second week, and if the third week's team advanced its work into the second week, there would then be three times as many street cleaners on the job in the second week. But the total over the month would remain unchanged. Similarly, Norman Ryder has estimated that 58 percent of the rise in the fertility rate and nearly half of the increase in annual births would have occurred even if the total number of babies borne by women throughout their lives had not risen at all. The difference between babies and street cleaners, though, is that while the street cleaners go home, the doubled-up babies born in any one year will stay with us and remain a bulge in the age structure for another seventy years.

That accounts for one-half of the baby-boom increase, but what of the other half? It was no timing shift but rather a real change in family size, one that saw the average American family increase by a full child in just one generation. From the low of 2.27 children for women in the 1908 cohort, completed fertility rates gradually increased to a high of 3.2 for the women who conceivably were their daughters, born in the 1933 cohort. These high-fertility women, who turned 47 in 1980, not only had more children than any others in this century but topped every other age group going back to 1885. If mothers were wines, 1933 was the vintage of the century.

What made women born in the 1930s have so many children? The usual answer is that their favorable lifetime experience promoted optimism and therefore fertility. The children of the 1930s did, after all, grow up on an upward slope. Born in the gloom of the Depression, they thrilled to the battles of World War II (but did not suffer from them) and, as young adults, entered the thriving, building economy of the 1950s. The first generation trained in modern, postwar technology, they enthusiastically embraced it as no one has since. The first man to walk on the moon was born in their generation. All along the way, nothing broke the optimism generated by rising hopes and even more exhilarating realities. Blessed with the good luck to be born at the right historical moment, they confidently decided to marry promptly and to have children who, they thought, would inherit an even better future.

Here, also, we had an American generation influenced as much by the discontinuity of its size as the era it grew up in. Because the family plans of their own parents were foreshortened by the Depression and World War II, they grew up as the first generation in the country's history smaller than the one before it. This meant they needed less from society but received more. One demographer, Carl Harter of Tulane, has christened them the "Good Times Generation." They were advantaged throughout their life cycle simply because of their small number. They were born in uncrowded hospital wards. They did not compete with as many brothers and sisters and received more attention from their parents. The number of children who were five years old in 1940, for example, was 25 percent less than ten years earlier. They, therefore, had more books, more teachers, and more classroom space. In 1950, when there were a quarter million fewer fifteen-year-olds than in 1940, they had that much better a chance of becoming class officers, joining athletic teams, or getting into college.

As adults, they found it easy to settle down and establish families. They faced less competition for houses, jobs, and promotions. And, yes, they someday will not have to elbow anyone for cemetery space. In short, the experience of the Good Times Generation was the opposite of the tumultuous coming-of-age that, as we shall later see, befell their children in the crowded baby-boom generation. Where the parents slipped easily into society, thanks to their small generation, the baby-boom children would be blocked and frustrated all along the way. The uncertainties about the future and doubts about values that trouble baby boomers today were unknown to their parents. David Riesman has tellingly quoted a self-assured senior in Princeton's Class of 1955 talking about how he saw himself fifteen years later:

Life will not be a burden for me at thirty-five because I will be securely anchored in my family. My main emotional ties will center on my wife and family—remember, I hope for five children. Yes, I can describe my wife. She will be the Grace Kelly, camel's-hair-coat type. Feet on the ground, and not an empty shell or a fake. Although an Ivy League type, she will also be centered in the home, a housewife. Perhaps at forty-five, with the children grown up, she will go in for hospital work and so on. . . .

Such staggering complacency seems unthinkable today. But the astonishing truth is that the generation David Riesman called "The Found Generation" saw many of its dreams come true. Harvard's Class of 1954 reported at its twenty-fifth reunion not only the expected material success—more than half earned over $50,000—but also unexpected emotional fulfillment. More than 95 percent said they were "sleeping well" and two-thirds were even "enjoying sex more." One architect drew what could be a metaphor for his generation when he wrote, "I have lived in the house I designed, and have seen the summer sunlight move through it as I had planned and hoped it would."

These lucky Americans, then, the ones who saw summer sunlight move through their lives, contributed most to the baby boom. A small generation, they acted together with impressive unity to create our largest generation. (It is still hard to believe that during the 1950s, when births were soaring over four million each year for the first time ever, the number of women reaching the peak childbearing ages of 20–24 actually *declined* by 3 percent.) They did it by marrying earlier, by having children faster, and by having more of them. But that generalization alone barely begins to describe the astonishing uniformity within the baby boom. It was a mass movement made by millions of families of all races and classes, making millions of individual decisions. Yet the result was strikingly similar for all families.

Imagine a typical baby-boom family. A vision leaps to most minds of a suburban house cluttered with six or seven children, toys, diapers, peanut butter, and bicycles. But that, strangely, is exactly what the baby boom was *not*. Cartoonists and jokes of the time notwithstanding, the baby boom was *not* a return to the large American families of the nineteenth century. In fact, the percentage of very large families in the United States actually *declined* during the years of the boom. In 1910, nearly one-third of women who had completed their families had given birth to seven children or more. In 1960, only about 6 percent of the women had that many children.

This apparent paradox can be explained by understanding the requirements of the Procreation Ethic. Before and during the baby boom, the Procreation Ethic was impressed on families deeply and constantly, like water dripping on a stone. Its rules were clear and unmistakable. Briefly, they were:

1. It was preferable to marry than not to marry. If a person chose to remain single, the onus was on him or her to explain why.

2. It was preferable to be a parent than a nonparent. A couple that did not have children would be considered unconventional and tacitly pressured to make an explanation. The only excuses accepted were medical or financial.

3. It was preferable not to have an "only" child, especially in the suburbs.

All of these strictures have since changed, but during the postwar era they were social law. If a couple met these obligations, they could have more children if they wanted, as many as five or six without raising eyebrows, but that was up to them.

If we look at the history of fertility before and during the baby boom, we can see the changes caused by families having what Norman Ryder calls the "normative" number of children (less than three) or "discretionary" children (three or more). During the Depression, when mothers were having fewer children than ever before, childlessness played a large part in the decline in fertility. One out of every five married women born early in this century never had a child of her own. Many of them simply could not afford to. But in the America of the fifties, the Procreation Ethic made childlessness deviant. Thanks to better nutrition and medicine, more women were able to have children; thanks to prosperity, more women could afford to. Consequently, the rate of childlessness dropped from 22 percent to an unheard-of 8 percent for married women born in the early 1930s. So many women were having babies, in fact, that astonished public health officials had to revise downward their medical opinion of the incidence of sterility within a population. These families seemed to be taking literally the warning John Donne had given his parishioners in a sermon in 1621: "To contract before that they will have no children makes it no marriage but an adultery."

The other major change in families was the move from one child to at least two. As the Procreation Ethic required, parents wanted not a single child but brothers and sisters. By 1958, the number of families with two or more children at home had increased to 16.4 million, a jump of 5.2 million, or 46 percent, in a decade. At the same time, the chances of any family having more than five children dropped steadily. What had happened, then, was not the creation of many large families but rather a movement away from spinsterhood, childless marriage, and one-child families. The range of family sizes was being narrowed at both ends, resulting in an enormous increase in the number and proportion of women who had two to four children. Norman Ryder has shown that fully 90 percent of the postwar increase in completed fertility (as opposed to the previously mentioned increase that resulted only from changes in timing) was within the range of "normative" childbearing—that is, in the rise in the proportion of women having at least two children. (It rose from 55 percent to 82 percent.) The pressure had always been there for women to have at least two children and, in the postwar era, an entire generation of women finally had the means to achieve the old ideal. There was a boom, all right, but it was a boom in small families, not large.

The increase in third and fourth children during the boom years originally led some demographers to suppose that American mothers had increased their "ideal" number of children from two to three. But as Ryder pointed out, 58 percent of the increase in *fertility* can be explained by the change in timing alone and has nothing to do with the ultimate size of families. Of the remaining 42 percent, which was the real increase in children per family,

90 percent of it was "normative" (people having fewer than three children) and only 10 percent was "discretionary" (three or more children).

Moreover, we now know that many of the third and fourth children were not planned. National Fertility Studies conducted by Princeton's Ryder and fellow demographer Charles Westoff in 1965 and 1970 reported that nearly 20 percent of all pregnancies in the postwar period were unplanned and that the number of babies actually unwanted might have been higher than anyone ever guessed. This leads to the interesting question of why the 1950s' mothers were so ineffective at birth control—especially after their own mothers had been so successful during the thirties.

One explanation is the fact that, because women were marrying younger and having children sooner, they were finishing their *intended* families earlier than before. Between the prewar and postwar eras, for example, the mean age of American mothers at the time their second child was born declined from 27 to 24. They were then left with the daunting task of avoiding another pregnancy for the next twenty or so years. It was an obstacle course with 240 monthly hurdles. What's more, by completing their desired families three years earlier than previous generations, they had not added just any three years to their "at-risk" period of pregnancy; they had added three years in their mid-twenties, when the chances of pregnancy are highest. Further, those who married earliest were leaping straight from sexual maturity into marriage. They never bothered to learn effective birth control because they never had to. They wanted to have their first two babies. But because they had never practiced birth control in their lives, before or during marriage, they developed what social scientists call a "trained incapacity." Those white women who had their first children before they were 18, for example, wound up with an average of four children apiece. When the time came to stop having children, they didn't know how.

The other reason why fifties' mothers got pregnant unintentionally can be thought of as the "What the hell?" syndrome. It is simply that, during the prosperous fifties, couples relaxed their contraceptive vigilance because the penalty for failure was not so harsh. In those prepill days, the common weakness of every method of contraception from condom to coitus interruptus was that they had to be used during each sex act. Sometimes, whether in the heat of passion or out of forgetfulness, these methods of contraception were . . . inconvenient. In the 1930s, couples were well enough aware of the cost of an unwanted baby that they gritted their teeth and abstained. But during the relaxed 1950s the bedroom conversation might have sounded more like, "What the hell? If an accident happens, we can afford it."

Returning now to the net effects of these changes, here is what we see. American families who once distributed children evenly along a range from zero to five or more were conforming to what was becoming a universal norm. On one end, bachelors and spinsters, childless couples, and couples with an only child all but vanished. On the other end, the odds of a mother with four children having a fifth or sixth declined, as did the actual proportion of families with seven or more children. What was left was an unprecedented concentration of children in smaller families. One of the most curious statistics of the era is that, throughout the population explosion of the 1950s, the *average* size of the American family barely budged, rising almost imperceptibly from 3.5 in 1950 to 3.6 in 1958. What had triumphed was the Procreation Ethic, which had extended the franchise of children to practically every family.

This helps us to understand, on a national scale, who made the baby boom and how they did it. But individual fertility is not just a function of a parent's age. Other factors—race, religion, occupation, and income, to name just a few—have influenced childbearing over the years. We might logically suppose that not even the baby boom could send its ripples evenly into every inlet of society. Scholars reasoned that if they could sort out some of the *differences* in the way groups of people behaved, then they might understand more about the reasons behind the boom itself. Yet, what the fertility sleuths uncovered was a phenomenon even more baffling: virtually *all* groups of Americans participated in the boom. So powerful were the forces behind the baby boom that they had apparently permeated every level of society and overridden all the usual "filtering" variables of race, class, education, and residence. It was a tide that lifted all the boats on the lake.

Demographic Transition theory held that modernization would reduce fertility among the urban and the educated classes. Those fertility differentials remained during the boom, to be sure, but instead of increasing they were diminishing. In fact, the groups that showed the greatest fertility surges during the boom were precisely the same ones that, according to theory, should have been least likely to. In a stunning reversal, the educated and the urban and the middle classes actually led the boom. It was as though, once having demonstrated that they could put the brakes on fertility if they wanted to, as during the Depression, they could release their controls just as easily. The lesson could only be that the boom could not be explained by parochial factors, particular to certain groups in society, but was a product of forces that were deeply historical and sweeping. Each special group that was studied bore out this conclusion.

EDUCATION. Traditionally, the higher the education of the parent (particularly the mother), the lower the fertility. Education presumably spreads information about birth control and understanding of the financial costs of children. But during the baby boom, the most spectacular increases in fertility showed up where it was least expected: among educated women. Women with high-school diplomas had the largest increase in fertility—70 percent—whereas women who never attended high school had the smallest. College women also experienced large rises in fertility: at one point the Class of 1945 averaged a 51 percent gain nationally in fertility over their counterparts in the Class of 1936. (The single most prolific was the Mormon campus, Brigham Young.) So many women were abandoning college to bear children that the female enrollment rate dropped after the war.

INCOME. Thorstein Veblen had commented in his *Theory of the Leisure Class* on the low birthrates of the upper classes, and subsequent history seemed to prove him right. (Such conspicuously fertile families as the Kennedys were usually attributed more to religion than to wealth.) But during the baby boom, this relationship, too, reversed. The rise in fertility was actually larger among upper-income families than among the poor. Lawyers and doctors and executives contributed *more* proportionately to the baby boom than did the farm and factory workers often thought to be fathers of the biggest families.

RESIDENCE. Country people traditionally had more children than city people, if only because they needed the extra hands to harvest the crops. But during the baby boom the city parents began to catch up. During the 1950s, the increase of rural fertility was considerably less than the fertility in the cities. In fact, one normally high-fertility subgroup—older, rural women with less than a high-school education—actually experienced a *decline* in fertility between 1945 and 1957. Technically, that means that these women were the only ones in America *not* to be affected by the postwar baby boom. Of course, these same older, less educated rural women have *always* had more babies than anyone else. The rest of the world was just catching up to them.

MINORITIES. There have always been as many different fertility patterns as there are cultures. During the baby boom, American Indians experienced the largest gains, Asian-Americans the lowest. But, in terms of absolute numbers, the most important group was black Americans. Throughout American history, blacks have consistently had markedly higher and earlier fertility than whites. The strange thing, though, is that the two groups have responded together in the same way. The parallels are almost eerie. Slave women, for instance, typically bore their first children about two years earlier than Southern white women. Today black women still bear their first children approximately two years earlier than white women. Times change, but fertility patterns prevail. In the late nineteenth and early twentieth centuries, black fertility declined along with that of white, even though there seemed little reason for the similarity. Unlike whites, blacks were still poor and rural and had not benefited from the forces of education and urbanization that, according to Demographic Transition theory, explained the decline in white fertility. They were effectively living in a Third World country within the borders of the United States. Yet, even though their life expectancy remained low and their infant mortality high, conditions normally encouraging high fertility, blacks were having relatively fewer and fewer children. This remarkable trend continued into the Depression. When childlessness increased among whites, it did so even more dramatically among blacks. What's more, the argument that black childlessness then was a product of poor nutrition or venereal disease does not bear up against the fact that childlessness was highest among educated blacks. As many as one-quarter of all black women born at the turn of the century did not have a single child, but among the black

36

women who went to college, nearly one-half were child-less.

The parallels between black and white fertility appeared in the baby boom as well, against all expectations and despite grievous differences in social and economic circumstances. Most black women then did *not* live in suburbs. They were not benefiting from the economic boom of the fifties. The majority of them were not full-time mothers but were in the labor force, a further inhibition against parenting. Yet they managed to average nearly four children per mother, the highest completed fertility of any group since the decade following the Civil War. They did it firstly by an extraordinary decrease in childlessness, which plummeted from 28 percent to 10 percent. Secondly, they had babies earlier and quicker, often becoming mothers shortly after puberty. Thirty percent of the black women born in the Good Times Generation of 1930–34 had two children by the age of 21. Sixteen percent had four children by 24, and 10 percent had six children before they were 27. Those who had their first child before 19 wound up with an average of five children each. Nearly 20 percent of all black women went on to seven children before they were done. Most of them lived in the South. In fact, region was as important as race in black fertility. Black women born or living outside the South had about the same number of children as did white women. Interestingly, when they reached upper-income levels, blacks and Hispanics did not participate in the baby boom. Instead of having more children, they had fewer. The family reasoning seemed to be that their newly-found economic position was precarious enough without the burden of additional children.

RELIGION. American Catholics, Protestants, and Jews have always reproduced in just that order: Catholics highest, Protestants next, and Jews lowest. (None of them, to be sure, has approached the Hutterites, a Mennonite sect of communal farmers in Montana and South Dakota, whose doctrine holds that birth control is sinful. Accordingly, Hutterite women have averaged between nine and ten births apiece, making theirs perhaps the fastest-growing population in the world.)

All of the major religions experienced increases in fertility during the baby boom. Among Protestant denominations, Methodists and Baptists were at the top of the scale, and Episcopalians and Presbyterians at the bottom end.

But the most disproportionate leap was made by Catholics, who had been previously declining toward the lower levels of other faiths. By the end of the 1950s, as Charles Westoff and others have shown, Catholic fertility was running 20 percent higher than that of the United States as a whole. College-educated Catholics had the highest fertility of all, a fact suggesting that the rise was not a result of failed contraception, since educated people usually have the best control over their fertility. (More recently, Catholic fertility has again dropped—as have church-going habits—until it is all but indistinguishable from other religions.)

As the baby boom surged on year after year, demographers felt like the Wrong Way Corrigans of social science. Their critics regarded them as harmless as hobbyists who build model ships in bottles—a fine skill but not one that is widely transferable or particularly useful. Instead of following the advice of the experts and shrinking from the 1946 population of 141 million, mothers reproduced with a vengeance. The boom thundered to 152 million by 1950 and then an incredible 180 million by 1960. The annual growth rate was approaching 2 percent a year, as much as some Third World countries. The theory of Demographic Transition lay in ruins. Who could ever again seriously argue that industrialization led to fertility decline? The most extraordinary baby boom ever was concentrated not in some underdeveloped land of peasants but in the most industrialized society the world had yet seen.

Demographers understandably resolved never again to be exposed as false prophets. After a look at the eye-popping figures from the 1950 census, the Census Bureau promptly revised its future population up a notch. Some experts projected a huge population in the United States by the year 2000 of 300 million or more. Others, like Philip Hauser of Chicago, pointed out that the continuation of existing growth rates would mean one billion Americans by the year 2050. Ansley Coale of Princeton performed a frightening academic exercise demonstrating that worldwide continuation of a high growth rate would result six thousand years later in our descendants multiplying into a solid sphere of live bodies expanding outward from the earth at the speed of light. And few would argue with Peter Drucker's conclusion in an otherwise remarkably prescient book, *America's Next Twenty Years,* that "the low birth rate of the Depression decade was a freak. The higher birth rate which reasserted itself in the early forties now appears to be the normal rate at which the American people reproduce themselves."

Drucker had the misfortune to make that categorical statement in 1957, the year the sigmoid curve of the baby boom reached its apogee. In eleven straight years, from 1954 through 1964, there were more than four million babies born annually. This extraordinary population explosion was based not on decreased mortality, as in underdeveloped countries, but on increased natality. But after 1964, women began having fewer children and annual births again dropped below four million.* The boom then took on the shape of a bulge, the pig in the python, and began moving up through the age structure. The shock waves rippled up the decades. In 1940, there were fewer than 11 million under the age of five; by 1950 it was 16 million, and by 1960 it was 20 million. Then in the 1950s the 5–17 age group, which had increased by only 52,000 in the forties, exploded by an additional 8.3 million. By 1964, four out of every ten people in the United States were under 20 and there were more children under 14 than there had been people in the entire nation in 1881.

This was the army of the baby boom. Seventy-five million strong at full force, it was mobilized by a generation of parents that was ready to give it everything. What had at first looked like a statistical oddity was becoming a nation within a nation. The sideshow was on its way to becoming the main event.

* Other measures based on fertility alone yield an earlier ending date of the boom period. But since it is the disproportionate number of people in the generation that concerns us, I use total births here to define the length of the boom.

Chapter 3

THE BIG BARBECUE

In the early 1950s, the huge Census Clock in Washington was clicking like a runaway taxi meter. Every seven seconds the Birth Light blinked off a new baby. Boys were arriving with familiar names like Robert, John, James, Michael, William, Richard, Joseph, Thomas, Steven, and David, making a Top Ten of favorite names that was proudly all-American. Girls were named Linda, Mary, Barbara, Patricia, Susan, Kathleen, Carol, Nancy, Margaret, and Diane. And perhaps thanks to Debbie Reynolds, "Deborah" would have a run all of her own later in the decade.

Like the steel industry, mothering was running at close to 100 percent capacity, and it was harder and harder to keep up. In January of 1952, General Electric decided to celebrate its seventy-fifth anniversary by awarding five shares of common stock to any employee who had a baby on October 15. Some public-relations whiz tried to predict the eventual number of winners by dividing the total of 226,000 G.E. employees by the U.S. crude birth-rate. Unfortunately, he forgot that G.E. workers as a a population were considerably more fertile than the United States as a whole, since they contained no one under 17 nor over 65. In the end, the company's guess that thirteen G.E. babies would be born amounted to underestimation on a grand scale. The workers, true to the thriving surplus economy of the era, came through with no less than 189 new G.E. babies that day.

But General Electric was not about to complain. It was investing $650 million in new plants and assembly lines over seven postwar years to prepare for the boom in babies. As early as 1948, *Time* noted that the U.S. population had just increased by "2,800,000 more consumers"

40

(*not* babies) the year before. Economists happily predicted that the new babies would set off a demand explosion for commodities such as homes, foodstuffs, clothing, furniture, appliances, and schools, to name only a few examples. *Fortune* pronounced the baby boom "exhilarating" and with an almost-audible sigh of relief concluded that the low birthrates of the 1930s were a "freakish interlude, rather than a trend." "We need not stew too much about a post-armament depression," the magazine wrote. "A civilian market growing by the size of Iowa every year ought to be able to absorb whatever production the military will eventually turn loose."

As the economic and baby booms surged on together, the cheerleading became almost feverish. Public-service signs went up in New York City subways reading, "Your future is great in a growing America. Every day 11,000 babies are born in America. This means new business, new jobs, new opportunities." After-dinner speakers began to talk about "Prosperity by Population" and lofted tantalizing guesses of up to five million new babies a year by 1975. Financial magazines editorialized about the joys of "this remarkable boom." "Gone, for the first time in history," announced *Time* in 1955, "is the worry over whether a society can produce enough goods to take care of its people. The lingering worry is whether it will have enough people to consume the goods."

The most euphoric article of all, perhaps, was a story *Life* printed in 1958, at the height of the boom. Three dozen children were crowded onto the cover along with the banner headline: KIDS: BUILT-IN RECESSION CURE —HOW 4,000,000 A YEAR MAKE MILLIONS IN BUSINESS. Inside, the article began with another headline—ROCKETING BIRTHS: BUSINESS BONANZA—and continued chockablock with statistics and photographs about new citizens who were "a brand-new market for food, clothing, and shelter." In its first year, *Life* calculated, a baby is not just a child but already a prodigious consumer, "a potential market for $800 worth of products." Even before returning from the hospital, an infant had "already rung up $450 in medical expenses." Four-year-olds are not just sugar and spice or puppy-dog tails but rather represent a "a backlog of business orders that will take two decades to fulfill." A rhapsodic *Life* then clinched its case by visiting Joe Powers, a thirty-five-year-old salesman from Port Washington, New York. He and his wife, Carol,

41

had produced ten children and were buying 77 quarts of milk and 28 loaves of bread a week, just for starters. Faced with examples like that of meritorious devotion to the Procreation Ethic, little wonder that some American mothers felt as if it were their *duty* to have children. Either they were pregnant or, if not, wondered whether they should be.

The baby-boom kids had kicked off in America a buccaneering orgy of buying and selling that carried all things before it. The only thing like it earlier was the Gilded Age of the post–Civil War 1870s, which the historian Vernon Louis Parrington so aptly dubbed "the Great Barbecue." Here was a feast spread out for an entire nation, and everyone scrambling for it. More food was spoiled than eaten, perhaps, and the revelry was a bit unseemly, but no one minded. Everywhere people were getting rich in a demographic debauch.

The spending boom started, literally, at the bottom. Diapers went from a $32-million industry in 1947 to $50 million in 1957. The diaper services (disposables had not yet arrived) also prospered. Mothers and fathers were paying $5 million annually (twice the preboom business) to have baby's shoes bronze-plated at L. E. Mason, Inc., in Boston. The under-5 appetite, which had grown from 13 million mouths to 20 million by 1960, more than one out of every ten Americans, was consuming baby food at a rate of 1.5 billion cans a year in 1953 (up from 270 million cans in 1940).

As the kids grew up, so did the markets. Throughout the 1950s, the 5–13 age group grew by an additional one million baby boomers every year. The toy industry set sales records annually after 1940, growing from an $84-million-a-year stripling to a $1.25-billion giant. Sales of bicycles doubled to two million a year; cowboy outfits became a $75-million subindustry; space-science toys claimed another $60 million. Children's clothes became a boom market, and packaging researchers suddenly discovered the troika of "family" sizes—Giant, Economy, and Supereconomy. At its peak, the juvenile market was ringing up a staggering $33 billion annually.

The rain of spending did not fall evenly on society. Rather, it was both a cause and an effect of what amounted to the opening of a new American frontier: the suburbs. Historians had already suggested that America's expansiveness during the nineteenth century was built on the common goal of settling the West. Now there was a new impetus behind the conquering of the suburban frontier: babies. The suburbs were conceived for the baby boom—and vice versa. Here in green garlands around the cities, Americans were creating new child-oriented societies, "babyvilles" teeming with new appetites, new institutions, and new values. Families who were asked why they moved to the suburbs first mentioned better housing and leisure, as if they were conforming to the old goal of a country place that began with the French aristocracy. But then, invariably, they added that they thought suburbia was "a better place to bring up the kids." The common acceptance of this goal united the suburbs. "Instead of the wagon train, where people leaned on one another as they moved across the continent," historian Daniel Boorstin remarked, "Americans in suburbs leaned on one another as they moved rapidly about the country and up the ladder of consumption." Author William H. Whyte found the same communal spirit in his examination of the mythical suburb of Park Forest. Families shared baby-sitters, cribs, lawn mowers, tea services, and baseball equipment. "We laughed at first at how the Marxist society had finally arrived," one suburban executive told Whyte. "But I think the real analogy is to the pioneers."

As an internal migration, the settling of the suburbs was phenomenal. In the twenty years from 1950 to 1970, the population of the suburbs doubled from 36 million to 72 million. No less than 83 percent of the total population growth in the United States during the 1950s was in the suburbs, which were growing fifteen times faster than any other segment of the country. As people packed and moved, the national mobility rate leaped by 50 percent. The only other comparable influx was the wave of European immigrants to the United States around the turn of the century. But, as *Fortune* pointed out, more people moved to the suburbs every year than had ever arrived on Ellis Island.

By now, bulldozers were churning up dust storms as they cleared the land for housing developments. More than a million acres of farmland were plowed under every year during the 1950s. Millions of apartment-dwelling parents with two children were suddenly realizing that two children could be doubled up in a spare bedroom, but a third child cried loudly for something more. The proportion of new houses with three or more bedrooms, in fact, rose from one-third in 1947 to three-quarters by 1954. The necessary *Lebensraum* could only be found in the suburbs. There was a housing shortage, but young couples armed with VA and FHA loans built their dream homes with easy credit and free spending habits that were unthinkable to the baby-boom grandparents, who shook their heads with the Depression still fresh in their memories. Of the 13 million homes built in the decade before 1958, 11 million of them—or 85 percent—were built in the suburbs. Home ownership rose 50 percent between 1940 and 1950, and another 50 percent by 1960. By then, one-fourth of *all* housing in the United States had been built in the fifties. For the first time, more Americans owned homes than rented them.

We were becoming a land of gigantic nurseries. The biggest were built by Abraham Levitt, the son of poor Russian-Jewish immigrants, who had originally built houses for the Navy during the war. The first of three East Coast Levittowns went up on the potato fields of Long Island. Exactly $7900—or $60 a month and no money down—bought you a Monopoly-board bungalow with four rooms, attic, washing machine, outdoor barbecue, and a television set built into the wall. The 17,447 units eventually became home to 82,000 people, many of whom were pregnant or wanted to be. In a typical story on the suburban explosion, one magazine breathlessly described a volleyball game of nine couples in which no less than five of the women were expecting.

Marketers were quick to spot what amounted to capitalism's Klondike Lode. "Anybody who wants to sell anything to Americans should take a long look at the New Suburbia," marveled *Fortune* in 1953. "It is big and lush and uniform—a combination made to order for the comprehending marketer." It went far beyond toys and diapers. In suburbia's servantless society, laborsaving devices were necessary adjuncts to having children. The number of washing machines sold in America went from 1.7 million in 1950 to 2.6 million in 1960. Sales of electric clothes dryers doubled during one two-year stretch. With a then-astonishing average family income of $6500 (compared to $3800 for everyone else), the suburbanites were creating an American way of spending organized around children and the needs they created. Retailers eagerly followed them to the suburbs, opening branch stores by the dozen and clearing the way for the later age of shopping malls.

The settlers of suburbia also brought with them beasts of burden. They had Fords in their future—and Chevys and De Sotos and Hudsons and Studebakers. The car, especially the second car, was the one indispensable suburban accessory. Car registrations soared along with the birthrate: from 26 million in 1945 to 40 million in 1950 to 60 million by the end of the decade. The number of two-car families rose 750,000 a year and doubled from 1951 to 1958. Station wagons, the housewife's version of the Willys Jeep, began crisscrossing the suburbs like water bugs, dropping off husbands, picking up children, stopping by the supermarket. "A suburban mother's role is to deliver children obstetrically once," said Peter De Vries, "and by car forever after." *Time* joked that "if the theory of evolution is still working, it may well one day transform the suburban housewife's right foot into a flared paddle, grooved for easy traction on the gas pedal and brake."

Even in those days, the automobile had seized its central place in the emotional life of the baby boom. It was the first entire generation to be driven before it walked. It was the first generation to grow up in cars, even to seek its entertainment in cars. Back in 1933 a chemicals manufacturer named Richard Hollinshead had turned a parking lot in Camden, New Jersey, into the World's First Automobile Movie Theatre. Fifteen years later, there were only 480 drive-ins in the country. But between 1948 and 1958 the number zoomed to 4000, equipped with everything from playgrounds for the kids to Laundromats for Mom. For millions of baby-boom parents, a night at the drive-in neatly solved the suburban dilemma of what to do if you couldn't get a baby-sitter. Much later, the adolescent baby boomers would find their own use for the passion pits. Here is Lisa Alther in *Kinflicks:*

> Mixed with the dialogue were the various sighs and gasps and sucking sounds from the front seats and blasts from car horns throughout the parking area as, in keeping with Hullsport High tradition, couples signalled that they'd gone all the way.

Nowhere was the postwar baby-suburb-car symbiosis more symbolically apparent than during the gasoline

45

shortage of July 1979 in the Philadelphia suburb of Levittown, Pennsylvania. There some 75,000 people live on 7000 acres of suburb. But, for a city of such density, it is served by little mass transportation. Threatened by the loss of their cars, angry young Levittowners staged the nation's first gas riot, burning cars, stoning ambulances, and battling police. Ironically, many of the 195 who were arrested belonged to the same families who had originally settled there during the baby-boom years and who, in 1960, won the Little League World Series for Levittown.

Meanwhile, the suburbs continued to grow and prosper and create a whole new sequence of bench marks for American Studies teachers. In 1956, white-collar workers outnumbered blue-collar workers for the first time. In 1970, the suburbs became the largest single sector of the nation's population, exceeding both central cities and the farms. By 1972, the suburbs were even offering more jobs than the central cities. Everyone was enthusiastically buying "on time" (as it was called then), and the number of Americans who thought installment financing was a good thing increased from 50 percent to 60 percent in ten years.

Sociologists began to pursue the suburbanites like doctors after a new virus. The baby-boom parents were poked and prodded and examined with the kind of fascination hitherto reserved for South Sea Islanders. They were, to be sure, pioneering a life-style (the dread word first came into currency then) that would be predominant in America. Often living in small houses filled with children, they moved outside to their patios and barbecue pits and created a new, rigorously informal style. Lawn and porch furniture sales went from $53 million in 1950 to $145 million in 1960. Hot dog production likewise zoomed from 750 million pounds to more than 2 billion pounds in the decade. Everyone first-named everyone and no one criticized the neighbor's kids (at least in front of a neighbor). Books of the time began to portray a strange netherworld of rathskellers and dens, of cheese dips and cocktails (the required icebreakers in a highly mobile society), or Kaffeeklatsches and card parties, and of outer-directed husbands and neurotic corporate wives.

Some of these studies no doubt revealed more of the anxieties of the examiners than the examined. (Did ordinary citizens really have "identity crises"?) But, if there was a common message, it was of the *sameness* of

46

suburbia. It was as if the same forces that produced prosperity and fertility also produced homogeneity. Parents had rediscovered the old verities—home, hearth, children, church. But they had also made a faith out of brand names, modular housing, and gray flannel suits. Everywhere were the same drugstores, the same franchises, the same music on the radio. The children, too, were being shaped by a world of repeatable experience. But they were not being molded by their parents or their teachers. Instead, there was another dominant presence in the early lives of the baby boomers. It was one that would forge their unity as a generation. It would mobilize them as a consumer force. It was television. In 1938, E. B. White prophesied that "television is going to be the test of the modern world and . . . in this new opportunity to see beyond the range of our vision we shall discover either a new and unbearable disturbance of the general peace or a saving radiance in the sky. We shall stand or fall by television—of that I am quite sure." In the year White wrote that, barely 2 percent of American families owned the small, flickering Philcos and DuMonts dwarfed in their elephantine cabinets. But in less than a decade, the age of television swept over us. From fewer than 6000 sets manufactured at the baby boom's outset in 1946, production leaped, almost impossibly, to 7 million a year by 1953. Eighty-six percent of American homes had television sets at the end of the decade and, by 1967, 98 percent of all homes had sets, effectively saturating the market. The exponential growth curve of television was steeper than that of any other technological innovation of the century—including the telephone, radio, and automobile.

It was also the most important new child-care development of the century, one that would redefine the environment in which Americans grew up. Some of the oldest baby-boomers remember when the first sets were lugged into their homes. But, for most, television was not an intruder in the home but what Buckminster Fuller called "the third parent," practically a family member itself. These children treated the glowing box not with the awe due a mysterious and wonderful invention but with the unquestioned familiarity of an old armchair or the kitchen sink.

Families wanted to stay home in the 1950s, and television made it easier. Aside from the growth in drive-ins, movies almost withered away during the baby-boom years. In 1946, the first year of the boom, Hollywood had recorded its biggest year ever: 400 features were released and 90 million went to the movies every week. Then in 1947, movie attendance dropped 10 percent as parents stayed home with their babies. By January 1953, when a record 50 million of them watched another baby-boom mother, Lucy Ricardo, have her baby on *I Love Lucy*, movie attendance had been cut to one-half the 1946 level, despite such lures as 3-D movies. (The first was *Bwana Devil* in 1952.) With most of its screens located in emptying downtowns instead of expanding suburbs—in New York City alone, 55 theaters closed in 1951—Hollywood lost an audience it would not even begin to reclaim until it squeezed theaters into suburban malls twenty years later.

Television, meanwhile, was giving the baby-boom children a series of vivid images that would color their memories forever. They all sang "M-I-C-K-E-Y M-O-U-S-E" with Karen and Doreen. (In those days, no one noticed that there were no black or Asian or Hispanic Mouseketeers.) They grew up glued to *Howdy Doody*, part of a vast Peanut Gallery in a national Doodyville. Mr. Bluster was a faintly disguised Ike, and as author Jeff Greenfield has observed, Clarabell was the original Yippie. Two decades later, in the aftermath of the Vietnam antiwar strife, Buffalo Bob and Howdy put together a road show that offered a burned-out student generation a return to a childhood myth that somehow seemed more real, or at least comforting, than the 1960s had been.

The baby-boom parents themselves were mirrored in nuclear-family dramas like *The Adventures of Ozzie and Harriet, Father Knows Best,* and *The Life of Riley.* Yet, on TV at least, the birthrate remained surprisingly low—evidently the bumbling Ozzie Nelsons and Chester A. Rileys were a lot more savvy about some family matters than their children ever could have suspected. (*The Brady Bunch*, with its amalgam of six children by two different marriages, was more of a postboom family that arrived ahead of its time.) Perhaps the prototypical baby-boom family was the Cleavers in *Leave It to Beaver*. Beaver Cleaver could have been penned by Norman Rockwell as a sort of Tom Sawyer relocated in Pasadena. The rumor that the actor who played Beaver, Jerry Mathers, had been killed later in Vietnam seemed cruelly symbolic of the death of the generation's own innocence. (The reality was, if anything, even more appropriate: Mathers had actually gone from selling insurance to real estate, while his klutzy buddy, Eddie Haskell, had really become a cop with the Los Angeles Police Department.)

As the baby boomers grew out of diapers, advertisers looked at the figures and discovered that American mothers had created the biggest market in history. Now technology had produced the tool to move it: television. The earliest ads had been silly jingles about chlorophyll toothpaste and chlorophyll chewing gum. But then a marketing consultant named Eugene Gilbert stumbled on a galvanizing truth: "An advertiser who touches a responsive chord in youth can generally count on the parent to succumb finally to purchasing the product." It was the Relativity Theorem of television: a law that changed everything. Money for commercials flowed like a river as TV went about the business of turning toddlers into consumer trainees. Tests showed that children could recognize the word "detergent" before they could read. They sang "Pepsi-Cola hits the spot/ Twelve full ounces, that's a lot" before they knew the national anthem. They were trained to buy. As Joyce Maynard wrote in her autobiographical memoir, published when she was all of 20, "We are, in the fullest sense, *consumers,* trained to salivate not at a bell but at the sight of a Kellogg's label or a Dunkin' Donuts box." This generation could not be organized socially or politically, Dwight Macdonald argued, because it had already been organized as a body of affluent consumers. Fittingly, the NBC program *Saturday Night Live,* which later drew its audience from the grown-up kids of the fifties, chose as one of its first satirical themes something they knew best: commercials.

Let's turn now to what was the most fruitful expression of the alliance between television and advertising and the boom generation: fads. Fads were so much intertwined with the social history of the fifties that it is easy to forget that they've always been a part of the American scene. This century had already given us everything from Mah-Jongg to marathon dancing to miniature golf. But there's one crucial difference between the earlier fads and the crazes of the fifties. Fads used to be started by young adults and then spread up and down to younger and older people. But the fads of the fifties, almost without exception, were creations of the children. They flowed *up*. Back in the twenties or thirties, for instance, it would have been impossible to imagine the under-ten group starting anything. They were just as demographically powerless then as they are now. But in the fifties, the critical mass of baby boomers entered the impressionable pre-school and elementary-school ages. And where the baby boom went was where the action would be.

Toy manufacturers have always gone straight for the jugular of childhood: imaginative play. What has always been the sustaining fantasy of American children? The West. In the suburbs, millions of pint-sized cowboys were riding the ranges. Hopalong Cassidy was their first hero, and by 1950 kids were wearing some $40 million worth of Hoppy's black outfits and six-shooters. Then Gene Autry, Roy Rogers, Wyatt Earp, and the Cisco Kid rounded up another $283 million on toy guns, boots, chaps, and lassos between 1955 and 1959. The generation that someday would passionately oppose a foreign war won its spurs early at home, acquiring a peacetime arsenal that rivaled the Pentagon's in firepower.

Television merchandised these Burbank cowpokes with enough success to make marketers look increasingly seriously at the young generation. Then, in 1955, the baby boom unleashed its economic clout once and for all in the biggest bonanza to date. The previous December, some 40 million Americans had watched as 29-year-old Fess Parker pull on Davy Crockett's buckskins on *Disneyland* (ABC, Wednesday night). As director Steven Spielberg remembered it:

> I was in third grade at the time. Suddenly the next day, everybody in my class but me was Davy Crockett. And because I didn't have my coonskin cap and my powder horn, or Old Betsy, my rifle, and the chaps, I was deemed the Mexican leader, Santa Anna. And they chased me home from school until I got my parents to buy me a coonskin cap.

By May, Davy Crockett was whooping and hollering into a seven-month shopping spree that saw more than $100 million change hands. A record, "The Ballad of Davy Crockett" by Bill Hayes, became one of the biggest hits of all time, with versions in sixteen languages, not to mention the "Davy Crockett Mambo." The wholesale price of raccoon skins jumped from 26 cents a pound to $8 a pound. More than 3000 different Crockett items were moving off the shelves, including sweat shirts, sleds, blankets, snowsuits, toothbrushes, and lunch boxes.

Then, at Christmas, Crockett collapsed. The kids had burned it out overnight. The price of Crockett T-shirts was slashed from $1.29 apiece to 33 cents and still were not moving. Crockett had "pancaked," *Variety* groaned in a headline. "He laid a bomb." Not exactly. Crockett turned out to be a different kind of pathfinder. The hold of Walt Disney on childhood imagination, building throughout the fifties, was stronger than ever. The "Frontierland" that Disney made a staple of his amusement parks owes it all to Fess Parker. More importantly, the baby-boom children had come into their own as consumers who could make or break entire product lines. The discovery was exhilarating. Surveying the thriving market of 1955, a Seattle banker announced, "Anybody who can't find cause for at least selective optimism is just congenitally morose." In its year-end review, *Time* concluded that "1955 showed the flowering of American capitalism."

For the rest of the decade, other fads swarmed like mayflies in the sun. In 1958, two Pasadena entrepreneurs imported an idea from another baby-boom country, Australia. Their Wham-O corporation began to manufacture simple plastic hoops at a cost of 50 cents each and sold them for $1.98. Hula-Hoops became a national infatuation. Upwards of 20,000 were manufactured daily and Wham-O and its imitators flooded the market with more than 20 million in a matter of months. (A loophole—or better, hoophole—in the patent law prevented Wham-O from cornering the market.) Then, like Davy Crockett, Hula-Hoops fizzled quickly in the winter. *The Wall Street Journal*'s epitaph: HOOPS HAVE HAD IT. But the unconscious eroticism the fad had released found another expression just two years later when the same kids started a swivel-hipped dance craze called the Twist.

All of these fads had an effect on the baby boom that made them unlike children of the past. They were the first generation of children to be isolated by Madison Avenue as an identifiable market. That is the appropriate word: *isolated*. Marketing, and especially television, *isolated* their needs and wants from those of their parents. From the cradle, the baby boomers had been surrounded by products created especially for them, from Silly Putty to Slinkys to skateboards. New products, new toys, new commercials, new fads—the dictatorship of the new—was integral to the baby-boom experience. So prevalent was it that baby boomers themselves rarely realized how different it made them. They breathed it like air.

Joyce Maynard remembered how a typical new product, Barbie dolls, arrived in her world "like a cloudburst, without preparation. Barbie wasn't just a toy, but a way of living that moved us suddenly from tea parties to dates with Ken at the soda shoppe." In twenty years, Mattel sold 112 million copies of Barbie, Ken, little sister Skipper, cousin Francie, and dozens of others to Joyce Maynard and her peers. Barbie has worn one thousand outfits, enough to make Mattel one of the top manufacturers of women's clothing in the world. Barbie herself, gifted with a high-breasted, wasp-waisted look and a plastic personality, was born in 1959 and turned twenty-one in 1980. For that matter, the prototype Barbie—designer Bill Barton's daughter Barbie—is also a baby boomer. That's the way it's always been for the baby boom. Products were made for the generation, and the generation was made for the products.

Chapter 4

FROM SPOCK TO SPUTNIK

In one of John Updike's best stories about Dick and Joan Maple, his archetypal suburban couple, we come across a moment of truth about baby-boom parents and their children. Over dinner, the Maples have just tearfully told their family the news that they are divorcing. The children are hurt and confused. "What do you care about us?" blurts their son angrily. "We're just the little things you had." Stung, Dick Maple tries to explain. "You're not the little things we had," he replies. "You're the whole point."

Exactly. Children were the whole point. This generation of Americans enshrined them. European visitors joked knowingly about how well American parents obeyed their children. American parents did seem to be making their kids their religion. Their resolve was supported by the grandparents, who never enjoyed such a wealth of offspring in their time. Nothing was too good for a generation lucky enough to be spared the scars of Depression and war. In the quarter-century after World War II, the parents had seen their family income double in real purchasing power. Affluence would now bring their children the best of everything. They would have more toys, more money, and more attention. They would have better schools and better books and better teachers. They would be, as William Manchester wrote in *The Glory and the Dream*, "adorable as babies, cute as grade school pupils and striking as they entered their teens. After high school they would attend the best colleges and universities in the country, where their parents would be very, very proud of them."

True, some people worried that they would also be a "spoiled" generation. The historian Richard Hofstadter thought that America was becoming the land of the "overvalued child." More recently, the heroine's mother in Lisa Alther's *Kinflicks* reflected, "If anything had been drummed into her in her years of motherhood, it was that you mustn't squelch the young. It might squelch their precious development. Never mind about your own development." But such criticism was rarely heard at the time. America seemed to have adapted advertising sloganeering to childrearing. Children could be as "new and improved" as detergent. John Dewey once remarked that the great discovery of the twentieth century was the child. Now American parents seemed bent on raising their discovery to a kind of Pygmalionesque perfection.

It began with Spock. By publishing *The Common Sense Book of Baby and Child Care* in June of 1946, Benjamin McLane Spock, M.D., achieved a triumph of good writing that was firstly a triumph of good timing. He caught the first of the successive waves of baby-boom mothers who eagerly reared an entire generation on what they just called "Spock." Unpromoted and unreviewed, the 35-cent Pocket Books edition sold 4 million copies by 1952 and sold at least 1 million a year for eighteen straight years, reaching 30 million copies in 29 languages, including Catalan and Urdu. It became the bestselling new title ever published in the United States. Veterans' wives called their toddlers "Spock babies" and it didn't hurt presidential candidate Jack Kennedy's standing among voting mothers when his wife announced in 1960, "Dr. Spock is for my husband, and I am for Dr. Spock." Most young mothers then would no sooner quarrel with the Spock canon than a parish priest defy the pope. Pediatricians sometimes grumbled that they were sick and tired of hearing from their patients' mothers "what Dr. Spock says," but all of them had to acknowledge his service to mothers. If as many mothers read Spock as bought him, one out of every five babies was a Spock baby.

What was Dr. Spock's secret? His book was enormously thorough and clearly and sympathetically written. Mothers said that he "understood" their problems. His tone was reassuring and folksy. "How to fold a diaper," decreed the good doctor with a twinkle, "depends on the size of the baby and of the diaper."

More importantly, perhaps, Dr. Spock offered a warmly human alternative to the rigid childrearing teach-ings of the thirties and forties. Thirty years previously, parents followed a set of Victorian rules that kept babies on schedule (both bottle and potty), frowned on breast-feeding, and advocated unbending discipline. The popular books of Dr. L. Emmett Holt threw the full weight of the scientific method behind "no more coddling of babies," especially such indulgences as playing, kissing, and rocking. Experts like Granville Stanley Hall agreed that they wanted "less sentimentality and more spanking." Grandparents of the baby boomers devoutly read behavioralist John B. Watson's *The Psychological Care of Infant and Child,* which told mothers never to hug or kiss children, never to let them sit in one's lap, to shake hands with them in the morning, and hold them to clockwork feeding and toileting schedules.

Attitudes had already begun to soften before Spock wholeheartedly told parents to trust their instincts and not be afraid of loving their babies. Relax, he said in effect. Children are individuals, too. Love and enjoy them. Cuddling can be as important as cleanliness.

His message was clear enough, but some parents took his emphasis on honesty literally. One fifties mother told *Time* that "a parent who says to a child, 'I don't know' is somehow better than one who says, 'I know for sure.'" To Spock's own dismay, the public began to associate him with "permissiveness." The confusion was between "permissive" social behavior and "permissive" feeding habits. Spock had come out for demand feeding, but even in his first edition had warned against giving up clockwork schedules abruptly. (Curiously, the incidence of breast-fed infants discharged from hospitals actually *dropped* from 65 percent in 1946 to 37 percent in 1956 to 27 percent in 1966. Since it rose again in the 1970s, the baby boomers wound up as the *least* breast-fed generation in our history.)

The charge of permissiveness returned when Spock joined the Vietnam antiwar movement during the 1960s. To his critics, Spock had thus revealed his real message. His theories of child care were somehow subversive and responsible for the opposition of so many young people to the war. President Richard Nixon tried such epithets as "Spock-marked" and Vice President Spiro Agnew fulminated against the children of "affluent, permissive, upper-middle-class parents who learned their Dr. Spock and threw discipline out the window." According to Agnew,

"The decree that infants should be fed on demand and not on schedule has been elevated to dogma up to age 30."

Scrutiny of *Baby and Child Care,* however, fails to uncover the basis of these charges. Spock had always been opposed to the "needless self-sacrifice" of parents martyring themselves to their children and, in his 1957 edition, had added more emphasis on the need for firm parental leadership. Nonetheless, he had become a symbol. As such, he meant one thing to the Agnews who found him permissive. But I think he was a symbol of something altogether different to parents. It was the idea that one could devote oneself entirely to raising the children. Further, these children could become the brightest and healthiest and most assured ever. Only later would the parents learn that one of the prices of their success would be that the bold and independent generation they raised would choose to make its own headstrong way in the world.

If Dr. Spock was the first millionaire made by the baby boom, then elementary and secondary education became the first growth industry. As early as 1947, the number of children entering kindergarten had jumped 10 percent because of babies born during the first year of the wartime draft. Then, in 1951 and 1952, the first wave of postwar babies surged into kindergarten and the schools began exploding. Between 1950 and 1970, elementary-school enrollment rose by two-thirds. At the crest of the wave were the students born in 1946–47, who would form a moving cohort 38 percent larger than the one immediately ahead of it. As they advanced through the grades, they forced each level to expand drastically to make room for it. For twelve straight years, each graduating senior class was replaced by a group of kindergartners that outnumbered it by an average of 1.5 million students and by as many as 2.5 million students. This vertiginous growth rate did not begin to ease until the 1946 cohort began graduating with the high school Class of '64. By that time, one out of four Americans was enrolled in the public schools. The absolute number of students would not turn down until 1970, when elementary- and secondary-school enrollment peaked at 51.3 million.

The schools thereby became the first of our institutions to feel the strains brought by the baby boom. They, after all, are as close to purely age-specific institutions as exist in our society: entrance and exit are determined by age and attendance is almost universal. When the total of Americans between the ages of 5 and 14 increased by 47 percent in a decade, there was nothing to soften a similar shock to the schools. As we shall see, their response to the problems posed by the arrival and departure of the baby-boom children could practically have been a paradigm for the identical experience in countless other institutions for the next thirty years.

To begin with, no one prepared for the baby boom. Demographers had predicted all along that the boom was likely to end "next year," after wartime parents finished having their welcome-home babies. Why should they build a new school, officials reasoned, if by the time it was funded and completed, the boom children could easily have moved on past it? Further, since most of the educational decisions were not made nationally but locally, regional differences in migration and fertility made consistent planning almost impossible.

The result was that the schools wound up jammed. In 1952, some 50,000 new classrooms were built, but they were hardly enough. That next fall, some 2 million more students headed for school. California was opening one school a week in the fifties, and Los Angeles was spending $1 million a week on new schools by the mid-sixties, opening 62 elementary schools, 26 junior highs, and 10 senior highs in less than a decade. But the nation still wound up short 345,000 classrooms despite frantic construction of new ones. Classrooms with 45 students to a single teacher were not uncommon, and three out of every five classes across the country were considered overcrowded. Upwards of 78,000 makeshift classrooms sprang up in churches and vacant stores across the country, and students found themselves sharing both books and desks.

Teachers were also in short supply. Each new surge in the birthrate resulted six years later in equivalent demand for more teachers. With more than a 50 percent increase in annual births from 2.8 million in 1945 to 4.3 million in 1957, the teachers colleges could not possibly keep pace. (One reason was that the supply had earlier drifted abnormally low because of the relatively small number needed to educate the Depression generation.) In the decade from 1956 to 1965, the City of Los Angeles hired 1000 new teachers each year but still could not keep up.

The teacher shortage hit 72,000 in the early fifties and, by 1959, nearly 100,000 of the nation's 1.3 million public school teachers were working with substandard credentials. In states like New Jersey, where the school population increased by 62 percent from 1950 to 1960, some 57,000 students were crowded into half-sessions and 48,000 were being taught by underqualified teachers.

It is not, I think, overstating the case to say that the arrival of the baby boom was an educational disaster for the United States. The system was on overload. To parents, who could see and hear the red lights blinking, it was practically a betrayal. The most promising generation America had produced was not getting the education it deserved. Moreover, as we would later begin to learn, the socialization of the young was also being crippled. Every society seeks to transmit its culture to the younger generation through parents and teachers—and now there were not enough teachers to go around. In times of rapid social and technological change, as during the fifties, this process is even more difficult. Some of the threads that bound generations together were being unraveled.

Who would help? In those days, the federal government stayed out of local education. Instead, aid came from the people who started it all, the parents. Suburban mothers became the chief guerrilla fighters for school expansion and reform. They formed militant PTAs whose common cause was the Best Possible Education. Across the country PTAs doubled their membership in six years to nearly eight million by 1952. Education was becoming the nation's secular religion, a crusade in which mothers marched not with crosses but bond issues. In 1950, we had spent $6.6 billion on our elementary and secondary schools. A decade later, the total had risen to $18.6 billion. In a single year, 1958, we built 62,000 new classrooms at an average cost of $40,000 apiece.

In his discerning book, *The Organization Man,* William H. Whyte, Jr., was struck by how suburbanites managed to link up idealism with their desire for a good life for their children. He visited one suburb where the school board was demanding that a $60,000 multipurpose room be added to a new school under way—even though the money was not there to pay for it. Why, he asked the young board president, did they need it? The man was astonished at the question. "Our children deserve the best," he replied heatedly. "Our children deserve the best."

So the best schools money could buy were built for the baby boomers. But just as they entered the schools, their education was cast into the shadow of the Cold War. On June 25, 1950, the North Koreans had invaded South Korea. That same year Dr. Klaus Fuchs admitted his guilt in passing nuclear bombs to the Soviets. Then in 1951 the Army began detonating nuclear bombs in the Nevada desert. That winter radioactivity was detected in the snowfall in Rochester, New York. By March 1953, there had been twenty nuclear tests in Nevada, and sheep were dying in Utah. A seven-year-old boy, Martin Laird, died of leukemia in Carson City, Nevada, seventy miles from ground zero, and became possibly the first baby-boom casualty of the atomic age. On November 1, 1952, the first H-bomb was exploded. Five years later, a radioactive isotope called strontium 90, which lodges in bone and causes cancer, was detected in cow's milk around the country. Mothers began telling the baby boomers *not* to drink their milk.

In the schools, baby-boom children began performing a bizarre weekly drill none of them has forgotten. "At a sudden signal," Jeff Greenfield remembered, "we would drop from our chairs, pull ourselves into a fetal position, and crouch under our desks, and wait until the A-bomb had fallen." In her novel, *McCarthy's List,* Mary Mackey also remembered the terror of those days:

> Obediently we would fold our bodies into that attitude of prayer and supplication known only to the children of the fifties: legs folded, head between the knees, hands raised to protect the fragile, invisible nerve that floated somewhere in the blackness behind our eyes.

In case the students missed the point, teachers passed out maps of cities upon which were superimposed ominous bull's-eyes showing the lethal reach of the bomb. The baby-boomers never forgot the lesson that their world could someday end in a flash of light and heat while they were crouched helplessly in gyms and basements among heating ducts and spare blackboards.

Or, if they were not killed at once, would their teeth and hair fall out in a slower, more agonizing death? This was not Tom Corbett and his Space Cadets and could not be explained by Mr. Wizard. It was a vague, ceaseless anxiety. Mary Mackey's protagonist, a consummate post-war child born on the very day the bomb fell on Hiroshima, remembers how

> At night I would lie awake in my bed and count slowly to twenty-five as each plane passed over, afraid to miss the flash of light that would be my only warning.

Here is another baby-boom writer in the *Washington Post*:

> Between the ages of about 10 and 20, I had fairly regular nightmares about the destruction of the world with nuclear weapons. These dreams almost always began with a flash of dazzling light, followed by a murky series of episodes in which I stumbled through rubble, always looking for someone—a friend—a member of my family—whom I could never find. Often I was chased by sinister figures, but my legs could hardly move. I would try to warn people that we were in great danger, but my mouth would be locked as if with tetanus.

The doomsday dread was pervasive in the boom generation. One woman, now a graduate student, remembered being awakened at the age of eleven by two sonic booms. She thought it was the end of the world. "I was paralyzed," she said. "I couldn't make any noise or call out. I just lay there and prayed."

Years later, students at San Francisco State reported having recurring dreams of nuclear bombs exploding. It was not just a grim joke when this generation made Barry McGuire's "Eve of Destruction" into rock's first protest song. One of the leaders of the antinuclear weapons movement in the late 1970s, Charles Hansen, dated his concern to the "shapeless fears" his mind held from the days of air-raid drills at his school in Seattle: "I remember watching President Kennedy on television when he talked about the Cuban missile crisis. He said the Russian ship was in the bull's-eye, and that upset me." It was no different after the Three Mile Island nuclear accident of 1979, when the first protesters to take to the streets were the same grownup kids who had marched through the air-raid drills a quarter-century earlier. Like the Japanese, they would never outgrow the feeling that they were all *Hibakusha,* survivors of the bomb.

The Cold War hysteria continued to shove its way into the schools. On October 4, 1957, Americans were jolted with the news that the Soviet Union had rocketed into space the first man-made satellite. The 184-pound "Sputnik," not much bigger than a beach ball, was whirling around the earth once every hour and a half, beeping out what Clare Boothe Luce called an "outer-space raspberry to a decade of American pretentions that the American way of life is a gilt-edged guarantee of our national superiority." Twenty-nine days later the Soviets put up a second Sputnik, this one with a dog inside of it, and American confidence was further shattered. The Russians had somehow seized control of the heavens themselves! How had we failed?

The scapegoating began with the schools. Suddenly the entire country discovered that, while American youths were idly humming Jimmie Rodgers's "Honeycomb" (the number one song that Sputnik week), little Ivan was ruthlessly studying long division. Alarming reports flowed from Russia of tough and purposeful Soviet schools, stressing the sciences and placing little stock in civics. Soviet teachers were creating little geniuses in the fourth grade and training them to develop bigger and even more frightening rockets and Sputniks. They were bravely shouldering formidable homework assignments while American kids played Davy Crockett. Rudolf Flesch's *Why Johnny Can't Read and What You Can Do About It,* which had barely made a ripple when it was originally published in 1955, was reissued and became a national byword. Reformers like James B. Conant and Vice Admiral Hyman G. Rickover argued that American know-how was failing, the missile gap was growing, and that the schools were somehow responsible.

Life added its worried voice to the national debate with a "Crisis in Education" series that flunked the entire system:

> The schools have been overcrowded for years. In their eagerness to be all things to all children, schools have gone wild with elective courses. They build up the bodies with in-school lunches and let the minds shift for themselves. Where there are young minds of great promise, there are rarely the means to advance them.

The nation's stupid children get far better care than the bright. The geniuses of the next decade are even now being allowed to slip back into mediocrity. . . .

Parents could hardly quarrel with such a resounding clarion call, though they were, in a way, the problem. From the time of Miss Frances and Ding Dong School, they had stressed the social values of education. This was to be a "well-adjusted" and "well-rounded" generation, one that would work well in groups, play cooperatively, express itself creatively. Report cards graded "gets along well with others" as highly as spelling. Pity the child who received failing marks in such categories as "cheerfulness"—though the nature of the remedy was left unclear.

Now these same parents were demanding that their schools be toughened. The National Defense Education Act of 1958 began the process with a typically American solution by throwing millions of dollars at the problem. But while everyone agreed on the goals, no one agreed on how to get there. Some educators called for less fluff and a "Back to Basics" approach. Others, contrarily, blamed textbooks for dumping masses of facts and rote learning on students without explaining the whys and hows of the subject. New programs and approaches began to sprout up like housing developments. Audiovisual programs gained as a method of "engaging" students pretrained by television. So did the New Math and the New Social Studies. Schools were built with green blackboards and modular classrooms that would expand and contract to accommodate a kind of free-form teaching.

Textbooks had always been under siege, but as the baby boomers came of age the attacks came from all directions. The John Birch Society attributed the North Koreans' success in brainwashing American POWs to earlier history textbooks which did not build character. Other right-wing groups saw a lack of anti-Red zeal in the schoolbooks. Later, in the 1960s, blacks began to weed out racial stereotypes from books which had either ignored black history or pigeonholed it in brief discussions of the contributions of Ralph Bunche and George Washington Carver.

But, as the writer Frances FitzGerald has pointed out, most baby boomers grew up reading schoolbooks that presented a singularly glowing (but unrealistic) account of American history. We were a kind and generous people.

We made mistakes, like cheating Indians, but also made amends. We welcomed immigrants to our "melting pot." We did not fight unjust wars. Rather, we were the champions of freedom and democracy. We were a tolerant people who had made a land where any shoeshine boy had a chance to go to the top.

The danger of such a sanitized representation of the American reality is that it leads almost inevitably to cynicism. Baby-boom children discovered in the sixties that they'd been given a Disney version of history. America was not perfect. There were injustices around them and tragedies in our history. The shock of recognition was all the more shattering because of the historical whitewash in their social studies courses. The concerned PTA mothers who fought to nurture patriotism in the schools in the fifties did more than they ever could have known to destroy it in the sixties. The war in Vietnam, the riots in the cities, and the assassinations were devastating to a generation raised on American righteousness. Dick and Jane could offer a bland misrepresentation of American life in elementary readers, but they could not get away with it in high school. FitzGerald has described the ultimate message of these books. "They give young people no warning of the real dangers ahead, and later they may well make these young people feel that their own experience of conflict or suffering is unique in history and perhaps un-American."

On May 17, 1954, the United States Supreme Court announced its decision in *Brown* v. *Board of Education:* desegregation would be the law of the land. *Brown* would have a profound impact on the lives of the baby boomers. But at first it barely changed a thing. Despite the headlines about places like Little Rock, where schools were integrated at bayonet point, there was pitifully little integration in the first decade, after Southern politicians effectively delayed, evaded, impeded, and otherwise blocked integration. Northerners did little better to desegregate the ghettos of the large cities.

Black and white baby-boom children did not really begin to see one another in classrooms until after the Civil Rights Act of 1964, the year the oldest baby boomers were graduating from high school. Back in 1968, 75 percent of all minority students were attending segregated schools, but by 1976, only 17 percent of black students were still segregated. The change was most dramatic in the South, where only one of every ten black students was in a segregated school in 1976, compared to twice as many in Northern schools. But for most baby boomers, integration really began in college, where black enrollment doubled in the seventies.

In the end, what made the baby boom different from earlier generations in race relations was less a question of integration than tolerance. If white baby-boom students did not actually march to class with the black girls in Little Rock, they at least watched them on television. Their preachers, parents, teachers, and schoolbooks paid considerable lip service to the rights of what were then called Negroes. By the time the Freedom Riders had gone south, and three young civil rights workers had been killed in Mississippi, the baby boom was largely committed to the principle—if not always the practice—of black progress. When a poll taken in 1979 by the National Conference of Christians and Jews asked if the rate of integration was "too fast" or "too slow," more than twice as many in the over-30 generation answered "too fast." On the other hand, twice as many of the under-30 group thought that integration was "too slow." Civil rights was the one history lesson that stuck.

Schools were not the only institution that the baby-boom kids joined in those years. It was the golden age of scouting. Actually, the Cub Scouts were the first to absorb the generation. Enrollment in Cub Scout packs doubled from 766,635 in 1949 to 1.6 million in 1956 and eventually peaked at nearly 2.5 million. In a single year, 1954, more than 200,000 tots clapped on their blue-and-yellow beanies for the first time and started tying square knots. Girl Scouts and Brownies likewise raced from 1.8 million in 1950 to 4 million a decade later. Young Americans, most of them living in the suburbs, were devoting themselves to woodland crafts with a passion that no doubt proved useful years later when some of them joined communes and moved back to the farms.

Baseball had its heyday then, too. The nostalgia and warmth that baby boomers would later devote almost exclusively to baseball among American sports began in the fifties as the number of Little Leagues expanded from 776 in 1950 to 5700 in 1960. More than a million kids were playing on Little League teams. One suburb, Lakeland, California, fielded 110 boys' teams with 2000 players. "The kids are the only ones who are really organized here," said one Californian at the time. "We older people sort of tag along after them." But that was not the whole truth. The elders were more like an army of Little League parents, motivated by love, but imposing a burden as well. Their children were becoming an overorganized generation with every spare moment preplanned. Their parents would have built lemonade stands for them, if they could, and they often did. Later, psychologists would find here the origins of frustration. Everything had been done *for* the baby boomers when they were young. They had been counted and grouped together in classrooms, teams, and packs because that was the only way society could sort out and contend with their enormous number.

The baby boomers were trained in groups. They looked not within themselves or even to their parents for guidance but to their peer group. They had an appreciation for the common good that was hitherto unknown in a country of individualists. They had, as William Manchester put it, marvelous radar but no gyroscopes. At first, whether in classes or in Cub Scout packs or on Little League teams, the organization was imposed from without. (In those days, one's closest friends were likely to be those whose last name began with the same letter as yours.) Later on, the baby boomers would organize themselves for another form of mass action.

This was also the golden age of disease. I do not mean that facetiously, since the baby boomers both caused and benefited from the epidemics of infectious diseases that swept across the country when they were young. Initially, the boom generation did not have enough medical care. The country could not hope to produce doctors as fast as it could produce babies. The supply of pediatricians in the country was barely adequate to cope with the generation before the baby boom. The Depression generation that might have been expected to train more doctors was itself so small that it faced a manpower shortage. When the boom babies began jamming maternity wards, there was no way to keep up. It takes ten years to train a pediatrician, from the time a student decides to become a physician until he or she is fully licensed to practice. Thus, something like 38 million potential sore throats and 76 million potential ear infections were born before the *first* new pediatrician arrived to do something about it. By 1959, there were five thousand hospital staff vacancies for doctors. Hospitals were running short of nurses, too. Why? Because many nurses, as well as women who might have become nurses, were busy having babies.

Astonishingly, the American Medical Association, which certifies medical schools and thereby controls the flow of new doctors, did almost nothing to increase medical care for the boom generation. After World War II, while every other segment of higher education was rapidly expanding, medical schools remained unchanged. In 1950, more than 5 percent of postgraduate degrees awarded in America were in medicine; in 1972, less than 3 percent were. The number of physicians per 100,000 citizens in the United States actually *declined* between 1950 and 1960. The shortage was eventually made up by doctors trained in other countries. More than one out of every five physicians practicing in 1974 received his or her training abroad.

Fortunately, the baby boom grew up during some of the most dramatic advances made during the history of medicine. The diphtheria vaccine introduced in 1945 meant that the boom generation never had to fear a disease that infected nearly 20,000 people annually during World War II. The oldest members of the boom generation will be the last to remember the fear of polio. More than 33,000 children were afflicted in 1950, and the 1952 polio epidemic of 58,000 cases left 1400 dead and thousands more in wheelchairs or steel braces. Parents warned their children to stay away from crowded swimming pools, and Mary Mackey relates in her novel how "my best friend, Joyce, lay in a big silver machine that did her breathing for her. At home we lived in a state of siege, boiling our water and keeping the windows closed so the flies couldn't get in." But then in 1955, with the contagion spreading through the generation, the crash program to develop vaccines paid off. Five years after the Salk vaccine was introduced, the number of new cases of paralytic polio dropped to 3190, and the disease was all but wiped out in the seventies.

The baby boomers were also the last generation to live with the worst epidemics of measles. Before the vaccine was introduced in 1963, there were 400,000 cases reported annually, though public health officials estimated that the true number was more like 4 million. More than 400 children were dying every year from measles. But by 1978 the number of cases of measles had been reduced by 95 percent and not a single death was reported. Similarly, German measles, or rubella, made its last stand in the winter of 1963–64, when pregnant women exposed to the disease had an estimated 20,000 miscarriages and 30,000 children born with birth defects. In 1978, the total number of rubella cases was down to 16,817.

Other dread diseases, thankfully, are now almost forgotten. Whooping cough, a leading cause of death at the turn of the century and still a feared child-killer in the thirties, had infected as many as 183,866 people in 1940. One out of every hundred children who caught it died. But, after the vaccine, the number of cases fell to 14,809 in 1960 and to 2000 in 1977. Mumps was cut from 152,209 cases in 1968 to 38,000 in 1976. Some surgical procedures also went out of style. Few baby-boom children survived into adolescence without at least one doctor making a grab for their tonsils. Entire families trooped into hospitals to undergo what was the nation's leading major operation as recently as 1971. Tonsillectomies are performed far less frequently now. Some generations would have sacrificed their right arms for their country; the baby boomers sacrificed their tonsils.

Hyperactivity, a condition unknown to previous generations, was first diagnosed in the baby boomers. The name is actually a catchall describing a variety of childhood complaints, including restlessness, inattention, impatience, and interruption of others. What is interesting is the treatment. In the sixties, doctors found that if stimulants like dextroamphetamine and methylphenidate were given to "hyperactive" children, they had the contrary effect of calming them. Most doctors who study the problem believe that hyperactivity afflicts between 1 and 5 percent of all children. The problem is that many more baby-boom children were so diagnosed, often by teachers unable to cope with them. There are examples of some teachers citing as many as seven children in a class of twenty as "hyperactive." How many of them were truly in need of medical attention? Or how many of them were identified because of a teacher's difficulty in contending with the crowding and large classes brought on by the boom generation? Doctors are only now turning their attention to follow-up studies of the many thousands of adults who were labeled "hyperactive" as children and lived on daily dosages of drugs throughout their schooling.

* * *

Those problems aside, the baby boomers could generally count their blessings. Thanks to medical advances, especially in infant mortality, a child of the baby boom could expect to live at least six years longer than one born before World War II. Parents who were striving to make their children perfect in mind and character were also succeeding in body as well. They had scrimped along eating Spam during the war. But here was a robust generation of children growing up eating steaks, milk, and Wonder Bread for strong bones and teeth. Look, the parents marveled, our children have so much more than we ever did. They will be bigger and stronger and healthier. They must seize this wonderful opportunity. They are the luckiest generation alive.

The message was not lost on the baby boomers. They, too, knew that they were *special*. Their parents had endlessly told them how fortunate they were. Their experience provided ample proof of their specialness: they'd had new schools, crisp new schoolbooks every year, homes so new that the putty was barely dry, toys of gleaming plastic. Their whole world was fraught with the promise and fresh smell of a new car. They were at home in the culture of the new.

In the early years of the baby boom, an unusually large proportion of the children born were eldest children. First children are not like the others—for a brief shining moment in their lives, before siblings arrived, their parents and their world truly seemed to revolve around them. They are often more self-confident than other children, less compromising, and more arrogant. In most years, eldest children soon confront a world that makes clear that their place is *not* the predominant one they originally thought. But, during the baby boom, all children were in effect told that *they* were the eldest children, that *they* were at the center of a benevolent world, that *their* needs were important, that *they* could shape events to their liking. It was as if the peculiar psychological makeup of the eldest child had infected all children. Many of them never lost the special expectation of an eldest child that the world is somehow organized *just for them*.

How, indeed, could they be blamed for drawing this conclusion? Everywhere they looked they would see evidence of their power. The landscape had been paved into suburbs; thousands of new schools had been built. Their economic power turned their casual fancies into national fads. Madison Avenue was aiming the most powerful selling medium ever invented—television—directly at them. So pervasive was their influence that it was difficult for some solipsistic baby boomers to distinguish it from everything else. A woman born in 1946 once remarked to me that for most of her youth she thought that *all* new generations were afforded such attention. Only much later did she realize, "This wasn't the way it always was; we were the ones who were different."

Chapter 5

THE TYRANNY OF TEEN

"ONE, TWO, THREE O'CLOCK, FOUR O'CLOCK ROCK . . ." Belting out those words, Bill Haley did more than anyone to forge the consciousness of the postwar generation. They are the opening lyrics to "Rock Around the Clock," a rhythm-and-blues tune sang, incongruously, by a white man, that became the "Internationale" of the rock revolution. But at first no one knew it, least of all Haley, then an obscure country balladeer with a spit curl plastered on his forehead. He had recorded the song written by James Myers (under the nom de guerre of Jimmy De Knight) as an afterthought, the B side of a single called "Thirteen Women" that was supposed to become his breakthrough hit. But when the record was released in 1954, it was "Rock Around the Clock" that became a minor hit—and then fizzled out.

The story might have ended there. But a year later "Rock Around the Clock" resurfaced on the opening credits of a movie about juvenile delinquents, *Blackboard Jungle,* and something clicked. In the context of teenage rebellion, the song made a statement that released the inchoate energies of a whole generation on something that was exclusively theirs. It was, as rock critic Lillian Roxon wrote, "the first song to have a special secret defiant meaning for teenagers only. It was the first inkling teenagers had that they might be a force to be reckoned with, in numbers alone. If there could be one song, there could be others; there could be a whole world of songs, and then, a whole world."

Remember the world "Rock Around the Clock" invaded. In the early fifties, older singers were still churning out tunes for an older audience. They listened to Rosemary Clooney's "Come on-a My House" and Perry

Como's sixth gold record, "Don't Let the Stars Get in Your Eyes." At a time when Patti Page could score with a novelty song like "How Much Is That Doggie in the Window?," the idea of selling millions of records to preteens was as unthinkable as writing music about them.

But here, with all the force of the giant generation gathering behind it, was a hit song unmistakably written for teenagers and reeking of their atavistic energies. The most symbolic moment in *Blackboard Jungle* came when the kids smashed a teacher's treasured collection of jazz 78s. Haley himself was a grown-up (a fact that would limit his career), but "Rock Around the Clock" nonetheless became the first international record hit, holding number one on the charts for two months in 1955 and surging on to sell 16 million copies before it was all over. Kids were rioting in England over a song that the bemused record company had marked on the label as "Fox trot with vocal." Other rock hits followed rapid-fire, many of them white "covers" of black songs. On Lucky Strike's televised *Your Hit Parade*, the ensemble of Snooky Lanson, Russell Scott, Dorothy Collins, and Gisele MacKenzie found it harder and harder to conform their cloying production numbers to rock's suggestive rhythms and lyrics. It was easy enough to handle "I Saw Mommy Kissing Santa Claus," all right, but what could you do when Leiber & Stoller were writing hymns to teenage lust and motorcycle gangs? The Hit Paraders and Raymond Scott's orchestra finally admitted defeat and went off NBC in 1958.

The oldest boom children were only eight when "Rock Around the Clock" came out. But from then on each wave of kids entered adolescence in a world permeated with rock. At the onset of puberty, a vulnerable point in anyone's life, they were overwhelmed by an energetic music whose sexual power was never far below the surface. (The term "rock 'n' roll" meant something altogether different to black bluesmen than it did to suburban parents.)

A generation gap was already forming between the kids who discovered rock and their older brothers and sisters. In 1956, ten-year-olds were learning the words to "Blue Suede Shoes," while their older siblings in high school were still swooning over Doris Day's "What Will Be, Will Be." Those younger kids became the cutting edge of the rock generation. As they aged, they took the beat with them. When the ten-year-olds of 1956 hit high school six years later, they embraced the Beatles. Then the rock audience extended through high school, but not through college, where senior proms still danced to Lester Lanin. When the rock generation entered college, they brought the Beatles and the Jefferson Airplane with them. And, as young adults, they became the thirty-year-olds behind the adult version of rock, disco.

In short, the baby boomers *were* the rock audience. Rock was the sound track in the movie version of their lives. They discovered it, danced to it, romanced to it, went to college to it, protested to it, got married to it, and someday will presumably be buried to it. The music consolidated their group identity, bridging the emotions they all felt inside with peers who felt the same way. Rock was a language that taught the baby boom about themselves. Before rock, the people who were born in the late 1940s and grew up in the 1950s might have thought of themselves as disconnected individuals who shared little other than a common interest in fads and TV. After rock, they were an army. "It began with the Music," Jeff Greenfield has written perceptively. "Nothing we see in the counter-culture—not the clothes, the hair, the sexuality, the drugs, the rejection of reason, the resort to symbols and magic—none of it is separable from the coming to power in the 1950s of rock and roll music." The Woodstock Nation was originally the Rock Nation. Kids all over the East Coast were sneaking upstairs, closing the door, and listening to disc jockey Alan Freed playing "Stagger Lee" on New York's radio station WINS, juiced up to 50,000 watts. Anyone from Los Angeles visiting relations in Chicago knew that, if all else failed, there was one sure way to feel at home: turn up the radio.

In those energetic early days of rock, the singer was less important than the song. The attention of an entire generation was focused on the excitement and thrill of the music itself. Rock was the message and the singers were merely the messengers. This vast audience could absorb a hit overnight and, while everyone was reeling, drop it, and move on to another. A maudlin single like the Kingston Trio's "Tom Dooley" was an intensely felt national event, blooming and dying in the space of a month. The artists were just as disposable. Bill Haley never came close to replicating his "Rock Around the Clock" miracle. Many others, like Guy ("Singing the

Blues") Mitchell and Jim ("The Green Door") Lowe, had even briefer lives.

But rock was still waiting for its first superstar. In Memphis, Sam Phillips of little Sun Records had always said that he could make "a billion dollars" if he could find "a white man who had the Negro sound and the Negro feel." He found him in a truck driver. Elvis Presley recorded Arthur (Big Boy) Crudup's "That's All Right, Mama" for Phillips in 1954. Two years later, Presley's "Heartbreak Hotel" and "Hound Dog" gave a compellingly magnetic personality to rock for the first time. Instead of the relaxed genteelisms of Perry Como and later, Pat Boone, Presley was hot and sullen and dangerous. Even now it is hard to overestimate the galvanizing excitement Presley released with his first records. He wore slicked hair, like a hood, sneered, and defiantly placed his feet wide apart. Yet in his eyes was a look of surprise, as if he were as startled as we were by the flooding emotions he had tapped. It was television, typically, that helped put him over as millions of preteens watched him on *Ed Sullivan* and wondered with delight what could have been so wildly wicked that the cameras could not show him from the waist down. In one year, 1956, Presley won an unheard-of five gold records; Perry Como was cut to one for "Hot Diggity." But by that time Sam Phillips had sold Presley's contract to RCA—not for $1 billion dollars but $35,000. He had found a true revolutionary, a destroyer of both the old musical order and also the hegemony of the older generation. Elivs Presley was more than a singer to the baby boomers. He was the catalyst for a new culture.

The symbolic importance the baby boomers later attached to Presley's role as a liberator explains in large part the extraordinary grief and denial accompanying his death. His mourners were not the teenagers of 1977 (though some were there). Rather, his mourners were the teenagers of 1956–63. Today Elvis imitators and Elvis conventions and Elvis memorabilia are part of the baby boom's iconography, circulated endlessly like slivers of the true cross.

But Dick Clark was the first real tycoon of teen. On August 8, 1957, his *American Bandstand* show on WFIL-TV in Philadelphia acquired its ABC network hookup for the first time. Baby boomers in sixty-seven cities across the nation sat down to listen to the first song (Jerry

Lee Lewis's "Whole Lotta Shakin' Goin' On") and watch Billy Williams lip-sync the words to his hit, "I'm Gonna Sit Right Down and Write Myself a Letter." The show was panned by *Billboard* ("Colorless juveniles"), but Clark was soon pulling 20 million weekday viewers, drawing 50,000 fan letters a week, and making $500,000 a year. He almost single-handedly built the careers of singers like Connie Francis and Bobby Darin—not to mention making trivia questions out of South Philadelphia kids like Kenny Rossi and Justine Corelli who regularly showed up to dance on his show.

· Eerily ageless and fresh-faced—is there a painting rotting away in his attic?—Clark has remained on the air in one form or another throughout the life of the boom generation. He survived the payola scandal (though he was asked to divest himself of his interests in some 33 music publishing and recording companies). He outlasted the Beatles and acid rock. As late as 1978, television executives understandably became convinced that Clark held the key to reaching what was becoming Madison Avenue's prime target audience. He was given a weekly prime-time slot. His sponsors had changed—from Clearasil to General Motors—but the audience was still the same. (Mercifully, the show flopped.) It is not hard to imagine Clark twenty years from now as the Lawrence Welk of the Pepsi Generation, spinning reprises of "Da Doo Ron Ron" for those who remember.

By the end of the fifties, rock had still not totally conquered the pop charts—Elvis was in the Army and older brothers and sisters were still buying songs like Sinatra's "High Hopes" and Como's "Magic Moment"—but it had brought the baby boom's young teens and preteens into the market with a bang. Retail sales of records had risen from $182 million in 1954 to $40 million in 1957 and then to $521 million in 1960. Dollar sales of record players had doubled in the same period. Yet all the while preachers had fulminated against rock 'n' roll's "immorality," parents had slammed doors, and even Frank Sinatra had erupted against a music he felt was "phony and false, and sung, written and played for the most part by cretinous goons." But the Mr. Blusters of the world would be thwarted again. The coming of "The Twist" in 1959 and 1961 (it was the only record to go to number one *twice*) conquered an older audience for the first time. The kids, meanwhile, moved on to the Watusi, The Hully-Gully, the

Slop and Swim, the Mashed Potato, and dozens of other new dances breeding as fast as adults caught on to the previous one. Danny and the Juniors were right: Rock 'n' roll *was* here to stay. Many of the baby boomers could concur with Bob Dylan, whose sensibility (if not age) was of their generation. "I just carry that other time around with me," Dylan once confessed. "The music of the late fifties and early sixties when music was at that root level —that for me is meaningful music—Buddy Holly and Johnny Ace are just as valid to me today as then."

The idyll of the fifties did not end for the baby boomers on December 31, 1959. Nor was it really over February 3, 1959, when Buddy Holly was killed at the age of 22 (along with Big Bopper and Ritchie Valens) in a plane crash near Mason City, Iowa. (In *American Pie,* singer Don McLean called it "the day the music died.") The time of innocence for this generation, in its own mind, ended on November 22, 1963.

On *As the World Turns,* a live CBS soap opera, actress Helen Wagner had just said, "I gave it a great deal of thought, Grandpa." Suddenly a BULLETIN card flashed on the screen. The disembodied voice of Walter Cronkite was saying that the president had been shot. For the next three and one-half days, 180 million people sat watching the terrible sequence: the return of Air Force One to Washington, the first "live" murder on television, the funeral of the president.

For the baby-boom children, this was the most mesmerizing moment of their youth. Time was frozen. They were the television generation and here was the ultimate television event: not even commercials were being shown. Nine out of every ten members of the generation participated by watching it. All Americans were affected, to be sure, but the impact fell heaviest on the young people who had grown up watching a vigorous young president. They knew him intimately because John Kennedy was the first president to become a TV star. He had debated with Nixon on television and had held the first press conference on television. They had seen him on television speaking in Berlin, toughing out the Cuban missile crisis, and talking about the Peace Corps. They had watched his wife show off the White House on television. His idealism was theirs. To the baby boomers, his death was as personally threatening as if a father had died. Here is how Jeff Greenfield, a slightly older writer, put it:

> To understand that this supremely confident, self-assured man could be slaughtered in broad daylight, his head blown off by some madman (or by some sinister conspiracy; no one could be sure) was to understand the fragility of life, the powerful forces lurking just under the surface of life. What our parents learned in a war, or in a struggle for survival, we learned that November. No one was safe; if not John Kennedy, than definitely not any of us.

The political scientist Sigmund Neumann once made the point that contemporaries are not merely people who coexist in the same period. He argued that generations are identified by "their common experiences, the same decisive influence, similar historical problems." Further, he proposed that generations could be distinguished according to essential impressions received around age 17. The baby boom fits the yardstick only too well. The first baby boomers born in 1946 turned 17 in 1963.

We can see just how deeply the assassination marked them by looking at the records its writers are leaving behind. Michael Medved and David Wallechinsky were well enough aware of its emotional impact that the opening pages of their 1976 best seller, *What Really Happened to the Class of '65*, dealt not with 1965 but with 1963 and the high-school classmates' memories of That Day:

> I guess it was probably the first time that everybody in that high school experienced one feeling together.

> You know, nothing had ever happened bad. All of a sudden these bad things were happening.

> The assassination was probably the single most significant event of my awareness over all those years. It affected me more deeply than anything else that happened, personally or politically. . . . After that, in French class, Mr. Pann made some talk about how this was a terrible tragedy but life had to go on as planned, that we had planned to sing that day. I thought it was the most wretched thing for him to put us through. He made us sing that day. To this day I

remember the songs we sang. If I ever hear them, I get a chill.

Playwrights like Michael Weller have made the assassination a leitmotif in their work. In *Moonchildren*, typically, one character wonders idly, "Did you hear something about an assassination?" No one answers. The *National Lampoon*'s famous parody of a 1964 high-school yearbook included, with cruel accuracy, a page dedicated to John F. Kennedy. Joyce Maynard also reflected on That Day in her autobiography:

> Like over-anxious patients in analysis, we treasure the traumas of our childhood. Ours was more traumatic than most. The Kennedy assassination has become our myth: talk to us for an evening or two—about movies or summer jobs or the weather—and the subject will come up ("where were *you* when you heard . . ."), as if having lived through Jackie and the red roses, John-John's salute and Oswald's on-camera murder justified our disenchantment.

The assassination thus became the marker event in the life of the baby boomers, a trail mark everyone could recognize. "It was the most important day of my life," says a character named Wanda in Robert Patrick's play, *Kennedy's Children*. "I measure everything as happening before it, or after it. I remember every detail, every instant, every little bit of information as it came in." So large, in fact, does the assassination loom in the minds of the baby boomers that they have distorted time around it in the fun-house mirror of memory. Events before the assassination receded as rapidly as if seen through the wrong end of a telescope. It is no coincidence, for instance, that neither of the two movies of the 1970s which most reverently celebrated the culture of the fifties, *American Graffiti* and *Animal House,* were really set in the fifties. Rather, they were both advanced to 1962, the last year of the American Eden before the center could not hold. Similarly, Jack Heifner's *Vanities,* the longest-running play in off-Broadway history and at one time the most-produced play of any kind in the United States, achieved an easy irony by beginning its saga of three Texas high-school cheerleaders on November 22, 1963. Looking back now at the life of the baby boom, we can track its growth the same way botanists detect ancient droughts by measuring thicknesses of tree rings. The assassination of President Kennedy was a constricting event. History was compressed into a single weekend; events and memories overlapped. But then, in the next five years, the baby boom experienced perhaps the greatest growth burst of its life. It was a period of expansiveness so sudden that time seemed to stretch to accommodate it. When it was over, America had passed through Alice's Looking Glass: the social order had turned topsy-turvy. Where we were once ruled by the old, we were now ruled by the young. The rough beast slouching toward Bethlehem was the Youth Society.

It began with the Beatles. Jerry Garcia of the Grateful Dead was still in high school the first time he heard "A Hard Day's Night." "Suddenly it was a good flash," he remembered later. "A happy flash. Post-Kennedy assassination. Like the first good news. It was a groovy thing." The Beatles were exhilarating proof that the baby-boom generation was emerging as an international phenomenon. What now hardly seems to matter at all—the *Englishness* of the Beatles—was amazing then. Here were four musicians who had listened to Chuck Berry not in St. Louis but Liverpool. Rock, once as much an American monopoly as musical comedy, had suddenly passed all borders. At a time when the assassination deprived the boom children of one thing to believe in, the Beatles arrived just in time with something new and fresh and altogether different. If Elvis was more like a threatening older brother, the Beatles were friendly contemporaries. The British rock invasion ended around the time of the 1967 Monterey (Calif.) Pop Festival, but the lesson lasted. Kids in London and Louisville and Larchmont were speaking the same cultural language. Youth was Power.

More than anyone realized at the time, the power was based on the entry of the baby boom into the teenage years. The number of teenagers in the United States had actually *dropped* by 1.5 million in the late 1940s, from 11.5 million to 10 million. But then, as the boom generation arrived, the growth rate of the teenage population took off at four times the average of all other age groups. In the 1950s, the teenage population expanded from 10 million to 15 million and would eventually hit 20 million by 1970. America had gained a critical mass of teenagers that was as fissionable as any nuclear pile.

At precisely the same moment more people were entering adolescence than ever before, the period of adolescence itself was longer than ever before. This was something new in history. The concept of "adolescence," with all its Freudian baggage, was introduced as recently as 1904 by G. Stanley Hall in his two-volume classic *Adolescence*. Previously, observers like de Tocqueville had been able to conclude without contradiction that "in America there is, strictly speaking, no adolescence: at the close of boyhood the man appears and begins to trace out his own path." Then universal public education began to change the life cycle of young Americans. In 1900, only 13 percent of children 14–17 were students. By 1930, the ratio had just passed 50 percent. But by 1950, the ratio had risen to 73 percent, and the culture had a new word: "teenager." By 1965, the proportion of children in school had risen to 95 percent, and total enrollment in public and private schools had doubled in just one decade. With more than half of high-school students going on to college, the age of adulthood did not begin until 20 or 21. Thus, America's largest generation was growing up in an age-segregated universe, cut off from outside society (which they typically called "the real world") and bound together by their own prolonged adolescence.

High schools became the first dumping ground for the baby-boom generation. There, in the absence of adults, they began to form a support system of their own. In some societies, as it happens, *Jugendkultur* is an essential agent of cultural transmission, the way a society passes on its heritage and maintains its continuity. In tribes like Africa's Nandi, the social machinery itself is centered in the creation of exclusive age groups, formed during the critical passage from adolescence to full adulthood.

But in America, the baby-boom generation had been deposited in an education system that seemed designed not to facilitate the passage into adulthood but to delay it. Thousands of junior high schools were built in the suburbs and filled with seventh, eighth, and ninth graders who knew no world but their own. In elementary school, they at least were responsible to teachers who acted as surrogate parents. But in the junior highs, where the same group of students traveled together from classroom to

79

classroom, the only continuity was provided by the group. Parents could not hope to compete with institutions like New Trier High School outside of Chicago, which offered a range of courses rivaling most colleges and routinely graduated senior classes of fifteen hundred students. The result was that the baby boomers inevitably began to look not to the adult community for guidance but to the only one it knew and trusted, its own. These kids had what they needed—affluence plus education—to set themselves free from the dictatorship of the adults. They had money, music, and a thriving culture based on their shared history, rituals, language, and values. They would do it their way.

Take, for example, the pattern of dating. Sociologist James Coleman has pointed out that the bonds shared by this generation operated against the old pattern of "going steady." They did *not* choose to imitate the adult model of a nuclear family. Boys and girls did not pair off but rather clustered together, adapting flexible group relationships that almost prohibited exclusive "commitment" (the highest virtue in old-style romance). It may not have seemed important then, but we are still feeling the result of this new romantic style in the rise in both unmarried and divorced Americans.

It was remarkably egalitarian. Since they had not yet joined the work force, the baby boomers were less preoccupied with class differences than older people. Instead, the generation was replacing the bond of social class with the bond of their cohorts. A woman from Los Angeles told me that she used to reassure her parents at the time that it did not matter if she had no plans for housing during a trip to Marin County. "Don't worry," she told them, "there's always a place to crash. Everything will work out okay. And it did. Everyone was really open to each other."

What we now think of as the calling cards of the youth movement—outrageous dress, music, and drugs—were at first less apparent than its homogeneity. In its cover story on "Today's Teenagers," published in January 1965, the first year that high schools were composed entirely of baby boomers, *Time* found a generation of conformists. "Almost everywhere boys dress in madras shirts and chinos, or perhaps green Levis," *Time* reported. "All trim and neat. The standard for girls is sweaters and skirts dyed to match, or shirtwaists and jumpers, plus blazers, Weejun loafers, and knee socks or stockings."

The school *Time* featured in that article was Pacific Palisades High, bordering on Sunset Boulevard in Los Angeles. The choice was appropriate. In the diaspora of the baby boom, California was the Promised Land. More boom babies grew up there than anywhere else. For three decades, millions of young parents had migrated to the state Arnold Toynbee had called "the New World's New World" and brought with them a fourfold increase in births. In the 1940s, California jumped from fifth to second place in population among states. The state next increased by some 15 million, or nearly 40 percent, in the 1950s and finally passed New York to become the most populous state in the country in 1964 (appropriately, the year the Beatles arrived). In a single decade, the number of children under the age of 4 expanded by 58 percent and the 5–14 age group *doubled*. By 1970, there were twice as many Californians between the ages of 6 and 4 as there had been in 1955.

Now we can see how California's reputation as the nation's lead indicator in fashion and fad—usually the provinces of the young—began in sheer numbers. Inevitably, the whole panoply of problems we associate with the emerging of the baby boom appeared first, most dramatically, in California. One out of every ten schoolchildren in the United States was attending school in California. At the end of the fifties, the state faced a shortage of 775 elementary schools which, as the baby boom worked its way up the educational pipeline, threatened to become an even worse shortage of colleges.

The state began to try to absorb the onslaught of children by building the most extensive state-supported system of higher education in the world. Yet it was already too late. The seeds of rebellion at Berkeley were planted not by Mario Savio but by the millions of ex-soldiers and their wives who had struck out West nearly two decades earlier. (Similarly, it helps to understand the street riots in Watts in 1965 if one remembers that the number of blacks in the Pacific states grew by a boggling 184 percent in the 1950s and then by another 113 percent in the 1960s.) The kids who turned up on the streets in Haight-Ashbury, seen this way, were not making a statement; they were just the inevitable spillover that the system could not absorb.

In California and elsewhere, the youth culture moved on four wheels. As they turned 16 and 17 in the sixties and earned their first driver's licenses, the number of car registrations in the country exploded from 61.7 million to 86.9 million. Cars would impart more pleasure and power to this generation than any other inanimate object (with the possible exception of marijuana). Drive-in restaurants were replacing corner drugstores as teenage hangouts, though they were somehow more ominous. As early as 1962, the nation was shocked to learn that a teenager had killed himself playing Russian roulette in, of all places, a drive-in restaurant.

The writers and artists of the baby boom would eventually make the landscape of the road one of the leitmotifs. Who, least of all Madison Avenue, could not be aware that the two major encounters of adolescence—with the opposite sex and with automobiles—were now occurring simultaneously? In the earliest movies of the era, cars like James Dean's 1949 Mercury in *Rebel Without a Cause* were practically a love interest. Archivists of rock have long cited Jackie Brenston's 1951 recording of "Rockett '88," which honors an Oldsmobile, as the original rock 'n' roll record. *American Graffiti* brilliantly fused the teenage preoccupations with rock and cars to make a romanticized (and lucrative) representation of adolescent culture. Director Steven Spielberg, whose suburban Scottsdale, Arizona, upbringing amounts to a quintessential baby-boom experience, brought cars and trucks to the screen more effectively than anyone in *The Duel* and *Sugarland Express*. Other youth movies like *Brewster McCloud, Two-Lane Blacktop, Grease, Corvette Summer*, and a hundred American International road epics likewise celebrated the automobile. And in his first feature, *Targets*, Peter Bogdanovich created a terrorizing metaphor of art striking back at the audience when a mass murderer climbs the scaffolding of a drive-in theater and, poking a hole through the screen itself, shoots unaware moviegoers helplessly isolated in their chariots.

The association of cars and the baby boom continues into the 1980s. Only now baby boomers are customizing vans equipped with Day-Glo paints, shag carpeting, and wall-to-wall stereos. They can be as much a surrogate home for this generation as a '32 Ford "deuce" was for their parents. During summertime van festivals, clubs with names like Sky High Truckers and White Rose Jammers arrive at Woodstocks-on-wheels and pull their vans into circles, like Conestoga wagons. "It's the gathering instinct," a van owner explained at one such convention. "These people are here because they want to belong to something. A lot of them are ex-hippies, people from the sixties who don't want to grow up yet."

In the mid-sixties, Roger Daltry of The Who sang "Hope I die before I get old" and, implausibly, no one was arguing with him. Not only had the kids stopped looking up to their parents for guidance, but the parents were instead looking down to them. The baby boomers had found the power to make their own way and to drag along everyone else in their backwash. They jettisoned the fifties' patois of "cool" and "hip" and "smooth." Instead they took aboard a harsher slang of their own, blunt spondees like "put-on" and "freak-out" and "hung up." Adults seized the new words as fast as they bobbed up and turned them into *Tonight Show* routines. Before long, New York's chic Bergdorf Goodman was using "right-on" in its ad copy and Fifth Avenue matrons were tricking themselves out in leather boots and hip-huggers.

To Harold Rosenberg, writing in 1959, generations really were little more than such matters of costume. "Their existence is established by a Look," he wrote. "Part of this look is the rhetorical makeup, the blend of ideas and phrases by which each generation creates the illusion of its intellectual character . . ." Rosenberg could not afford to write that about the boom generation. What was unique about it was not merely its generational chauvinism but its magnetism. It simply could not be ignored. If it was gerontophobic, we were gerontophobic. In their awesome confidence, these young baby-boomers were not far from the spirit of the pre-World War I generation of dramatist Carl Zuckmayer:

I would not have defined what all this was about that had laid so strong a spell on me, but it was *our* time, *our* world, *our* sense of life that came rushing upon me, and suddenly I awakened to a consciousness of a new generation, a consciousness that even the most intelligent, most aware, and unbiased parents could not share.

The world was hardly ready for the new generation

emerging out of America. Before the baby boom, for example, American youths knew how to behave when they traveled abroad. They went continental. In the fifties and early sixties, all those haggard-looking students in sweaters curled up reading Sartre at the Deux Magots were almost as likely to be from Peoria as Paris. But then airlines started running $107 charter flights from Los Angeles to London and a new group of tourists was getting off. They were big and blond and wore cutoff jeans and sweatshirts with the letters UCLA on them. They did not try to blend in. They traveled in prides, leonine in their confidence, with identical nylon-and-aluminum backpacks. They did not try to learn French. Why should they? They were what was happening. In fact, the word "foreigner" was barely part of their vocabulary at all, since they saw their peers around the globe as extensions of themselves—other baby-boom "kids" facing the same hassles they were facing. The Europeans were stunned and even outraged by the appearance of millions of strapping, corn-fed Americans who obviously cared not a whit about absorbing their cultures. But they proved to be no better able to withstand the cultural imperialism of the baby boom than the generation's mothers and fathers at home. Before long, students at the Sorbonne were reverently wearing faded Levi's and Big Ten sweatshirts to their haunts on the Left Bank.

Back in the States, meanwhile, merchandisers were preparing to drill into the teenage market like wildcatters after oil. The last traces of the gloom of the 1930s had been erased as the economy surged forward five straight years in the early sixties. According to *Time,* "The amazing U.S. economy could defy even the law of physics: what goes up need not necessarily come down." All agreed that the primary stimulus behind the economic boom was the unprecedented surge in teenage demand. In 1964, the nation's 22 million teenagers were increasing their number three times faster than the overall population and 3.7 million baby boomers were celebrating their seventeenth birthday, 1 million more than the 1963 crop of 17-year-olds. Loaded up with then-indulgent allowances averaging $6 a week for boys and $4 for girls, they were letting the cash flow out of their hands like water. Teenagers were spending something like $12 billion a year and, counting the money their parents were spending on them, the total market was heading for a spectacular $25 billion. What's more, to advertisers' delight, much of it was *discretionary* income. That is, teenagers were not locked into buying durable goods like washing machines and sofas. They were buying lipstick ($12 million annually) or records because they wanted to or because their friends were.

What did it mean? It meant that teenagers accounted for 55 percent of *all* soft drink sales, 53 percent of *all* movie tickets, and 43 percent of *all* records sold. They owned 10 million phonographs and were spending $100 million a year on records *before* the industry had its biggest years. More than one out of every five high-school seniors drove his or her own car. Others were adding "seconds" to a family's accumulated goods: a second TV set, a second car, a "children's" phone. Teenage girls, only 11 percent of the total population, were spending one-fifth of all the money devoted to cosmetics and toiletries. The boys were likewise handing over $120 million a year for hair cream, mouthwashes, and deodorants. At the time, Purdue polled two thousand teenagers and asked them what was the gravest problem facing American youth. One-third had their answer ready. It was acne.

The fifties had earned it, as the saying went, now the sixties were spending it. But who had the handle on the market? Businessmen were at first unsure how to reach this vast but somehow different generation. They did not respond to traditional "sells." Admen could flood the media with millions of dollars of razzle-dazzle and promotional stunts, but who could tell if it would take? You could call an Oldsmobile a Youngmobile, but the kids would not buy it. Strange success stories were heard—of herbal lines like Celestial Seasonings or hip capitalists who'd made millions selling T-shirts. A few traditional businesses, like Thom McAn shoes, managed to turn their companies around by importing rock bands and throwing light shows in their stores to lure in the kids. "If you can't succeed with them, you can't succeed at all," judged the firm's president back then. "What they demand today, their elders will demand tomorrow."

Fashion, which used to flow *down* through the age groups, had reversed. Now fads and trends were bubbling *up*. Furthermore, reversing another historic trend, they were flowing from the lower classes to the upper. Adolescents, to be sure, have always identified themselves with the poor: both groups see themselves as powerless. And one of the affectations of upper-class parents has always been to dress their children in the garb of the working classes. Children are thought to look cute in overalls and mackintoshes. But now, implausibly, rich parents themselves were dressing like laborers in denims and fatigue jackets. The style of the young, if not yet the sensibility, was spreading through society. "Money, status, and power no longer have the same meaning," said Rudi Gernreich, a fashion designer particularly attuned to such distinctions. "Now fashion starts in the streets. That's why I watch the kids."

All armies travel on their stomachs, and the youth movement was no different. During the sixties, the baby boom got hungry. Teenagers require 20 percent more calories than normally active adults. The massive appetite whetted by the baby boom fueled an enormous expansion in the food industry, particularly in fast foods, a business that catered to the world of mobile youth who lived—and ate—in their cars.

Baby-boom parents felt the same way. Why stay at home in a hot kitchen, they reasoned, when they could load the brood into the station wagon and let Ronald McDonald or Colonel Sanders clean up the mess? Dollars spent on food eaten out of the home mushroomed from $22.5 billion in 1950 (in 1972 dollars) to $34.5 billion by 1970. Fast-food franchisers were enjoying runaway growth of 20 percent a year and becoming Wall Street's choicest stocks. One hundred shares of McDonald's stock that cost $2250 in the mid-sixties were worth $141,000 in 1972. Kentucky Fried Chicken outlets were saturating the country from Montauk to Monterey; the number of outlets increased from 400 in 1964 to 3317 in 1971. Within ten years of the surge in pizza sales, nationwide consumption of oregano had increased by more than 2000 percent. The baby boomers, in fact, were supplying the fast-food market on both ends: with millions of consumers to eat the food and with millions of gangly kids to put on paper caps and serve it.

Writing later about what she called her "junk-food generation," a despairing Joyce Maynard found "a slackness to our will, a numb, unthinking indifference in our grandstand munching—the way we reach for crackers on a plate simply because they're on it, the way we forget which flavor of ice cream we're licking . . ." Others, though, rejoiced in their conditioning in a kind of reverse snobbism celebrating junk food. Not atypically, baby boomers like Steven Spielberg freely admitted to being junk-food freaks because, as he explained, junk food is the ultimately repeatable experience. Repetition, whether on television or in movies or in food, is a quality the baby boom values. With the noise of technological and social change crashing in their ears through their lifetimes, it is somehow comforting to baby boomers to know that a Big Mac purchased in Phoenix can be trusted to taste generally like a Big Mac bought in Boston. It was not for nothing this generation made a hit out of an otherwise forgettable song called "Junk Food Junkie."

The junk-food psychology also found its way into pulp literature of the times. Traditional magazines like *Seventeen* were being crowded on the newsstands by a host of pilot fish with names like *Teen Times, Hollywood Teenager, Teen World, Teen Parade, Modern Teen,* and *Teen Screen.* Newspapers were running teenage advice columns alongside "Dear Abby." The most popular of the pulps, however, was not a magazine or a book but Stan Lee's Marvel Comics. The baby boomers had already learned to read on Walt Disney's *Comics & Stories* and further refined their taste for simplistic, linear narration by watching television. In the sixties, Lee was able to build an empire out of larger-than-life characters like Spiderman, The Fantastic Four, The Incredible Hulk, and The Mighty Thor. Psychologists might theorize that the popularity of all-powerful heroes suggested the natural feelings of frustration experienced by most young people. And, in a way, the prototypal Marvel Comic hero—someone of superhuman power but also afflicted with doubt and angst about using it—paralleled the reality of the boom generation in society. It was feeling both power and frustration. Even now, baby boomers have maintained their allegiance to the Marvel Comics, bidding up prices on the originals at comic-book conventions and creating an audience for television shows based on various superheroes. *Charlie's Angels* and movies like *Star Wars* owe no small part of their success to the grip of comic books on the imagination of the baby boom.

By the mid-sixties, then, the size and economic power of the boom generation had helped it muscle its way onto the center stage of the nation's life. Most Americans were delighted at what they saw. The generation of the young was richer and stronger than theirs had been. It was confident and articulate about its dreams. Its ideals were outstripping those of previous generations bogged down by Depression and war. Its education and affluence were offering it the golden means of achieving its own great expectations. Its hopes for itself were matched only by ours for it. The editors of *Time* honored the "Under-25 Generation" as its Man of the Year in 1967. In its lifetime, *Time* wrote, this promising generation could land on the moon, cure cancer and the common cold, lay out blight-proof, smog-free cities, help end racial prejudice, enrich the underdeveloped world and, no doubt, write an end to poverty and war.

These were heady responsibilities with which to burden the young, but this ambitious, earnest generation seemed eager to assume them. "Few of these young men and women have any doubt that they will one day be part of our society," said Kenneth Keniston at the time. "They wonder about where they will fit in, but not about whether." It would be left to someone like David Riesman to suggest a reservation about what he was witnessing. "One can go into many modern homes," Riesman wrote, "and get the feeling that it is the parents, especially the father, who are marginal, who are in a precarious position, who are the frightened conformists, while the children hold the strategic initiative."

PART II

The Invasion of the Barbarians

People try to put us down
Just because we get around
Things they do look awful cold
Hope I die before I get old.
                    —The Who

Chapter 6

THE ARCHIPELAGO OF YOUTH

> Every old man complains of the growing depravity
> of the world, of the petulance and insolence of the
> rising generation.
>
> —Samuel Johnson

In his first edition of *Baby and Child Care,* Benjamin
Spock bothered to include only a few pages on adolescents, characterizing them generally as wayward Huck
Finns who would soon leave their rafts behind. But by the
mid-sixties, after national enrollment in the four high-
school grades had nearly doubled from 7 million to 13
million in a decade, the *Sturm und Drang* of adolescence
was impossible to ignore. In the previous decade and a
half, America had swallowed the new generation in a single gulp. Now the pig was moving inexorably through the
python, changing each age group it entered. In the sixties,
the number of 14–24-year-olds increased more in a single
decade than it had in the rest of the century altogether
and was continuing to grow at five times the rate of the
previous seventy years. Feeling the hot breath of youth,
Dr. Spock prudently added almost a full chapter on the
psychological stresses of puberty to the next edition of his
book.

For most parents, it was too late. Beginning in 1964,
the cutting-edge cohorts of the boom generation—those
babies born in 1946 who had absorbed the first shocks of
their size—began turning eighteen. In the next six years,
more than 20 million of them entered the 18–24 period in
which most people leave home and make decisions that
will affect them the rest of their lives. Some went to college, some went to work, some joined the military, some
married and had children. Others, however, did not join

the society but opposed it: some committed crimes, some had car accidents, some rioted, some dropped out, some left their families, some left their jobs. None of this was surprising. The years from 18 to 24 are the most volatile time of everyone's life, a period roiling with inner turbulence. In some fields like mathematics and music the boldness and iconoclasm of youth are linked to imaginative acts of discovery. But more often, the 18–24-year-olds feel that society is not freeing them but shackling them. From their ranks come the mass movements that change history.

It is no coincidence, then, that the six years from 1964 to 1970 saw the outbreak of the most prolonged and dislocating domestic turmoil of this century. These were the same years that the first baby boomers massively entered the dangerous years. Princeton's Norman Ryder, who has pioneered cohort theory in demography, argues that throughout history the younger generation has challenged the older as it enters this life stage. The young are cultural insurrectionaries, *agents provocateurs* with no allegiance to the past. The task of the older generation is to control this "invasion of barbarians" and shape their energies so they become contributors to society. Only then, by recruiting the young, can the culture maintain its continuity.

This process is never easy. Both the generation in charge and the generation to be recruited feel the smoking frictions of the transition. Further, in times of rapid change, the tension builds faster and hotter. Fissures appear warning of earthquakes to come. When Americans were leaving the farms and moving to the cities in the early years of this century, the gulf between the older, traditional, rural generation and the younger, bolder, urban generation—the "Flaming Youth" of the 1920s—cracked open. Similarly, educated youth may feel as remote from the experience of uneducated parents as the first generation of immigrant children born in America felt from the old-world ways of their parents and grandparents.

Year after year, nonetheless, we have managed to convert the "barbarians" into contributors. The primary agents of socialization—the families and the schools—have carried out their work peacefully. In most of the nation's history, this job has been made quantitatively easier by the simple fact that the proportion of the young in society has been decreasing as more Americans live longer.

But what if the odds were reversed? What if a generation of barbarians appeared that, for the first time, abruptly threatened to overwhelm the defenders by force of numbers?

This is exactly what happened in the middle of the 1960s. As the baby boom entered the most rebellious years of youth, it gave them a weight and impact they never had before. The difficulties were compounded by the social and technological upheavals of the sixties. Freed from its moorings, the baby boom became a loose cannon on the deck of society, rolling and smashing whatever stood in its path.

The table printed here shows the changes that have and will be brought to the 18–24 age group by the baby boom.

YEAR	SIZE (IN THOUSANDS)	PERCENT CHANGE
1900	10,307	
1910	12,748	+ 23
1920	13,018	+ 0.02
1930	15,463	+ 0.19
1940	16,616	+ 7
1950	16,075	− 0.03
1960	16,128	+ 0.003
1970	24,687	+ 53 (!!)
1980	29,462	+ 19
1990	25,148	− 0.15
2000	24,653	− 0.02

SOURCE: 1950–2000. U.S. Bureau of the Census, *Current Population Reports*, Series P-25, No. 704, "Projections of the Population of the United States: 1977 to 2050," U.S. Government Printing office, Washington, D.C., July 1977. Table H, Series II, 1900–1940. U.S. Bureau of the Census: U.S. Census of Population: 1970. *General Population Characteristics, United States Summary*. U.S. Government Printing Office, Washington, D.C., Table 51.

Over the first sixty years of the century, the 18–24 group grew slowly but erratically—and in the two decades from 1940 until 1960 it actually *decreased* in size. Then, in the single decade of the sixties, the numbers of young people aged 18–24 expanded by an unparalleled 8,559,000, more than in the rest of the century put together. In the Western states, the increase was even more spectacular, as the 15–24 age group grew by 83 percent in the cities and nearly 100 percent in the suburbs.

As early as 1963, demographers like Donald Bogue and Philip Hauser began to post warnings about the hurricane of youth ahead. If nothing else changed, they predicted, we were doomed to see increases in teenage unemployment, juvenile delinquency, race tensions, teacher shortages, and traffic accidents. What is more, as Ryder has pointed out in a brilliant essay, our ability to deal with these problems was being eroded by the abnormally small size of the older generation. Many of the 25–64 group, responsible for devoting the time, energy, and skill necessary to socialize the young (not to mention providing the tax funds), had been born during the low-fertility years of the thirties. A small cohort hammocked between two larger ones, they did not have the same numerical advantages over the young enjoyed by previous generations. The result was that in the 1960s, for the first time in two centuries, the ratio of young to old was increasing in this country. (A curious fact in that regard is that, as numerous as 18–24-year-olds were in the sixties, their *proportion* was actually higher in the 1930s and much higher at the turn of the century because there were fewer old people. What mattered, though, was that their proportion had been slowly *declining* since Colonial times—until the sudden dislocation of the baby boom sent it soaring.)

Millions of baby boomers were pouring out of the high schools every year. We were surfeited with youth. If the young people attempted to find jobs at the same rate their parents had, then the job market would be flooded. Then unemployment would surely rise and, with it, crime. The armed forces could soak up some but not all of the surplus. (Not until the Vietnam years would the draft begin to siphon off young people.) In the end, we decided in effect that the economy was not prepared to absorb the baby boomers after they left high school. All we could do was to delay their arrival. That meant lengthening the time required to socialize the "barbarians" until we could deal with them later. Thus, the educational system, which had borne the brunt of handling the boom generation in the fifties, would have to make room for it again in the sixties. Only now the front line had moved from the schools to the colleges.

Looking back, we can see just how dramatically the entry of the baby boomers changed higher education in this country. Before World War II, more than one-half the students who entered fifth grade did not make it to high-school graduation. Only 38 percent of all young people received high-school diplomas, and only a third of that group went on to college. In the forties and fifties, the available pool of college-age youths actually declined as the small Depression-era cohorts passed into the 18–24 group. The only thing keeping colleges growing was the fact that enrollment rates were simultaneously increasing because of family prosperity and the demand for college-trained workers generated by a booming economy. The enrollment rate among 18–24-year-olds—that is, the proportion of them who went to college—was rapidly rising from 9 percent to 20 percent. The net result was that colleges were growing by about 2 percent a year despite the shrinking number of potential students.

In the sixties, public education became so pervasive that 75 percent of the boom children were receiving high-school diplomas. The overall college enrollment rate was simultaneously continuing to grow from 20 percent in the fifties to 30 percent in the sixties as more than half of the high-school graduates, or 1.2 million students, were going on to college. Only now the smaller, Depression-era student pool was being replaced by the massive baby-boom group. Thus, two trends at once were building college enrollment in the sixties: the enormous increase in the total number of available students was being redoubled by the continuing increase in the percentage of them who actually went on to college.

The result was a $100-billion boom in higher education. In the decade from 1963 to 1973, total enrollment at all institutions of higher learning doubled from 4.7 million to 9.6 million—five times as many students as were enrolled in 1940. The annual growth rate of colleges rose from 2 percent to nearly 9 percent. Five new professors were being hired for every older professor who retired or died. Eventually, the number of college graduates in the population at large went from 10 million in 1965, before the first baby boomers arrived, to 19 million in 1980, when the boom's peak years were graduating. The percentage of college graduates within the overall population likewise increased by more than two-thirds, from 9 percent to 15 percent, most of them baby boomers.

The point is not merely that colleges were busily filling dormitories in these years. Rather, it is that the parents had neatly solved two problems at once. College was a way of giving their children a better education than they ever achieved. Simultaneously, it solved the problem of what to do with this vast generation. De Tocqueville, as usual, had noted more than a century earlier that Americans have always taken a distinctive, almost Rousseau-esque view of youth and turned naturally to education as the solution to every problem, public and private. The irony no one would anticipate, however, was that the concentration of the baby-boom generation in the fortresses of learning was about to cause as many problems as it solved.

The first thing many of the men and women of the baby boom discovered was that the act of going to college meant that their peers were also their competitors. Previously, the competition caused by numbers had seemed more remote and less personal. If they had once been competing for pediatricians, or for school desks, or for the time of their teachers, they were not aware of it. It was abstract. But, in the mid-sixties, the colleges discovered that they could not admit all the boom-generation students who wanted to go. The process of sorting, evaluating, and selecting would come to characterize the baby-boom experience for the rest of its life.

Everyone, rich and poor, was being evaluated on the basis of class rank and on Scholastic Aptitude Test (SAT) scores and on their leadership ability. The most prestigious universities were openly boasting of their highly competitive admissions policies. Students who in the past could have counted on getting into Ivy League schools were uncertainly looking elsewhere—and were not sure about that, either. The state universities were toughening up standards and flunking out 40 percent of some new freshman classes. How else could they deal with this generation? There were too many of them.

Now that competition was direct and personal, baby boomers had to look at their peers differently. Who was smartest? Who was the best athlete? A whole new layer of stress had been added to their lives. Senior year in high school, once golden for Henry Aldrich, had taken on a darker and less joyous quality. The most important day of the year was not Graduation Day but the day the college acceptances or rejections arrived. Would you be rejected by the college of your choice? Would you let your parents down? Would you be judged and found wanting? It is not surprising that, after surviving this Darwinian ordeal, the baby boomers later became the most fiercely anticompetitive generation in our history.

Once they arrived at college, the teeming numbers of students overwhelmed the teachers and educators waiting for them. Higher education was facing the same dilemma in the sixties that parents had in the fifties. What could they do with this number? How could they house them and feed them? Parents had resorted to institutions, turning their children over to the schools, television, and the Cub Scouts. In the sixties, the colleges and universities were no better able to handle the load. The result was that the baby boom began to undertake its own socialization in places like Berkeley, Boston, Austin, New Haven, and Ann Arbor. Communities of students and ersatz students circled the major universities like penumbras around a hundred suns. Madison, Wisconsin, became "Mad City," where the population of 170,000 was dominated by 40,000 students and thousands more faculty and staff. After they got the vote, the students of Madison elected a baby-boom mayor who was all of thirty-three *after* six years in office. And as early as 1967, baby boomers comprised 30 percent of the population of Ann Arbor, Michigan.

We called them "youth ghettos," and the analogy was not inaccurate. Baby-boom youth in the sixties resembled nothing so much as an unassimilated minority group. Membership in the baby boom was determined at birth, just like any other ethnic group. They had their own rituals, traditions, and language, usually at variance with the outside society's. They suffered from substandard housing and conflicts with both landlords and police. They were not required to carry IDs in these Sowetos, but they might as well have. Student dress and long hair marked them as ghetto dwellers in the outside world—and acted as passports admitting them into other student homelands as they restlessly traveled around the country.

Youth was no longer a stage of life but a community, a *Jugendgemeinschaft*. Rock remained such an integral part of it that, when the Beatles' *Sergeant Pepper* album was released in 1967, at least one critic called it "the closest Western Civilization has come to unity since the Congress of Vienna in 1815." In the youth ghettos, the residents did not read James Michener but Vonnegut, Richard Brautigan, Alan Watts, Ram Dass, Timothy

Leary, Herbert Marcuse, Hermann Hesse, and *I Ching*. In Alison Lurie's scathing academic satire, *The War Between the Tates,* her Professor Brian Tate felt that he was not "living in present-day America, but in another country or city-state with somewhat different characteristics. The important fact about this state, which can for convenience' sake be called 'University,' is that the great majority of its population is aged eighteen to twenty-two. Naturally the physical appearance, interests, activities, preferences and prejudices of this majority are the norm in University. Cultural and political life is geared to their standards, and any deviation from them is a social handicap." As an alien, Professor Tate "speaks differently, using the native tongue more formally, the local slang infrequently and as if in quotation marks; he likes different foods and wears different clothes and has different recreations. Naturally, he is regarded with suspicion by the natives."

Other adults, contemplating the youth archipelago at greater distance, were even more mystified. Some, like downtowners imagining a Harlem of their minds, supposed that students led wildly romantic lives, sustained by drugs and sex. If they were poorer than most folk, well, they were having fun. Some grown-ups led expeditions into the darkest regions of the country of youth, returning months later clutching thoughtful analyses of the bizarre tribes they had witnessed. The cultural processes at work on this group, they reported, were unlike anything they had ever seen before.

Genuine anthropologists were quick to point out that segregation by age group is nothing new in humankind. The Nykyusa, a Bantu-speaking people who live at the northern end of Africa's Lake Nyasa, have traditionally herded boys of ten or eleven into "age villages" to live on their own for several years while preparing for the passage into manhood. Likewise, the Hamitic cultures of East Africa developed an "age grade" system cutting across family lines that bound together generations early in adolescence. But these highly structured, adult-sanctioned youth societies were drawn up precisely to ensure cultural transmission. The youth ghettos of the sixties were the first true countercultures, set up in what often became fierce opposition to adult society. (Like L.A.'s Watts and Cleveland's Hough, they even had their own riots.) In *The Pump House Gang,* Tom Wolfe noticed that "Surfers, not to mention rock and roll kids and the hot rodders . . .

don't merely hang around together. They establish whole little societies for themselves."

Wolfe had noticed what English social anthropologist A. R. Radcliffe-Brown called "sibling equivalence," the extension of the peer group. In the youth ghettos, the baby boomers had finally managed to unite to realize the power so far denied them in adult society. As always in their lifetimes, they achieved their greatest success en masse, not as individuals. The youth ghettos were as much shows of strength and sources of fulfillment as coonskin caps were and Woodstock and ten-kilometer races later would be. They were not complete environments any more than school was. But they were *exclusively* of the young. A Yankelovich poll in 1973 showed that college youth then identified more strongly with other students (84 percent) than with family (68 percent). The concentration and segregation of young people in the youth ghettos explain more than a small amount of their behavior then. It was, they hoped, the first step in a revolution of the young, by the young, and for the young.

Back in 1959, the University of California's Clark Kerr had predicted, "The employers will love this generation. . . . They are going to be easy to handle. There aren't going to be any riots." But in the fall of 1964, when the first wave of baby boomers entered the campuses nationally, the new freshman class was 20 percent larger than the previous one. The pressures did not take long to show. On October 1, 1964, a crowd of students at the University of California at Berkeley spontaneously formed a sit-in to prevent campus police from arresting a nonstudent for trespassing. The issue then was simple and even parochial, involving the right of student organizations to solicit funds on campus, but its reverberations would be felt as far as Kent State, six years later. Kennedy was gone, the Beatles had arrived, and the new era had begun. Students were angry and frustrated. "I am a human being," the slogan went. "Don't fold, spindle, or mutilate." With it came a new idea: student power.

Originally, the forces behind the student movement were political and educational. (Not until later would the cultural revolution join up.) Students wanted control over their lives, *Lernfreiheit* (student freedom) instead of the Mr. Chips doctrine of *in loco parentis*. Socially, they wanted coed schools and coed dorms. Pedagogically, they wanted "relevance" in their courses. That meant more sociology and psychology and religion, disciplines to help them cope with modern life. It also meant courses in subjects youth was interested in. Berkeley had a course in comic books and Wayne State added one in monster literature. The University of Wisconsin created a Division of Contemporary Trends, designed to foster classes requested by students.

History, on the other hand, was out. Why waste their energies in irrelevant time-based disciplines, students reasoned, when they could be building models to understand today's society? History was the academic equivalent of the voice of their parents, harping on an irrelevant past. Why should they compare their experience to anything else? The whole point was that theirs was a *unique* generation, without parallel, *sui generis*.

Indeed, that was exactly the conclusion reached by psychologist Kenneth Keniston. By prolonging education and preventing young people from producing in the economy, he argued, we had created a new and previously unrecognized stage of life for the baby boom. He called it Youth. Youth was found on campuses and in youth ghettos and anywhere students gathered. Youth occupied a limbo between adolescence and adulthood. Neither child nor father, Youth was left dangling. In fact, it was a dysfunctional life stage in which its members were adults in every sense except independence. Blocked from functioning in adult society, and exhilarated with the energy of their own, they found traditional roles and institutions and values as useless to them as saddle shoes and letter sweaters.

Parents did not understand Youth. To begin with, education had opened a gap between them and their children. What we would later call the generation gap was at first an education gap. Eighty-five percent of the baby boomers born from 1947 to 1951 completed high school, compared to only 38 percent of their parents. More than half of them had gone on to college, a proportion unthinkable in their parents' era. The fathers of nearly two-thirds of today's college graduates, for example, did not go beyond high school.

What did this mean? Certainly that the younger generation would be more open to change. Polls have consistently shown that people attending college have more liberal attitudes about politics, sex, childrearing, and religion. Among the first lessons of American education, after all, is that change and modernity must be understood and welcomed. If college-educated people are more receptive to the facts of social, technological, and cultural change, it is because their education has taught them to be.

Further, the level of education is a fact that marks a generation throughout its life-span. The baby boom will always seem different from other generations if only because no generation, before it or after it, has produced so many college graduates. Superior education is a fact that will follow the baby boom to its grave, distinguishing it just as clearly as religious reform or immigration separated previous generations. The most relevant difference between today's 25-year-olds and 75-year-olds, for example, is not that fifty years of aging has fossilized the older generation. Nor is it necessarily that the older generation was born just after the turn of the century in what was still a largely agrarian society. Rather, the most telling difference between the two generations could well be that while only one out of every ten Americans born in 1905 had any college training, one in every three born in 1955 has been to college. In short, they think differently.

The distinction holds just as true within the baby boom. Those who went to college formed their values and attitudes in a completely different world from those who did not. Baby boomers who did not go to college were not part of Youth. They were forgotten. In fact, the point of view of college youth became so pervasive in the sixties and seventies that it was the mass of working-class youth, once the backbone of the American system, who showed the most evident signs of alienation. Daniel Yankelovich, the market researcher and opinion analyst, has documented how the liberal values of college students have typically spread to their noncollege peers after a five-year gap. (Along the way, some strange reversals have taken place. In the sixties, long hair was the universal badge of the college student. But by the late seventies, long hair was the sure sign that the wearer was *not* in college.)

Social classes now cluster just as naturally around levels of education as they once did around levels of income. During times of rapid social change, the gap between the educated and noneducated becomes all the more pronounced. One does not have to look far to see this. At one Ivy League university, student activists passionately spoke of their commitment to help the working classes in the university's community. But then, during an open

university meeting, these same students found themselves—
to their own embarrassment—giggling despite themselves
at a working-class university policeman who made the
unpardonable error of speaking ungrammatically. The
feeling of class distinction was as strong as if he were a
hod-carrier and they landed gentry in Victorian England.

It just made the parents nervous. The generation that
had tried to do so much for the children of the baby
boom were beginning to feel that they had created an alien
and even hostile culture. "My parents had to worry
whether I'd get drunk at a dance or get suspended for
breaking curfew," remembered one father. "I have to
worry whether my sons will disappear into some strange
offbeat life before they even know what they're leaving
behind." The authority of age seemed irrelevant in dealing with a younger generation that spoke a different language. It was as if the bodies of their children had been
invaded by some creatures from a science-fiction movie.
They often looked and acted the same but, safe in their
peer-governed world, they were beginning to talk of radical politics and drugs and perhaps worse. This generation
did not seem to have its quota of alienated "hoods"—the
Fonzies of the fifties—because they *all* looked and
sounded alienated.

The changes that we once thought were biological and
therefore passing—"Don't worry, dear, they'll grow up"
—were beginning to look historical and possibly threatening. It was a dramatic change since 1965 when, according to a newsmagazine, "Teenagers today do not think of
themselves as 'knights in shining chinos'. riding forth on
rockets to save the universe. But even the coolest of them
know that their careers could be almost that fantastic."
According to writer Jacob Brackman, a generation was
now coming of age in America "that doesn't take the news
straight, that doesn't take the utterances of public figures
straight, that doesn't take social games straight. It suspects
not only art but the whole range of modern experience."

The concept of the generation gap had reared its hoary
head. Not that the much-discussed idea was particularly
useful. It dated to antiquity, and George Bernard Shaw
had erupted in *Misalliance* that between the generations
"there's a wall ten feet thick and ten miles high." Like
any stock phrase, generation gap was a cliché, one we
slathered on like spackling putty to plug up leaky theories.

101

We could not build a lasting edifice with it—but it temporarily served our purposes.

During the hardening years of the sixties, the children had no use for the parents' skills or wisdom and did not need their money. Generational conflict was beginning to replace social conflict as the critically divisive social issue. On the one side stood a formidable youth culture which drew its strength from its own number. Like David Riesman's "other directed" types, the baby boomers had made their peers their ultimate authority. Further, they were abandoning what they said was the sterile, empty, materialistic world of their parents to shop in a supermarket of new ideas and life-styles.

The child-oriented parents of the forties and fifties, who had made their children their religion, were devastated. The idea of their children—so fortunate in the affluence and attention lavished on them—rejecting the society that made it possible seemed almost obscene. They had seen enough of human waste during the Depression—but at least they could understand that tragedy. But how had they failed their own children? Was it, as some psychologists suggested, a function of the modern division of labor? The absence of the working father from the home was said to have left an unresolved Oedipal conflict which was being transferred to society and, later, to the government. Or, the parents wondered, were they more directly to blame? Erik Erikson has said that one generation revives the repressions of the generation before it. Had the shackles of the Depression and war deprived the parents of a necessary adolescent rebellion which only now was finding its outlet in their children?

Later, when the counterculture was in full bloom, *The Wall Street Journal* got into the debate, worrying that "what troubles the older generation is the nagging thought that this ill-mannered rebellion is reward not for its failure but for its success." That is, these parents, the first to raise children in the modern era, had succeeded magnificently in liberating their children from the Victorian strictures of their own youth. Instead of ruling their children by parental fiat, they had been flexible and understanding. They had shown their children both the complexities and the shining possibilities of life and given them the independence of mind to pursue it. Yet when the children did show how confident and independent they had become, the parents were shocked. They had never dreamed that, by throwing out the old code of behavior and not re-placing it, they had left it to their children to draw up their own.

Another way to put this is that the baby boomers had been cut off from their past. They were raised in a post-industrial world in which accelerating change was making the rules obsolete. Instead of futilely binding them to the values of the old order, their parents had cut them adrift to chart their own course into the future. The popular idea at the time that "there's a new generation every three or four years" is a function of the rapid turnover of social change. Think of the world as a home. The parents of the baby boom grew up in a house furnished with the famil-iar sofas and armoires that had been in the family for years. But the baby-boom cohorts were growing up in an unfamiliar house with new furniture—and every three or four years someone was redecorating. "We live in a time that's divorced from the past," Norman Mailer said. "There's utterly no tradition any more." Bruno Bettelheim has gone so far to argue that the decline of the fairy-tale tradition accentuated generational discontinuity since, in the absence of reinforcing myths, children come to feel that their parents inhabit a world irrelevant to their own. It is not surprising, then, that students called for "rele-vance" in college courses. What use is nineteenth-century history to Protean Man, who never finds a fixed identity because he has to keep changing just to stay on his feet? The new idea the baby boom was bringing into the world was not that we could not know the future; it was that we did not need to know the past.

In her lucid study of the generation gap, *Culture and Commitment,* Margaret Mead put forth a theory distin-guishing between three different kinds of culture—*postfig-urative,* in which children learn primarily from their forebears, *cofigurative,* in which both children and adults learn from their contemporaries, and *prefigurative,* in which adults also learn from their children. According to Mead, our grandparents grew up in a postfigurative world, one in which the process of change was so incremental that they could not conceive of a future differing from their own past. But the America of the early postwar era was more of a cofigurative society: the wisdom of the grandparents useless to children growing up in a world the grandparents had never known. The solipsistic youth ghetto, in which members create its own standards, is a cofigurative society in microcosm. The young could disregard the guidance of their parents, in effect saying to them, "You have never been young in the world I am young in, and you never can be." This, as Mead points out, is the common experience of immigrants and their children, who also found themselves living in ghettos in an unfamiliar land.

In the third, prefigurative stage of culture, social change is so rapid and so disorienting that everyone born before World War II is transformed into an immigrant—not in space but in time, struggling to adapt to an unfamiliar and transformed world. But the younger generation is like the firstborn in a new country. "They are at home in this time," Mead writes. "Satellites are familiar in their skies. They have never known a time when war did not threaten annihilation. Those who use computers do not anthropomorphize time; they know that they are programmed by human beings." The parents, on the other hand, were uneasy in the modern world. They had not grown up with television. They saw a world of contending Great Powers, not Spaceship Earth. They could no longer teach the young but only follow them. No elders could know what their children did. They might well have felt like Eskimo grandparents, cast out into the snow after they'd outlived their usefulness.

Mead's argument, and others like it, seem antiquated now with their apocalyptic views of the generation gap. They believed that the changes they were witnessing were not just based in this generation but rather were broad, sweeping, and historical. If we had to learn from our children in one generation, they reasoned, the pattern was bound to repeat itself. Our children, in turn, would presumably have to learn from their children. The gap between young and old was here to stay, a fact of modern life as inevitable and unavoidable as the technological juggernaut that caused it.

This scenario has not prevailed. We had thought Youth was here to stay. In the sixties, the boom generation did not yet look like a bulge that could move on. Rather, the phenomenon of Youth seemed a permanent prominence on the American landscape, as immutable as the Grand Tetons. Only later, when births began to decline, did the baby boom come into focus as aberration. If it could end, so could the youth culture. As the boom generation left the preschool ages, we stopped worrying about preschoolers. As the baby boom left high school, the teenage culture lost its energy. As the baby boom left the colleges, the colleges returned to normal. As the baby boom entered adulthood, the rivers of ink that had been spilled on the subject of the generation gap seemed to dry up overnight.

There was a generation gap, all right. But it was not between the young and old. It was between the many and the few. It was between the large generation of the boom, painfully swollen with its own numbers and trying to find its place in the world, and the small generation in power which was just as firmly resisting it. The real struggle of the young was not with parents but with a society that could not accommodate them. Mead herself observed that the turbulence experienced then by adolescent Americans was not typical of adolescents in the South Seas cultures she had studied. The unique event in America was an abnormally large generation which we could not pacify. The two generations were contemplating one another with suspicions, like armies aligned on either side of a chasm. The question was whether the young would make peace and lay down their arms, as previous generations had, or would their strength of numbers tilt the generational equilibrium in their favor and convince them that the struggle was theirs to win?

Chapter 7

THE VIETNAM GENERATION

Vietnam, a nightmare still coiled deep in the generation's consciousness, began in the watershed year in the life of the baby boom. It was 1964, the year the Beatles arrived and the unrest at Berkeley began. It was the first year after the presidential assassination, the first year of the new era in which the fifties images were already becoming tinged with nostalgia. It was the last real year of the baby boom itself. After 1964, the boom generation became a closed population that no one else could join.

On August 4, 1964, the U.S. Congress approved the Tonkin Gulf resolution and the Vietnam Era began. Over the next decade, the entire generation was clapped between the hands of war. All the festering tensions and strains that had been slowly building up during the boom's first years finally erupted. In the end, they were as marked by Vietnam as their great-grandparents had been by the Great War. (The 1914 soldiers were "poor children, fascinated and lost," said the French writer Pierre Drieu la Rochelle, unable to escape the memory of war and its "mystical dream.") It was a war the baby boomers hated. To them, it seemed as if the adult generation was solving the problem of its noisome presence by sending them straight from the schools to the battlefield. For most baby boomers, and especially those born between 1946 and 1954, Vietnam and the draft were the most cauterizing events of their young lives.

In retrospect, the confluence of Vietnam and the boom generation seems eerily exact, a hellish blind date arranged by history. Between 1964 and 1965, the months immediately after the Tonkin Gulf resolution, the number of draft-eligible 18-year-olds went up faster than at any time in the nation's history. In 1964, the pool of draftable

18-year-old men was 1.4 million; a year later it had jumped 35 percent to 1.9 million. By July 1, 1965, the overall draft reservoir was one-third larger than in 1963.

Then, immediately after the number of 18-year-olds peaked in the middle of 1965, the Vietnam draft calls began. In September 1965, the Selective Service called 27,500, more than in any month since 1953. By December of 1965, the monthly call was up to 40,200. Four times as many young men were drafted in the last six months of 1965 as in the same period in 1964.

Strictly in the sense of manpower alone, Lyndon Johnson had decided to go into Vietnam at the best of times. The nation's parents had just presented the military with the largest supply of potential soldiers ever. So massive was this generation that it looked as if we could train and field an army with a minimum of domestic dislocation. Fathers could be spared. So could graduate students and undergraduates. In the Vietnam years, some 27 million men passed through the draft-eligible ages. But only 11 million actually had to serve in the military and, of them, only 1.6 million saw combat in Vietnam. In other words, we were able to fight the longest war in our history using only 6 percent of the eligible generation. By comparison, an individual's chances of being drafted were much higher during the Korean War, when monthly draft calls were running at the 80,000 level. Moreover, in 1959, when the smaller Depression generation had diminished the size of the draft pool, the odds of an individual being drafted—in peacetime— were actually *higher* than they were during the height of the Vietnam War. It is interesting to speculate just how much worse the domestic turmoil might have been if Vietnam had broken out when a small, rather than a large, generation was growing up. The draft would have reached into a far larger percentage of families and drastically disrupted the economy. On the other hand, there would have been fewer youthful troops on the home front to lead the resistance. The large size of the boom generation *contributed* to the war effort. Their numbers made it easy. The Reserves—potentially a political headache if they were ever called up—never had to be mobilized. Because the potential supply of draftees was more than the Pentagon could ever need, the government had the luxury at first of treating people preferentially. On one end of the socioeconomic scale, a thicket of deferments allowed dispensations for college students, graduate students, married men, men with children, and a host of occupations judged "in the national interest." This had the dual benefit of protecting the influential, wealthy, and educated classes from the horrors of the draft and, further, protecting the government from their wrath should they be called. On the other end of the social scale, minimal educational and physical standards were drawn up that had the result of keeping many of the poorest urban minorities out of the draft.

There was, however, a fatal flaw in this system that Congress failed to correct when the Selective Service Act was renewed in 1963. Deferments—and most noticeably the II-S student deferment—meant that men were vulnerable not in just one year but rather over a minefield of eight years, from their nineteenth birthday until their twenty-sixth. They had their entire student careers to worry about the draft and the injustice of the war and to build up resentments against the system that had caused it. Further, even if only some students would be needed by Uncle Sam, the deferment had put *all* of them in jeopardy. We fought the war with just 2 million troops in the war zone, but to procure them we threatened 25 million more baby boomers. It is no wonder that they hated the war. In addition to their moral and intellectual disgust, which was real enough, the war was plainly not in their self-interest.

The result of the draft policy was that the men of the boom generation found themselves unwillingly pitted in another Darwinian struggle for survival. The losers would wind up in Vietnam; the winners would go to graduate school, or join the Peace Corps, or find a friendly doctor to certify their asthma, or fake craziness or homosexuality, or enlist in the Reserves, or attempt any number of humiliating devices to avoid their military liability. For every man taken, two or three others were dodging from deferment to deferment like children playing hide and seek. All the while they concentrated on the draft, they were delaying decisions about marriage and family and career and were becoming increasingly angry. "My whole life style, my whole mentality was cramped and distorted, twisted by fear of the United States government," remembered one Palisades High graduate. "The fear of constantly having to evade and dodge, to defend myself against people who wanted to kill me, and wanted me to kill." In their excellent study of the Vietnam draft, Lawrence M. Baskir and William A. Strauss estimate that 15 million men—60 percent of the generation—could be classified as draft "evaders"—those who were eligible for service but did not serve a single day. As one resister accurately commented, "Almost every kid in this country [was] either a draft evader, a potential draft evader, or a failed draft evader."

Contrary to the impression given by movies like *Coming Home*, incidentally, America was not then divided between one army of soldiers blindly or helplessly shipped to Vietnam and another army of committed war resisters back home. The largest army dodged both confrontations. Of the 27 million draft-age men, just over half a million committed draft violations and fewer than 9000 were convicted. Of them 3250 went to prison. Only 24 soldiers were convicted of deserting under fire. These numbers remain minuscule beside the 15 million who solved the moral dilemma of the war simply by keeping it out of their lives.

Who, then, did serve? The evidence, not surprisingly, is that the war was fought by the poor and the powerless. What is surprising is that the worst inequities were not racial, as is commonly supposed, but educational and economic. College graduates and men who never made it to high school were *least* likely to serve. Only 9 percent of college graduates saw combat duty. High-school dropouts were twice as likely to see combat and four times as likely to be drafted. One study in Chicago discovered that men from low-income neighborhoods were three times as likely to die in Vietnam as men from upper-income neighborhoods.

The feeling of class discrimination in Vietnam service was brought home to one baby-boom writer, James Fallows, when he showed up for a preinduction physical. He and his Harvard classmates were adroitly finding their outs from the draft. Fallows had starved his six foot one inch frame down to 120 pounds, and his friends were armed with advice from draft counselors and letters from lawyers and doctors. Then they saw a busload of "thick, dark-haired young men, the white proles of Boston," arrive at the center. "They walked through the examination lines like so many cattle off to the slaughter," Fallows noticed, feeling strangely ashamed, while "the children of the bright good parents were spared the more immediate sort of suffering that our inferiors were undergoing."

Of 600 Harvard men in the Class of 1970 who answered a questionnaire for their fifth reunion, only 56 said they'd entered the military and only 2 went to Vietnam. In his college community of Buffalo, New York, Leslie Fiedler wrote that he "had never known a single family that had lost a son in Vietnam, or indeed, one with a son wounded, missing in action or held prisoner of war." The class protection similarly extended into high school. Michael Medved and David Wallechinsky reported that, of their 500 classmates at well-to-do Palisades High, not one died in Vietnam. The children who had grown up with the greatest expectations—the elitest of the elite—did not reckon that their destiny was in Vietnam. A Rhodes Scholar reflected the unconscious arrogance of his caste when he said, "There are certain people who can do more in a lifetime in politics or medicine than by getting killed in a trench." If you had money or intelligence or education, you would escape. If you did not, you fought. (By comparison, losses among the European elite in the world wars were appalling. Only one-third of Germany's 15,000 *Wandervögel* returned from World War I alive. Of 5588 Etonians who fought for England, 1159 were killed and 1469 were wounded. In World War II, the British Bomber Command alone lost 55,888 men, a figure comparable to America's total losses in Vietnam.)

Even as the war grew in ferocity, and monthly draft calls were rising to 46,000, the highest since the Korean War, the government continued to try to find ways to protect the vocal and powerful student generation. In 1966, Defense Secretary Robert McNamara announced a new program to rehabilitate "part of America's subterranean poor." Rather than ending the student deferment and taking *more* qualified men (and therefore more vocal critics of the war), the government went the other way: they would *lower* physical standards and take *less* qualified men. The Pentagon made it seem more like the War on Poverty than the War in Vietnam. It would reclassify upwards of 100,000 draft rejects and retrain them with the skills, the government promised, that would help end unemployment at home. It all sounded like the government was sending these recruits to college. The catch was that some of them would wind up with body bags instead of book bags. Four out of every ten of the "Project 100,000" recruits were black. Though blacks were only 11.6 percent of the total population, and were *less* represented in the military service than whites, they accounted for 24 percent of combat deaths in Vietnam in 1965. The Pentagon succeeded in reducing the incidence of black fatalities to 16 percent in 1966 and to 13 percent in 1968, but the association between racism and Vietnam had been made. Ironically, although many blacks joined the service to escape racial discrimination, subsequent surveys have shown little positive effect of military training on the civilian market.

Reform of the draft finally came in 1967—but in a way that solidified the opposition of the bulk of boom babies in college even more. The new law passed on July 2, 1967, ended graduate-student deferments and put them in the pool to be drafted along with graduating seniors that following June. The result was that the entire college class of 1968, most of whom were born in the boom's first year of 1946, suddenly lost their most reliable avenue of escape. In an angry editorial called "The Axe Falls," the *Harvard Crimson* complained that the end of special treatment to graduate students was an act of "careless expedience" that was "clearly unfair to students."

The students hit on a less lonely and in many ways less hazardous type of resistance. They would accept deferments, if they could get them, but they would also fight in the streets and in the classrooms. In 1968, the first year that colleges were composed entirely of baby-boom students, academe erupted in opposition to the war. The genteel "teach-ins" of the previous year, a hangover from the idealistic faith the boom had originally placed in education, gave way to sit-ins and protests. In the first five months of the year, nearly 40,000 students participated in 221 major demonstrations on 101 campuses. Thousands were arrested, including the generation's guru, Dr. Spock.

To the older generation, the Tet Offensive had come home. The barbarians were at the gates. Among the 18–24 age group, the liberal position on the war had gained from 29.5 percent in 1964 to 54.6 just three years later. Student turmoil was spreading to other countries as their baby-boom generations came of age. "Stop us?" rejoiced the French firebrand Daniel Cohn-Bendit. "Slap at water."

Historians were beginning to draw parallels between 1968 and 1848. Kenneth Keniston, who had called his earlier book about youth *The Uncommitted,* did a U-turn to write *Young Radicals: Notes on Committed Youth.* Before long, Jerry Rubin would be shouting that "the first point in the Yippie program is to kill your parents! . . . We ain't never, never gonna grow up! We're gonna be adolescents *forever!*" It was as if Vietnam had unleashed the nation's nightmares: Clarabelle had cut Howdy Doody's strings and the two of them were garroting Buffalo

Bob. How far had we come from those first demonstrations in 1960 in San Francisco, when police arrested a clutch of students protesting a hearing by the House Un-American Activities Committee? Even the Students for a Democratic Society's original Port Huron Statement of 1962 seemed relatively mild by comparison, asserting only that "We are people of this generation, bred in at least modest comfort, housed in universities, looking uncomfortably to the world we inherit." As recently as 1965, the press was nothing if not optimistic about the men and women of this docile generation. In Vietnam, one magazine had cheerfully noted, the American soldier's "main concern in off-duty hours is aiding the Vietnam civilian" and that, among the fighting men, there was "a good deal of the Peace Corps ardor that animates their peers back home."

But now their idealistic peers were less interested in building irrigation ditches than in stopping the war machine. Many of them embraced the radical catechism of poverty, racism, and war. They would operate from their power bases: the campuses and the youth ghettos around them. And their technique would be the strongest card the baby boom had to play: mass action. Says Rona in *Kennedy's Children:*

> We were, all the young, reaching out to each other through wild crazy means like that: the top ten charts, and our hair, and the way we dressed. I got taken for Dylan once. And the other side knew something was happening, but they couldn't figure out what. They fired Leary from Harvard, and they killed Kennedy, but they couldn't stop what we started. Boys began evading the draft, a lot, and we all became aware of that mindless horror going on under *our* name in Vietnam! And we marched! For peace and civil rights and everything we marched. I don't know how many marches we were on. We'd hitchhike or take busses and trucks and travel anywhere to march.

The baby boomers produced few leaders, even during their peak antiwar activity, and those who did emerge— Tom Hayden, Abbie Hoffman, Jerry Rubin, David Harris, even Dylan—were from an older generation. Only together, it seemed, could they meet the test of idealism their parents and teachers had been prepping them for all along. The kids did not accuse their elders of false values but rather of not living by the ones they taught. They actually believed those homilies about fairness and justice Jim Anderson was preaching on *Father Knows Best*. If killing is wrong, they said, it is just as wrong in Vietnam as in Dallas.

The massed energy of the boom made its first political show of strength in Eugene McCarthy's "Children's Crusade" in March 1968. Thousands and thousands of political novices proved in the New Hampshire primary that footpower and envelope-stuffing power could make up for all the computers in the world in the right arena. The technique of calling on nearly every voter in the state worked. McCarthy's strong showing ended Lyndon Johnson's presidency. The second show of strength came at Columbia University later that spring. The "Battle of Morningside Heights" and the take-overs that followed drew their driving energies from mass action. The students could shut down the university! They could show America the evil of the university's racism and complicity in the war! They could smoke President Kirk's cigars! Columbia students encamped in university buildings shared their delight by calling long-distance to friends at Sara Lawrence, UCLA, and Antioch. They had danced together and now they would build barricades together. In the American Gulag, the revolution was beginning in the Peanut Gallery. In his book *Time's Children*, Thomas Cottle reports a conversation he had with a typically self-involved college student of that time. "We're right at the center of everything," the student exulted. "You remember when you're a child, and your younger brother is the big star, or your big sister is doing all the things? Now it's us, we're right in the center, reading about ourselves in the newspaper. It's youth. Everything is youth and us."

So it seemed. But the thrill of revolution was not shared by the New York policemen, many of them not much older than the demonstrators, who reacted to the epithets of "pig!" with particularly brutal arrests. How galling it was to the police to witness the spectacle of upper-middle-class kids squandering the educational opportunities they could never enjoy. Their rage was shared by working-class students at Columbia—though it was consistently misrepresented as a political disagreement when it was more correctly a class issue. The demonstrators were locking out the lower-middle-class students on scholarships, whose parents were depending on them to lift their families out of their economic plight.

One of the ironies of Vietnam is that the opposition to the war was led by college students, who were safely deferred, while its support often came from young laborers—*The Deer Hunter*'s steelworkers—who were doing the actual fighting. For all the press and attention generated by the demonstrators, theirs was a leadership of the minority. Almost every public-opinion poll taken during the war years showed that youth, in the aggregate, disproportionately *supported* the war. (Surprisingly, the most "dovish" age group turned out to be people over fifty-five.) Similarly, in 1968 George Wallace's third-party campaign drew disproportionate support from the young and less-educated. Not until later would the values of the college students begin to spread to the generation at large.

By 1969, the best of this generation were becoming increasingly politicized and alienated. A full 50 percent of the students in a "forerunner group" interviewed by *Fortune* agreed with the proposition that American society was sick (and that was *before* Kent State). Harvard —Harvard!—had experienced its own fugue of idealism, building take-overs, and violence. A typical experience was that of a woman from Los Angeles, who once put a FREE HUEY NEWTON sticker on the bumper of her father's car. "My dad had never in his life so much as touched me," she remembered. "But that day he came outside, tore off the sticker and hit me."

The groupings of baby boomers, meanwhile, were becoming larger and larger. Woodstock, as we shall see later, convincingly demonstrated the size of the army that the generation could mobilize. In the March on Washington in November of 1969, hundreds of thousands more effectively put on a political Woodstock in opposition to the war. (The Nixon administration ringed the White House that day with tour buses, wagon-train style, as if to ward off barbarians.) If the baby boomers could not be heard as individuals, they were delivering a testimony of bodies that was deafening.

Opponents of the peace movement were given at this time to drawing largely unfair comparisons between the demonstrators and Hitler Youth (a charge that was returned with equal hyperbole by students charging "Fascist" police tactics). But there is one analogy between the periods that is worth making. It is that young people become conspicuous during times of rapid population growth.

When the post-World War I Depression hit the Weimar Republic, the older generation running the country had already been weakened by war. The young adult age group from 20 to 45, moreover, was the largest in German history and comprised more than 40 percent of the population. Thus, it is easy to see that the Depression hit Germany at the worst possible time: there were fewer jobs but more people who wanted them. It is not surprising that Hitler was able to move this restless generation of "barbarians" to overthrow their outnumbered elders. After Hitler came to power, interestingly, the number of Germans in the youngest age cohorts actually shrank, thereby decreasing the chances of a counterrevolution.

Let me add that I am not maintaining that social change is *caused* by discontinuities in youth any more than Nazism was *caused* by youth. Rather, social change is carried out by youth. The student unrest of the 1960s saw upheavals not just at Columbia and Berkeley, but in England, Italy, France, Germany, Holland, Sweden, Spain, Belgium, Japan, Formosa, Poland, Hungary, Yugoslavia, and Czechoslovakia. The demographics of the postwar baby boom were not to blame in each of these countries. Other forces were plainly at work. But, because youth is the messenger, any increase in the number of youth in society carries with it the potential for activating those forces. Herbert Moller, a historian who has studied youth and change, put it this way: "The presence of a large contingent of young people may make for a cumulative process of innovation and social and cultural growth: it may lead to directionless, acting-out behavior; it may destroy old institutions and elevate new elites to power; and the employed energies of the young may be organized and directed by totalitarian rulers." In the end, America may have been fortunate that its democratic tradition was strong enough to resist assaults from willful minorities of any persuasion during the 1960s.

The spring of 1970 was at once both the height and the beginning of the end for the student movement. On April 30, President Nixon announced the movement of American and South Vietnamese troops into Cambodia. On May 4, four students were killed and nine wounded at Kent State. On May 14, two more were killed and twelve wounded at Jackson State. Campuses across the country were swept by a prairie fire of protest. In all, 448 campuses were either on strike or were completely closed down. Columbia President McGill called it "the most disastrous May in the history of American higher education and, in a Gallup poll, the American public called campus unrest the nation's most important problem. Momentarily, at least, the baby boom had burst out of control.

Yet, by that fall, campuses had turned quiescent. Many students campaigned for peace candidates, to be sure, but they were surprisingly inconspicuous. Most others were returning to their books, as if shocked by the terror of Kent State and Jackson State.

Several things had happened. The radicals lost credibility after students saw them blowing themselves up with bombs in Greenwich Village and blowing up innocent people in Wisconsin. The popular support behind the antiwar movement faded. A Gallup poll in the spring of 1970 showed that most young people were more opposed to the excesses of the peace movement than they were to the war. Furthermore, the most common theme in demonstrations on campuses was *not* the war—it was student power. The efforts by the students to make reforms favoring students—adding pass-fail electives, election recesses, and the like—eventually paid off.

Still more important, though, in defusing opposition to the war was a new Selective Service law passed by Congress. In November of 1969, the Nixon administration set up the system of a draft lottery. It succeeded where no one had before in separating the twin issues of opposition to the draft from opposition to the war. Almost all young Americans hated the draft. Far fewer hated the war. The master-stroke of the new law was limiting all men—students and nonstudents alike—to one year of draft vulnerability after their nineteenth birthday. If their lottery number was high enough, they could forget about it. Thus, with more than one-half of all students instantly freed from the possibility of going to Vietnam, the antiwar movement lost its most immediately compelling issue. The animosity against the war would be a little less personal. The baby boomers would never again so intensely feel the fear of Vietnam at their backs. (The bulk of protests in 1970 were more in outrage over killings at

116

Kent State than in Cambodia.) One can only wonder how many students would have marched against the war if the draft lottery had been enacted back in 1964.

The protests took a grim toll. Some baby boomers disappeared into their anger and alienation and never came out on the other side. Leon Botstein, who was president of Franconia College and Bard College by the time he was thirty, told one writer, Mary Alice Kellogg, how it was for him:

> It was a tumultuous period emotionally because you were constantly sorting this stuff out. The lure of really radical involvement was always there. A lot of my friends disappeared. Some went underground. My first girlfriend in grad school, the brightest student in the history department, vanished. You struggled with the issues. It was very hard.

On the other hand, as in any war, the protests also brought the participants together in what many of them still remember as their finest hour. The sixties were an inspiring lesson in the power of ideas and in the power of numbers. Everyone was taking sides. "In California," a woman remembered, "we were utterly convinced that the revolution was coming and that we were making it." Another baby boomer, now a magazine editor in New York, agreed. "We went through a hell of a lot. If you went through it and emerged from it, you emerged so much stronger. I think there is a way of seeing the worst. You know you're not going to see it that bad anymore. Therefore, you have a lot more strength and drive to go on and get about your life and do well. I weathered my father's death, a suicide, and the sixties. Nothing scares me." What the playing fields of Eton were to the generations of British soldiers, the exhilarating battles of Columbia and Harvard and a hundred other campuses were to a generation of young Americans. They had been tested and met the test. The justness of their cause was proved by the dossier of cases lost by the government: the Chicago Seven, the Harrisburg Seven, the Camden Seventeen, the Seattle Seven, the Kansas City Four, the Evanston Four, and the Gainesville Eight. Even Dr. Spock's conviction was later reversed. Rona in *Kennedy's Children* expressed the phosphorescence of the generation's dreams then. "European visitors told us how students had always been

117

a political force in Europe," she says. "But we were the first like that in America. We were something terrifically exciting and frightening. We were America's big chance for change—everybody's chance for change."

The terrible price of Vietnam was paid by the entire country. But no one felt it more directly or more personally than the 26.8 million men of the baby boom who came of draft age between 1964 and 1973. In Vietnam, there were 58,000 killed and 153,000 wounded, the overwhelming majority of them baby boomers. The war created 35,000 widows and orphans; some 275,000 Americans experienced a death in their family; 1.4 million saw someone in their family wounded. Millions more suffered invisible scars at the hands of the war that was—and is—a generational obsession. The compromises forced by the draft, said Kingman Brewster, the former president of Yale, resulted in a "cynical avoidance of service, a corruption of the aims of education, a tarnishing of the national spirit." Many men of the boom are still walking around with three-year holes punctured in their lives, whether they served or not.

Vietnam still lives with us in the person of the 6.5 million baby boomers who served in the armed forces during the Vietnam Era. More than a million of them saw combat. Even if they were not wounded, many of them have faced staggering problems as a result of their Vietnam service, ranging from unemployment to suicide, guilt, depression, anger, rage, and rejection. An estimated half-million Vietnam veterans suffer from "post-traumatic neurosis," periods of terrifying nightmares and flashbacks. The number of Veterans Administration alcohol treatment centers is growing 13 percent a year. The suicide rate among Vietnam vets currently runs 23 percent higher than that for nonveterans. Vietnam veterans have been unable to reintegrate themselves easily within the society. Unemployment among younger veterans still runs higher than average. The education and careers of countless others were interrupted to the extent that they have been unable to rejoin their generation. The movies about Vietnam —*The Deer Hunter, Coming Home, Apocalypse Now, Who'll Stop the Rain?*—have helped end the taboo about popular discussion of the war. But they have hardly helped cleanse the veterans of their stigma as junkies, psychos, misfits, and crazed Sergeant Rocks. Like Agent Orange, the lethal herbicide that was sprayed during the war, the memories of Vietnam can lie dormant only to reappear much later to claim their victims. Vietnam is like a death in the family. The country has moved through three of the four stages of mourning—denial, anger, and depression—but is only beginning to confront the fourth —acceptance.

The experience of Vietnam was not unlike that of the generation of 1914 in World War I. Novelist Erich Remarque felt that the Great War had destroyed his generation both physically and morally. To Robert Wohl, the 1914 war both fortified "the consciousness of a new generation and gave plausibility to the idea of its unity by creating an overwhelming sense of rupture with the past." So, too, Vietnam crystallized the boom generation's identity by setting it in opposition to the world of its parents and giving it a common fund of experience it would draw on the rest of its life. The war, coming at a time of youthful transition for the first half of the baby-boom generation, also brought with it another disturbing indication that their great expectations might not be met.

The optimism and hope that the boom generation took into the Vietnam years only made its eventual disenchantment more devastating. They had been young and idealistic and Vietnam made them old and cynical. Their parents had come out of World War II with renewed confidence, but the boom generation came out of Vietnam with little to believe in of its own. Typically, the closest thing to war heroes Vietnam produced were, as Baskir and Strauss pointed out, the returning POWs, most of whom were older pilots from another generation. It is trite now to say that Vietnam marked America's end of innocence. But the boom generation did receive then its first personal taste of life as tragedy. One mother, whose son was killed two weeks before the end of his tour, summarized it well: "My son was a victim, my family was a victim, all boys of draft age were victims in one way or another."

Chapter 8

THE ROAD TO WOODSTOCK

Q. Will you please identify yourself for the record?
A. My name is Abbie. I am an orphan of America.
Q. Where do you reside?
A. I live in Woodstock Nation.
Q. Will you tell the Court and jury where it is?
A. Yes. It is a nation of alienated young people. We
   carry it around with us as a state of mind in the
   same way the Sioux Indians carried the Sioux
   nation around with them. It is a nation dedicated
   to cooperation versus competition, to the idea
   that people should have better means of exchange
   than property or money, that there should be
   some other basis for human interaction.
Q. Can you tell the Court and jury your present age?
A. My age is 33. I am a child of the '60s.
Q. When were you born?
A. Psychologically, 1960.
                        —Testimony of Abbie Hoffman at
                        the trial of the Chicago Seven

If you wanted to dramatize the split that marked the
youth movement from the start, you could not do it better than the baby boomers themselves did at their gather-
ings. At protest rallies in Berkeley, for example, the writer
Sara Davidson heard one group of students singing "We
Shall Overcome" and another singing "Yellow Subma-
rine." During antiwar demonstrations at the Pentagon, it
was not always clear whether the real objective was to
liberate it or to levitate it. James Simon Kunen, who participated in the 1968 Columbia take-over, candidly admitted later that he went to the Poor People's March on
Washington not out of a passionate sense of injustice but

to get two girls' addresses and a tan. The difference between Kunen and his fellow radical Mark Rudd aptly summarizes the church-and-state schism in the youth movement. Some were cultural revolutionaries, others were political revolutionaries. While the political revolution initially attracted the most fevered attention in the press and in the minds of the public, the cultural revolution was the most representative of the boom generation and the one that ultimately would come closest to prevailing.

Both wings of the youth movement grew from the common feeling among baby boomers that they could not adjust to society. Or, rather, that society could not adjust to them. Their numbers were too many, their needs too compelling, and their energies too robust. Realizing this, the political side of the boom generation struck out to seize power directly from the elders. Vietnam was not the only political issue of the sixties, but it was the one most fatally intertwined with the destiny of the baby boom.

The style of the cultural revolution, on the other hand, was not confrontational. It was less a product of the politics of the sixties than the cumulative experience of the boom generation. The lessons hammered in by parents, teachers, television, rock 'n' roll, and the youth culture were taking hold. The people of the boom generation believed that they were something new under the sun: a new generation with a unique sensibility and the power to use it. Theirs was a revolution of rising expectations. They were special. They would *not* be like their parents. In fact, they believed it was their *duty* not to choose adult roles that were plainly unsatisfactory and unfulfilling. Their parents had practically told them as much by their constant striving to make their children better. Who, the kids seemed to be saying, would even want to get integrated into the adult community when the alternative—a vibrant world of youth—was so much better? Here was an enthralling sense of community, of contemporaneity, and of spontaneity.

Then, too, lurking somewhere in the back of the boom babies' minds was the disturbing idea that they were not needed. The Pentagon did not need all of them to fight its war and neither did the labor force need all of them to fire the satanic mills. Their numbers had rendered them unnecessary and their long education had made them a marginal elite, prepared for a world that was not prepared for them. But this superfluity did not need to be depressing. If there was not enough room for everyone to crowd through the door at once, then fewer needed to make the effort. The others could go in another direction: they would make a competing culture, drawing its authority not from the elders nor from organizations nor from traditions but simply from one another.

They called it a counterculture and, during the ephemeral "Summer of Love" in 1967, it flourished on the streets of Haight-Ashbury. Scott McKenzie sang to be sure to wear flowers in your hair if you came to San Francisco, so they did. They wandered hand in hand at the Monterey County Fairgrounds, listening to the Mamas and the Papas, a hippie group that wore funny hats and fringes but which had rescued rock from the English. Mama Cass was great at The Monterey Festival. So were Janis Joplin, Otis Redding, Jimi Hendrix, and Keith Moon of The Who. (Sadly, all of those performers would die later, giving the movie of *Monterey Pop* the doomed quality of the hippie movement itself.)

Psychedelic art meant that art was imitating the swirling, teeming, drugged-up life of the sixties. Density and clutter were everywhere. At a Berkeley party brought to life in Sara Davidson's *Loose Change,* people wore "Edwardian velvet gowns, spaceman suits, African robes, cowboy regalia, Donald Duck hats and Indian war paint." The kids who had been born free from what *Time* called "the cold pressures of hunger and mortality" were turning into refugees from affluence. Dismissing the Protestant Ethic of their parents—hard work, competition, and material success—they were moving into tepees and adobe huts and giving their children names like Morning Star. Their friends were their "brothers" and "sisters" and all part of the tribe. "God knows many of them are fools, and most of them will be sellouts," Lillian Hellman said. "But they're a better generation than we were." (Hers was a minority reaction, however. Now that the counterculture is part of Pepsi ads, it is hard to remember the frightening and often irrational hostilities hippies provoked in the older generation.) Eventually, buses would shuttle in tourists to gawk at the spectacle of middle-class kids scorning their class status. Tougher elements would not be far behind. The flower children never numbered more than a few thousand, and they soon faded. But they left something behind that fascinated the media. They were telling the world that the generation everyone voted Most Likely to Succeed did not want to be part of a society that was (pick one) corrupt, repressive, materialistic, closed, demented, joyless, and militaristic. Their values would be (pick all) free, open, joyful, pure, spontaneous, giving, and loving. "California was a second chance," said Rona in *Kennedy's Children*. "The streets in Haight-Ashbury were a carnival. Incredible young people, tripping and digging each other and dying to live. The Big Be-In, the first be-in they called a be-in, in 1967—that was the peak."

Be-ins. Happenings. How appropriate. The political revolutionaries wanted to send Washington a message with their feet. But the cultural revolutionaries would send it with their hair. In both cases, the real discovery was that the mass was the message. They really were brothers and sisters! Their whole was greater than any of their parts. In fact, their real message could be seen *only* in the mass, like the massive letters spelled out by cheering sections at Big Ten football games. And the message to the parents was, Leave Us Alone. "The baby boom grew up under parents who were not like their grandparents," said one college student who wound up selling newspapers on the street of the Haight. He continued:

> I talk to my parents and ask how they were raised. It's the usual thing, "Children are to be seen and not heard." But our parents didn't operate that way. They could remember their childhoods, the coolness of their parents, the selfish dullness of love. Both of them resolved that when they had children they wouldn't do that to them, that they would give their children time and love and patience. When you give that much love and that much attention to a whole generation of people . . . (he shrugs). It was almost a resentment. Get off my back. I don't want it. I want to be myself.

Just what did the doctrine of independence embrace? It meant that an influential college-educated minority of baby boomers were attacking virtually every belief and value cherished by their parents. These Forerunners, as Daniel Yankelovich named them, left nothing unchallenged:

> They rejected economic well-being as an indispensa-

123

ble source of the freedom and dignity of the individual. They derided society's definition of education as the royal road to success and achievement. They belittled the efforts of the average person to cope with the economic harshness of everyday life and his struggle to stand on his own two feet and retain some measure of autonomy within the complex conditions of modern life. They professed beliefs that seemed to flout faith in marriage, work, family, patriotism, democracy, competition, and equality of opportunity. They downgraded traditional American aspirations for more material comfort—more money, more education, more leisure, and more opportunities for one's self and one's children. They challenged established authority in the larger society in every one of its forms—the law, the police, the universities, the elected officials, the professions, the corporate structure, etc. They countered the traditional social institutions of marriage and church with new styles of communal living and new forms of religious expression. They scrutinized each element of traditional sexual morality for opportunities to try something different. They countered the alcohol culture with the drug culture. They met the old emphasis on private careers with a new craving for community—the list could be continued indefinitely.

On the campuses, where at least some of these views were shared by students, the quest for personal salvation found an unlikely guru. When Hermann Hesse died in 1962, *The New York Times* obituary-writer not unreasonably pronounced the German writer "largely unapproachable" for American readers. Yet in the next decade, implausibly, Hesse became a literary cult, selling eleven million books as he went from obscurity to become the most widely read German writer in America. Millions of baby-boom readers identified with his protagonists and their spiritual odysseys through a corrupted world. Steppenwolf became the name of a rock group and a Berkeley bar, and Siddhartha was seen as the original flower child. Novels like *Demian,* with its theme that life offers no rewards beyond the search itself for personal value, provided fictional justification for a generation of adolescent angst and rebellion. If nothing else, Hessomania convincingly demonstrated that the religious eclecticism and mysticism usually identified with "hippies" had a far broader base. As the leading edge of the boom babies passed beyond college, and their needs for spiritual reassurement dissipated, the Hesse boom disappeared almost as fast as it had arrived.

Unlike novels, newspapers and magazines are better equipped to shift with the vagaries of fashion and taste. So many publishing properties later became symbiotically tied to the baby boom that now it is easy to forget that at one time youth publishing was a no-growth field. The purchasing power was there, all right, but no one had found the key to turning it on. Youth was in revolt but the teentown magazines were still writing about acne preparations.

What made the difference? Inevitably, rock 'n' roll. In just five years, for example, rock releases had grown from 15 percent of the Columbia Records list to 60 percent. The record industry was exploding at a quantum growth rate of 20 percent a year. Radio was really the first music medium to save itself with the youth market. Television had drained off the network radio audience in the early fifties, as radio use in the average home dropped from 3 hours and 42 minutes a night to 24 minutes. But, backed by record advertising, AM rock stations were taking over the big-city market, and FM radio, once a backwater, was thriving with new life. In the youth ghettos, proliferating underground newspapers were becoming social institutions with their eclectic mix of idiosyncratic reporting, headshop ads, bizarre personals, and record ads. Some music magazines—most notably *Cheetah* and *Eye*—were aiming for the youth market but seemed to be missing the target.

Then, in 1967, a 21-year-old baby boomer named Jann Wenner (b. January 7, 1946) dropped out of Berkeley and with $7500 started a magazine that changed the business. *Rolling Stone*, Wenner said in his first editorial, "is not just about music, but also about the things and attitudes that the music embraces." That meant politics, drugs, and the music business—all delivered with iconoclastic reporting that took nothing for granted, including its readers' prejudices. What interested Wenner were the changes related to rock 'n' roll. "Rock and roll is more than just music," *Rolling Stone* announced. "It is the energy center of the new culture and the youth revolution." Thus, while other publications were listing personnel changes in bands, *Rolling Stone* was pulling no punches as it went after its subjects with a vengeance. Its critics

125

called it the rock generation's *Pravda* but it was more like *The Wall Street Journal*. At its best, it was the generation's publication of record. "Dope, rock and roll and taking a billy club over the head are the experience of young people today," Wenner once said. For good measure, he could have added the name of *Rolling Stone* to the list.

When the youth revolution found its Thomas Paine, he was not, as one might expect, someone of that generation. Instead, a 42-year-old law professor at Yale articulated better than anyone the revolutionary romanticism of the era. In *The Greening of America*, Charles Reich became the shaman whose vision was of "a revolution coming. It will not be like revolutions of the past. It will originate with the individual and with culture, and it will change the political structure only as its final act. It will not require violence to succeed, and it cannot be successfully resisted by violence. It is now spreading with amazing rapidity . . ."

Reich built his apocalyptic analysis on what he described as the evolution of human consciousness. All history was divided into three parts: Consciousness I was the realm of individualistic Natty Bumppos and entrepreneurs who built capitalism. Consciousness II was the habitat of the other-directed makers of the corporate state. Consciousness III was the New Era that the young were building. They were the nurturers of a warm and embracing humanism that, Reich argued, pervaded everything they touched. They were rejecting competitiveness, materialism, and the work ethic itself. Instead, they tried drugs which can "add a whole new dimension to creativity" and bell-bottoms which "give the ankles a special freedom, as if to invite dancing right on the streets." Where did he see Con III flourishing? In the college class of 1969, which had left high school with *What Really Happened to the Class of '65* class, and which was born in the birth cohort of 1947, at the leading edge of the baby boom.

The problem with Reich's theory was that it had a kind of Silly Putty quality that seemed to fit whatever he or anyone else, even his critics, wanted to make of it. Reich, for instance, could have it both ways. If bell-bottoms were good because they were free and loose, well, so were tight jeans which revealed the true contours of the body. His Con III seemed about as economically viable as Oz, floating off without the necessary affluence and technological base that could only be guaranteed by the drudges of Con II. It was even harder to make a general principle out of what ultimately was a phenomenon confined to a minority of students on a minority of campuses. And, as Kenneth Keniston pointed out, "People who really live in organic, tribal, symbiotic and shamanistic cultures generally can't wait to escape into the world of affluence, science and technology."

At the same time, the flood of controversy spilled by Reich's book—it boiled in *The New York Times's* Op-Ed columns for months—showed that he had tapped into something important. But what? He thought it was an era of lasting change: American youth was the vanguard ushering in a New Man. But we know now that the New Man never really arrived. He just got older. Reich's fallacy, I think, was in not recognizing that the changes he was witnessing were not historical but generational. The youth movement, with all its manifestations, was a creation of the baby boom and was exclusive to the baby boom. Its enormous size has always forced it to break the rules. But there is no reason to expect subsequent, smaller generations to behave the same way. They lack both the size and the sense of mission that characterized the boom generation. As the baby boomers moved along, they would eventually take the youth movement with them—only it would become the middle-aged movement. In short, it was not the times that were a-changing, it was the generation.

The gong rung by *The Greening of America* reverberated through the country. Suddenly everyone wanted to know what kids were thinking. Reporters swarmed onto the campuses. Kids fresh out of college were being handed book contracts to write not of their dreams but their memoirs. Joyce Maynard published her bittersweet autobiography as a 19-year-old Yale sophomore. The media hothouse intensified the boom generation's acutely felt self-awareness. "My friends and I became preoccupied with the common nostalgic assertion that 'these are the best years of our lives,'" Kunen remembered. It was not easy to live up to the standards they were setting for themselves. They must not cop out and they must not squander their dreams. They were what was happening. The richness of the 1960s experience was such that baby boomers were turning historians even before the decade was over. Writers struggled to put it down on paper, no matter how bizarre the result. Here is how a mystery writer, Roger Simon, typically tried to compress most of the history of the times into a single paragraph in a neo–Sam Spade novel called *The Big Fix:*

> Lila had always been like that—one of those intense people who went through the sixties like a wine taster, sampling each vintage and moving on. FSM, SDS, shooting pads in the Haight, the Hell's Angels, bus trips with Kesey's Pranksters, sunshine at the Fillmore, communes in Taos—she did it all. The first time I met her we were being firehosed down the steps of the San Francisco City Hall at the HUAC protest in May 1960.

Peter Townshend of The Who came closer to describing his formative feelings of generational solidarity in this passage:

> As a force, they were unbelievable. They were the Bulge, the result of all the old soldiers coming back from the war and screwing until they were blue in the face. Thousands and thousands of kids—too many kids, not enough teachers, not enough parents, not enough pills to go around. The feeling of being a mod among two million mods was incredible. . . . Everybody looked the same, everybody acted the same and everybody wanted to be the same.

The baby boom did not always seem so homogeneous. There were so many of them that words like "youth" and "adolescent" and even "postadolescent" began to lose their utility. The press began to zero in on whole new species: "preteens" and "subteens" and "postteens" and, most barbarically, "teenyboppers." A typical refrain among older baby boomers, as their noise level rose in the background, was, "If you think I'm weird, wait until you meet my little brother!" During the most vertiginous years of the sixties, college and high-school classes began to fragment into separate but distinct subgroups, each with life expectancies as ephemeral as those of Olympic swimmers or second lieutenants in combat. Even the old idea of three generations to a century was beginning to seem an anachronism. The baby boom was changing all that, too, embracing older and younger people alike.

One group, however, was made oddly ambivalent by

the boisterous presence of the baby boom. Not the parents—there was never much ambiguity about where they stood. Rather, it was the group immediately older than the boom babies. They were the big brothers and sisters who had arrived just before or during World War II. They became an in-between generation, straddled between the parents, whom they would not identify with, and the boom babies, whom they could not identify with. Just when they thought the world was theirs to inherit, they had been shoved aside by their aggressive, abrasive —but fascinating—younger siblings.

They were the Left-Out Generation. They had not grown up with *Romper Room* pulsating in the background. In fact, television was not necessarily in the house when they grew up. They had accepted the authority of their parents instead. Their music was not rock but folk. The fictional hero who spoke most directly to their concerns was not Siddhartha but Holden Caulfield. They were teenagers when teenagers were still an emotionally deprived class. They thought of themselves not as a community of interest but rather as lonely individuals wrestling with personality problems. A "Silent Generation" in college, they had lusted after Natalie Wood and climbed on the corporate ladder before their kid brothers and sisters told them that corporations were corrupt. They married and made lifetime goals that were later declared obsolete. Never forced by the war or the draft to take sides en masse, the Left-Out Generation remained uncommitted. Too young to be part of the older generation and too old to join the younger, they were estranged from both. When a student leader named Jack Weinberg told everyone at Berkeley not to trust anyone over 30, they feared he was talking about them.

The sibling gap continues today, but the lines of demarcation are less clear now. The older brothers and sisters did suffer, after all, from many of the same economic and social stresses of the postwar period; they shared the same musical heroes as the baby boomers; they even watched the same television shows. What made their experience more favorable, however, was their smaller number. We were able to absorb them. If they sometimes suffered from generation envy, lacking the strength and certainty and attention-getting ability of their younger siblings, the older brothers and sisters will always have the one consolation of knowing that society will always have room for them.

In recent years, an astute investor might well have contemplated putting a bundle into Robert Burton Associated, Ltd. of New York. In just six years, the company boosted its sales from $400,000 to $7 million and its net worth to $1.2 million. Likewise, an investment in the Adam's Apple Distribution Company of Chicago would have paid off handsomely. It zoomed from sales of $40,000 in 1971 to $10 million in 1977. What was this growth industry? Computer parts? Some energy-saving device? The answer was hardly so glamorous.

It was cigarette paper. Specifically, it was roll-your-own cigarette paper, the flimsy stuff that cowboys used to wrap around Bull Durham. The boom generation, however, wrapped it around marijuana, millions and millions of joints. Unit sales of booklets of cigarette papers tripled from 50 million in 1968 to 150 million in 1977. (Meanwhile, lest there be any doubt about what was in those reefers, the industry sales of actual roll-your-own cigarette tobacco slumped from 12 million pounds to less than 6 in the same period.) As the marketers of, respectively, E-Z Wider and Job rolling papers, Robert Burton and Adam's Apple were cashing in on yet another burgeoning industry created in the backwash of the baby boom. And they were Johnnies-come-latelys. The leader of the $200-million cigarette paper industry, U.S. Tobacco Company's Zig-Zag, saw its sales increase on the average of 25 precent a year in the decade from 1964 to 1974.

Cigarette papers are only a small fraction of the drug industry. Other legal drug-oriented accessories include such items as acrylic and glass bongs, water pipes, roach clips, and colored lights. The bit payoff, of course, was marijuana itself, an illegal billion-dollar industry created almost exclusively for and by the boom generation. From 1960 to 1970, the number of young people who tried marijuana went from a few hundred thousand to an estimated eight million. By 1977, more than two-thirds of all college students were getting high at one time or another. And, even though marijuana use has unquestionably spread to older and younger age groups, it remains overwhelmingly a baby-boom activity, one that dates people of this generation almost as accurately as a birth year.

For years, smoking dope was a ceremonial rite of initiation into the youth movement. Friends turned on friends to become better friends. Best of all, adults did not do it and did not necessarily understand it. Not surprisingly, drug culture contributed most of the additions to the English language that have been made by the boom generation. The most recent edition of *Roget's Thesaurus*, for instance, added words like "down," "downer," "turned off," "turned on," "spaced out," "stoned," and "zonked" —all parts of the drug vocabulary.

In the sixties and early seventies, marijuana and an entire pharmacopoeia of chemicals spread from the colleges into the high schools and eventually into the elementary schools. In 1976, more than half of the high-school seniors surveyed by the University of Michigan smoked marijuana regularly and 10 percent did *daily*. In true Elmer Gantry style, Hollywood was making movies like *The Trip* and *Cisco Pike* and *Dealing* that dwelled delightedly on the evils of drugs.

It all could have been a lark, another baby-boom put-on, but drugs were also the pathology of this generation. Too many kids were taking off on trips and not coming back. The drug experimenters were this generation's Lewis and Clark: they disappeared into a deepening wilderness of drug use—acid, hash, peyote, angel dust, PCP—and only occasionally reappeared to tell us of the wonderful things they found there. Others lost their inner maps; either they never returned at all or, if they did, they might as well have not been there. Every baby boomer has a friend or two from school who did not make it back and wound up dead or effectively lobotomized by drugs. Here is what a Los Angeles woman remembered about a drug party in high school:

We were all stoned, really stoned. And this girl friend of mine had O.D.'d on something, and no one knew what it was. So someone called the hospital, and while we were waiting for the ambulance and police to come, I was sitting there trying to hold her. I remember thinking, Oh, my God, the insanity, the absolute insanity.

Another New York woman remembered that she

stopped taking drugs in 1969 when my friend and I were hitchhiking from Provincetown to Boston and got a ride from some rough trade. They were on morphine and driving all over the road. A cop saw us and tried to pull us over. These guys were passing me packets of morphine to hide under the seats and pulling on sweaters so the cops wouldn't see the needle marks on their arms. And here I am asking God to get me out of this. If I didn't smoke dope, I wouldn't have been in the car in the first place. So that was it. No more dope. I haven't smoked since. I don't pick up hitch-hikers, either.

Just as the fifties did not really end until 1963, the sixties waited until just a few months before the end of the decade before finding their most resonant event. It came in August 1969, during sixty wet, weary hours in the farm town of Bethel, New York. There, on Max Yasgur's dairy farm, some 400,000 people came together for the rock concert that briefly gave its name to the generation. Woodstock encapsulated all the forces that had been churning through the sixties: drugs, rock, rebellion, mass action, idealism, and, ultimately, disenchantment. It produced so-so music, but that was not the point. It also produced 400 LSD freak-outs, three deaths, and two births —and that was closer to the point.

As usual, the generations disagreed about what it meant. *Newsweek* called it "the official coming-out party for a generation abandoning politics for psychedelics." Newspapers like *The Wall Street Journal* were revolted by the spectacle of hundreds of thousands of our children rolling naked in the mud. (At Monterey Pop, a more genteel audience had listened decorously in folding chairs.)

To the kids, though, the mud and the drugs and the music were all incidental to what to them was a Statement as fraught with meaning as Luther's Ninety-five Theses. In those days, before disco and after swing, rock itself was political theater—ungodly, ugly, unpatriotic, and worse. When Peter Townshend smashed guitars onstage, he was speaking clearly to his audience. And when half a million baby boomers showed up in one weekend to watch him, it was power. Woodstock was the last time that rock would speak so directly to the needs of its audience before turning pandering and escapist in the seventies. "The New York Thruway is closed, man!" Arlo Guthrie shouted to the multitude, adding triumphantly, "Lotta freaks!" At Woodstock, what they best demonstrated, as always, was their numbers.

132

"It was like an incredible huge people show," said Jerry Garcia. "You could just wander around from people scene to people scene. It was like I knew I was at a place where history was being made. You could tell. You could be there and say, 'This is history. This is a historical moment.'"

In a strange kind of reversal, the kids at Woodstock even took pride in some of the very qualities they found oppressive in adult organizations. The United States had sent a man to the moon a month before, but, look, at Woodstock the freaks had organized themselves, too. They had created the third-biggest city in New York State overnight. And it had fewer crimes and good medical care. Helicopters were dropping in and evacuating the wounded, oddly like Vietnam. Boasting about their free kitchens and clean-up details, the volunteers of Woodstock sounded for all the world like the Chamber of Commerce of Rochester, the real third-biggest city in New York.

The massing of thousands of their brethren has always been a purposeful activity of the baby boom. It has an analogy in nature. Years ago, the English ethnologist, V. C. Wynne-Edwards demonstrated how starlings periodically flock in the thousands to conduct what amounts to a census of their population. (The "epideictic displays," as Wynne-Edwards called them, helps the birds control their food supply by regulating their birthrate.) For the kids, who had already been grouped everywhere from hospitals to playgrounds to lecture halls, the convincing display of their numbers was a strengthening reinforcement of their generational identity. Their prolonged adolescence seemed to have conditioned them with a craving for group support. The music at the concerts was no more important than the ritual: the cheering and waving of lighted matches had all the emotional richness of a religious revival. Before many rock concerts, hundreds of students would wait in line overnight, huddling in sleeping bags and passing joints from hand to hand.

At Woodstock, they could meet and see more people than anyone could ever imagine. "The roar after a song!" remembered Country Joe McDonald. "It was scary, God, I had never seen so many people." Kids who returned from Woodstock spoke less about how Jimi played, or what Joe Cocker had said, than they did about sloshing together—together!—in the rain and the mud. The actual

133

attendance at Woodstock was less then half a million, but twice as many would later claim that they'd been there. And many millions more felt as though they'd been there. The generation had achieved its own Beau Geste effect— the few who were there convinced us of the army behind them. Just as Arlo Guthrie had promised in "Alice's Restaurant," 50 people could look like a movement. To that degree, Woodstock was a success. (It is interesting that the attempts to organize a reunion concert there a decade later failed. The promoters missed the point. The pilgrims of 1969 had not come to Woodstock to see the musicians; they came to see one another. The youth of 1979, however, were not subject to the same centripetal forces and psychological needs that brought the boomers together ten years earlier.)

It has become a journalistic cliché to say that the spirit of Woodstock died at Altamont. The comparison is too facile. On December 6, 1969, not even four months after Woodstock, the Rolling Stones gave a free concert at the Altamont Speedway in California. More than 250,000 spectators showed up; 4 died, one of whom was stabbed to death by Hell's Angels before cameras filming a Stones' movie, *Gimme Shelter*. But if Woodstock was never so wonderful as its mystique, Altamont was not so awful. When Cleveland held a "World Series of Rock" ten years later, it resulted in two deaths, five shootings, ten stabbings, eight robberies, fourteen car thefts, and countless drug overdoses—all with only 65,000 fans.

But there was nevertheless a gnawing sentiment that the spontaneity of the youth movement was becoming institutionalized and cheapened by its self-indulgence. Instead of reforming the world, they were entertaining it. The titillated over-30 generation was romanticizing their every moment and *Life* was lavishing four-color spreads on subjects like "The Commune Comes to America." The worst of all were scholars rhapsodizing about long hair as the "rejection of the phallic way of life" and the like. *Hair* itself had moved to Broadway.

After the florid display of Woodstock, youth lost its bloom as quickly as if it had been sprayed by the kind of herbicide that kills by overstimulating its growth. The peace movement marched in the cities in November of 1969 and then made its last stand the following May. The leaders were still walking, but the media had blown the movement into a caricature of itself. In 1971, Bill

Graham closed his Fillmore rock temples on both coasts. "What happened with the music and with the young generation is that it went into a period of wanting to forget the world around them and using gasoline to get there," he said. "The young people used rock 'n' roll to say to the world, 'We can be independent. This is our way of life. We're revolutionaries. This is the background.' There was nothing wrong with it except that there was very little doing. There was a lot of thinking and a lot of escaping."

Now the Woodstock Nation seems about as substantial as Brigadoon. It appeared, we blinked and rubbed our eyes, and it was gone. In 1979, on the tenth anniversary of Woodstock, most commentators mulled it over with the kind of archaeological interest usually reserved for pre-Columbian digs. The fact, however, is that more of Woodstock has remained than most of us realize. The twinkle-toed, bell-bottomed look is gone, but many of the attitudes nurtured at Woodstock lasted through the seventies and are part of the baby boom today. This has been confirmed by Daniel Yankelovich, whose polls have documented the spread of what he calls the "New Values" from the college-educated minority to a growing majority:

Apart from the impact of the war, the 1960s were not an aberration, but an inherent part of our cultural continuity. The war was like having a despised stranger living in your home at the same time that a baby was born to a family. With the departure of the stranger, the situation may at first seem to return to what it was earlier, but it soon became apparent that the new baby has created its own pattern of changes in the life of the family. The war was vivid and traumatic while it lasted, but the enduring heritage of the 1960s is the new social values that grew on the nation's campuses during that same fateful period and now have grown stronger and more powerful.

The Greening of America was not the gospel of the New Era. But it wasn't an epitaph, either.

Chapter 9

CHILDREN OF THE MEDIA

It seems inevitable that all changes in ways of life . . . continuously alter the perceptual world of the developing organism. New behavioral patterns and new problems of social adaptation inevitably result from such environmental changes; these, in turn, impart to individuality some characteristics that are shared by most members of a particular generation.

—René Dubos

In a well-known scene in *The Graduate,* a touchstone film of the sixties, Dustin Hoffman is cornered by a businessman at a party. The man, breathing Babbitry from every pore, has just a single word of advice for Benjamin, the character Hoffman plays, about his future. The word is "Plastics."

Plastics???? The line is embedded in the collective memory of the baby-boom generation as firmly as "Play it again, Sam" was for an earlier one (even if Bogart didn't say exactly that in *Casablanca*). That line still draws laughs at movie festivals. Plastics was precisely the future the boom generation did *not* see for itself. Plastics? They had not grown up heeding the assertions of their parents and teachers that they were the best and brightest America could produce only to dissipate their promise on some kind of phony merchandising. Plastics? Plastics was everything they saw wrong with America. Plastics was not honest. It was artificial. For a generation that insisted on honesty and naturalness, plastics was a fake.

Millions of boom children flocked to see *The Graduate* and made it one of the biggest-grossing films ever. They had always watched movies on television, even *Casa-*

blanca, but now Hollywood was making films that were speaking directly to them. The message was never really threatening—in fact, it usually confirmed their values more than challenging and extending them the way real art does—but it was *their* art. They were the Media Generation.

The romanticism that made the youth movies of the sixties succeed now seems almost touchingly naive. In *The Graduate,* Hollywood was asking us to relate to the angst of a sports-car-driving suburbanite who could not decide whether to float on a raft in his parents' swimming pool or make love to his girlfriend's mother. But it did have the assertion of middle-class rebelliousness that characterized the decade. In *The Graduate,* all the themes were falling into place. The antimaterialism. Parental hypocrisy. Sexual initiation at the hands of an older woman. The iconoclasm (when Benjamin interrupts the adult ritual of a wedding). The triumph of love and "natural" feeling over a sterile culture. Even the sound track by Simon and Garfunkel spoke directly to the special concerns of middle-class youth.

Thanks to *The Graduate* and *Bonnie and Clyde,* another film which deftly captured the antiauthoritarian esprit of the times, total attendance at movies in 1967 turned up for the first time since World War II. It was the first good news for Hollywood since television began drawing off the mass audience during the baby boom's youngest years. Earlier movies like *Rebel Without a Cause* had caught the spirit of the new generation but made the mistake of using an urban setting. Disney films like *The Shaggy Dog* were set in suburbia but could hardly build a movement out of turning Tommy Kirk into a dog. But with *The Graduate* and dozens of "youth films" to follow, Hollywood discovered that millions could be made by bringing the needs and fantasies of the baby-boom elite to the screen. Unmarried youth, after all, was traditionally the biggest single segment of the film audience. Kids needed to get out of the home to find privacy, and movies offered it. Home was where the teenage heart was not. Hollywood, which could deal with themes that could not be shown on television, was finding its salvation as a medium for adolescents.

The route to the youth audience was orginally paved by Samuel Z. Arkoff and his American International Pictures. Such primordial baby-boom heroes and heroines as

Annette Funicello and Frankie Avalon were reborn in AIP films like 1960's *Beach Party* and a whole series of surf-and-sand epics like *Bikini Beach, Beach Blanket Bingo,* and *How to Stuff a Wild Bikini.* The formula was simple: parental or authority figures were rarely shown on the screen and, if they were, only to look ridiculous. Arkoff also tapped teenage fantasy (*I Was a Teenage Werewolf, I Was a Teenage Frankenstein*) and delusions of grandeur (*Wild in the Streets, The Wild Angels*) in films that captured the anarchistic mood of the sixties better than most efforts of the big studios. Hollywood did not catch on to alienation until 1969, when *Easy Rider, Last Summer, If . . .,* and the underrated *Alice's Restaurant* all made their runs at the youth market. (Even in that year, the youngest baby-boom cohorts could still command considerable clout at the box office. The top-grossing movie of 1969 was not *Butch Cassidy* or *Midnight Cowboy* or even *Funny Girl.* It was Disney's *The Love Bug.*)

What was the lesson of the youth movies? In many ways, it was a bleak one. They rejected the values of the adult culture, but offered little else to take its place. At the end of *The Graduate,* Dustin Hoffman has foiled the grasping and sinister adults around him but is left facing an uncertain future. *Zabriskie Point,* a failed youth movie, managed to demean both its young heroes and the police they opposed alike with its tendentious and self-serving cynicism. Movie critic Pauline Kael remarked that young people then seemed to be looking *for* something in movies, not just *at* them (a search that may say more about their intellectual habits than anything else). Movies were offering an affirmation of generational solidarity, but it came at the cost of generational continuity. Hollywood was reinforcing the strong sense of specialness and separateness that had always been a part of the life of the baby boomers. Ultimately, what the youth movies were celebrating was youth itself—a cause that, in the long run, could only lose.

When *Star Wars* came out in the mid-seventies and started its surge to become the biggest-grossing film ever, the movie-company executives were startled by an attendance phenomenon they had never seen before. Many teenagers were not just coming back to see the movie twice—the previous pattern for a blockbuster hit—but they were coming back three and four times. Some were even watching it twenty or thirty times, not unlike the laboratory rats who keep pressing a bar sending shocks to the pleasure center of their brain until they collapse from exhaustion or starvation. The older generation was mystified. Why see a movie three times if you could get the message the first time? But that was precisely the McLuhanesque point: for this generation, the medium *was* the message.

Reared on television, records, and movies, the boom generation became our first Media Generation. Along with the new modes of thinking that may or may not imply came a new idea: entertainment as a natural and necessary part of life. Entertainment was joining, and even replacing, work and education as an expectation of every young person. Most entertainment was communicated through the electronic media—whether on records or TV sets or movie screens—and more and more people were spending more and more of their time with the media. According to a 1976 study by Cleveland State University, the number of hours devoted to media by the 18–24 age group rose from 13.9 in 1965, when only a few baby boomers were in that category, to 18.5 in 1975, when it was composed entirely of that generation.

The medium that shaped the boom generation most profoundly was television. It is rivaled only by the automobile and perhaps the long-playing record as the technological innovation which has set the baby boom apart from previous generations. In one four-year stretch from 1948 until 1952, the number of television sets in use in the United States jumped from a few thousand to 15 million. After that, childhood was forever altered. Parents of boom babies who at first looked to television as their helper, an electronic baby-sitter, found that instead it was their foe, an implacable competitor that was winning the battle for their children's minds. Urie Bronfenbrenner of Cornell has reported a forty-year decline in the amount of time children spend with their parents, much of the recent loss due to television. The earliest and most affectionately recalled memories of many Americans born after 1946 often consist not of interactions with their parents and families but of shows watched on television. In the 1950s, as historian Eric Goldman has observed, a workable definition of a home could be the place where the television set was. Now we know further that the "family room" in

American homes is not necessarily where the family eats or plays but rather is where the television set is located.

If their parents owned a TV set, and most of them did, the children of the boom started using it when they were about 2. At 6, they had watched up to 5000 hours in their short lives and were dedicated TV consumers, with regular viewing times and favorite programs. They watched more and more as they grew older, reaching an early peak in sixth grade when the average child watched 4½ hours daily and upward of 6½ on Sundays. During the sixties, when most boom children were forming their TV habits, average viewing time rose a total of about an hour a day. By the time an average child of the baby boom reached the age of 18, he or she would have been under television's hypnotic influence an average of 4 hours a day for 16 years. The total of roughly 24,000 hours—one-quarter of a person's waking life—is more than children spend in classrooms or with their parents. The only activity that consumes more of a child's time is sleeping. In just six years, from 1960 to 1966, the proportion of Americans who named television as their favorite leisure activity doubled to 46 percent.

This prodigious investment of time came with a cost. Of all the machines that have entered our lives in this century, television was the most ravenous of time. When television entered the home, for instance, the amount of time individuals spent with all media combined rose by only fifty-eight minutes. But television itself was eating up time in three- and four-hour chunks. That meant that it was robbing time from every other endeavor. We read fewer magazines and books and newspapers. We spent less time going to movies, socializing, conversing, traveling, thinking, daydreaming, and even sleeping. When the television entered the home, children began going to bed later and were less likely to be read to by their parents. When—or if—they did learn to read, children with television spent less time reading than children without television.

The glowing blue light also plunged the boom children into an environment that was as alien to their parents' experience as if they'd moved to never-never land. It was an alternate reality that was absorbing but strangely discombobulating. In the new world inhabited by children three or four hours a day—call it Televisionland—there was violence but rarely blood or pain. There was death but never emptiness. People did not work regularly but were rarely hungry or in need. In fact, economic realities were not present at all. There was little unemployment in Televisonland and no food stamps. Fathers were not wage earners but hapless buffoons, outwitted by both their children and their wives. There was desire in Televisionland, but lust and greed were somehow mixed up with cravings for prettier hair and whiter laundry.

The age segregation that had always been a part of the baby boom's experience was reinforced in Televisionland. The population there was loaded with striking women in their twenties and craggy-faced men in their thirties and forties. Characters over 65, however, made up only 2 percent of the TV population. A viewer exposed to 300 speaking characters over a week would meet only 7 over 65. What little human ugliness or misery that was visible in Televisionland was confined largely to people over 65. According to one recent study, three out of every ten older people shown on television were likely to be robbed or beaten. (The real-life figure is less than 1 percent.) These senior citizens were usually portrayed as eccentric, stubborn, nonsexual, inept, or silly—almost as if they deserved to be mugged.

This fun-house mirror reflection of reality inevitably distorts more than it informs. For example, heavy television viewers who watch more than thirty hours a week typically believe that old age comes earlier in life than it really does. They are particularly gloomy about the ravages of old age in women—perhaps because so few women over the age of 35 ever appear on television. In Televisionland, the middle-aged woman is the real lost generation. Viewers watching series enter a kind of time machine in which the past disappears. Heroes can turn into villains and villains into heroes. Characters can be routinely replaced by different actors on soap operas and the show goes on. Actions have no consequences in Televisionland. When everything is subject to change or cancellation, life becomes absurd. Little wonder that many baby boomers had trouble fitting the chaotic events of their adolescence into an understandable context. No one —not their teachers, not their parents, and certainly not television—had ever told them how.

From the start, educators and psychologists agreed that television was somehow influencing the intelligence, imagination, and behavior of the young generation. But there was less agreement on precisely *what* television was doing to children and *how* it was doing it. Barely a year has gone by since 1954 without a report or study mounting a quixotic charge against the windmill of antennas. In fact, the evils these studies pointed out have almost told us more about particular problems afflicting society at any given time than they have about television's role in them. At various times, we have faulted television for causing juvenile delinquency, crippling reading ability in schools, impoverishing family life, narcotizing the imagination, promoting mindless acquisitiveness, shortening attention spans, eroding respect for authority, and increasing everything from drug use to the divorce rate. So pervasive is television's impact that it is difficult to find social issues that have *not* been attributed to its pernicious influence at one time or another.

But even if we assume that television's omnipotence is at least in part overstated, the problems it has presented are just as real. The earliest advertisements for television sets, for instance, usually showed a happy family of several generations—Grandma was right there along with the tykes—grouped around the set watching their favorite show. Off in the kitchen, presumably, TV dinners were smoldering in the oven. The message was that television would bring families closer. Yet the fact is that most people who watch television watch alone. Instead of bringing families together it isolated them further into their own worlds. Parents began buying second sets for the kids. The children of the baby boom absorbed a prodigious amount of information about the adult world by watching television but understood less about the human problems their parents actually faced.

At the same time, the television series the baby boomers watched were relentlessly programming a vision of the American family that was either unrealistic or unattainable. No one, as Jeff Greenfield has pointed out, is ever alone in Televisionland. There is little real despair. Problems can be worked out and almost always are. More TV parents are widowed than divorced. Anger is cute, rarely ugly. A child who would believe television would believe that most problems are soluble, usually within the half hour, and that sacrifices and compromises rarely involve human pain. Beaver Cleaver never had to worry that his parents would announce a trial separation. And if Ozzie Nelson had a drinking problem or was otherwise unemployable—why else was he always hanging around

142

the house?—no one worried about it. Even after TV producer Norman Lear discovered social realism, the reassuring lesson of television was that differences are funny, and families can stick together. Life is fair. Little wonder that the boom generation has had a difficult time coming to grips with some of the uncomfortable realities of family life.

Advertisers were spending upwards of $140,000 a minute to reach the audience that commanded the largest chunk of disposable income in the economy. By the time an average baby boomer reached the age of 21, he or she had been bombarded by as many as 300,000 commercial messages. It is difficult to sort out the effects of this prolonged sell, but, as Paul Goodman said, the only part of television which has fulfilled its promise is the commercial. Baby boomers grew up brushing their teeth with Bucky Beaver and made commercials so much a part of their learning process that, when *Sesame Street* went on the air in 1969, it deliberately adapted the sixty-second spot to teaching. During the sixties, some baby boomers seemed to revolt against the intimate connection television made between material acquisition and status and happiness. But their narcissistic style in the seventies returned at least in part to the assumption of all TV commercials that personal gratification is the primary objective in life.

Television also gave the baby boom its first lessons in the little dishonesties of adult life. The numbing repetition of Saturday-morning ads for candied cereals and electric toys did not turn every child into a drooling consumer. Many of them simply developed built-in truth detectors. They assumed that the commercials were less than truthful, that grown-ups lied, and made judgments accordingly. (Was Watergate really a surprise to the TV generation?) Television comedies further presented an image of domestic life based largely on trickeries. How would Lucy Ricardo hide from Ricky the awful truth of her shopping spree? Would Ralph Cramden lure Norton into his latest get-rich-quick scheme? Adult life had lost its mystery. "We grew up old," said Joyce Maynard. "We are the cynics who see the trap door in the magic show, the pillow stuffing in Salvation Army Santa Clauses, the camera tricks in TV commercials."

Schoolteachers, meanwhile, were reporting that they were seeing a different kind of student. Many of them, especially at the youngest ages, were more sophisticated about the grown-up world than their predecessors ever had been. But they were oddly passive. They asked fewer questions and volunteered fewer answers. Studies have consistently linked television viewing with poor academic performance. At the age of 5, children who watch television heavily have shown less imagination than their peers. A study in Evanston, Illinois, as early as 1954 found that children in the lowest quarter of high-school classes watched, on the average, six hours more television a week than other students. More disturbingly, the brightest students also seemed to be affected—as if they found the bright stimulation of television more compelling than schoolwork. Television was cutting into homework time, too, and even those who did their lessons at home often worked with the television on. Some teachers decided that if they could not compete with the tube for their students' attention, they would join forces with it by assigning viewings of *Playhouse 90* and the like. The schools had become what educator Neil Postman calls the Second Curriculum; the First Curriculum was television, which was imparting more information in a day than a teacher could in a week. Television was reshaping education and producing a generation characterized by poor verbal skills, inability to concentrate, and a reluctance to read. Even the boom generation's language tics—usages such as "like" and "y'know" and "sort of"—bespoke its lack of precision.

The most hotly debated question of all, especially during the time of social unrest in the sixties, was televised violence. How was a daily regimen of beatings and murders and mayhem—whether on cartoons or on *Mod Squad*—affecting the first generation to grow up with it. Crime rates were mounting each year? Was this younger generation inherently more violent than others? Or was it growing up in a more violent time? In 1972, the surgeon general reported a "modest" link between violence on television and aggression among children. Subsequent studies have strengthened the relationship. Leonard Eron, a psychologist at the University of Illinois, began a ten-year study of third graders in semirural New York State convinced that the impact of television on children was no worse than that of fairy tales. Afterward, though, he concluded that there was a "direct, positive relation" between television viewing and aggressive behavior. Similarly, William Belson, a London researcher working on a grant from CBS, found strong evidence that high exposure to televised violence increases the chances that adolescent boys will engage in serious violence themselves.

For that matter, a viewer does not need to be a victim or a criminal to suffer from the pathology of TV crime. After examining the question for a decade, a group at the University of Pennsylvania concluded that, regardless of whether television increases actual violence, it inevitably increases the fear of violence. The depressing result is that an entire population suffers. Compared to light viewers, for example, heavy television watchers live in a darkening world of anxiety. They greatly overestimate the proportion of people involved in violence, the danger of walking alone at night, and the number of criminals in society. (While criminals represent only 1 percent of the actual population, they make up 17 percent of all characters on television.) Heavy viewers are also more likely to mistrust the motives of other people and, when asked if it is all right to hit someone if you are mad at them, they answer "almost always" in significantly higher proportions.

So it is not at all hard to see how, for the baby boomers, television raised the level of difficulty people have understanding the outside world. Commercials and domestic dramas indoctrinate them with a fantasy of family life that is rarely achieved in reality. The police shows, at the same time, taught them that violence is a frequent and even acceptable method of resolving problems. The world thus becomes a fearful, dispiriting place that falls far short of one's expectations for it. Seen this way, aggression is a predictable response to a frightening environment. Students who called policemen "pigs!" at protests revealed, besides their unconscious class cruelty, the extent to which television had distorted and made almost incomprehensible what policemen really do.

The latest judgment against television holds that content is only part of the problem. The larger issue is that the act itself of watching television is changing consciousness. For thousands of years, as this argument goes, humanity passed along its culture within an oral tradition. Like all spoken language, it was sequential and linear. Then, for the past several centuries, the job of transmitting knowledge passed to books and the printed word. But the method was still logical and symbolic. The mind filled in the symbols with images and made the imaginative leaps to understanding.

Now, however, after watching TV the greatest part of its waking life, the baby boom has become the first generation to skip this process. We do not need to use our imagination or intelligence to fill in the images while watching television. It does it for us. Tests have shown that television is not perceived by the left hemisphere of the brain, where the activities of reading, writing, and reasoning are controlled. Rather, television goes directly into the mysterious right hemisphere, which is visual, audial, spatial, intuitive, and holistic. Once there, according to brain-wave studies, television promotes the production of alpha waves, a relaxed state usually associated with semiconsciousness or daydreaming. Time is distorted. A man who sits down to watch the news will wake up hours later during the late show, his mind glazed over as if he were staring into an electronic fireplace. Television does not penalize reduced concentration; it rewards it. In 1977, the *Detroit Free Press* offered to pay 120 families $500 if they would go without television for a month. Ninety-three of the families turned the offer down flat.

Educators have already seen some consequences of what amounts to television's programmed inattention. Students in classes typically crave stimulation and show greater impatience with long expositions, as if their concentration spans have shrunk to the length of a half-hour sitcom. They want learning to be easy and entertaining. The National Assessment Test has revealed an altered writing style that owes less to literary models than to the oral rhetoric common on television. That is, they are learning to write as Howard Cosell talks. We once dreamed of revolutionizing education by plugging students into a wired university. The problem with television education turned out to be that information that was broadcast did not stick. The facts did not process. Watching television is pleasurable and mesmerizing but it is no more related to learning than looking is to thinking. "There is a desire on the part of young people for messy shows," William Paley of CBS once admitted. "They don't want a good beginning, middle, and an end. They want the damn thing to sort of float around, and they either read something into it that the older generation can't, or they feel comfortable in not having things too carefully spelled out. The spirit of it is more important than the story part."

Television does work directly on the emotions, a fact that the antiwar protestors in Chicago in 1968 were counting on when they chanted "The whole world is watching" as police routed them before the cameras. But the demonstrators made the mistake of thinking that the presence of television alone was enough to communicate their message and to invest them with power. People do not want television to disturb them; they want it to relax and to reassure them. So serious is this emotional need that it can provoke passions of its own. In prisons, one of the most frequent causes of cellblock violence is disagreement over which programs to watch on the rec room set. Not that prisoners are any more irrational than law-abiding citizens. When Roper Reports asked 2000 couples what was their leading cause of marital discord, 25 percent of them said it was choosing which shows to watch on television.

The influence of television cannot be avoided any more than the air we breathe. For years, for example, the town of Essex, California, did not receive television. Journalists would regularly visit there and report with amazement the reactions of the natives when told of such phenomena as, say, Johnny Carson. Then in December of 1977 television finally came to Essex. The visitors went back and found that the citizens of Essex had joined the American race. They wanted soap operas. And they watched Johnny.

We will now be led for the rest of this century and into the next one by the first generation born and bred on television. It would be foolish to think that television is the sole decisive factor in their lives. We still know relatively little about the way television has altered our sensibilities and our capacity to think and act. But no product of technology is more intimately involved with the people of the boom generation than television. From *Howdy Doody* to the streets of Chicago in 1968, the baby boomers sought to validate and legitimatize their life on television. Television has molded their style and controlled their daily habits. It has helped bind them to their peers while driving wedges between them and their parents. It has given them economic power and a spurious sense of omnipotence. It has given them sophistication without understanding. It has taught that self-gratification is no farther away than the off-on switch.

Now the first young generation raised on television is becoming the first generation of parents who have spent their lives with television. If we know little about how television affected them as children, we know even less about its long-term effects on adults. The baby boom is the first generation of adults whose attitudes about marriage, family, and consumption were formed during a lifetime of television use. It will eventually become the first generation of elderly people to have grown up with television. How will that life stage be altered? The worrisome question that remains is whether we will become the masters of this powerful medium—or vice versa.

Chapter 10

THE MYSTERY OF THE DISAPPEARING SCORES

The baby boom is not given to cryptic behavior—openness and visibility have unavoidably been its calling cards —but over the past 20 years it has left behind a puzzle that still has not been satisfactorily solved. Like all good mysteries, it began when it was least expected.

The victim was the reputation of the boom generation. All through the fifties and sixties, even during the times of trouble, the one unshakable article of faith held by every baby-boom parent and child had been the idea that this was the smartest generation ever. The parents believed it because they had financed the newest schools and colleges. The children believed it because they had been told it for so long. In the sixties, we had marveled over the language labs and open classrooms and sophisticated methods at work in the schools and colleges. We were witnessing "the successful transformation of U.S. secondary education," said a magazine article, and educators agreed. "We're on the fringe of a golden era in education," predicted one. "It's going to come slowly but we're heading there."

But something went wrong. It was not the flowering of long hair in the schools or the rebellion of college students. It did not have anything to do with student power. In fact, the problem could not honestly be blamed solely on the schools. Year after year, baby-boom senior classes in high school had marched en masse to take the Scholastic Aptitude Test. A national exam given to two-thirds of all students who enter college, it seeks to predict freshman year performance by measuring reasoning ability developed both inside and outside of school. It was a generational rite of initiation in which the battlefield was a multiple-choice question and the weapon was a No. 2

149

pencil. The competition was clear and so were the results: the best would go on to the colleges of their choice, the others would not.

For years, the scores on the SAT tests had remained reassuringly steady. When the scores drifted up a bit in the early sixties, educators proudly concluded that the post-Sputnik educational push was finally paying off. In 1963, the average SAT verbal and mathematics scores reached highs of, respectively, 478 and 502, on the 200-800 scale. Then the scores started dropping steadily, year after year. The downward drift was slow at first but speeded up in the 1970s. In a single year, 1975, the combined scores plunged 18 points. By 1979, the SAT scores had failed to go up for sixteen straight years. Moreover, the decline coincided precisely with the period the children born during the baby boom were taking the test. The reasoning ability of a million or so high-school students going on to college had been measurably diminished in almost every year the baby boom was examined. (The scores for the first postwar babies born in 1946 were recorded in 1964, the year the decline began. But most of the first big wave of boom babies graduated with the high-school class of 1965, affecting scores for that year.) After believing all along that they were the best and the brightest, the baby boomers were suddenly facing distressing evidence that they were the dumbest.

SAT Score Averages for College-Bound Seniors, 1963-79

Year	Verbal	Mathematical
1963	478	502
1964	475	498
1965	473	496
1966	471	496
1967	466	492
1968	466	492
1969	463	493
1970	460	488
1971	455	488
1972	453	484
1973	445	481
1974	444	480
1975	434	472

1976	431	472
1977	429	470
1978	429	468
1979	427	467

What was wrong? Bewildered, Americans began groping for causes. Had we spoiled our children? Were they
an intellectually sloppy generation that craved instant
gratification and a spurious freedom of expression at the
cost of disciplined learning? That suspicion was enough to
set off another back-to-basics movement, which are as
periodic and practically as predictable in American education as sunspot cycles. If only we toughened up standards and cut out frills, the argument went, then students
would shape up. Others blamed the test itself for somehow becoming too difficult or losing touch with what
students were really learning. But American College
Testing, which gives an examination that competes with
the Educational Testing Service's SAT, reported that it,
too, had observed a similar decline in test scores. In fact,
there is some evidence that the SAT actually became
easier during the decline. A control group was given both
the 1973 exam and the 1963 exam. If the 1973 test were
harder, the group presumably would score lower. Instead
it actually scored *higher* on the 1973 test, suggesting that
it was easier and that the real decline was *greater* than
previously believed.

Aside from the usual docket of suspects—television,
drugs, and liberal education—blame was also pointed at,
among others, the New Math, increased numbers of
married female teachers, Communist subversion, and
court-ordered busing. Some suggested that chemical ad-
ditives in foods—shades of the fluoridation battles of the
fifties!—were addling the minds of our children. Others
theorized that the increased incidence of induced labor in
pregnancy, Cesarean deliveries, and anesthesia during
childbirth had produced mentally damaged babies. A
University of Pittsburgh professor has argued with conviction that the decline was due to radioactive fallout affecting babies still in their mothers' wombs.

Finally, the College Entrance Examination Board,
which administers the SATs, sought to cut through the
increasingly befogged question by sponsoring its own investigation of the long decline. This was no lightweight
committee designed to leave behind a pitter-patter of

press releases and little else. Instead, a twenty-one-member committee headed by former Secretary of Labor W. Willard Wirtz sniffed around the problem for two years before releasing a cautiously qualified document that nonetheless found "clearly observable evidence of diminished seriousness of purpose and attention to mastery of skills and knowledge" among American students.

Its first conclusion, to be sure, was almost reassuring. Half of the total decline in SAT scores and three-fourths of the decline before 1970 could be traced to the broadening composition of the student group taking the test. In the beginning, the SAT was taken most frequently by upper-middle-class students as a passport to the most exclusive private colleges. But then education went democratic in the sixties as the huge boom generation came of age. From 1952 until 1970, the proportion of students staying in school through twelfth grade went from one-half to three-quarters. Of those, the proportion that continued on to college went from one-quarter to one-half. Now students headed for community colleges were taking the test along with putative Ivy Leaguers. Most of the increase in test takers came from three groups—the poor, minorities, and women—all of whom had traditionally scored lower on the SATs than middle-class white males. Examination of the SAT curve showed that the greatest declines were on the lower end of the scale while there were just as many high scorers as always. Those baby boomers born from 1946 until 1952 were not necessarily any less advantaged than their older brothers and sisters. To the contrary, they had participated in a laudable widening of educational opportunities across the country.

After 1970, however, the pattern changed. The Wirtz Committee found that by then the composition of the test-taking pool had all but stabilized. The historic extension of college to an increasing range of different groups in society seemed to be completed. At the most, barely one-quarter of the subsequent change in the SAT scores could be explained as resulting from the influx of a group of traditionally lower-scoring students. Yet, paradoxically, the score decline not only continued but accelerated, particularly sharply between 1972 and 1975. Moreover, the number of top achievers—those scoring over 600 on the SATs—had started to fall alarmingly. In 1972 there were 53,794 students who recorded verbal

SAT scores over 650. A year later, as the mean verbal score dropped by 8 points, only 39,779 scored over 650. In short, the weakness was at the top of the scale as well as the bottom. Valedictorians' scores were dropping. So were the scores of salutatorians. In fact, the averages of every subgroup—rich students, poor students, public schools, private schools, big schools, little schools—were falling.

What had started out as a simple whodunit was getting complicated. With a shift in the test-taking pool ruled out, the investigators had lost their smoking gun. But they pressed on and eventually mounted a case that could be tried on circumstantial evidence. No one factor, they said, could produce such sweeping changes as the SAT scores had recorded. It could only be a combination of forces, acting on the members of the boom generation from as early as childhood, that had made their intelligence measurably different from the generation before them.

The first suspect was the schools. During the years of the baby boom's education, elective courses in high schools had become as plentiful as popcorn—and about as nutritious. Courses like film appreciation were booming at the cost of the harder skills of reading and writing. During the two-year period from 1971 to 1973, enrollments in Advanced English dropped 50 percent nationally. Most students were still claiming to be taking "English" courses, though it was hard to say just what that meant. In Massachusetts, the two most frequently added high-school "English" courses from 1971 until 1976 were science fiction and radio/television/film. While one-quarter of all Massachusetts high schools were adding courses in filmmaking, the absolute number of eleven-grade English and world history courses decreased. It was no different across the country. In California, enrollment in English composition classes dropped 77 percent in 1972–75 but doubled in electives like children's theater and mystery and detective story. Not surprisingly, those schools which had most enthusiastically added electives frequently showed the largest drops in SAT scores, while those who had rigorously stuck to English fundamentals often showed no decrease or even improvement in the scores of their students. The Wirtz Committee went so far as to speculate that one reason math scores have not declined as precipitously as verbal scores is that there are fewer math electives.

If Johnny could read at all he didn't read well. The SATs may have even underestimated the decline with a multiple-choice format that places more emphasis on terminology and facile comprehension than on good writing. (Some critics have suggested that the fact that students can score well on the verbal SAT without being able to write coherently has, in a kind of ironic feedback effect, contributed to the decline in verbal abilities. Teachers, it seemed, were preparing students for the SATs, not for college, and neglecting reading and writing skills.)

Dozens of studies have documented the fact that the decline in literacy began during the mid-sixties with the arrival of the boom generation. As recently as 1978, a test of 42,984 college freshmen in New Jersey showed that 39 percent could not fully understand written prose and that 41 percent were unable to construct grammatical sentences. Each year 40 to 60 percent of the entering students at the University of California are required to enroll in what used to be called "remedial" English. (The word remedial was dropped in 1976 when the university logically concluded that if a majority of students required remedial attention, it should no longer be labeled as such.) At Stanford, with its supposedly first-rate student body, only one-quarter of the students were able to pass the English placement test in 1975. The broadest survey was conducted by the University of Texas, which found in 1975 that 20 million adult Americans—about one-fifth of the adult population—were unable to perform such tasks as calculating change, reading a want ad, or addressing an envelope. Zeroing in further, the Texas researchers found the then 30–39 age group to be by far the most competent and that, surprisingly, the presumably best-educated 18–19-year-old group was down on a level with the older 40–49 year olds. That is, the group of adults who finished high school between 1964 and 1975, all baby-boom years, wound up with a higher rate of functional incompetence than the less educated generation before them. One example of the human cost of this educational dry rot became apparent when George Washington University refused admission to the valedictorian of Western High School in Washington, D.C. The young man's grades were impeccable, but his SAT scores were a dismal 280 in mathematics and 320 on the verbal test. Puzzled, George Washington asked the student to take a series of private tests. They confirmed the SAT results.

"My feeling is that a kid like that has been conned," said the admissions dean at George Washington, in his brutally candid appraisal. "He thinks he's a real scholar. His parents think he's a real scholar. He's been deluded into thinking he's gotten an education."

Who was to blame? When in doubt, Americans of all persuasions have scrutinized the reading materials on hand for evidence of sinister influence. In the 1950s and early 1960s, textbooks had been dominated by the reassuring Americanism of books like David Saville Muzzey's *An American History*. But Muzzey's blind spots—for example, his chest thumping chauvinism and downgrading of pluralism in American history—were not suitable in the politically sensitive aftermath of the sixties. His resolutely "literary" books were replaced by a new breed of textbooks. They were not written but were "developed" by editorial teams. His closely packed type was replaced by pages gussied up in glossy graphics, short paragraphs, and great frozen seas of white space. The reassuring certainties of the earlier books were retired in favor of problem-oriented books that challenged students to fend for themselves with the dilemmas of history.

Frances FitzGerald has rightly pointed out that these books wound up presenting a bland, confusing view of American history as a sort of crazy quilt of events. The grand panorama of history had been robbed of passions and convictions. Worse, the new books were also stripped of literary excellence. According to the standard Dale-Chall readability formula, the revised textbooks had dropped anywhere from one to four grades in difficulty. A student had to be in eighth grade in 1974 to know what a sixth grader knew in 1964. As a McGraw-Hill official admitted, textbooks today have to be "much more carefully constructed in language to appeal to students brought up with the visual experience of television. There is a great need to check the overall readability of a textbook because of the declining verbal skills of students." So the tests were wrapped in appealing packages and served up to students in easily digestible bits. This was not education; it was pasteurization.

If interest in American history was running low, it had sunk out of sight for foreign cultures and foreign languages. In the 1970s, the total number of students taking college and high-school language courses dropped by 30 percent in five years. Only 16 percent of all students were studying modern foreign languages, compared to 36 percent in 1916. Colleges made the attrition easier as the proportion of them requiring foreign languages for admission declined from 34 percent to 8 percent, and the number requiring foreign language credits for graduation declined from 73 percent in 1967 to 53 percent in 1974.

Ironically, young people in America were becoming more parochial at the exact time their dependency on other nations was increasing. The result was almost pathetic. Young foreign service officers were being posted to countries where they could not speak the language. While there are 10,000 Japanese salesmen in the United States, all of whom speak English, there are only 1000 American salesman overall in Japan. So far, the boom generation has shown little inclination to do anything about it. It sent the musican Ravi Shankar back to India after a brief flirtation with Oriental culture. It is as if, after exporting music and tourism and an entire youth culture to Europe in the fifties and sixties, the boom generation found it difficult to take seriously the idea that events would ever be dominated by anyone but itself. Losing the human connection with other languages and cultures was bad enough but there was another kind of damage done as well. Study of foreign languages deepens understanding of one's own lauguage. As A. Bartlett Giamatti, the president of Yale, put it: "In the last fifteen years, certainly in the last ten, any American college student who knew anything about the dynamics of English—its struts and cables, its soaring spans, the way it holds together and works—knew it by analogy from the grammar of a foreign language."

Giamatti's architectural metaphor was about as meaningful to the Media Generation as a deed to the Brooklyn Bridge. Why read when you could watch? "We never *had* to read," said Joyce Maynard. "There was always TV, and so we grew accustomed to having our pictures presented to us, our characters described on the screen more satisfactorily, it seemed to many of us, than five pages of adjectives." Schools built shining new Developmental Reading Rooms and outfitted them with plastic charts and audiovisual equipment. But there were often no books in the Developmental Reading Rooms. Writing assignments emphasized self-expression and creativity of thought more than the boring rules of grammar.

As language was impoverished, so was its natural ally, thought. Reading is difficult because it involves concentration. But the baby boom craved stimulation above all. Instead of concentrating, it changed the channel. In the sixties, the natural level of expression was a T-shirt with a Kiss Me, I'm Irish slogan and a Smile button. In a world of easy answers, thought is a bumper sticker and philosophy is a lapel button. Even now, baby boomers have their most passionate cocktail-party discussions not over books but over movies. They can count on their peers to have seen the same movies they have, just as Victorian gentlemen could count on their peers to have read the latest Dickens. No opinions are more easily formed than those gathered at the movie houses. You just sit there and let it wash all over you.

Perhaps I am overstressing this point. Paperback publishers and others have argued that the increase in college graduates has increased the literacy of the population. In 1977, for example, some 530 million paperbacks were sold. But it is difficult to feel a rosy glow of optimism about a generation the consumes novelizations of movies and fotonovels. The consummate art form of the eighties may be the media tie-in. The decline in value of the "literary" novel is enough to declare it an endangered species with prime specimens preserved in formaldehyde in schools and universities.

Good teachers might have made a difference during the baby boom. Experienced teachers were spread thin, with the result that many young, unseasoned teachers were forced to handle the largest generation of students ever. In 1961, the average elementary-school teacher was 41 and had been on the job for 13.3 years; fifteen years later, the typical teacher was 33 and had worked only 8 years. Inevitably, standards suffered. As the proportion of students finishing high school went up, so did the absentee rate, often running to 20 or 25 percent in some schools. Meanwhile, as if to make the idea of attending school more palatable, teachers were cutting homework assignments by 50 percent around the country. Cereal could be sugarcoated; why not education?

Not surprisingly, the Wirtz Committee indicted television as a conspirator in The Case of the Disappearing Scores, but the problem was proving the crime. In 1956, when the scores were beginning to fall, 95 percent of

American homes already has sets. More than half of the young people who took the SAT had been exposed to TV for ten years or more. So had many of their older brothers and sisters—whose scores had not dropped. But the lack of a control group of non-TV watchers who had taken the test made it hard to build a convincing case. While television's fingerprints were everywhere, proof was not. In the end, the Wirtz Committee confessed to a "subjective" feeling that television was involved in the SAT decline but admitted that it could not explain how or why.

Families were changing, too, but just how those changes translated into point declines on the SAT was equally hard to establish. On the face of it, the relationship would seem to be obvious. Social scientists like Christopher Jencks and James Coleman have convincingly demonstrated that the learning that goes on in school is closely related to the stability of the family environment at home. And no one could doubt that the baby boom grew up in a time of unusual change within the family. The divorce rate was starting to rise every year. The proportion of children under 18 living with both parents has dropped from 89 percent in 1960 to 80 percent in the mid-seventies. The absolute number of children who had seen their parents divorce had doubled in just ten years. More than half of all mothers with school-age children were working outside of the home. All of these variables were intriguing but none of them converted automatically into five-point losses on the SAT chart. Again, the suspicion was there but not the proof.

In an interesting but not verifiable conjecture, the Wirtz Committee advanced the notion that students of the late sixties and early seventies had been unnerved by "a decade of distraction." Students who took the SATs from 1972 through 1975—the years of the sharpest declines—were the same ones who in elementary and high school had witnessed some of the saddest and most disillusioning events in American history. They were the Vietnam War, the draft, the assassinations of 1968, the protests, the burning cities, and the spectacle of Watergate. If divorce and television and disintegrating schools were not enough, the argument went, then politics alone was enough to throw this generation off its stride. Why should these students motivate themselves to study or to score highly on exams when society was shredding all around them? What did better educational achievement have to do with solving the crises of their times? What did school matter when the outside world was so aggressively shouting its demands? It is worth remembering that the high-school senior class of 1964, the one who gave the SATs the first shove on their sixteen-year slide, actually took the exam in the academic year that saw the most appalling event of their lives: the assassination of John Kennedy.

Running through all these hypotheses is the idea that something—or was it everything?—in the experience of the baby boom had made it unique. The 17-year-olds of 1975 were markedly different creatures from the 17-year-olds of 1955. Among those differences was a decline in tested reasoning ability. The Wirtz Committee and others struggled mightily with the problem of isolating specific social and educational causes that might have contributed to the decline. To their formidable list I can add but one further consideration. However, I think it is essential. It is the unavoidable fact of the unprecedented size of the boom generation itself.

It surely is no coincidence that the number of 18-year-olds in America jumped by more than a million at the same time the SAT scores started down. And in the same years the SATs plunged most sharply—from 1972 until 1975—the tests were taken by the babies who were born in the high-water years of the boom, 1954 through 1957. In 1954, the total number of births passed 4 million for the first time and the number rose each year until 1957, when births reached their all-time peak.

We might have expected the addition of millions of the boom children to have *increased* the test scores. As we have seen, the boom generation was disproportionately composed of children in the higher social and economic brackets—precisely those who score best on tests. But, educational opportunities were simultaneously being extended to whole new segments of society, the actual increase reflected in the number of SAT test-takers tilted toward the lower-scoring groups of students.

The crucial factor, I believe, is that the enormous size of the baby boom, which gave it such power en masse, acted to the detriment of its education. The competition of numbers was so strong that it inevitably led to a feeling of hopelessness. Why run the race if the track is overcrowded? Why try to climb out of a teeming mass if only a few will succeed? It was not hard to imagine that the odds on the tote board of life—not to mention the bell curve of the SATs—was rigged against you. The oppressive effects of size upon the baby boom's group psychology cannot be proved any more easily than the effects of television on it. We necessarily must rely on circumstantial evidence. But if we cannot so easily deal with people in a generation, we can see what the press of numbers can do to people in families. It is to families that we must now turn to see the forces operating on the generation as a whole.

In Great Britain, the National Survey of Health and Development followed the progress of 5386 postwar children born in the first week of March 1946. The survey found that the larger the family size in which the children were reared, the worse off the children were likely to be. Many of the differences were physiological. Children in large families weighed less and were shorter than children in small families. They also got sick more often, at least partially because of infections carried by siblings. The amount of medical care per person diminished in large families, despite the fact that the need was clearly greater. Now, none of this ought to be particularly surprising; parents of large families would seemingly always have less money to go around per child. What is surprising, though, is that the pattern shows up regardless of income. In the United States, for example, the Department of Agriculture found in 1960 that families of six spent 40 percent less per person on food than families of three *at every income level*. Not all the difference can be explained by the economies of scale.

Just how does this relate to the baby boom? During the fifties, after all, the biggest increases in births were registered not by large families but by small- and middle-sized families. But that leads us to another surprising finding. It is that the welfare of each additional child in a family is a bit lower than its predecessors. That is, firstborn children in England were heavier and taller and healthier than second-born children, and second-born children were similarly advantaged over third. Further, the addition of each child seemed to drag down the welfare of older siblings; the eldest child in a family of five was measurably worse off than the eldest in a family

160

of four, on the aggregate, almost regardless of economic status.

Returning now to the years of the baby boom, what do we find? The average size of the American family did not increase appreciably then. But the average birth position within the family changed dramatically. During the war and immediately afterward, as couples married and started families, there was a disproportionate number of first children born each year. Then, as the boom rolled on and the families had more children, the number of firstborn children each year dropped back while the births of younger siblings grew dramatically. If differences did exist between children of different birth order, and if the distribution of birth orders within a cohort was changing, it was possible that an entire generation could take on a different character.

Folk wisdom has always identified various personality traits with order of birth. Eldest children are said to be responsible, dutiful, and ambitious. They learn to read and talk and write earlier. They are also the most driven and uptight, most anxious to please their parents, and riddled with fears of failure. Firstborn children are over-represented in *Who's Who* and even in space, where 21 of the first 23 astronauts who flew on missions were either firstborn or only children. Stranger still, a 1970 report on stripteasers found that 89 percent were firstborn. Firstborns, it would be fair to say, are show-offs.

Middle children, on the other hand, pick up adjectives like cheerful, stubborn, and happy. They are more adroit socially than their big brothers and sisters and are more willing to compromise. Last children, finally, are introspective, emotional and mischievous. Outnumbered from the start, they have to raise their voices and sometimes just raise hell to get attention. Often overshadowed by successful older siblings, they are the errant Billy Carters and Donald Nixons and Sam Houston Johnsons and Teddy Kennedys.

None of these personality traits can be easily traced by birth order within large populations. But intelligence can be. What if it turned out that, in addition to height and weight, intelligence was also distributed predictably to different birth positions in the baby boom? If, say, average position of birth rose or declined within successive cohorts of children, one might expect their overall intellectual ability to vary accordingly. Specifically, if test-taking excellence was linked generationally to the firstborn children, then the gradual reduction in the percent of the firstborn in boom-generation cohorts over the years could at least partially explain the parallel drop in SAT scores.

That is exactly the implication of test results. In the Netherlands, for example, one examination was given, when they were 19, to 386,114 men and women born between 1944 and 1947, nearly the entire population of that age group at that time. It found that, as birth position fell within the family, so did scores on the tests. Likewise, Hunter Breland of Educational Testing Service studied 800,000 American students who applied for National Merit Scholarships. He found that children from small families scored higher than children from large families and that children born earlier in families scored higher than those born later.

The harder question was figuring out *why* a generation's elder children excel. The assumption had been that mothers give more time to firstborn children. But that did not explain such anomalies as the fact that only children, who presumably enjoyed the undivided attention of their parents, typically scored lower on tests than first children in families.

The most important contribution to this debate has been made by Robert Zajonc, a psychology professor at the University of Michigan. Zajonc has proposed an imaginative and novel theory of intelligence that does not depend on race, genetics, income, or social class. Instead, in what he calls a "confluence model," the relation of an individual to a family is like that of a current to a river; the current helps form the river and the river shapes the current. Thus, the intellectual growth of an individual both contributes to the family environment and is determined by it.

Here is how it works. Think of a family's intellectual environment as the average of the total intelligence of each of its members. The older someone is, the more intelligence units the person has. But a newborn arriving in the family would at first add an intelligence contribution of zero. The entry of each additional child further lowers the family's intellectual average. While a first child might enjoy the stimulating dinner-table conversation of two adults, a fifth child is more likely to be influenced by his four older siblings. This model might

162

suggest that intellectual performance inevitably declines with birth order. But, as Zajonc points out, the crucial variable is the age spacing between siblings. A sufficiently large gap between siblings can equalize or even overcome the negative pull of lower birth order. Test results in fact confirm that widely spaced pairs of siblings typically perform better than children born closer together.

The beauty of Zajonc's theory is that it neatly explains an entire range of intelligence mysteries. His model predicts, for example, that twins would perform poorly on intelligence tests because they are born with the shortest possible interval between births. Test results not only bear him out—twins score considerably lower than others —but add the clinching fact that twins who are separated at birth (thus nullifying the age-spacing factor) are nearly indistinguishable from nontwins. It follows that children who live in a single-parent household should suffer intellectual losses. Indeed, fatherless students scored in the 55th percentile on the American College Entrance Examination Test, while another group from intact homes scored in the 65th percentile. The longer the parent's absence, or the younger the child when it occurred, the greater the difference in scores. The gap shows up in all income groups and even in families when one parent is away frequently because of work responsibilities. Conversely, the presence of grandparents or other adults in an extended family has a measurably beneficial effect on test results.

Zajonc similarly finds that family configuration can explain the differences sometimes found between racial and ethnic groups in test performances (a subject of inflammatory rhetoric in the past). In 1960, when most baby-boom children were living at home, the American white family contained on the average 2.27 children and the black family 3.05. Black parents also have their children sooner and at closer intervals than white parents. The proportion of single-parent families is much higher among black Americans than white. All of these factors, in Zajonc's model, would inhibit test performance. Jews, on the other hand, benefit under the model because they typically have small families and a high proportion of parents living together.

The single discontinuity of this theory is caused by only children, who consistently score below the level that would be expected if intelligence was inversely related to family size. Zajonc hypothesizes that the difference is that only children lack the "teaching benefit" that eldest children have. An older brother or sister has the opportunity to explain to the younger sibling how to draw pictures and play games and tie shoes. He or she also instructs the young in the rules of behavior. This chance to apply knowledge helps clarify and focus it in the minds of the students and the teachers.

We can now see the relationship between the SAT scores posted by the baby boom and the evolving numbers of first and later children within the entire population. In 1947, nearly one out of every two babies born that year was the first child in its family. When those same babies took the verbal and mathematics SATs eighteen years later in 1965, they averaged 484.5. In subsequent years, the scores dropped, as did the proportion of firstborn children taking the test. By 1955, as many baby-boom families were adding their third and fourth children, the percentage of firstborns had dropped below 30 percent. And when those 1955 babies took their SATs in high school in 1973, the average score had dwindled over 20 points to 463.

In a way, they were becoming a generation of kid brothers and sisters who had stumbled into the baby boom's own generation gap. They had never really enjoyed the bright promises and hopes that had given the lives of their older siblings such high drama—and their SAT scores reflected it. The last children can never know the heady conviction of the firstborn that the world was created especially for them. They were like actors who had wandered into the play in the second act. Everyone else knew his or her part, but they did not. Even in youth, the later-born baby boomers had the unavoidable feeling that they had somehow missed the action. "We felt cheated, many of us," reflected Joyce Maynard, who was born in 1953, "which is why we complain about inheriting problems we didn't cause."

Eldest children continued to lose ground in families until 1962, when they added up to only 27 percent of all American children born that year. Since then, however, the trend has slowly reversed. The children born in the first year to show an increase in firstborns, 1963, will be taking their SATs during the 1980—81 academic year. Accordingly, Zajonc has taken his argument to its logical conclusion and has predicted that the test scores will begin to rise then, give or take a year or two. He has already cited improving test scores from junior high schools as giving advance notice of improvement in intellectual aptitude in those grades.

It hardly needs to be added that test-taking ability is not the only judgment of the worth of a person or a generation. The SATs say nothing about responsibility, creativity, leadership, social competence, morality, motivation, or self-confidence. The kinds of computer-generated truisms that emerge only after quantifying millions of families do not necessarily apply at all to human relationships in any single family. And it may have been naive all along to expect that three-fourths of a population could be—or would even want to be—raised to the intellectual level achieved not long ago by only one-half of the population. It is the fallacy of the educated elite to believe that everyone *ought* to be just as book-read as they are. The most heretical thought may be that many of the students who took SAT tests in the sixties and seventies had no business going to college in the first place. They would not have gone a generation earlier and, judging from recently dropping enrollment rates, will not be there in the future.

Still, it is the overall fate of the boom generation that must concern us. The victories achieved by these barbarians were Pyrrhic even before their education ended. The achievement of a youth culture came at the cost of cultural continuity with their elders. Their embrace of television and the movies and the media way of life came at the cost of their own literacy and, perhaps, measured intelligence. The huge numbers that had once given them such strength were beginning to look like a liability. Standing together by the millions, shoulder to shoulder, the men and women of the baby-boom generation uncertainly faced the end of their schooling and their entry into the workplace.

Chapter 11

THE CRIME BOOM

Anyone who read crime statistics during the 1960s, or listened to politicians and editorialists, might well have concluded that Americans were going mad. They were killing, shooting, stabbing, and robbing one another at an alarming pace. In the decade from 1960 to 1970, the number of violent crimes jumped by 10 percent a year. Murders climbed from 9000 in 1960 to 15,700 in 1970 to more than 20,000 by 1975. Reported rapes increased from 27,600 in 1967 to 63,000 in 1977. Robberies were growing by 18 percent a year in the five years between 1965 and 1970. In the fifteen years after 1960, the number of serious crimes had soared by 232 percent and the number of arrests of persons under 18 had tripled.

The country seemed to be dividing itself into armed camps. On one side was a criminal underclass of youthful robbers, muggers, rapists, and murderers. On the other was a larger group of frightened victims. In between was a no-man's-land roamed by anxious public officials and curious criminologists. More than half the residents of cities reported that they were afraid to walk outdoors at night. The Jules Feiffer play, *Little Murders,* in which gun battles are as routine in the cityscape as garbage trucks, hardly seemed to exaggerate the real situation. In 1970, Richard Nixon and Spiro Agnew unfurled the banner of "law 'n' order" (originally hoisted by Herbert Hoover nearly a half-century earlier) and vigorously took their fear campaign out on the hustings for Republican candidates.

Coming after the tranquil fifties, the crime wave was as mystifying as it was terrifying. What could be the cause? The list of candidates included unemployment, divorce, poor schools, racial tensions, substandard housing, poverty, lax law enforcement, increased social mobility, permissive parents, television, and the general erosion in respect for tradition and authority. One scholarly paper even linked the decline in executions to the rise in murders and concluded, almost cheerfully, that the act of passing an electric current through just one man's body could potentially deter upwards of 155 murders.

Others like historian Richard Hofstadter suggested that the astonishing fact was the capacity of Americans, in the light of their bloodied past, to think that they had ever been otherwise. In this view, the aberration was not the storm of crime but rather the lull that preceded it. In the peaceful fifties, Americans had been able to revise their expectations about crime. But in the sixties, the middle class was suddenly getting worried. It had previously counted on residential segregation to protect it from the "criminal classes," who usually were left to prey on themselves. Crime was largely confined by geographical barriers to the other side of the tracks or across the river. But, as new highways and transit lines webbed the cities, crime was following wealth as surely as trade follows the flag. If the victims of burglaries, muggings, and rapes were poor and black, well, that was sad but inevitable. But as soon as violence showed that it could be upwardly mobile, too, crime became the Social Issue.

The real fact is that the crime wave of the sixties was in large part a fraud. The individual crimes were real enough, to be sure, but what seemed to be a nationwide breakdown in law and order was a predictable result of the coming of age of the baby-boom generation. The pig was continuing to force its way through the python, only now it was crowding prisons instead of maternity wards and schools.

This point was well understood by a group called The Campaign to Check the Population Explosion, which in 1969 placed a full-page advertisement in *The New York Times*. Among other chilling statements, the text asserted, "Last year, one out of every 400 Americans was murdered, raped, robbed, or beaten." Who was to blame? "Youngsters account for almost half the crimes," the ad went on, adding ominously, "And in a few short years millions more of them will pour out into the streets at the present rate of procreation."

It is not clear if Americans immediately adopted more

effective birth controls in an effort to avoid muggings. But the connection the ad made between population increase and crime was not inaccurate. To see how the baby boom affected the crime rate we have to understand that America's real criminal class is not the poor or the black or the otherwise disadvantaged. Violence, rather, is a sport of youth. Young men, especially, live dangerously. The leading causes of death among the 15–24 age group, for example, are accidents, suicide, and homicide. (Among young blacks, homicide is *the* leading cause of death.) The most frequent accidental death comes in a motor vehicle. Thirty percent of the 4000 people killed on motorcycles every year are under 20. The 20–24 age group includes only 13 percent of all licensed drivers but 21 percent of those involved in fatal accidents. As the baby boom started driving, the total number of auto accidents a year zoomed from 10 million in 1960 to 17 million in 1972 and fatalities went from 38,000 to 54,000.

Crime, it turns out, is almost as age-specific as driving, diapers, and dentures. Teenagers and young adults dominate crimes of violence and crimes of property. Nearly one-half of all the people arrested in this country are between the ages of 14 and 24. In 1960, the 14–24 age cohort included only 15 percent of the population but accounted for 69 percent of all arrests for serious crimes. Compared to those 25 and over, the younger age group commits twice as many murders, five times as many forcible rapes, six times as many robberies, nine times as many larcenies, ten times as many burglaries, and twenty times as many car thefts. The peak age of violent crime in the United States is 18. (Auto thieves and burglars are 16; murderers are 20.)

We have already seen how the stability of society depends on the ability of the older generation to assimilate the invasion of "barbarian" youth. The outcome of the battle can be predetermined by the birthrate eighteen years earlier. During the 1940s and 1950s, for example, the country had enjoyed a time of relative tranquillity thanks to the low birthrates of the twenties and thirties. The older generation had the edge in numbers and authority. Lawlessness was further reduced during World War II—not as much because of patriotism as the fact that 3½ million young men in the volatile 20–29 age group had been sent overseas. There they presumably were releasing their antisocial energies on military foes.

After 1960, however, millions of baby-boom children began flooding into the most crime-prone ages in society. In ten years the 14–24 cohort grew by more than 50 percent and 13 million people, a larger increase than in the rest of the century before it. Its growth rate was six times the increase of all other age groups combined. Thus, the most crime-prone age in society was expanding rapidly. The implication was obvious. Just as an increase in babies would mean a proportionate increase in the market for pacifiers, any increase in a social group with greater-than-average propensity for committing a certain crime would yield a proportionate increase in the incidence of the crime itself.

This is exactly what happened in the sixties and early seventies. In Washington, D.C., police officials were at first alarmed to discover that, at a time when the overall population was decreasing, the rate of serious crime had risen 350 percent. Then they looked more closely at their census figures. They discovered that, even as the total population was shrinking, the number of persons in the 15–24 age group had increased by 33 percent—enough to explain a considerable portion of the crime increase. Among the first categories to feel the wallop of the boom generation nationally was what used to be called juvenile delinquency. Even in the 1950s, the delinquency rate had set off a minor stir when the 15–19 group increased by 27 percent. But that was nothing compared to the 42 percent increase in the age group during the 1960s. At the same time, the number of persons arrested under 18 had exploded from 1 million in 1965 to 1.6 million in 1970. Robberies had increased less than 4 percent a year in the first half of the sixties. Then, from 1965 to 1970, the robbery rate shot up 18 percent a year. Why? Largely because more Americans turned 18 in those five years than ever before in our history. In its final report in 1972, the Presidential Commission on Population Growth and the American Future estimated that about 28 percent of the reported increase between 1960 and 1970 in the number of arrests for serious crimes could be attributed to an increase in the percentage of the population under 25. Another 22 percent of the increase could be explained by the growing size of the population and other demographic factors. Thus, population change alone demonstrably accounted for about one-half of the reported increase in the number of arrests for serious crimes during the worst crime wave the country had ever seen.

If we narrow our sights further to a single criminal category, the baby boom's impact looms even larger. Take homicide. Statistically, at least, homicide has a certain appeal. Everyone agrees what it is and, since it is usually discovered, it is less subject to the kind of prior underreporting that may have made the rise in rape, for example, seem larger than it really was. From 1900 until 1930, the homicide rate gradually increased until it reached a Depression peak in 1933. For the next twenty-five years, the rate gradually sloped down and widespread violent death began to seem a hangover from America's roistering past that we were glad to forget.

Then, beginning around 1960, Americans began killing one another again at a rate that had briefly seemed inconceivable. At a time when death rates in every other health category were decreasing, death due to violence was becoming a nationwide plague. Among men, the murder rate doubled in ten years. On charts, in fact, the increases looked strangely like an epidemic of infectious disease. It was a contagion that was increasing exponentially and spreading from young to old and from poor to rich. But instead of lasting a season, the epidemic of homicide lingered a decade. At its height in the mid-seventies, fifty-five persons a day were dying from it. On the average, the most dangerous day was Saturday; the least dangerous was Wednesday.

Murder also resembled disease in that it was selective. Murder, like sickle-cell anemia, discriminates racially. Its most likely victim was a young, poorly educated black man living in a central city. Young blacks were five times as likely to be murdered as whites, and nonwhite women were twenty times more likely to be murdered than white women. Though the usual explanations for black vulnerability to homicide suggest socioeconomic causes—unemployment, discrimination, and poverty—there is also a demographic explanation. Because black fertility is higher than white, blacks were more heavily represented in the young, aggressive boom generation than whites. And because they were overrepresented in the baby boom, they were overrepresented in murder. Most murders, as it happens, are committed by persons of the same race as the victim. Recently, though, some observers have become concerned over the rise in the number of interracial murders. But instead of accepting that statistic as evidence of rising racial tension, at least one criminologist, Marvin Wolfgang of the University of Pennsylvania, has managed to put an optimistic spin on the trend. What the rise in interracial killings really shows, he argues, is not racial hostility but rather the encouraging progress of integration. The problem is that if people live together, they can also kill one another.

By 1973, some 20,000 persons were being killed every year and the murder rate had topped the previous record set forty years earlier. One of the sadder statistics of the period is that, during the first four years of the 1970s, more Americans were slain at home than died during the decade of the Vietnam War. Further, whether it was Da-Nang or Detroit, the victims and their assailants were mostly baby boomers. In 1972, those babies born from 1943 through 1957 accounted for 40 percent of all murder victims and 60 percent of those arrested. Boom children from the expansive first half of their generation, they had felt more acutely than anyone the successive shocks of expansion that they'd generated in the society. Like Pogo, they could honestly say, We have met the enemy and he is Us.

If we examine other countries that experienced baby booms, the result is no different. Though the United States has by far the leading homicide rate in the world, the next in line are Canada and Australia, two of the three other countries which had seen similar booms. The third, New Zealand, has a negligible murder rate. From 1964 to 1971, however, the number of convictions for common assault doubled in New Zealand as its boom children elbowed their way into adolescence. Thanks also to boom-generation drivers, Canada and Australia shared with the United States a sharp rise in car accidents at a time when safety was improving in countries without dramatic population shifts.

There is always the possibility, of course, that the relationship between the baby boom and murders or car accidents is not what it seems. That is, some mysterious third force in a nation's past could provide the animus behind both high fertility rates and high homicide rates. Poverty has traditionally been suggested, though it hardly seemed relevant to the years of the baby boom. Yet the enormous increase in the number of criminal-aged people in the United States cannot itself account for

171

all of the increase in crime. The baby boom was large and it was also different. In addition to giving us more murderers in a generation, it also gave us a more murderous generation. There was no safety in these numbers. An individual passing between the ages of 20 and 24 was now twice as likely to be murdered as his predecessors fifteen years earlier.

A lawyer interviewed by Charles Silberman for his exhaustive study of criminal violence told him of "a terrifying generation of kids" that emerged during the late 1960s and early seventies. When she began practicing, she told Silberman, adolescents and young men charged with robbery had, at worst, pushed or shoved a pedestrian or storekeeper to steal money or merchandise. But, she said, members of the new generation killed, maimed, and injured without reason or remorse.

The older generation, to be sure, has rarely applauded the criminal style of the younger. But in its criticism now was a tone of bitterness and even defeat. In crime, as on the campuses, the invading generation of barbarians had outnumbered the defenders. Emboldened by their critical mass of numbers, as well as a hitherto-unknown degree of economic independence, the baby boomers had wrestled their freedom from their parents. Eventually, the older generation had become so uncertain of its values and confidence that it had gladly turned the task over to the schools and eventually the courts. It is not surprising that, given such a lack of external or internal restraints, not to mention the pressures of both their numbers and their peer-based culture, the boom generation yielded a higher-than-average pathology. As Silberman pointed out, the adolescent need for money, combined with the weakening of adult controls, produced a lethal criminal force.

Crime is but one symptom of the baby boom's tumultuous coming-of-age. This generation has always lived dangerously—and paid for it dearly. When the first boom children reached the 15–29 age group after 1960, young people of that age started dying faster from *all* causes. The death rates in the 15–29 age group had previously declined for the entire previous century. But in the decade after the baby boomers arrived, death rates among 15–29-year-olds reversed and rose an unprecedented 20 percent. That is the only sustained increase in mortality experienced by any age group in this country since 1900. It is hard to find any reason for it other than the excesses of the baby boomers themselves. Some of the cause was, no doubt, their aggressiveness. Others involved heavier risk-taking than previous generations. Their ties to stability and tradition were weaker. For that matter, belief in the future—an important index of mental health—also seemed to be waning in this generation. Accidents, homicides, and suicides still account for three out of four deaths in the boom generation. And, almost unbelievably, the best-raised, best-fed, and best-cared for generation America has produced still had a *higher* death rate in 1977 than the same age group did twenty years earlier.

Are we now doomed to an anxious, fear-filled future at the hands of this criminal generation? Will the baby boom have to be garrisoned to protect themselves from their murderous peers? Not at all. There is a prediction implicit in any discussion of age structure and crime. It is that the generation that made the crime wave can break it, too. Just as they inexorably grew into the high-crime ages, the boom babies will inevitably grow out of them.

The process has already started. Automobile theft, always the most popular crime among young teenagers, was the first to feel the change. Previously, from 1965 until 1970, the number of car thefts had increased annually at a runaway—rather, driveaway—clip of 12 percent a year. Then in the next five years, auto thefts sputtered to less than a 1 percent gain per year. The rate of increase in homicide also dipped sharply after 1975. Then in 1976, the total rate of violent crime in the United States fell 4 percent, the first such decline in sixteen years.

Law-enforcement officials embarked on a round of hearty self-congratulation. The decline in lawlessness, said the U.S. attorney general, provided ample "evidence that progress is being made in the fight against crime." But the credit was misplaced. It did not belong to more scrupulous law-enforcement or even to the millions of dollars that were poured into government social welfare programs during the sixties and early seventies. Rather, in this case, the best crime-fighter in the world was the calendar.

The bulge of the baby boom was moving on. In the ten years from 1965 until 1975, the 18–24 age group had filled up with 7.5 million additional persons. But in the next five years, as the last baby-boom cohorts passed through that age, it grew by less than 2 million and its proportion of the population actually decreased. Now, in the 1980s, the size of the 18–24 group will decline by 4.3 million. As an echo, then, of lowered birthrates following the baby-boom years, we can expect the opposite of the sixties' experience. All the behavior characteristics we associate with adolescents and young adults will diminish. There should be less drug abuse, fewer traffic accidents, reduced auto insurance rates, and even less venereal disease. (In 1974, the 15–24 cohort accounted for 67 percent of all cases of gonorrhea.) Using projections based on existing crime rates, the President's Commission on Population Growth and the American Future was able to predict more than a decade earlier that the number of rapes, robberies, assaults, burglaries, larcenies, and auto thefts should decline by 1985. By 1990, if other factors do not change, the number of violent crimes in the country could decline by one-fourth because of population change alone.

This is heartening news for urbanologists, who see in the lessening of crime rates another chance for the renewal of our cities. People have always named their fear of crime as one of the major drawbacks of urban living. The safety in the cities is already a less heatedly debated public issue now that the baby boom is moving on. In the late seventies, homicide rates dropped in ten cities, including such onetime criminal centers as Chicago, Los Angeles, Boston, and Newark. In 1977, violent crime decreased in New York City in every single category, except for rape. In Detroit, crime dropped 30 percent in two years. Recently, in fact, the center of urban crime has shifted out of the older cities of the Northeast to the new cities of the Southwest, where the population is also younger. In 1979, the murder capital of the nation was Houston.

None of this is to suggest that the aging of the baby boom means that we are entering a kind of utopian, crimeless state. The prisons will not be empty; they will have a different kind of prisoner. The sociologist Emile Durkheim has said that even a society of saints would invent its own crimes, presumably for such transgressions as rudeness, chewing with the mouth open, or smoking cigars in public. As the boom ages, the growth areas of crime will switch from violence to more refined activities. Criminologist James Alan Fox of North-eastern has pointed out that violence decreases with age not because of rehabilitation but because the commitments of family and career discourage the violent response. In adolescence, violence can pay off, but the middle-aged criminal may find embezzlement more to his or her tastes. Criminals will swap up a notch. Mugging will be out; graft will be in.

During the coming decade, moreover, the victims of crime will shift from individuals to institutions. Bank robberies are already gaining favor. But robbery itself will be displaced by what should be the heyday of white-collar crime. In 1978, embezzlers took three times as much money from banks as robbers did. The average bank robbery nets $10,000, but the average computer crime nets $193,000. The average street robbery makes $338, but the average arson-for-profit makes $6403. Fines levied for corporate price-fixing rose from $3.7 million in 1976 to $12 million in 1978. Congress has estimated that white-collar criminals cost businesses and consumers anywhere from $50-$200 billion a year (compared to $4 billion for crimes against property). Bribery, extortion, and public corruption will all rise throughout the eighties, not simply because of a breakdown in public morality, but because the opportunities will be so great. The 1980 congressional Abscam scandal was as appropriate for its day as car theft was in 1965. Seen this way, Watergate was ahead of its time. It would have fit right into the criminal style of the eighties. The FBI has doubled its percentage of agents assigned to white-collar crime but may need to do more. In the future, the real threat the boom generation faces is not from a drug-crazed addict but from the accountant in the office next door.

Chapter 12

WHY JOHNNY CAN'T EARN

> In ancient times people were few but wealthy and without strife. People at present think that five sons are not too many, and each son has five sons also and before the death of the grandfather there are already 25 descendants. Therefore people are more and wealth is less; they work hard and receive little.
> —Han Fei-tzu, Chou Dynasty (ca. 500 B.C.)

> The baby boom generation may never achieve the relative economic success of the generations immediately preceding it or following it.
> —1980 United States Budget

In the 1976 presidential election, the Democratic candidate, Jimmy Carter, attacked on the economic flank, charging that more people were unemployed in the United States than at any time since the Depression. The Republican incumbent, Gerald Ford, stoutly replied to the contrary that more people were employed than at any time in American history. Who was right?

Actually, they both were. In the late sixties and early seventies the boom generation had surged from the schools into the offices and factories and carried out a wholesale transformation of the economy. The civilian labor force, which had grown by only 7.5 million in the fifties (11.5 percent), leaped ahead by 12 million in the sixties (18 percent), and then an astonishing 20 million (24.4 percent) in the seventies. But even that was not enough to accommodate the boom generation. Unemployment had grown just as rapidly and a host of other problems were not far behind. Teenage joblessness, especially for blacks, was running at a crisis level. The worth of a college degree was devalued. Inflation had hit double-digit levels. Productivity was falling faster than at any time in American history. Opportunities for career advancement were suddenly limited. Each of these problems was related in one way or another to the invasion of the boom generation.

The result was that the economic position of the boom generation was being reversed. Once our affluent generation, it was economically disadvantaged by the competition of its own numbers. Each time the boom generation climbed into an older age group, the unemployment rate shot up in that age group while its earnings power declined. The difficulties were made all the harder to bear because the boom generation's lengthy education had nurtured such high expectations. Eventually one of the prime articles of faith in the American credo—that a college education will pay off—was undermined. That was not the worst of it. Economists were concluding that the competitive stresses that had marked the baby boom's early years could only become stronger. Forever shackled to the oversupply inherent in its large numbers, the boom generation would be doomed to a life of low earnings, career disappointments, and personal struggle.

The most persistent and paradoxical problem at first was unemployment. In the fifteen years from the end of World War II to 1960, the size of the crucial 15–29 age group, when most people enter the labor market, remained virtually unchanged. But then, by the ineluctable process of aging, the baby boom began to move from the schools to the work force. In the next fifteen years, from 1960 to 1975, the 15–29 age group exploded from 35 million to 57 million.

The first wave of baby boomers hit in 1964, when the number of 18-year-olds was larger by 1 million than the group a year earlier. Over the next decade, the average net growth in the number of baby boomers seeking jobs doubled to 1.7 million a year. The overall work force was expanding twice as fast as the population. The concentration was strongest in the youngest years. The representation of 16–19-year-olds in the total work force increased by 46 percent; the 20–24 group grew by nearly 60 percent.

The result was that, even at a time when the national unemployment rate was humming along at 3.5 percent a year, teenage unemployment was fluctuating wildly between 12 and 17 percent, six times higher than other workers. Since no new jobs were being created in the sixties for teenagers, their entire yearly increase of 240,000 new workers—six times the rate in the previous decade—was being dumped straight into the reservoir of the unemployed.

Teenagers, to be sure, have always had chronically high unemployment. Inexperienced, they change jobs often, spend more time looking for jobs, work part-time, leave the labor market to return to school, and so on. Moreover, during the sixties they were meeting increased competition from older women who also desired the same kinds of entry-level jobs, typically clerical or manual. During the five years from 1965 to 1970, the number of women working increased faster than it ever had—almost 4 percent a year. The simultaneous addition of millions of baby boomers looking for work created a surplus. Projecting from earlier figures, one congressional budget study estimated that the sheer increase in crowding alone contributed 4 percent to the rate of teenage unemployment.

By the end of the sixties, the total labor force had increased from 72 million to 86 million. More than half the total growth consisted of young workers between 14 and 24, who expanded their forces by 7 million. Some of them began to make their impact felt at once. With the track to the top greased by the absence of a large generation ahead of them, baby boomers began to move into the system in the late sixties. The median age of partners began to drop in law firms. Companies were so eager for the services of young business school graduates, attuned to the youth market, that they bid up starting salaries faster than oil-lease rights. Teaching jobs were easy to get, especially for the oldest members of the baby boom, who were desperately needed to teach their younger brothers and sisters.

Though it hardly seemed possible at the time, considering the runaway rate of teenage unemployment, the real impact of the baby boom on the work force was hidden during the sixties. As Norman Ryder has shown, the economy did not then absorb the full brunt of the boom generation. Instead, it had postponed the problem by delaying its arrival, sending millions of baby boomers to college and into the armed services during the Vietnam years.

Then in 1969 the first college class composed entirely of baby boomers graduated. Now there was no way to hide them. In both that year and the next, the labor force grew by two million workers, by far the biggest increases in American history, excluding the post-World War II readjustment. Between 1969 and 1976, the total labor force increased by one-sixth, twice the rate of 1955–62 and nearly three times the growth of the nation's population in the same period.

The issues that would shape the economics of the seventies were now coming into focus. The old "equilibrium unemployment" goal of 4 percent, which seemed reachable during the sixties, became unworkable as unemployment averaged 6.2 percent in the seventies *despite* the huge increases in numbers of jobs. In 1975, for example, we would have had to add 2 million jobs just to keep even with the number of new job seekers and hold unemployment near 5 percent. Instead, the number of jobs plummeted by 1 million during the 1974–75 recession and unemployment leaped to 8.5 percent. Even during the economy's strong rebound from that recession, when 12 million new jobs were created, unemployment was cut only by 2 million. The problem was that we had made babies faster in the forties and fifties than we could make jobs for them in the sixties and seventies.

Nowhere was the stress more acutely felt in the seventies than among college graduates. The boom generation had made itself the biggest college generation ever and, from the late sixties to the mid-seventies, the number of college graduates moving into the civilian labor force doubled. The new B.A.s had every hope of achieving the comfort and status that a college degree traditionally confers in America. Instead, they received an unsettling blow. For the first time in recent American history, the relative earnings of college graduates *declined*. As an investment, college was costing more but was worth less. The oversupply of college graduates dates to the degree mania that swept across the country after World War II and produced the GI Bill of Rights. But even though enrollment rates (that is, the percentage of high-school graduates going to college) rose during the forties and fifties, the actual number of students in college barely increased at all. The small Depression generation actually provided fewer college-age young men than its predecessors. Thus, while the *proportion* of young people enrolled in college increased by 15 percent between 1940 and 1960, the college-educated proportion of the adult population increased only from 4.6 to 7.7 percent.

The overheated American economic machine, meanwhile, was rapidly running out of managerial talent. The huge demand for college-educated workers quickly sucked up the available Depression generation and began driving up salaries. As in the classic Adam Smith paradigm, supply began to rise to meet demand. The Harvard economist Richard Freeman has likened this process to the "cobweb feedback system" in which the future supply of hogs or corn is determined by market conditions several years earlier. Drawn by the rich opportunities awaiting college graduates, more and more young Americans began entering college.

In its first stage before 1964, the increase in college enrollments was created not by a larger pool of available students but by increased participation from a smaller pool. Even during the time of excess demand, there was surprisingly little net increase in the number of new college graduates seeking work. During the fifties, colleges actually saw the lowest average of enrollment growth of the century, 1.9 percent.

In the sixties, as we have seen, the baby boom entered the college-age population with a bang. The same enrollment rates were now producing twice as many real students, thanks to the larger pool. Growth in higher education leapfrogged from 1.9 percent annually to 8.5 percent. By 1969, one-half of all white males of college age were enrolled, and higher education was an industry, employing more workers than either automobile or steel. Between 1969 and 1972 the net number of new college graduates seeking work relative to the entire work force increased threefold. By 1975, one-fourth of all people 25–29 had completed four or more years of college, an increase of 50 percent in five years. The boom generation had caught an educational wave, riding the demand of the forties and fifties to the heights of the sixties and seventies.

The only problem was that demand dried up long before the supply did. The Bureau of Labor Statistics reported that the first employment difficulties among college graduates started developing after 1969. Soon, more than 11 percent of the class that graduated in June of 1972 had not found the jobs they wanted by October. The situation was worst in the academic marketplace. In

1974, only 15 of 62 English Ph.D. graduates from Berkeley were able to find jobs. Of 1225 history Ph.D. candidates seeking jobs nationally in 1973, only 182 found them. By 1975, it was painfully clear that the labor market for college graduates was saturated with baby boomers but that the production lines of the education industry were still running overtime.

These fresh young college graduates, their eyes dancing with enthusiasm, could not just be stockpiled like so much excess inventory. They had to do *something*. But what? The answer was what the Labor Department, in one of its most egregious barbarisms, calls "recredentialization." To the baby boomers, that meant the now-familiar specter of a physicist working as a cabdriver, an economist waiting on tables, or an English Ph.D. repairing driveways. All across the economy, overtrained graduates were spilling out of the job categories they had prepared for. During the years from 1969 until 1976, some 8 million baby-boom graduates—twice the number of the preceding seven years—entered the labor force. More than 2.1 million of them, or 27 percent, were forced to take jobs they had not been trained for—whether clerical, blue collar, or agricultural—or were unable to find work at all. (By comparison, only 7 percent of the graduates of the earlier period suffered that fate.) One of the ironies of the period is that the older baby boomers hurt the job opportunities of their younger brothers and sisters in two ways. First, they snapped up most of the available jobs, effectively blocking future advancement from below. Second, by not having as many children as their parents they helped kill off one of the most fertile job-hunting fields: education. Teaching had provided one job in five for all male college graduates of the sixties but only took one in ten during the first half of the seventies.

The situation will get worse before it gets better. Between 1976 and 1985, an estimated 10.4 million college graduates will compete for the 7.7 million jobs traditionally filled by college graduates. That means that 2.7 million baby-boom graduates—about one-quarter of the total—will have to accept the kinds of jobs not taken by college graduates during the sixties.

We can only guess at the amount of bitterness and resentment engendered by the collapse of the job market for college graduates. Millions of baby boomers who had been promised everything from their education were being delivered nothing. And they were not alone in their frustration. Those college graduates who found good jobs soon discovered that, because the market was glutted, neither their pay nor their prospects were worth as much as they thought they were. As one recent graduate put it, "The Latin words on my degree ought to be *caveat emptor.*"

Historically, of course, Americans had thought of college as an "unlimited good." Like gold or precious gems, its marketable value held up regardless of how many people owned it. The proof was in the record. From the thirties until the late sixties, college graduates consistently earned 50 percent more than high-school graduates. Only later, as Stephen Dresch has pointed out, were we able to see that the relationship then between education and income was exceptional. For one thing, the economic boom that had powered demand for highly educated labor for three decades could not last. For another, the small supply of young people, which actually had declined during the fifties, was about to be replaced by the biggest generation in America's history. As the number of workers in the younger group began multiplying, their wages dropped relative to the older workers. We can see this by comparing salary discrepancies between young and old in different decades. Back in the mid-sixties, for example, a person in the 45–54 age group earned on the average 74 percent more than someone between 20 and 24. In the seventies, however, the premium paid to older workers increased to the detriment of the baby boom. In 1975, the 45–54-year-olds born in the 1920s had upped their salary advantage to a full 100 percent more than the younger workers born between 1951 and 1955. Thus, while prospects were getting better and better for the small Good Times Generation, they were getting worse and worse for the big Bad Times Generation.

This relative disadvantage was particularly painful for college graduates, who had expected to be riding steep earnings curves most of their lives. Traditionally, while a college graduate might start at a salary not much higher than a blue-collar worker's, the college worker would see his or her income rise throughout a career. The income of a blue-collar worker, on the other hand, usually peaked out far earlier in working life. After the baby boom, however, a larger percentage of the labor force was crowded into those high-velocity careers. The inevitable result of oversupply was smaller raises and fewer promotions and a flatter age–earnings curve.

In addition to losing value compared with previous generations, degrees were also losing value within the boom generation itself. In 1969, college graduates earned an estimated 53 percent more than high-school graduates. But by 1974, college graduates were earning only 35 percent more than high-school graduates. The National Longitudinal Study of a group of baby-boom men conducted by Ohio State University recently showed that the demonstrated wages of college graduates had fallen. '(For that matter, it also disclosed a drop in the relative wages of high-school graduates as well!) Similarly, the flood of law school graduates admitted to the bar, who tripled from 11,000 a year in 1963 to 33,000 in 1977, has driven down the value of lawyers. According to an American Bar Association poll, the median income of lawyers dropped $2000 from $32,000 in 1975 to $30,000 in 1976.

The disturbing fact confronting the boom generation was that their education had been devalued. Richard Freeman has calculated that the estimated return on each dollar invested in higher education has declined from 11 or 12 percent for the graduates of the late fifties and early sixties to 8.5 percent for the graduates of the seventies. The brass ring of higher education—on which so many disadvantaged people have placed their fervent hopes of improving their lot in life—seemed to have turned into tin. What they saw ahead was lower wages and poorer promotion opportunities. Even the assumption that any college graduate can easily earn a comfortable living was suspect.

It is not surprising, given the erosion of incentives, that the later cohorts of the baby boom began to back away from higher education. Between 1973 and 1976, the percentage of high-school seniors entering colleges the year of their graduation suddenly dropped from 62 percent to 54 percent. Later in the decade, the proportion of all students going on to college began to drop. Economists are now estimating that, from a peak of perhaps one-third of all 24-year-olds completing college in 1980, the proportion could decline to 15 percent at the end of the decade. With the expenses going up, and the rewards going down, students were finding it harder and harder to turn on to higher education.

At the end of the 1960s, Americans strongly agreed that the number one problem facing the country was student unrest.

At the end of the 1970s, Americans even more strongly agreed that the number one problem facing the country was inflation.

These two issues—student unrest in the sixties and inflation in the seventies—might seem to be worlds apart. But the point I will be developing here is that both of these issues were grounded in the proliferating numbers of young people who had grown up in the baby boom. We have already seen how the invasion of baby-boom "barbarians" contributed to the unrest of the sixties. But what did the boom have to do with inflation? Richard Easterlin and his colleagues Michael and Susan Wachter of the University of Pennsylvania believe that the problem lies largely in our unsuccessful attempts to integrate the baby boom into the work force.

The most commonly accepted goal of American economic policy is full employment without inflation. Ever since the Employment Act of 1946, the federal government has sought to achieve this goal through the Keynesian tools of monetary and fiscal policy. If unemployment went up, the theory went, the government could step in and, by cutting taxes, leave consumers with more money to spend. The spending would create demand for more goods, which would embolden manufacturers to produce more by hiring more workers, which in turn would reduce unemployment.

The problem in the seventies, though, was that the economy saw both high inflation *and* high unemployment. The government's steps to stimulate demand raised inflation but could not budge unemployment. Why? The problem, Easterlin argued, was that high unemployment in the seventies was not due to low demand for goods and services. To the contrary, high demand was already exerting inflationary pressure. Instead, unemployment was really due to the disproportionate number of young workers in the economy—that is, the boom generation—and that any attempts to reduce unemployment by stimulating demand were not only ineffective but were making inflation worse. The reason that unemployment could not be reduced by stimulating demand was the lowest feasible level of unemployment—known as "equilibrium" unemployment—was tied to the relative numbers of young and unskilled workers in the economy.

We need to back up a bit to see this. Earlier, as Easterlin pointed out, the character of the labor supply was not always so bound up in its age composition. Before the restrictive immigrant legislation of the twenties, for example, changes in the labor supply were responsive to swings in demand. When the economy was heating up, workers flooded to America. And when the economy was in recession, reduced demand dried up immigration. By the forties and fifties, however, immigration had been stabilized. Now the future growth of the labor supply was dependent as never before on the natural growth of the population and on the fraction of working-age people participating in the work force. Further, since demand was being stabilized at a high level because of the government's fiscal and monetary intervention in the marketplace, the result was that fluctuations in the size and age composition of the labor force during the postwar era were not governed by the business cycle or by immigration but by the lagged effect of the birthrate. If lots of babies were born, there would be more young workers twenty years later. If fewer babies were born, there would be fewer young workers twenty years later. Unemployment, unfortunately, is not an equal-opportunity unemployer. It discriminates by age. At any given time, the total unemployment rate is an amalgam of two divergent rates: a high rate for young workers and a low rate for older workers. Recently, for example, nearly one-half of all unemployed persons in the country were in the 16–24 bracket, even though those ages amount to only one-fourth of the total labor force.

We have seen some of the reasons why youth chronically suffers from high unemployment. Inexperienced, tentative, and lacking credentials, young workers take longer to find jobs or take longer between jobs. Often unhappy in entry-level jobs, they change jobs frequently, further contributing to the "frictional" unemployment caused by mobility. Some drop out of the work force from time to time to have children or to go back to school. Older workers, on the other hand, are far more committed to working and have less turnover.

It follows that, even if both the overall size of the work force and the age-specific unemployment rates remain unchanged, any increase in the proportion of young workers will induce an increase in the overall unemployment rate. The opposite is equally true. The unemployment rate in the fourth quarter of 1977, for example, was 6.6 percent but would have been 5.8 percent if the age distribution of the labor force had been the same as in 1956.

To these factors we add the crowding effect we have already seen. Just as the critical mass of baby boomers increased both the number of murders and the murder rate, so too did it increase both the number of jobless and the jobless rate. The unemployment rate of 5.9 percent in 1949 was higher than the 5.3 percent in 1971. But by age, the small generation of 16–17-year-olds in 1949 actually had a *lower* age-specific unemployment rate (13.7 percent) than the large generation of 16–17-year-olds in 1971 (18.6 percent). The crowding effect, then, further raised unemployment rates as the age structure of the labor force shifted from a scarcity of young labor in the fifties and early sixties to an oversupply of young workers in the late sixties and seventies.

Consider now what happened to the baby boom. As the young generation of workers flooded into the labor market, keeping salaries down and unemployment up, the government's initial response was to soak up the unemployed by turning on demand. But instead of improving the lot of the baby boomers, the aggressive demand-side policies heated up inflation even further. At the same time, the welfare of the boom generation continued to decline relative to the older generation.

What went wrong? The problem, according to Easterlin and the Wachters, is that monetary and fiscal policies designed to raise the level of aggregate demand could not adjust for the structural nature of unemployment, which was the surplus of young workers relative to older workers. The worst unemployment was concentrated in the youngest baby-boom workers, many of whom were untrained and unskilled. They could not be substituted for older, skilled workers. Demand policies that did not take into account the age imbalance generated by the boom generation did very little to create jobs and actually generated higher prices and the dilemma of "stagflation."

186

Easterlin illustrates this point with an example of the classic widget manufacturer:

> In response to increasing demand for widgets, he has hired as many skilled older people to operate his widget-making machines, and as many experienced supervisors, as he can find. He has also hired as many unskilled, inexperienced young workers to feed raw materials into the widget machines, wrap finished widgets, pack and stack them, etc., as his supervisors can supervise and his machine operators can keep up with. If there are still plenty of young, unskilled, inexperienced workers swelling the unemployment rolls, the government may increase demand even further by another tax cut.
>
> However, our friend the widget maker, having already hired all the experienced machine operators and supervisors he coud find, cannot respond to that increased demand by opening another factory—because he can't staff a new factory solely with young, inexperienced feeders, wrappers, packers, and stackers. So how will he respond to the increased demand for his limited output? He most likely will raise his prices.

So it was that, despite widespread unemployment, many companies were desperately searching for qualified machinists, draftsmen, toolmakers, and computer programmers. The government's attempts to ease the problem by regulating demand only contributed to the many forces fueling more inflation. Ultimately, the solution will lie with matching supply to demand, something that can only come with widespread training or vocational programs. Or with time.

Viewing persistent unemployment as a structural problem caused by age imbalance in the labor force can also help us understand one of the most melancholy aspects of the baby boom's life. It is the worsening job situation of blacks born in the boom generation, especially black teenagers. To some degree, of course, unemployment, like crime, is at least partly a function of the disproportionate numbers of blacks represented in the boom generation. But the statistics are more depressing than that. Among black youths, unemployment has risen from 3.4

187

percent in 1955—before the boom arrived—to just under 40 percent in 1980. Black teenagers have become a permanent underclass whose economic prospects are far worse today than they were for anyone during the Great Depression (when unemployment peaked at 25 percent).

That is only half of the story. More alarming than the fact that the unemployment rate for black teenagers is twice that of white teenagers is the disturbing trend: the gap is increasing. From 1965 to 1974, the black teenage population was growing at the high rate of 4.5 percent a year while their employment was growing only 2.2 percent. During the same period, the white population was growing 3.5 percent a year and its employment grew 3.9 percent. The message was clear: the labor market would try to keep up with expanding cohorts of white teenagers, but could not for blacks. Recessions seemed to make the difference even worse. After the 1975 recession, the unemployment rate for white teenagers dropped from 16 percent to 12 percent. For black youths, though, it rose from 37 percent to 38 percent.

By October of 1977, an estimated 700,000 nonwhites between the ages of 16 and 24 were looking for work but couldn't find it. And that figure includes only those who were trying. Each recession has shaken more and more black men out of the work force. They have just given up, instead entering what social scientists call the "underground economy" of theft, numbers games, and hustling. Some economists now think that as many as one million blacks may have dropped out of the system altogether and that the true rate of black youth unemployment is closer to 60 percent. For black teenagers, incidentally, unemployment is usually more debilitating than it is for whites. Nearly three-quarters of all white teenagers live with two parents who could presumably support them if necessary. Of blacks, however, half of unemployed teenagers live in a female-headed family and only 60 percent have a relative who works. The devaluation of education has come precisely at the moment when blacks and other minorities have been counting on it to relieve their economic plight. Labor Department statistics show that of recent black high-school graduates who did not go on to college, only one-third had jobs of any kind six months after graduation.

In short, all those forces operating against the boom generation in the seventies were intensified against blacks.

Their numbers in the job market were increasing faster than whites, but they were receiving fewer jobs. If white teenagers were suffering from their surplus, black teenagers were suffering even more. Many of them will pass directly into adulthood with little or no links to the working world—a fact that has been shown to injure a person's job prospects permanently. Often the sons and daughters of unemployed workers, they are a second generation of jobless, are written off by white America and condemned to a widening whirlpool of social pathology, personal hopelessness, and despair. Inevitably, this intractable unemployment became linked to crime. According to the U.S. Law Enforcement Administration, an estimated 48 percent of the nation's chronically unemployed black youths can be expected to commit crimes amounting to $5.9 billion a year.

Looking around at this point in one's life cycle, a typical baby boomer might have felt like a man who has just been in a car accident. He heard the squeal of brakes, saw the impact coming, and felt the crash. Now he was gingerly feeling around to see if his arms and limbs were still intact. Yes, the boom generation was still alive and well, at least in numbers. But its collision with the working economy had left some injuries. Its dreams had been bottled up by competition, its opportunities closed off by the older generation, its economic gains diminished by oversupply. The biggest and best-educated group of men and women in American history was beginning to feel as if it had entered some kind of negative growth cycle; the older it got, the worse things looked. Instead of rappelling itself up into adult society, it remained entangled in its own mass. Certainly, there were success stories in its midst— the Leon Botsteins and Jann Wenners—but their visibility only made the frustration of the majority more poignant.

The boom generation now faced the prospect that it had been almost as damaged by its passage into the world of work as the generation of 1930 was by the Depression. Its feeling of injustice was heightened by the realization that it might *never* recover its economic loss. Its earnings curve had been dropped down a notch, effectively flattened by the high unemployment, low wages, and slow promotions that threatened to follow the baby boom like an albatross for the rest of its days.

When did the youth society die? Demographically, it

was in 1977, the first year that the median age in the country turned up (to 28.2) after dropping more than two decades. But it also ended when the boom generation saw its future and for the first time realized that it did not work. The older generation had opened the door but the younger generation could not squeeze in. The conviction of the sixties—that youth would *prevail*—was looking more and more like the boom generation's grand illusion. The human metaphor for its situation was no longer the phalanx but the queue. This was the generation doomed to wait in line: first in hospitals, then in schools and colleges, then in the Army, then to get jobs, then to be promoted, and presumably someday to get into nursing homes.

PART III

The Baby Boom in Midlife

The meek are supposed to inherit the earth someday, and so it seems the baby boom generation will, too.

—article in *BBDO Magazine*

Chapter 13

ROSIE'S DAUGHTERS

"You keep forgetting that besides being a woman,
I'm an Egyptologist."
—heroine of Robin Cook's novel, *Sphinx*

Nobody ever figured Rosie the Riveter for a revolutionary. But there she was on the munitions assembly lines during World War II with her sleeves rolled up, her hair tucked beneath her cap, and a smile as wide as the Mississippi. As the wartime posters plainly showed, she was doing a man's work. Not that there was anything new about that. Women had always worked hard in America, from the farms to the mills. Before Rosie came along, however, most younger women had dropped out of the job force as soon as they married. But Rosie was different. She was already married and she was still working. And she was beginning a transformation of the American ways of life and work that by any yardstick—social, psychological, or economic—amounted to one of the most significant social changes since the Industrial Revolution.

Twenty-five million women followed Rosie into the labor force in the three decades after World War II. Ten million of them would have been expected to anyway, given previous trends. But 15 million—60 percent of the total increase—were women no one expected to go to work. They were largely the young baby boomers who have made up the bulk of the increase in working women over the last fifteen years. These women, Rosie's daughters, forever altered the labor force. Overall, three out of every five new workers since 1947 have been women and their portion of *all* workers has risen from under 30 percent in 1950 to more than 42 percent in 1980. Around 1972 the number of working women surpassed the number of housewives, and in June 1978 the proportion of women 16 and over in the labor force passed 50 percent for the first time in U.S. history. In less than a single generation, then, the typical environment of the American woman had moved from the home to the workplace.

This historic change rippled through almost every aspect of American life. Children were raised differently; husbands and wives were married (and divorced) differently; families ate out more often; stores stayed open later; charities ran short of volunteers; neighborhood friends were replaced by office friends; sales boomed in women's tailored two-piece suits; and magazines came out with names like *Working Women* and *Working Mother*. Women were reporting stress-related health problems once exclusive to men. Even arrests of women for property crimes increased from one out of six in 1960 to one out of three in 1977.

To understand how this happened, we need to return to 1890, when the United States first began keeping statistics on the employment of the sexes. Back then, only 3.7 million women—18 percent of the total—were working. But the figure was deceptively low. It did not include, for example, unsalaried rural wives who were as much a producing part of the family farm as field hands. In the cities, female employment was almost exclusively the activity of young women before marriage. In 1890, more than 40 percent of all single women were in the work force, a figure surprisingly close to today's.

Throughout the first half of this century, the percentage of women working slowly rose. In 1900, one woman in five worked; in 1940, it was one in four. Most of them were young, single, and often economically deprived women who worked out of economic necessity in both clerical jobs and garment-industry sweatshops. Then World War II changed everything. The shortage of male workers could only be eased by women—single women, married women, any women. More than 6 million took jobs, doubling the size of the female labor force. The original Rosies in the shipbuilding industry went from 36 such female riveters to 160,000. Suddenly 38 percent of federal office workers were women. The country was getting used to seeing the sight of working women who were married and over 35—a whole new class of workers. By the end of the war, 20 million women were in the labor force and nearly half of them were married. The door of economic equality had been opened for the first time and would never again be so firmly shut.

Immediately after the war, all the Rosies were expected to pull off their overalls, tie on aprons, and begin tidying up their kitchens. The proportion of women in the job force did in fact ebb, to 30 percent at the start of the postwar era. Only then, instead of staying at home, more and more older women began looking for jobs. The labor participation rate of white women edged up to 33 percent in 1950 and passed the wartime peak in the middle of the decade. The rise confounded government economists, who consistently had predicted that women would return to their prewar patterns. (The Bureau of Labor Statistics puffed along behind women for the next few decades, publishing a set of projections in 1973 that predicted a participation rate for women in 1980 that was actually exceeded in 1974.)

Why did so many women want to work? They did because of an unprecedented shift in labor demand. Traditionally, most women who worked had been single because married women were still needed in the home. In preindustrial America, when the families were productive units, women were functioning parts of a home-based economy. Only in the modern world did it become possible for women to achieve economic independence by working outside the family. As economists see it, the loss of women from the home threatened the family. So the "solution" in postindustrial society was to allow unmarried women to work in certain highly specialized jobs. Once they married, though, they were expected to return to the home and the traditional nuclear family.

The specialized jobs that women took most often were rigidly sex-typed. Women were teachers, hairdressers, clerks, sales workers, dressmakers, maids, nurses, librarians, telephone operators, housekeepers, and secretaries. This was the Pink Ghetto. Many of these jobs were left to women simply because the requirement of brute masculine strength was not required. Usually, the pay was low and unemployment high—possibly another effect of occupational segregation. There was also a high degree of substitution between younger and older female workers; employers did not much care if a seamstress was 25 or 55. (A similar lack of distinction was unthinkable in most male jobs.) By the end of World War II, as Valerie Kincade Oppenheimer of UCLA has shown, women had all but monopolized entire fields like nursing and elementary-school teaching and four out of five women were working in jobs sex-labeled as "women's work."

After World War II, though, America began a historic changeover from a manufacturing economy to a service economy. Between 1950 and 1974, only 1 million out of the 27 million new jobs created were in goods-related industries like steel, agriculture, mining, and construction, all of which largely employed men. Instead, the fields in which women outnumbered men—finance, insurance, services, real estate, and teaching—were thriving. The result was that demand for female workers was far outstripping demand for male workers.

Consider now what was simultaneously happening to the supply of female workers. As the demand swelled, the number of young single women—hitherto the slender backbone of the service economy—was declining by nearly 50 percent because of the small number born during the years of the Depression. Furthermore, many of these women had effectively taken themselves off the labor market by becoming pregnant with the baby-boom children. It was a roundelay: elementary schools desperately needed teachers to handle the growing hordes of baby-boom children—but the women who were needed to teach were at home making more baby-boom children. Other factors such as the rise in female college attendance and the lowered age of marriage also contributed to reducing the supply of young, single female workers. By 1960, according to even the lowest estimate of demand that year, the supply of young women was only one-third of the number needed by the booming economy.

The jobs had to be filled. Once the supply of young single women was exhausted, employers began to look to a less preferred group—older women. For the first time ever in peacetime, women over 35 began to be drawn into the work force by the glowing economic opportunities they saw there. Since most female jobs were not in careerist paths, they were able to take the jobs that younger women had entered in the past. As Richard Easterlin has pointed out, the economy adjusted in different ways to the scarcity of male and female workers. If men were in short supply, their salaries went up. But if women were in short supply, their salaries stayed low and the difference was made up by reaching out to older women. In the decade of the fifties, for instance, the proportion of married women 35–44 in the work force increased 27 percent. The historic pattern had been reversed: women were now working both before marriage and, for the first time, after it as well.

What is most remarkable about this extraordinary change in the living and working habits of women is that it came about in the absence of support systems like organized feminism. Indeed, all through the years of baby-boom fertility, the Procreation Ethic continued to glorify home and hearth. Addressing the class of 1955 at Smith College, none other than Adlai Stevenson told the seniors that their job was to "influence us, man and boy" and urged them to "restore valid, meaningful purpose to life in your home," keeping their husbands "truly purposeful." *Newsweek* stressed that the proper corporate wife needed to understand the tensions of her husband's job. Women's magazines consistently portrayed the most fulfilled women as those who had made their careers at home.

Most women did serve the Procreation Ethic. But perhaps the greatest unreported story of the fifties is how many of the mothers of the baby boom did not. The revolution in women's employment was started by the very women who supposedly were devoted to domesticity. During the fifties, the percentage of working mothers with school-age children *rose* from 25 percent to 40 percent. Two-thirds of the Radcliffe Class of 1954 either went back to work or tried to after the birth of their first children. When Princeton's Class of '54 came to its twenty-fifth reunion in 1979, the university's sociologists were amazed to discover that, although two-thirds of the wives of the Princeton men were homemakers, one-third of them had jobs and one-fifth of them worked full time. All in all, while the number of men in the labor force increased 12 percent between 1947 and 1962, the number of women gained 45 percent and the number of married women working jumped an amazing 97 percent.

After 1965, however, the first wave of baby boomers ended the shortage of young female workers. Now employers were able to turn again to younger women alone to staff the desks and counters of the service economy. In the sixties and seventies, older women started finding it harder to get jobs in the face of competition from the flood of younger baby-boom women. All of them, it seemed, wanted to work. The normally reserved Bureau of Labor Statistics groped for adjectives and settled on "phenomenal" to describe the surge in employment of baby-boom women. Between 1960 and 1979, the proportion of women 25–34 working grew from 36 percent to 64 percent—all the more remarkable since the majority of these women were married and many had children. Among women under 25, the change was even more dramatic. Fewer than half of the women born in the 1930s worked in their early twenties. But when the first baby-boom women born in 1946–50 crossed into their twenties, the proportion working leapfrogged to 58 percent. And by the time the younger baby boomers born in 1956–60 reached that age in 1980, no less than 69 percent of them were at work.

One reason so many baby-boom women were able to work during their twenties was because they had not yet married. That part of their experience, at least, was consistent with their mothers and grandmothers. But, unlike their mothers and grandmothers, they did not stop working when they married and had children. They remained in the work force in mounting numbers until nearly two-thirds of the 33 million baby-boom women in their twenties and thirties are now working.

The most unexpected gains have been made by the hitherto least employable women: young wives and young mothers. More than half of the nation's wives are working (compared to one-fourth in 1950) and earning a quarter of their families' incomes. Moreover, half of the working wives are mothers with children under eighteen. And most dramatically, the number of working mothers with children under six—traditionally the most homebound of all women—has nearly doubled since 1965 and tripled since 1950. Financial need, considered under the Procreation Ethic to be the only acceptable reason for a mother to work, no longer seemed relevant. Some studies have shown that the likelihood of a wife's employment *increases* with the income of her husband.

By working despite the fact of young children, the baby-boom mothers have redefined the nature of a woman's lifetime work experience. The old assumption that a woman would work only for a few years before marriage could no longer wash. Two out of every three women between 20 and 24 were working and half of the wives were. In the sixties and seventies, the number of married women working rose by 12 million and accounted

197

for nearly half of the total increase in the female labor force. They did it by leaving the home for the office, by taking full-time jobs instead of part-time jobs, and by staying in the same jobs longer. Opportunities in the economy, however, cannot solely explain why increasingly large numbers of baby-boom women continued to enter the labor force in the 1980s. Economic growth in the seventies was nothing like that of the fifties and sixties.

There must have been other forces working on the women of the boom generation. But which? Most explanations hold that the women's movement raised female consciousness sufficiently high to make them overcome domestic sex-typing. Women's lib undoubtedly did play some role in breaking down stereotypes. But the evidence, surprisingly, is the contrary. Feminism was not so much a cause of employment gains made by women in the sixties and seventies as a result. Studies made by sociologist Karen Oppenheim Mason and her colleagues at the University of Michigan show that the most profound changes in attitudes about women's sex roles began *before* women's liberation started receiving widespread media attention in about 1970.

Instead, Mason found that two other variables influenced women more. One was the simple fact of working itself. Working taught women more about sexism than Betty Friedan or Gloria Steinem ever could. (Most of the feminist leaders, not surprisingly, were older women from the generation that first paved the way before the boom generation arrived.) The women who were working carried home their convictions about their ability to perform equally with men. Attitudes, in other words, were adapting themselves to the fact of the working women, not vice versa.

The Michigan researchers also noticed that the biggest changes in women's attitudes came about after the late sixties. What was different then? The baby-boom generation had come of age. Furthermore, it was the generation of American women that had received more education than any other. Education always increases aspirations, and there was no reason to think that the women of the baby boom would be any different. Indeed, like their brothers, they, too, had the fact of their extraordinary promise drilled into them year after year while they were growing up. They had been richly educated and planned to use it. At the end of the seventies, married mothers

198

with some college were 20 percent more likely to be working than those mothers who had not finished high school, and the gap was growing.

That meant they had rearranged their priorities. Back in 1967, 44 percent of first-year college women had endorsed the personal goal of home and family. Ten years later, at the height of the baby boomers in college, only 20 percent of them did. Education was becoming the identifying field mark of an entire generation. We might have expected urban women to be more likely to work than suburban women, if only because the suburban women were more consumed in childrearing. Instead, suburban women were slightly more likely to work than their city sisters. Why? Because more suburban women have been to college. When Princeton's Class of 1973 returned for its fifth reunion, only 2 percent of the Princeton women classified themselves as "homemakers," while 22 percent were either doctors or lawyers.

It hardly needs to be added that the baby-boom women who were reshaping the workplace were doing the same to the marketplace. It was not just a question of making it tougher for daytime deliverymen to find anyone at home. Working wives with working husbands now account for more than half of all families. A two-career couple with a pooled income of $50,000 will spend its money far differently from a couple in which the husband alone brings in $50,000. Families with two earners typically spend more on household help (good for maids), less on home entertainment (bad for liquor), and more eating out (good for restaurants). Working couples also have fewer children and therefore more discretionary income. Working women also spend more on fashions and cosmetics than nonworking women, buying the kind of $200-$300 suits once worn in movies by Joan Crawford. Charles of the Ritz brought out Enjoli, "the eight-hour perfume for the 24-hour woman." Some entrepreneurs even started day-care services for pets abandoned during working hours by two-career couples.

By pooling their incomes, the working husbands and working wives of the baby boom have been able to overcome some of the economic difficulties that had pursued them. In the seventies, the country suffered through the deepest recession since the 1930s and the highest rates of inflation since World War II. But many of the baby-boom children were able even then to continue to achieve the affluence they had always enjoyed. Today almost one-half of the total family income in the country flows to homes where the wife is employed. And, according to Fabian Linden, an economist with the Conference Board, the working-wife household will soon be the dominant segment of the U.S. market.

This has meant an almost incredible rise in ability to buy the good life. No less than 77 percent of all upper-income families have at least two persons in the work force. With combined incomes of young college-educated couples frequently running in the $60,000 range, they have been able to buy not out of need but out of pleasure. These are the couples stepping up from Sears to Bloomingdale's, renting weekend cottages at the shore, driving BMWs, hiring full-time housekeepers, and submitting to everything from psychotherapy to tennis lessons. (In some instances, the desire of the baby-boom couples to keep up standards has led to some peculiar compromises. *Business Week* described a young couple with a combined income of $50,000 who owned half an airplane, belonged to two tennis clubs, took frequent ski vacations, spent $1000 a year on art—and lived in a $28,000 house.)

By going to work, the women of the baby boom have further widened the income gap in the United States. The traditional relationship between a husband's income and a wife's work reversed. Wives used to work to help bolster a husband's income. But the baby-boom women broke the link between need and work. Now the wives of relatively prosperous husbands began taking jobs. Employment of wives whose husbands earned more than $30,000 a year increased by 38 percent between 1967 and 1974, while the figure for those whose husbands earned between $2000 and $6000 nudged up only 11 percent. What's more, the well-off women joining the work force were also skimming off the best jobs. In both cases—going to work and getting better jobs—the difference was surely made by the superior education generally received by the prosperous wives of the boom generation.

We come now to the inevitable result of any revolution as sweeping as that experienced by young women in the past fifteen years. It is stress. Women who wanted the dignity and self-respect (not to mention financial independence) of a career discovered that they'd bought the whole farm: anxiety, ulcers, and all. The sheer dexterity of balancing husband, career, and children can be overwhelming. Two out of every three patients who seek psychological help in the United States are women. It might be argued that the women are actually not more troubled but rather just more likely to look for help. But it's also true that twice as many women as men are admitted to hospitals for depression and are twice as likely to use the two most popular tranquilizers, Valium and Librium. Four out of every five amphetamine prescriptions are written for women. Women in high-pressure vocations feel the most stress. Female doctors, for example, have the highest suicide rate among working women. The problems they and other working women face include the pressures of keeping their families happy while pursuing their own careers, and somehow avoiding the insidious guilt about their own achievements that sometimes plagues successful women. Even among the women of Princeton's Class of 1973, of whom more than one-third chose not to take their husband's names, more than two-thirds admitted that, even though they and their husbands were equally pursuing careers, they wound up cooking every night.

One of the paradoxes of these times is that, the more the baby-boom women have sought to improve their position by working, the more the competition of their own kind has hurt them and resulted in less overall improvement. On the face of it, this contradicts the evidence. There are now three times as many women enrolled in law school and double the number of female judges and lawyers. Since 1960, we have doubled the percentage of women doctors from 6 percent to 13 percent. At the same time, however, the enormous influx of women into traditional entry-level jobs has preserved the income and vocational inequities of the Pink Ghetto. Half of all working women still work in job categories that are 70 percent held by females; a quarter of working women work in jobs that are 95 percent filled by women. In 1967, a woman earned on the average about 67 percent of what a man made. By 1980, women were earning less than 60 percent of what men made. The average woman with four years of college education still earns less than an average male high-school dropout. One woman in four earns an annual income of less than $4000, but only one man in eighteen suffers that fate. In other words, while many women have improved their situations at one end of the socioeconomic scale, many millions more have entered the labor market at the other end and depressed the average.

In the end, what the country had seen was a twenty-five-year surge in which the American working force was remade by women. Of the 43 million women now working—more than half of the adult female population—some 9 million of them, mostly baby boomers, joined in the 1970s. It is no longer worth asking, as we once did, whether these events amounted to a real social change or just a transitory fad involving a small percentage of women. When historians of the future look back on our times, one event that will surely stand out will be the large numbers of baby-boom women who made working part of their lifelong experience. Rosie the Riveter may have thought that she was going to work to preserve the traditional American Way of Life, but she really subverted it. Rosie's daughters became the first generation of American women to spend their adult years not at home but on the job. That, in fact, has given the baby boom one more unique distinction: it was the last generation to be reared by housewives.

Chapter 14

THE MARRIAGE SQUEEZE

In 1979 a woman identified only as "Mrs. X" wrote to *The New York Times* about a dilemma in her life. She had just learned that her husband had been carrying on an affair for two years. Not an unusual problem, she admitted, but she was confused about what to do. In an earlier time her role would have been clear: she might have taken to bed, or had fainting spells, but she would also have put up a Brave Front and tried to carry on stoutly as if nothing had happened. "I would have kept my home, my shell, my outer battlements whole. And society would not only have approved, it would have frowned if I had chosen otherwise."

Now, however, the prevailing winds have shifted. Society not only condones divorce, it practically demands it. "When we see a home still standing after a marriage of 15 or 20 years, do we smile on the man and woman inside and thank them for adding to the general sum of social stability?" Mrs. X asked. "Not at all. We ask what wrenching inner compromises they have made." Society was transmitting a different set of signals to her. It did not matter if she summoned up forgiveness for her husband or simply remained a victim. Her inner integrity and self-worth, she was told, insisted that she rid herself of a corrupted marriage. "Only a short time ago society would, for the sake of its stability, have applied sanctions to keep my home together," Mrs. X concluded. "Now it has dropped its sanctions and no longer seems to think that it has any stake in marriage at all."

Marriage was the next institution entered by—and altered by—the baby boom on its journey to maturity. And, like every other institution before it, marriage was not easily able to assimilate this giant generation. In the space of a decade, the baby boom changed all of our rules about courtship and marriage. In doing so, it came precariously close to balkanizing our basic unit of cultural transmission: the family. The baby boomers married less often, married later, and had fewer children, divorced more often, left more children in single-parent homes, and have done more to undermine kinship than any previous generation. We have had to create an entire new vocabulary to describe the new, transitory relationships that are replacing the family—cohabitants, mates, "blended" or "reconstituted" families, and so on. In short, the boom generation was doing all it could to break the hold of the family over the individual.

THE SINGLES SOCIETY

The changes brought by the baby-boom generation actually began before married life with the creation of a new life-style: swinging singles. In 1964, with the kind of brilliant timing he never could have predicted, a lonesome Navy ensign named Michael O'Harro started in Washington, D.C., what is credited as the country's first singles bar. That same year, happily for O'Harro, the first wave of baby boomers was turning 18 and leaving their parents' homes faster than any generation before them.

The baby-boom kids themselves could not wait to get out. In 1904, the average age of departure of men from their parents' homes was 23. By 1970, the average male was leaving home at 19. Women, too, were discovering a new and increasingly important stage in their life cycle: Where they once went straight from their parents' home to their own families, now they were living on their own in colleges and cities. For the first time, then, large numbers of young, single adults had both the will and the financial means to make their own lives.

For the parents who had conceived and raised the children of the baby boom, this was one of the saddest moments of their lives. They were being left to preside over the biggest empty nest in history. Poignantly, a sample of baby-boom parents later surveyed by the University of Michigan singled out the launching of their children as the single most unhappy period of their lives. They had given so much to make their children independent and strong; now the penalty of their success was an enormous, generationwide sense of emotional loss.

For entrepreneurs like O'Harro, however, the arrival of the first generation of swinging singles was a bonanza. As they congregated in the cities, the process of sorting out sexual and marital problems began on a grand scale. From 1960 until 1978, the number of 14–24-year-olds living alone zoomed sevenfold from 234,000 to 1.6 million. And they were getting acquainted on production lines. There was O'Harro's in Washington and Friday's and Mr. Laff's in New York. In Boston, a group of students put potential dates on computers and called it Operation Match. In California, where the largest numbers of singles were swarming, life became a Marina Del Rey landscape, filled with singles bars, singles apartment complexes, singles magazines, and singles tour groups. Some were looking for Mr. Goodbar; others were just looking for a good time. In a sense the singles ghettos in the cities were not that much different from the youth ghettos in the colleges: removed from the proximity and therefore scrutiny of the older generation, they were free to develop values that placed them outside the adult mainstream. But while the organizing principle of the collegiate ghettos was, at least ostensibly, education, the organizing principle of the singles ghettos was sex.

The baby boomers were obsessed with sex, and because they were and because there were so many of them, the country became obsessed with sex as well. They were the first generation to *talk* about sex—obsessively, continually, sometimes neurotically. Every generation discovers its libido in adolescence. When the baby boom found its sexuality in the sixties and seventies, its astonishing discovery could hardly be kept a secret any more than its preoccupation with coonskin caps and rock and roll could be ignored in earlier times. "Life was free and so was sex," Sara Davidson wrote of Berkeley in *Loose Change*. "Mmmmmmmmmm sex, the ripe scent percolated in the air." Unlike the weather, people were both talking about it and doing something about it. The surveys said so. One national sample showed that the percentage of unmarried teenage women who were sexually active increased by one-third from 1971 to 1976, from 27 percent to 35 percent. In a Johns Hopkins poll the number of women 15–19 who said they were sexually experienced went from 30 percent in 1971 to 41 percent in

1978. The Urban Institute predicted that, while about 64 percent of females born in 1950 engaged in intercourse before the age of 20, some 90 percent of those born in 1962, near the end of the boom, would do so by 1982.

But if sex was a recreational sport to the baby boomers, it was something altogether different to other generations. The experience that made him decide to write about sex in America, Gay Talese said, was his first visit to a Manhattan massage parlor:

> there were young women in jeans—girls of the Woodstock generation—and a young man behind the desk who looked like a rock musician. Then there were the customers. Men in suits and ties, men 35 to 55 years old, middle-class men like myself. The young people were there to service the erotic needs of the older men. They were capitalizing on the older generation's inhibitions. But it was more than that. The young women were really teaching sexual freedom, a style they themselves had discovered, and they were teaching it to their fathers' generation.

These changes in sexual habits—or at least in the willingness to talk about them—has a dimension not often appreciated by the generations who thought they missed out. Pressures to perform sexually have increased on college campuses to the extent that therapists are overwhelmed by students reporting sexual dysfunction of every kind. Joyce Maynard recalled her first semester at Yale as a sort of sexual supermarket in which everyone was shopping. "The scarlet letter these days," she concluded, "isn't 'A' but 'V.'" Men, in turn, were feeling pressures from women who for the first time were insisting on their right to sexual fulfillment as well. The carnival doubtlessly produced much sexual sophistication but little intimacy. Indeed, many therapists on college campuses believe that the problem of lack of intimacy in sex has caused sexual dysfunction. The error of the baby boomer was believing that sex can satisfy without commitment. Their expectations were high but not all of them were willing to make the commitment necessary to make it work.

Scholars may be arguing one hundred years from now about whether the baby boomers really had as much sex as they seemed to (and, likewise, about whether their parents were as chaste as they seemed). Researchers like Phillips Cutright have recently argued that the much-discussed rise in teenage sexuality is bogus, a media "discovery" in our times of a historical fact like hunger or bigotry that has always existed.

In any case, the most important thing may be not that unmarried people were having sex but how they were doing it. They were living together without benefit of clergy, or even gift china, in what sociologists called "trial marriages." Some were short, others were long, most led eventually to marriage itself. But it was a permanent change. Cohabitation had become a fixed feature of love and marriage.

Before the baby boomers came along, for example, the only image of an unmarried couple was likely to be that of a wealthy older woman, often a widow, living with a younger man. If society did not condone them, it at least gave them a genial wink. What was there to worry about? If the woman was past menopause, she would not produce an illegitimate child—the taboo against which, after all, lay at the heart of society's interdiction against cohabitation.

But now, armed with the pill and liberalized abortion laws (which they had vigorously campaigned for), the men and women of the baby boom faced a greatly reduced chance of having a child out of wedlock if they lived together. (Most illegitimate births, as mentioned earlier, resulted from teenagers who were not living together.) As the baby boomers came of age, the number of unmarried couples living together in the United States doubled in just ten years to well over a million (or 2 percent of all couples). The sharpest change was among cohabiting couples under 25, who increased ninefold after 1970. The Census Bureau, to be sure, rather skittishly makes no assumptions about *why* people live together and has pointed out that "non-related persons of the opposite sex" can also be non-romantic roommates or lodgers. If anything, the figure of one million cohabiting couples underestimates the real change that has taken place in life-styles. We may have one million couples living together at *any one time*—but cohabitation is a high-mobility state. Individuals move in and out of it frequently. Thus, many millions more young people may spend at least some times of their life living out of wedlock with someone else and, among the most recent baby-boom cohorts, the numbers of sometime cohabitants may be approaching a majority.

Even if the Census Bureau still persists in placing cohabitating couples in its "non-family" category, other segments of society have moved quickly to recognize the new institution. The language itself is adjusting. Maternity wards now include provisions for hospital visits not by "husbands" but by a "significant other" person—as in, "How's your Significant Other?" The Ford Foundation sends invitations to addressees and "a meaningful associate." Airlines have changed the "family fare" to the "company fare." Phrases like "spouse equivalent" and "domestic associate" and "current companion" have been lofted like hot-air balloons on the winds of change. The least euphonious addition to the language, however, is not "your special friend" but "your marvin," honoring Lee Marvin's celebrated "palimony" case.

Demographers at the Census Bureau cast their eyes over the most marriageable generation in history. In 1946, the parents of the baby boom made what was then a record 2,291,000 marriages. After dropping from the postwar peak, the number of marriages began to rise again in the late sixties and early seventies as the baby boom entered the marriage-prone years. In 1973, the total of 2,284,000 marriages approached the 1946 record. But the following years, even as millions of more baby-boom children continued to grow up, the number of marriages dropped off significantly for the first time since World War II. In 1979, the record that had lasted 33 years was finally broken when the children of the baby boom made 2,317,000 marriages. But marriage rates were continuing to drop off—down 22 percent nationally between 1970 and 1977 and, in California, the decline was an even more drastic 34 percent.

In addition to marrying less than their parents, the baby boomers were also marrying later. Previously, the median age at which women married had remained relatively stable for a century. High during the 1900s and again during the 1930s, the median ages of marriage had slowly dropped to the all-time low in 1956 of 20.1 for women and 22.5 for men. Since the mid-fifties, however, the ages of marriage have been edging up and baby-boom men and women are marrying a full eighteen months later than their counterparts a generation earlier. (In 1979, it was 24.4 for men and 22.1 for women.)

This was a wholesale retreat from the altar. Traditionally, a woman was most likely to marry between the ages of 20 and 24. In 1960, seven out of every ten women in those ages were married. But by 1979, only half were married in the same ages. During the sixties, as the baby boomers were transforming the marital status of the younger 20–24-year-olds, women in their late twenties were still marrying at the usual rates. But then after 1970, as the baby-boom women moved into the older group, the proportion of unmarried women 25–29 doubled in a decade. Among college graduates, the marriage bust was most striking. When Princeton's Class of 1971 returned for its fifth reunion, fewer than half of them, men and women, had married.

The fact that the baby boomers were taking so long to get married did not necessarily mean that they were following the advice of Linda Ronstadt's "I Never Will Marry." But the evidence is that, if only because delaying limits one's options, a substantial number of baby boomers will remain single the rest of their lives. It will not be the first time. During the Depression, 9 percent of that cohort of middle-aged women never married. The proportion dropped to an all-time low of 4 percent for the baby boom's mothers.

Society has necessarily become more supportive of unmarried people, especially women. Back in 1957, when the Procreation Ethic was in full power, a University of Michigan poll asked Americans what they would think of someone who had decided he or she would never marry. Most of the answers indicated that the person would be thought of as sick, asocial, or selfish. By 1976, however, the opinions had flip-flopped. The baby boom's men and women were especially supportive of the unmarried person and a minority said that they would be *positively* impressed with someone deciding to remain single. (Polled again 19 years later, the women in the 1957 group were still unsympathetic to single people—a fact that suggests that this attitudinal shift was carried by changing cohorts, not by changing times.)

Now, with an enormous influx into the labor force of 4.6 million men and 3.3 million women *who have never married*, it is hard to imagine that social pressures will ever again so strongly compel Americans to marry. If the present unmarried group of baby-boom women continues to marry off at the rate of previous generations, as many as 9 percent of them will remain single for the rest of their lives, twice the level for those women presently in middle age. In the rest of this century we will have more bachelors and spinsters (the words now have an outdated and even cruel ring) than ever before in our history.

Why was there a marriage bust? What was the link between the men and women of the baby boom and their grandparents in the Depression thirty years earlier that led both generations away from marriage? This is a topic of much academic speculation, because of its importance to fertility. The median age of marriage and the marriage rate are intimately tied to fertility rates. To explain why Americans married early in the fifties is to close in on the reasons for the baby boom itself. To know why the baby-boom children have done the opposite is to understand the fertility trends that will shape this country for the rest of the century.

The marriage bust began with the marriage squeeze. Unlike fertility decisions made by individuals, marriage decisions have a marketplace dimension. That is, they depend on supply and demand in the larger population. The marriage market, in turn, is shaped by fluctuations in the birthrate twenty years earlier. We can best understand the marriage squeeze as a result of the fact that women typically marry men several years older than they are. For the supply of available men to equal the demand of women, though, the cohort of slightly older men must be the same size as the cohort of slightly younger women. But that, as the boom women learned, depends on past birthrates. The first large cohort of baby-boom women born in 1946 and 1947 reached the marriageable ages in 1966 and 1967. Their prime market of potential marriage partners would be those men born during the last years of World War II. But those cohorts were considerably smaller than the baby-boom cohorts—up to 35 percent smaller. The scarcity of men gave older men an advantage in the marriage market, but the surplus of women disadvantaged baby-boom women. They could wait and hope to find a husband in the diminishing crowd of men—or they could change their market and marry men their own age or younger (which many did). Or, finally, they could withdraw from the marriage market altogether—a solution taken by an increasingly larger number of women today.

The marriage squeeze can explain some but not all of the marriage bust. Other forces were operating on the baby boomers to inhibit marriage. The one that we must inevitably return to is the one that has shaped so much of the boom generation's history: its size.

We have already seen how the masses of baby boomers disadvantaged an entire generation in the job market. Compared to the Good Times Generation before it, the baby boom was the surplus generation: it suffered from overcrowding and overcompetition and wound up with relatively lower wages, reduced promotion opportunities, and higher unemployment. Starting with that fact, among others, Richard Easterlin and his colleagues at the University of Pennsylvania fashioned an ingenious "relative income" hypothesis that related the size of a cohort to its marital history, its fertility, and, for that matter, the entire range of its lifetime experience.

Easterlin began by asserting that the likelihood of young men and women marrying and having children depends on their feeling of relative well-being. If young men and women find it easy to make money and to establish homes in the style they want, then they feel confident enough and optimistic enough about the future to marry and have children. But if they find it hard to earn enough money to equal their aspirations, they are discouraged and are likely to defer marriage and children. And what is the critical determinant of their feeling of well-being? It is the relative size of the generation they were born in. When young adults grow up in a small generation, they are in short supply in the labor market and their employment opportunities improve. They are free to step into the footsteps left by a larger generation which would have already created the college classrooms, and jobs, and opportunities necessary for advancement. The small generation, then, is encouraged to settle down and begin families. The large generation, on the other hand, is disadvantaged by its size. It must fight its way into shrinking markets and diminishing opportunities. Its feeling of well-being deteriorates and it is reluctant to start its families. Thus, in both cases, the critical difference is supplied by the relative size of the generation.

What is the record of our recent history? The Good Times Generation was born during the years of low fertility in the 1930s. As it grew up, the fact of its small size benefited every individual in it: they had more room to breathe, compete, and flourish. Their generation was like a row of lettuce seedlings that grows fastest once thinned. The Good Times Generation did not feel the stresses of competing for schools, jobs, and meals. It developed relatively modest aspirations during the trials of the Depression and World War II. But then it came of marriageable age during the capitalistic orgy of the fifties. Short in supply, it found markets booming, salaries growing, and more demand for its labor than anyone could have dreamed. No wonder, then, they felt confident and secure enough to marry at a record pace and begin their families.

But what of the boom babies? They grew up plentifully during the fifties and formed their career and consumption aspirations by observing the prosperity of their parents. Then they started stumbling over one another. Schools were crowded, colleges hard to get into, and jobs even harder to find. Comparing themselves to their parents, they felt cheated and even betrayed. Their feeling of well-being plummeted. They were inhibited and defeated by a world glutted with baby boomers. And the more difficult it became for them to find jobs and settle down, the longer they delayed their entry into marriage and family.

That, in its simplest form, is the Easterlin hypothesis. Its strength and appeal lie in its aesthetic elegance and parsimony as an example of academic model-building. Yet it is also the object of the most furiously contested debate in demography today. The reason is that, in addition to proposing an explanation for the last half-century of American marriage and fertility, it also suggests a theory of the future. In Easterlin's model, cohorts wax and wane like the moon. Large cohorts, dispirited by the pressure of numbers, will inevitably produce small numbers of children. Small generations, on the other hand, will be emboldened by their myriad opportunities and begin to marry early and produce large numbers of children.

The empirical evidence behind Easterlin's theory is striking. For example, women born during the five Depression years of lowest fertility, 1933–37, are the same women who grew up to record the highest fertility during the baby boom. Thus the generations ride a seesaw from small to large and from large to small.

Other characteristics of the baby boom are just as prominent but are harder to relate directly to the marriage bust. The more education a person receives, for example, the less likely he or she is to marry early. One in every four people of marriageable age now will complete college, nearly twice as many as the proportion two decades ago. As more and more young women go to work, they are acquiring the financial security they could once obtain only through marriage. (If Mary Tyler Moore could be an unmarried career woman, why couldn't they?) Cohabition has further encroached on some benefits previously exclusive to marriage—namely, companionship, support, and sex. The widespread availability of contraception and abortion has also reduced what was once a notorious cause of early marriage—the shotgun wedding.

Some baby boomers were scared off marriage after witnessing the example set by their parents. Statistically, at least, those marriages formed after World War II by the parents of the baby boomers were among the most successful and stable in history. The baby-boom parents married earlier and stayed together longer and more often. But in those days the divorce statistics did not necessarily reflect the number of couples who stayed together "for the sake of the children." As one baby-boom writer, Paula Cizmar, remembered, some parents paid an inner price for their outward allegiance to the Procreation Ethic:

> My generation saw marriages that were little more than compromises between two warring parties; marriages that were filled with dashed expectations for husbands and indentured servitude for wives; marriages that were brought on by pregnancy in a pre-marital sex, pre-abortion morality; marriages that existed for no reason other than they fit into the expected birthday/high school prom/wedding/baby shower/funeral templet. It was ugly to look at.

DIVORCE, BABY-BOOM STYLE

In the mid-1970s, something funny happened to divorce. People were laughing about it. A comic strip named *Splitsville* began lampooning newly separated couples. Blondie and Dagwood were giving one another funny looks . . . would they be next in divorce court? Divorced characters began showing up on prime-time television more often than cowboys used to. Rhoda and Phyllis had dumped their husbands. Maude was threatening to. Meredith Baxter Birney had split from her guy on *Family* and Stockard Channing tried a short-lived sitcom, *Just Friends,* that seemed to be about nothing but her divorce. One short-lived show about the combat zone of modern marriage, *United States,* hovered between situation comedy and situation tragedy. We had come a long way, it seemed, from the day when the network had refused to allow Mary Tyler

213

Moore's production company to present her as a newly divorced woman instead of the bachelor girl she ultimately became.

People were laughing about divorce and looking to television for cultural clues because they were uncomfortable. Out there in the real world divorce was no joke. In the 1970s, as the baby boomers married and began families, the national divorce rate doubled. In the youngest age groups filled entirely by baby boomers, the divorce rate tripled in a decade. Of all marriages contracted in 1980 by young baby-boom couples, an estimated 40 percent will end in divorce. And if they should choose to remarry, the chances of that marriage surviving are worse than for the first. Millions of children, meanwhile, were growing up in a disorienting world where daddies and mommies lived across town and strange men and women were showing up for breakfast.

The divorce epidemic was carried almost exclusively by the baby boom. Young people before the boom couples arrived did not suffer from it so grievously, nor do older couples now. To put it in perspective, before 1940 the divorce rate in the country had languished as low as 2 divorces per 1000 marriages. In 1946, as hasty war marriages confronted the realities of peacetime, the rate doubled to a then all-time high of 4.3. That record was not equaled for the next twenty-seven years. Couples who married from 1946 through 1958 enjoyed tranquil unions, at least on the face of it. By 1960, the divorce rate had ebbed to the prewar level of 2.2.

Then the divorce rate turned upward. Demographers were not altogether surprised. Early age of marriage is perhaps the best predictor of divorce, and during the forties and fifties couples had married younger than ever. The men and women leading the divorce trend in the sixties did prove to be older couples who were splitting up, many of them over the age of 45.

The baby-boom couples did not really have a chance to start getting divorced until the late sixties and early seventies. But when they did, they sucked the wind out of all the old ideas about the immutability of marriage. In 1968, both the number of divorces and the divorce rate jumped by 12 percent. In 1969, the number of divorces passed the all-time high of 1946. In 1973, the divorce rate record of 1946 was surpassed. In 1975, the number of divorces passed one million for the first time. By the end of the seventies, America had twice as many divorced persons in its borders as in 1970 and a divorce rate of 5.1 per thousand marriages, one of the highest divorce rates in the world.

Who was getting divorced? The rates were up in every age group. But by far the most dramatic increases—three of every four divorces overall—were in the age groups of the twenties and thirties, precisely those ages that had been entered by the baby boom during the seventies. The earlier pattern had been reversed. Instead of the older women leading the way, now the younger women were (an almost eerily similar process had brought women into the work force). These were not tired suburban couples finally filing for divorce after sending all their children off. These were young couples divorcing before they even had a chance to get a seven-year itch. The divorce rate has quadrupled for couples under 30 since 1960 and increased 50 percent for couples under 25 in just seven years. One demographer, Robert Michael of Stanford, has calculated that while men and women in their twenties comprised only about 20 percent of the population, they contributed 60 percent of the growth in the divorce rate in the sixties and early seventies. What was causing the divorce plague? Was it the bad economy? Younger couples just starting their marriages would presumably be more vulnerable to economic strain. A more relevant factor, perhaps, is that the rise in divorce closely paralleled the increase in women working. Working frees women from economic dependency on men. In premodern times, when the family was the basic unit in the economy, the man was both the husband and the employer. He controlled production, income, education, housing, savings, and even the welfare of the grandparents. The women of the baby boom, however, were the first generation to escape what was previously the primary economic basis for marriage—the security provided by a working husband. If a marriage came under pressure, they no longer had to accept it. Now they had the economic power to use the option of divorce to solve their problems. Women who enter the workplace also enjoy new confidence, new friends, and an expanded view of their place in the world that does not necessarily include their spouse. For working women, the pain of divorce is eased by their new horizons as well as their income.

This interpretation of the divorce rise may seem overly

deterministic or even cynical but is supported by considerable evidence. At Syracuse University, sociologists have found that women about to separate or divorce are more likely to be working than other women and typically have incomes 20 percent higher than women who remain married. Similarly, the National Longitudinal Survey of Mature Women undertaken at Ohio State found that the higher a woman's income in relation to the total income of her family, the more likely she was to seek a divorce. These women form high expectations for marriage and have the psychological (as well as economic) independence to end it when it disappoints. Writers and moviemakers have intuitively known this all along. In Michael Weller's play about the post-Woodstock era, *Loose Ends*, the ex-wife tells her ex-husband just how she feels about working as a photographer:

> You don't understand something, Paul. It's important to me to make my own living. I'm proud, too, you know. I never liked taking money from you. I never liked taking money from my family. Now I don't have to and it feels good. Real good.

Hollywood studies of marital breakups almost invariably link the woman's newfound confidence to her work. It was as if all the marriages made under the old order were being tested by the changing roles of women: some adapted and survived, others did not.

The departure of women from the home was not the only stress tugging on baby-boom marriages during this period. Those marriages made in the late 1960s and early 1970s suffered during their earliest years from a variety of unusual strains. Wartime mobilization historically raises the divorce rate, and Vietnam was presumably no different. The economic decline from the sixties through the seventies hurt marriages made at a time of higher expectations. (One study, for example, has shown that the chances for divorce are greater if the husband does less well, relatively, than the wife's father.) The increase in teenage pregnancy among the youngest baby-boom women added another layer of complexity to marriage. Almost one out of four newlywed women under 25 in 1972-76 had either given birth to a child before marriage or was pregnant arriving at the altar—meaning that nearly one-quarter of all newlyweds began their married life in a situation of some stress. Divorce laws were also liberalized during the baby boom generation's earliest years of marriage, but the relaxing of legal and social constraints against divorce were less a cause of marital dissolution, I think, than a result of it. Attitudes, as always, were playing catch-up to real behavior.

The forces I have been describing so far have all been essentially external. That is, they have been outside social and economic changes that have acted on the individuals of the boom generation. Many of them undoubtedly have shaped this generation's marital experience. Yet I want to add here one further consideration. It is the possibility that within the particular psychology of the baby boom— itself a product of its turbulent history—lies the essence of its problems.

Erik Erikson has argued that the critical problem facing an individual in his or her twenties is developing the capacity for intimacy—that is, "to commit himself to concrete affiliations and partnership and to develop the ethical strength to abide by such commitments." The boom generation has not had an easy time with commitment. It was able to commit itself politically and socially all right, to everything from Hula-Hoops to the protest movements. Those commitments were made ensemble, *as a mass*. The baby boom's strongest and most effective statements have always come through the larger group. Only in the aggregate could they find the necessary intensity and emotion to fulfill their needs. But the baby boomers, so decisive and passionate as a generation, were practically paralyzed on the individual level. It was as if life in the here and now could not deliver on the expectations they had always had for it. Why should one limit one's prospects when the choices still ahead were so thrilling?

Loose Ends is a play that crystallizes the ambivalence the baby boomers have felt about intimacy. The young couple scrupulously respects each others' freedom and independence. At first, this was an exhilarating new world where they were free to determine for themselves what they felt about sex, fidelity, parents, children, and careers. But, as Michael Weller makes abundantly clear, they had lost something as well. They had kept their options open and their expectations high—but somehow it wasn't working. Here is how the husband, Paul, reacts in confusion

217

when confronting an emotion he was not prepared to feel, jealousy:

> We've always had this kind of an understanding, not like a formal thing, just we picked it up talking to each other that it'd be all right if we . . . in theory, that is, in theory it was O.K. if we, we weren't like exclusively tied down to each other, you know, if we were attracted to someone . . . and we didn't have to necessarily tell each other if we ever, unless we were afraid it was getting out of hand, like it was getting too serious and we couldn't handle it. But the thing is, we've never been unfaithful. Unfaithful. Funny how it comes back to words like that.

Weller is saying that life is somehow less satisfying and certainly less secure under the permissive ethos than it had been under the old, discredited standards of the parents. When the *Loose Ends* couple eventually divorces, it is not from lack of love. It is from lack of commitment.

But what made commitment so difficult for the baby boom? In Erikson's theory of the life cycle, a person cannot move on to the next stage unless he or she has satisfactorily resolved the conflicts of the previous one. Before facing the problems of marriage and intimacy, the baby boomers had to deal first with the *Sturm und Drang* of adolescence. In adolescence, the central problem of an individual—and by extension a generation—is that of ego-identity. Ego-identity, in Erikson's words, "is the accrued confidence that the inner sameness and continuity prepared in the past are matched by the sameness and continuity of one's meaning for others, as evidenced in the tangible promise of a career."

But what did the baby boomers encounter in adolescence? A culture being ripped up by its roots. How could they hope to reconcile the dreams of their past with the disillusioning present? Nothing made sense. This wasn't the way they were told it would be. It is not surprising, considering the discontinuities of their coming-of-age, that the baby boomers found that, like Biff in *Death of a Salesman*, "I just can't take hold, Mom, I can't take hold of some kind of a life."

Unsure of their identity, the baby boomers were emotional transients, hesitant to commit to others in intimate relationships. "We had the most prolonged adolescence of any generation," wrote novelist Lucian Truscott IV. "We were simply too alienated and hedonistic to grow up. We were emotional adolescents." The result, Erikson said, is that a youth without ego-identity "shies away from interpersonal intimacy or throws himself into acts of intimacy which are 'promiscuous' without true fusion or real self-abandon." Erikson wrote that sentence in 1967, but he might as well have been describing the college campuses, singles bars, and young marriages of the seventies. Sex was present—indeed, omnipresent—as in *Loose Ends*, where we first meet the archetypal baby-boom couple naked on a beach. But good sex was never the problem. That was easy. Intimacy was the problem.

Unable to give themselves unconditionally to others, the baby boomers began to look inward instead. As Erikson put it, "a fear of ego loss may lead to a deep sense of isolation and consequent self-absorption." The human-potential movements and narcissistic excesses of the "Me Decade" are now as familiar a sign of the seventies as divorce. If the boom babies could have instant gratification on television, why could they not in a marriage partner as well? Previous generations were taught that life is hard, sacrifice is necessary, and unhappiness a cross that sometimes must be borne. But the baby boomers were not willing to make the risky and often painful compromises their parents did. Just as they had great expectations for themselves, they had great expectations for their marriages. Life was too short to live with an unhappy marriage. If they could switch to another TV channel, why not switch husbands or wives? In fact, their satisfaction and sense of self-obligation practically demanded it. As Norman Ryder has pithily phrased it, frequent divorce is the understandable consequence of making the satisfaction of the individual the test of a good marriage. The burden of proof, he added, has shifted from what the individual can do for the family to what the family can do for the individual.

Like the shocks radiating from an earthquake, the consequences of the divorce boom have spread out erratically from the epicenter of the boom generation and have been registered in different ways by different people. Within the baby boom, we have created a cohort that is growing up divorced. The idea that the normal destiny of a man or a woman is to live within one family has been broken. These baby boomers have first families and second families and stepchildren and a whole new raft of relations with unfamiliar names. (New grandparents? Old grand-parents? Ex-brother-in-law? Ex-stepsister?) Moreover, the experience of divorce is not just something that the boom babies have during their twenties and thirties. It is a characteristic that they will carry with their cohort until old age. Very few people presently over 65 are divorced. In the future, millions of them will be—thereby further increasing the generational loneliness that is already a feature of old age, especially among women, who are less likely to remarry than men and tend to live longer.

The black women of the baby boom have been hit par-ticularly hard by the divorce boom. The ratio of divorced black women to married ones is twice that of whites. The probability of becoming poor increases markedly with marital disruption, for either race, but black women suffer a double whammy: they have the handicaps of both dis-crimination and divorce. The government now classifies more than one-half of all divorced black women as "poor" and 70 percent as "relatively poor." *Julia*, Diahann Carroll's groundbreaking TV series about a hap-pily divorced middle-class black woman, was about as realistic as *Wonder Woman*.

Divorce also cut off whole generations from the baby boom. At present, nearly half the children born to baby-boom parents are likely to spend some time living with only one parent before reaching the age of 18—a fact that surely will affect generational continuity. Then, too, some of the worst shocks were felt by the parents of the baby boomers adjusting to the divorces of their children. Theirs was the generation that had invested so much emo-tional capital in the idea of marriage. But now, as they neared old age, they would not be taken in by nuclear families like their own. Instead, they anxiously surveyed a deteriorating extended family. Their children were casting aside their families and, most painfully, their grandchil-dren. Like absentee fathers, the grandparents are being reduced to infrequent visitations with an entire generation of grandchildren, many of them out of reach and out of touch, living with ex-daughter-in-laws in distant cities.

When the generations divide, youth will know only youth; the aged will know only the aged. And, as always, the boom generation will know only itself.

Chapter 15

THE BABY BUST

Young women are gradually being imbued with the idea that marriage and motherhood are not to be their chief objects in life, or the sole methods of obtaining subsistence; ... that housekeeping is a sort of domestic slavery, and that it is best to remain unmarried until someone offers who has the means to gratify their educated tastes. ... If this view of the case is correct, the birth-rate will not only continue low in the United States compared to former years, but it will probably become lower.

—Dr. John S. Billings, writing in *Forum*
(now *Current History*), June 1893

Of all the surprises fathered by the baby boom, perhaps the most utterly confounding was the baby bust. Without warning, and at a time when such a turnabout was least expected, American parents began turning off their fertility. They were having fewer children. In fact, they were having millions and millions fewer children. The bust came with a swiftness that, like the boom before it, left demographers floundering in its wake, not to mention baby-food manufacturers, pediatricians, educators, and parents. The bust, moreover, was not happening to all women. It was happening to the young women of the baby boom. As much as any change of such wide magnitude can be laid to a single generation, the baby bust is the exclusive creation of the baby boom. It was the boom's ironic joke on the future: the largest generation we had produced would not return the investment. It was not replacing itself.

As recently as 1957, births had hit the all-time high of 4.3 million. For the next seven years, they cooled only slightly to just over 4 million. Then, as the first cohorts of baby-boom women were entering their prime years of childbearing, the bottom dropped out of fertility. In 1965, births dropped below 4 million for the first time in twelve years. Over the next fifteen years, virtually every measure of fertility dropped to the lowest levels in American history. By 1980, when the baby boomers dominated the childbearing years, they had transformed family life. Families of the type that once had two or three children were having one or two or possibly none at all. The number of children under 15 was plummeting at a time when virtually everyone thought it would be increasing. The Procreation Ethic had been abandoned.

We are still trying to sort out what the baby-boom parents have done and how they did it—a task that will yield no final answer until the last baby boomers complete their childbearing around the year 2000. The subject has ignited a lively scholarly controversy as well as some morbid curiosity on the part of baby boomers. "The best of our generation," says someone in *Loose Change*, "and we're not reproducing." What caused the boom generation not to reproduce itself? The pill? Inflation? The women's movement? Or was it a case of this giant generation, whether reluctant or unable to be assimilated into the adult culture, drawing the line at parenthood in order to cling to its youth? None of these suggestions alone suffices to explain what was happening. Somewhere between Dr. Spock and Dr. Leary, between Silly Putty and Acapulco Gold, between getting married and getting divorced, something happened to turn the baby boom against the Procreation Ethic. Nowhere was the break between the parents of the baby boom and the baby boomers themselves more clear than over the matter of childbearing. The baby-boom generation, like any other social class or ethnic group, was once again drawing up its own norms and going its distinct way.

Back in the 1950s and early 1960s, when many businessmen and economists were convinced that population growth generated the necessary energy for prosperity, the idea of a baby bust was unthinkable. In 1959, *Fortune* speculated without undue alarm that births might reach five million yearly by 1970. The director of the Census Bureau noted that while each new baby added a mouth to feed, he or she also added two more producing hands, hands that would add to the flood of goods and services in the American economy. The 1964 New York World's

Fair opened with a 45-foot map of the United States blinking like a Christmas tree as lights flashed for births and deaths in every state. When the Census clock officially clicked off its 200 millionth American on November 20, 1967, many Americans felt a swelling of national pride.

At the same time, however, some alarming reports were coming in from academe on the negative effects of crowding. An ethologist named John Calhoun had decided to test Malthus by allowing rats to breed out of control in a contained pen in Rockville, Maryland. It turned out to be a rodent holocaust. The rats became severely pathological: some became aggressive and cannibalistic; others became bisexual and sadistic. Female rats were unable to carry pregnancies, and the rearing of their young was disrupted. It sounded like a disco, but Calhoun called the eventual social breakdown a "behavioral sink" and warned that his study might "contribute to the making of value judgments about analogous problems confronting the human species." (His point was not lost on Manhattan residents who endure population densities of up to 400,000 per square mile during working hours.)

The baby boom, of course, grew up as the overcrowded generation that waited in line to get into the bathroom, to get into rock concerts, to get into college, and to get jobs. (It is not clear that the baby boomers felt the same negative effects as the Swedish commuters who in one study were shown to pump more or less adrenaline into their blood depending upon how crowded their train was.) With the specter looming of a teeming, overcrowded future, Americans began to think seriously for the first time about the flip side of population growth. How could the quality of life be maintained for 380 million citizens (as the Census Bureau was then projecting) by the turn of the century? As early as 1957, a well-known Pittsburgh banker, James Neville Land, had warned about the dangers of overpopulation. Now even *Fortune* was beginning to worry about "whether all the squalling millions of new babies represent unalloyed good news." In an article in *The New York Times*, David Lilienthal shuddered that overpopulation could "threaten the very quality of life for individual Americans," not to mention "undermine our most cherished institutions."

What could we do? Leadership was not forthcoming from the White House. When President Eisenhower, asked about government sponsorship of birth control research, retorted, "I cannot imagine anything more emphatically a subject that is not a proper political or government activity." John Kennedy, a Catholic, became the first president to give even limited endorsement to population control at an August 1963 press conference when he said he would not stop government research into fertility and human reproduction. Some people were beginning to envision drastic and even Draconian antinatalist measures. In 1964, one economist proposed licensing children as the only solution offering "maximum of individual liberty and ethical choice." Others wanted to remove the tax exemption for children or deny college loans to parents with large families. One measure talked about (but never, thankfully, taken seriously) was to put fertility-depressing chemicals in municipal water supplies. A Harvard demographer, thinking further ahead than some, observed that by the year 2000 there would be two Americans for every foot of coastline in the country. How to preserve bathing space? The answer he came up with was to build offshore islands for twenty-first-century bathers to have their own strands.

When Paul Ehrlich published *The Population Bomb* in 1968 and helped found Zero Population Growth a year later, it seemed to some minds to be just in the nick of time. America, demographers knew with certainty, was due for still *another* baby boom, a seismic aftershock of the first. The problem was the boom itself, the hapless pig that was traveling through the python. The bulge of the boom was about to enter the prime ages of childbearing and increase the number of fertile women by one million a year. If they had anything close to the fertility rates of their mothers, the potential for growth was astronomical. The prime baby-producing 20–24-year-old group, for example, which had declined (!) in the forties and fifties, was about to explode by 50 percent in the sixties. Between 1960 and 1980, the number of women aged 15–34 was going to increase by two-thirds. This "baby echo," as demographers called it, could possibly be a thunderclap of millions of babies. Projecting ahead on the basis of current fertility rates demographers were aghast to discover that there could be as many as 6 million babies born annually by 1976 and 6.5 million in 1980. Suddenly housewives were wearing buttons with slogans like "Stop at Two," "None Is Fun," and "Jesus Was an Only Child."

But even before the movement to curb "popullution" be gan to heat up, a funny thing had happened. Birthrates were dropping back to prewar levels. Observers were puzzled, but agreed that the erosion would be shored up just as soon as the baby-boom mothers arrived in force. But the decline just got steeper. In 1967, as the country passed 200 million, the crude birthrate dropped to the then lowest level in history. Magazines began speaking of the "curious decline." Hospitals were reporting vacancy rates in maternity wards of 60 percent and more. By 1970, we were faced with the astonishing fact that, even though there had been a 29 percent increase in women of childbearing age, and a 52 percent increase in the most fertile period of 20–24 year olds, the number of preschool children in the country had *declined* by 3 million.

Demographers, however nervous, were not about to be proven disastrously wrong twice by the same generation. Almost without exception they discounted the downward trend, confident that it would be swept away by the tidal wave of baby-boom mothers. Some of the babies of the oldest baby-boom women, they noted, had been "delayed" but were coming sooner or later. At the Census Bureau, demographers were equally determined not to repeat the humiliations of the forties and fifties when their projections were continually outstripped by real growth. They would not be lulled into thinking the years of high fertility were over. But American mothers had another surprise for them. After watching their projections fruitlessly chasing real births *up* the hill during the baby boom, the census demographers were about to watch their projections chase real births *down* the hill in the sixties and seventies. In 1958, the Census Bureau issued a "moderate" projection for 1980 of 261 million. In 1964 the moderate projection was revised downward to 245 million. Then in 1966 it was revised yet again to 242 million. Eventually, the actual 1980 population of 222 million was almost 40 million lower than the "moderate" projection made only twenty years earlier.

The story of the seventies was that of the sixties, but more so. The experts continued to agree that the pressure was building up on the baby-boom mothers to deliver on their baby-making potential. They could not, after all, wait forever. The birthrate did edge up slightly in 1969 and 1970. About then, Fabian Linden of the business-backed Conference Board predicted in the "early seventies . . . a new birth boom which will roughly match the magnitude of the earlier experience." Using "simple arithmetic," he calculated that the U.S. population would grow by 30 million to 230 million in 1980. In that year, he added, a "conservative projection" yielded an annual total of births of 4.5 million. (He stands to be off by 1 million for the year and 18 million for the decade.)

The facts certainly seemed to be with the experts. In the seventies, women in the 20–24 bracket increased by one-fourth and women in the 25–34 bracket increased by one-half. By 1985, the army of potential mothers between 20 and 34, who account for three of every four births, stood to gain 10 million new recruits. That, said *Fortune*, will "virtually guarantee there will be a rise in births." Philip Hauser, the eminent University of Chicago demographer, saw "a new tidal wave of births" on the horizon. And in 1972, the President's Commission on Population Growth and the American Future, which had been created by President Nixon in response to the growing clamor about overpopulation, concluded that "there will be no year in the next two decades in which the absolute number of births will be less than in 1970." As it turned out, the Population Commission was wrong. Births did drop below the 1970 total, not after two decades, but in the very next year, 1971, which was the year *before* the Population Commission report came out. Fertility behavior was changing so fast that experts not only could not forecast accurately, it was difficult even to backcast until all the figures were in hand.

Birthrates then all but fell off the cliff in 1972. Though there were *900,000 more women* in the childbearing ages than the year before, there were *300,000 fewer births* and the smallest total since 1945. For the first time in American history the total fertility rate, which measures how many children a typical woman would have in her life if she bore them at age-specific rates for that year, dropped below the "replacement" level of 2.1. The decline continued in 1973, but then in 1974 the total number of births rose for the first time in five years. The increase was practically imperceptible, but it was enough to give new life to the "baby echo" argument. In a thoughtful article in *Science*, June Sklar and Beth Berkov argued persuasively that the time was up: the baby-boom women would have to start producing their babies.

What happened? In 1976, the total fertility rate bottomed out at its historic record low of 1.768, a rate of childbearing less than one-half of that posted by the baby-boom's mothers twenty years earlier. Total births, to be sure, bottomed out and even fishhooked up slightly at the end of the decade. But that increase in no way matched the number of new potential childbearers, and fertility rates continued to languish near their all-time low.

By this time, safety workers at the Census Bureau were on the verge of removing roller towels from rest rooms and locking windows on the upper floors. The luckless demographers had been forced to abandon almost every forecast they'd made since the Depression. They had been wrong on the low side before and during the baby boom and then wrong again on the high side during the bust. The bleached bones of their "projections"—their guesses were no longer called "predictions"—littered the landscape. In the decade and a half since the first baby-boom babies reached the minimum childbearing age of 15, the number of potential mothers had increased 35 percent but the number of actual births had dropped 25 percent. In a single year, eighteen New York City hospitals closed down their maternity wards. Diaper services were going bankrupt. Elementary schools in San Francisco enrolled only half as many students as they had in the mid-sixties. Pediatricians were looking for patients, and orthodontists were getting worried. The only maternity service that had increased its volume was Cesarean sections, which had tripled in ten years.

Like the baby boom before it, the baby bust was universal: no one escaped it. Fertility declined for rich baby boomers and it declined for poor baby boomers. Though the differences were relatively small, the groups that felt the bust most acutely were those who had had the highest fertility during the boom: blacks, American Indians, Mexican-Americans, and low-income groups. What seemed to matter most, however, was not minority-group membership; it was the fact that *all* Americans were moving away from large families. Some of the sharpest drops during the baby bust were in the category of families of four or more children, especially those in the Deep South. A unique feature of black fertility, for example, is that it is highest at the youngest ages. At times, black women under the age of 20 have had more babies faster than any group ever measured in all of history (and their fertility rates today still compare with those in Third World countries). Ultimately, the decline in black fertility came not from younger black women but from older black women who drastically curtailed their fertility, stopping at two or three children instead of four or five. Similarly, despite Church doctrine, the fertility of Catholic women also declined precipitously. Back in 1962 the president of Gonzaga University in Spokane, Washington, had predicted that Catholics would be an American majority in fifty years because of their higher birthrates. Instead, Catholic women born in the first five years of the baby boom, 1946–50, cut back their childbearing so dramatically that today their fertility is all but indistinguishable from non-Catholics.

In electing *not* to have millions of babies, the boom generation acted with the awesome uniformity of their parents twenty-five years earlier when they decided to have their babies. In fact, the forces that came together to produce the bust are strikingly familiar—*in reverse*—to the forces that produced the boom.

A crucial factor once again was the *timing* of births. In the fifties, the baby boom had resulted in considerable part from a "bunching" of births into a few years. Older women were having babies later and younger women were having them earlier. The baby bust, however, was the exact opposite. Now, as the accordian was expanded, births were thinning out over the sixties and seventies. Older women had had their babies earlier and younger women were having theirs later. The net effect was to remove babies from the two decades, creating a hammock in the yearly birth totals.

Looking first at the older women who had given birth to the baby boom, what do we see? In their younger years, they had created more babies faster than any generation in history. One-third of them had three children by the age of 25. The birth cohort of 1938, for example, set an all-time record for speed. On the average, every 1000 women born in 1938 had issued 1457 children by their 24th birthdays. But, because they had so many children while young, they began to cut back drastically as they grew older. By the time the 1938 cohort reached the age of 30 in 1968, it had reduced it childbearing considerably. In other words, a major factor influencing the decline of the sixties was the fact that babies we might have once expected to have been born then had been shoved ahead into the fifties. The entire group of women largely responsible for creating the baby boom, who were born between 1925 and 1940, had extraordinarily high fertility in their younger ages but lower-than-average fertility when they were older—a time that corresponds to the beginning of the baby bust.

The second change in birth timing arrived when the giant cohorts of baby-boom women entered their reproductive ages. We had expected them to generate another boom, or at least a boomlet. But the unique economic and social history of the baby boom meant that it carried with it new assumptions about marriage and parenthood. They did not have children as quickly as their parents. Instead, they postponed both marriage and children, pushing births back in time and deepening the trough of the baby bust.

The delay in childbirth actually began with the delay in marriage. The fact that baby-boom men and women married on the average 18 months later than their predecessors inevitably raised the median age of childbearing, regardless of fertility within marriage. Eighteen months may seem a small difference, but they came directly out of the 20–24 prime time of childbearing. Unmarried women in those years were effectively removed from the pool of eligible mothers. Their opportunity to have children, to be "at risk" of pregnancy, was substantially reduced. Likewise, the rise of cohabitation inhibited fertility. The postponement of marriage also freed many baby-boom women to keep working and to become more attached to their careers than to the idea of parenthood.

Divorce, meanwhile, was cutting into marital fertility from the other end. Between a typical divorce and remarriage is a turnaround span of three and a half years. Those years, too, are effectively removed from a woman's most fertile period. There is a further cancellation factor on either side of a divorce: couples contemplating divorce are unlikely to plan more children and remarried couples are usually less eager than they were the first time around. The net result of both delaying marriage and divorcing was that a dwindling proportion of young baby-boom women wound up living with their husbands during their peak years of childbearing. The proportion of unmarried women in the 20–24 age bracket, meanwhile, rose from 28 percent in 1960 to 49 percent in 1979, a historic transformation that we are still feeling.

Once they finally did marry, the baby-boom women delayed again by not hastening to bear their children. They took longer to have their first child than their mothers did and longer still to have their second. Their ultimate goals of family size may have been the same—indeed, during the first years of the baby bust, mothers consistently denied planning smaller families even as they were doing it. Still, just as the acceleration of births inflated fertility rates during the fifties, the slowed pace reduced fertility rates in the sixties. It helps in this context to think of births as a group of actors parading across a stage. If they start to walk slower, there will be fewer actors onstage at any given time—a year, in the case of fertility rates—but the same number will eventually cross. Or, to use another analogy, trying to anticipate completed fertility by looking at current fertility rates is roughly like trying to figure out how far a car is traveling by looking at the speedometer. It can tell us how fast we are going but says nothing about how far we are going. All we know is that, if we slow down, it may take longer to get there.

These timing factors—the delay in marriage and the delay in childbearing—combined to give the young women of the baby boom the lowest fertility in history. In 1960 for example, 1000 married women between 20 and 24 had produced an average of 1441 babies. But in 1978, married baby-boom women of the same age, born in 1950–54, produced only 908 children, 37 percent fewer than the previous generation. Similarly, while 1000 women born in 1927 had given birth to an average of 2171 children by their 30th birthdays, a later cohort of baby-boom women born in 1947 had produced only 1700 babies by the same age.

Another indication of the baby boom's abandonment of childbearing early in marriage is the enormous increase in childlessness. Between 1960 and 1979, the years corresponding to the maturing of the boom cohort, the percentage of married women age 20–24 who had not yet had a baby nearly doubled from 24 percent to 41 percent. The rise was even sharper for women in their late twenties. No one, of course, thought that all these women would go the rest of their lives without children. Indeed, when asked, only 5 percent said they planned to remain childless, suggesting that the ideal, if not the reality, of marriage and children was still intact. The expectation that they would eventually have their children sustained the notion of the inevitable "baby echo" for most of two decades. The rise in childlessness may yet prove to be a

230

temporary result of the delay in childbearing. But the growing suspicion was that, for these women of the boom generation, "later" might eventually mean "never."

Using the same analysis he had done on the earlier baby boom, Norman Ryder attempted to sort out how much of the baby bust was a matter of timing—that is, births that had been delayed but still could arrive later—and which families were not having children. He found that 55 percent of the fifteen-year decline in births could be explained by changes in timing alone. In other words, more than half of the drop we experienced in fertility in those years would have occurred even if the number of babies born by women throughout their lives had remained fixed. The remaining "quantum" half of the decrease represented that real change in the size of families. And what Ryder found there was that more than half of it was a decrease in "discretionary" births—that is, a decrease in the percent of families having more than two children. Most of the real difference between the baby boom and the baby bust was in the proportion of parents having a third child. The parents who made the baby boom often had a third child; the baby boomers grew up and did not have a third child.

Demographers had already demonstrated that many of the babies born during the baby boom were unwanted. The 1965 National Fertility Study showed that one out of every three of the mothers who made the baby boom admitted to having had at least one unwanted child in her life. Two demographers, Larry Bumpass and Charles Westoff, further concluded that 16 percent of *all* births to these women were unwanted and that, if not for the natural reluctance of any woman to brand a child sitting in the next room as "unwanted," the real total might have been even higher.

The baby boomers, on the other hand, were the first generation to enter the childbearing ages with the opportunity to plan the children they wanted and to prevent children they did not want. (These two factors are related, since a delay in having a wanted second birth reduces the time a woman is later "at risk" of having an unwanted third.) The modern methods of contraception —the pill, IUD, and sterilization—clearly made the difference in fertility regulation. Unlike their parents, the baby boomers did not rush into marriage and childbearing and thereby had time to "practice" effective contraceptive habits. Modern contraceptives, moreover, did not have to be employed with each sex act and therefore resulted in fewer "mistakes." By 1975, more than three out of four boom-generation couples were using the modern methods, compared to only one out of three parents a generation earlier.

This is not to say that the pill *caused* the baby bust. For one thing, the first oral contraceptive, Enovid, was licensed on May 9, 1960, *after* the fertility decline had begun. As late as 1964, only 10 percent of all married couples were using it. American parents of the thirties, after all, had succeeded remarkably well in controlling their fertility without any modern contraceptives. And during the fifties, when more information about contraception was available than ever before, fertility increased fastest among educated Americans. What seems safe to say, though, is that modern contraception enabled many couples to have the small number of children they previously wanted but had been unable to attain. Westoff has argued that the decline in births in the sixties is associated almost entirely with the reduction in unplanned babies. Contraception helped baby-boom parents to postpone marriages (the shotgun marriage was not the threat to the baby boomers that it was to previous generations), to space out their children after marriage (which in turn reduced births in the short run), and to evaluate every pregnancy in terms of its possible costs and benefits.

Legal abortion may also have helped the baby boomers bring down birthrates, though it too is difficult to measure. Officially, the number of legal abortions administered in the United States increased from 50,000 a year in 1969, before the Supreme Court's 1973 decision, to more than 1 million by 1979. In Washington, D.C., there are twice as many abortions as births, and even such exurban locales as Bridgeport, Connecticut, now report more abortions annually than births. Two of every three current abortions are performed on baby-boom women. The generation has clearly felt the impact of abortion in its life. What is less clear is the ultimate impact of abortion on fertility. In 1969, for example, there were an estimated 500,000 *illegal* abortions, making the rise through the seventies less steep than it at first appears. Abortions can cancel out contraceptive failures, but since they can still be replaced by later births, some experts tend to discount the net effects of abortion on fertility.

Nothing mentioned so far necessarily means that the baby boomers wanted smaller families. Changes in the tempo of childbearing do not necessarily affect the final total of childbearing, as proponents of the "birth echo" pointed out. The crucial question is, how many children did the baby boomers want? Or, to put it another way, was the baby bust a decline in unwanted births alone or a decline in the number of births that were wanted?

The answer, as much of it as we have, is both. This conclusion, however, can only be tentative because not a single baby boomer had left the years of childbearing by 1980. The peak cohort of the boom, those women born in 1957, had not even left the high-fertility 20–24 category and thus have fifteen years or more left of potential childbearing. So far, though, the drastically reduced fertility of the boom-generation mothers argues convincingly that they want smaller families and are better able than any mothers before them to stop at the number they want.

For the first time we now have a family average composed not of three children, as during the baby boom, but two children. This has come about not by an even reduction in size of all families but by a decline in the number of large families. In fifteen years, the odds that a woman with two children would have another in any given year dropped 50 percent. At the same time, the proportion of married women with fewer than two children rose to 40 percent. What was happening was a movement away from three-child families and a concentration of families of one and two children. Thus, the baby bust differs from the baby boom in one interesting way: the boom was mostly a rise in the number of small families; the bust was a decline in the number of large families (presumably due to superior fertility regulation). With the baby bust, as with everything else, when the baby boomers moved, they moved as a generation, massively and uniformly.

Over the years, both the Census Bureau and pollsters like Gallup have periodically asked women about their fertility intentions. But if any one conclusion emerges from the polls, it is that they most accurately reflect not what will happen but what has already happened—albeit with a slight lag. At first, despite mounting evidence to the contrary, baby-boom mothers professed to have no intention of reducing the size of their families from the ones produced by their mothers. Not once did the baby-boom women anticipate their baby bust. In fact, it took

233

them a while to realize that it had started. In 1963, five years after the fertility decline began, white women told Gallup that they wanted an average of 3.5 children apiece; in 1966, the "ideal" had slipped only slightly to 3.1. Even then, two-fifths of the women considered the ideal number of children to be four or more. (The fact that many of them then began working for ZPG may be a classic case of what psychoanalysts call "cognitive dissonance." Confronted by the incongruity between their stated ideals and their contrary behavior, these baby boomers tried to justify their reduced childbearing by promoting birth control for others.)

Not until the 1970s did baby-boom women begin to admit what they were doing. By then, the number alleging a preference for two-child families had doubled and those who considered four or more the ideal number of children had been halved. Sixty percent of the mothers of the fifties expected three or more births; now only one-quarter did. But they still had not caught up completely with their baby gap. Today many older women with no children or just one are still saying that they expect to have at least two—even as the sands continue to drain from their hourglasses.

Why did the boom children have so few children of their own? It certainly was not from lack of sexual initiative. A study by Westoff showed a 17 percent increase from 1965 to 1970 in the frequency of sexual intercourse by married couples. The highest frequencies belonged to the youngest women. Women born in the baby boom, for instance, had intercourse with their husbands an average of eleven times a month compared to eight times for all women. If the general estimate that human sexual intercourse is performed two thousand times for each one that produces an offspring, then the Churchillian line can be modified: Never have so many done so much for so few.

There are two reasons why children fell out of favor. The first is that the forces of modernization, which had eroded fertility for two centuries, were once again prevailing. The second is that women of the baby boom came of age at a time when women were first developing personally and economically satisfying alternatives to motherhood. For many years the greatest rewards society had for women came from the bearing of children. But now society had developed a different set of rewards for *not* having children. These rewards were largely enacted by baby-boom women who had carried with them from childhood a conviction of their great expectations. And, as the first generation to grow up with reliable and readily available birth control, they were uniquely capable of freeing themselves from what they saw as the burden of children.

All across America women were telling their husbands that they did not want to be baby machines. Their own mothers, by God, had warned them about the mother trap. They had told their children how smart they were, how independent they were, how much better they were. They could have chosen motherhood, all right, but they had a higher obligation to themselves to be free. The archetypal baby-boom couple in *Loose Ends* divorces after the wife conceals an abortion from her husband so she can continue her newfound career. Women's magazines were filled with anguished accounts by women struggling with the dilemma of modern motherhood: to be or not to be parents. "We go about our business, but always in the hard way," wrote one feminist, Paula Cizmar, about her generation, "taking all the old values off the shelf, blowing the dust away to see what is underneath. It has become a habit of our living." Why should they endure the shackles of children when their foremost obligation was to themselves? Perhaps Betty Rollin said it best and briefest in the title of her famous 1970 *Look* article, "Motherhood: Who Needs It?"

And what did women want? Freud himself had given the answer in his definition of mental health. It was *"Lieben und arbeiten"* ("to love and to work"). But what these women loved *was* work. We have already seen how millions of baby-boom women poured into the labor force during precisely the same years their fertility rates were drying up. The association between the women's work and women's fertility is hard to miss. The more women worked, the more they became attached to their careers, and the less they seemed inclined to drop out to have babies. A young *Wall Street Journal* correspondent, Jo-ann Lublin, put it like this in an unusually frank column: "I can't see easily relinquishing my journalism career to be a fulltime mother and housewife. It would radically change my work-oriented life and restrict my professional mobility." In a group of recent female graduates of Princeton, four times as many women identified themselves as lawyers than as housewives. Only one in five

235

had children and, compared to the population at large, twice as many were single and twice as many married women were childless. When Harvard's Class of '69 returned for its tenth reunion in 1979, only eight women answering a poll called childrearing their main occupation.

Like college-educated black women born around the turn of the century, half of whom never had a child, these educated baby-boom women hesitate to risk their hard-earned professional gains by having a baby. Just as children were a liability for the black grandmothers, so they could be a liability for the young women of the baby boom. Moreover, the very state of parenthood is limiting. One's options are suddenly curtailed. And options—*possibilities*—have always been one value treasured by the baby boomers. Why commit themselves to one way of life when so many more beckon? Childlessness offers, among other things, the youthful illusion of unlimited opportunity and growth. The heady feelings of power that the baby boom earned in its adolescence could not easily be forgotten. In this way, the baby boomers were reluctant to proceed into adulthood. By working and playing, they could postpone adulthood along with their children and remain, as Dylan had promised them, forever young.

As compelling as the relationship between women's work and women's fertility seems, there is one problem with it. Which causes which? It is easy enough to see that work and high fertility are negatively correlated, but the casual connection is more elusive. Did the baby-boom women choose to enter the labor force because they were able to have fewer children? Or did they choose to have fewer children because they were working? Or are both independent variables that have no relationship at all?

Fortunately, there is one promising theory recently developed by two California demographers, William Butz and Michael Ward, which seeks to resolve this conundrum. On the face of it, Butz and Ward were proposing a standard economic theory of fertility. It holds that babies are consumer durables which are "bought" just like washing machines or cars. In good economic times, people have more money to spend on lawn mowers and dishwashers and babies. Fertility goes up. But in bad times they have no income with which to "buy" babies and fertility goes down. History seemed to support this notion. During the Depression, fertility ran at then-record lows. And during the prosperous fifties parents seemed to be "buying" more babies with their greater spending power.

But after 1960, Butz and Ward pointed out, the classic formula no longer worked. In fact, it had turned upside down: during the expansive periods of the sixties and seventies, birthrates went *down;* during recessions, they went *up.* What was causing the contradiction, they hypothesized, was the fact that the multitude of baby-boom women entering the labor force had made female wages just as important as male wages in determining fertility. But there was a crucial distinction between male and female wages. Higher male wages had traditionally increased family income and led to increased demand for children. Increases in female wages raised family income, too. But—and this is the crucial difference—they also raised what economists call the "opportunity cost" of having children. That does not mean maternity fees or diapers. Opportunity costs are the real wages that a woman gives up to have children. As her earnings rise, the time she spends at home becomes more costly. If they go down, or she is out of work altogether, the time she might spend to bear children is less costly. Thus, the more women work and the more money they earn, the higher their opportunity cost of childbearing. If enough women are working, the traditional relationship between business cycles and fertility reverses: now good times mean higher wages and fewer children; bad times mean lower real wages and more children.

What happened in the fifties according to Butz and Ward, was that men's wages went up tremendously. Women, who were not then working in nearly the numbers they are today, were able to afford to stay home and bear the baby boom. But then the overheated demand began to draw more and more women into the labor force. The only available category left was one that had not been used much before in peacetime: young married women with children. So, in the historic postwar transformation, they too were sucked into the labor force for the first time.

Once they were working, the boom-generation women began to find they preferred more paychecks to more pregnancies. Their new income brightened their opportunities for better housing, better vacations, and a better life. The only thing that became more expensive was having children. In prosperous times, the wages forfeited to parenthood began to hurt. According to one 1969 estimate, the net loss per baby was 400 income-producing hours a year. And that did not include the thousands of dollars paid to full-time babysitters if a new mother decided to return to the office. Previously, babies returned on their parents' investment by producing needed labor or security in old age. But those virtues had been devalued by modern society, as had the "psychic income" available to mothers during the baby boom. In short, a baby's return on investment had never looked so meager.

At first, the working baby-boom women resolved this dilemma by postponing births until "later." For some of them, "later" came during economic recessions when earnings and therefore their opportunity costs were lower. Accordingly, Butz and Ward argue that the interruptions of the fertility decline during the recessions of 1970 and 1974 were produced when women compressed their delayed childbearing into those years. Ultimately, they contend, women increasingly realized that their new work roles were incompatible with the family size they'd originally planned. Their response then was to begin to scale back on the number of children they expected to have. To sum it up, the fertility mechanism constructed by Butz and Ward is based in general on the total income of the family and in particular on the different effects of male income and female income. An increase in the husband's income will raise the demand for children. An increase in female earnings increases family income but also increases the opportunity cost of having a child. The more women working in the labor market, then, the more this effect depresses fertility.

This brought demographers unexpectedly back to an idea that had almost been laughed out of the classroom during the baby boom: the Demographic Transition. It was the long-term trend of declining fertility that had once been theoretically linked to, among other things, modernization and urbanization. But the America of the baby boom was the most developed, industrialized, urbanized nation in the world. The theory also tied reduced fertility to increased education, especially among women. But births among educated women were disproportionately high during the boom years. Discredited and dismayed, the experts had shivered and shelved the theory while groping for new explanations to explain the baby boom.

But now, after the baby bust, the Demographic Transition was beginning to look like a healthy theory again. All of the developed countries of Europe were reporting record low fertilty rates that had sunk below replacement levels. No cohort of Swedish women, for instance, had repaced itself since 1885. In both Germanys, population was in absolute decline, and one West German demographer had worried—shades of the 1930s!—that "beneath the blankets, we are a dying people." Fertility rates were dropping sharpest in the countries that had seen baby booms. In New Zealand, where the total fertility rate had soared to 4.16 in 1962, the highest of any developed country, the postwar birth cohorts were not reproducing themselves, and the annual growth rate of the population had dropped 80 percent in just four years. Canada's fertility rates were also skidding, most dramatically among the French-Canadian (and Catholic) Quebecois, who had previously posted some of the highest birthrates on record.

Perhaps the most remarkable transformation came in Japan, which halved its birthrate in a decade, the sharpest decline of any large population in modern times. Japan's experience was colored by one of the oddest dips in births on record. According to the superstition of *Hinoeuma*, women born in the Year of the Fire Horse in Oriental astrology will murder their husbands. Not surprisingly, many Japanese parents feel that daughters born in Years of the Fire Horse are poor marriage prospects. Fortunately, *Hinoeuma* comes only once in every fifth cycle of the Japanese zodiac, or every sixty years. It had last appeared in 1906 and was due again in 1966. What happened? Japanese births shot up in 1965, plunged by half a million in the fatal year of 1966, and then rebounded ever sharper in 1967. A similar bobbing of the birthrates occurred in Japanese populations in Hawaii and California. Over all three years, the sum of births is what would have been expected anyway. The difference was that Japanese parents successfully managed to keep their babies out of 1966. The strangest fact of all, though, is that, of the babies actually born in 1966, there was an unusually small proportion of girl babies. These parents had not outwitted Mother Nature. Rather,

239

the parents of females born early in January and late in December had pre- and postdated birth certificates to take the girls out of the dreaded year of 1966 and preserve their daughters' chances for a happy marriage.

In America, demographers were looking with renewed interest at the charts showing the long-term decline in fertility that had begun back in 1800. The baby boom had seemed to end it. But now that birthrates had dropped back down again, even lower, the boom looked less like a new trend than a brief fluctuation. In fact, if we had projected future birthrates on the basis of the trends of the twenties and thirties, the straight-line decline would have dropped almost exactly to the present level. The downward trend had continued after all. The once-humiliated demographers of the thirties and forties had been right all along about the long-range decline. Their only mistake was timing. The baby bust had simply come a generation later than everyone thought.

Just as America will be living with the consequences of the baby boom for the next half-century, so it must also live with the baby bust. By failing to replicate itself, the boom generation had once again defined itself in bold relief against all other generations. If, for example, the baby boomers had continued the high birthrates of their parents they would have created a secondary boom all but indistinguishable from the first. High birthrates would have been seen not as an anomaly—the pig in the python —but as a fact of a dangerously expanding population. The baby boom would have been the shock wave bringing in a whole new way of life.

But that did not happen. Instead of swelling the population further, the grown-up baby boomers left a void. Now the boom generation had given itself a beginning and an end—and turbulence at both extremes. As it continued to churn through society, it was forcing adjustments both fore and aft: at one end we struggled with expansion and at the other we struggled with contraction. We could now see for the first time that the problems caused by the baby boom were not those associated with youth or whatever age the boom generation was passing through at the time. The problems were associated with the generation itself. And instead of fading away, they would remain with the baby boom forever.

Chapter 16

THE BABY BOOM AS PARENTS

Somewhere, hidden in the rec room of memory, every baby boomer carries around a notion of what family life is *supposed* to be like. Families live in towns like Mayfield at addresses like 211 Pine Street. Fathers are named Ward and mothers are named June and, if a kid is named Theodore, everybody just calls him Beaver. In its six-year run from 1957 until 1963, *Leave It to Beaver* was the quintessential celebration of what Leslie Fiedler called "the cult of the child." Fiedler thought that the domestic excesses of the fifties represented the "most maudlin of primitivisms." No family, after all, could have been as innocent as the Cleavers. Where was the independent career woman struggling to escape from June? Why could Ward never bring himself to ask for a divorce? Why did Beaver and Wally enslave their parents to their childish needs? Theirs was plainly an unauthentic family.

But what did the baby boomers have left to put in its place? The wild ride from the domesticated fifties through the shattered sixties and self-absorbed seventies dislodged most of our ideas about parents and children. Marriages no longer lasted and mothers no longer stayed in the kitchen. Therapists report that many married couples of the baby boom now feel confused and even alienated because the roles that they had once expected of husbands and wives and parents had changed so drastically from their own childhood. Theirs is the last generation of Americans raised in the traditional patriarchal family. Now they are so unsure about what parents are supposed to be that in a recent report on foster homes, the Children's Defense Fund felt obliged to list some reasons why parents are probably good for children (for

241

example, they make them feel wanted and accepted, they provide continuity in relationships, they give guidance with the problems of growing up, and they lend a regular, dependable quality to a child's life).

The rearing of the next generation remains a primary task ahead for the baby boom. It must transmit the culture if the culture is to last. But which culture? Theirs? Or their parents'? Unsure, the boom generation was initially able to defer action by having children later and less often. Now, as adults, the baby boomers have become the first generation of parents to be widely unavailable to their children. The cult of the child has become the cult of the adult. The result is that the entire concept of a parent's responsibility toward his or her children has been eroded. How has this happened? Two separate trends, both reinforced by society, have changed the nature of parenting. The first is the massive entry of baby-boom women into the working force. Dick and Jane are not being cared for by Daddy or Mommy but by relatives or friends or teachers. Or by no one at all, as in the case of the many thousands of latch-key children who return after school to darkened homes to wait for their parents to come back from work. Which is assuming that they have two parents. Because the second trend changing parenting for the baby boomers is divorce. Today divorce is doing what death did one hundred years ago in creating one-parent families. It is estimated that nearly one-half of all children born today will spend a meaningful portion of their lives before 18 in single-parent families. Already one out of every six children lives with a single parent, usually the mother, double the portion in 1950. If a child is living with two adults, they are increasingly less likely to be his or her biological parents. One-quarter of all school-age children today do not live with their real fathers.

Literally from the moment their children were born, the baby boomers announced to the world that parenting would no longer be the same. For most of America's history, the same dozen or so given names had held their popularity, with changing fashions only shuffling their order within the list. But now that they were parents, the baby boomers were not going to be any more conventional about picking out names than anything else. No longer would girls' birth certificates give us old standbys like Mary and Jane and Susan. Boys would no longer be

Tom, Dick or Harry. Here, instead, are the ten most popular boys' and girls' names for 1978:

GIRLS	BOYS
Jennifer	Michael
Jessica	David
Nicole	John
Melissa	Christopher
Michelle	Joseph
Maria	Anthony
Lisa	Robert
Elizabeth	Jason
Danielle	James
Christine	Daniel

Where were all the Lindas and Sandys and Patricias and Barbaras of the fifties? And whither William—*Bill!*—a name more American than Uncle Sam's? There had been nothing short of a revolution in nomenclature. New names had risen out of obscurity and traditional leaders had been cast aside. Of the girls' names, only one—Elizabeth—remained from a similar list of baby-boom names in 1950. And how could the previously disdained Jennifer shoot to number one on a girls' list otherwise notable for its Francophilia? Half the boys' names remained, but minus such former reliables as Stephen and Charles. Instead, short, crisp names like Brian, Jeffrey and Scott were gaining in popularity.

No sooner had the mothers come home with their Kimberlys and Joshuas (two other popular names) than many of them promptly turned around and went to work. Nearly one-third of married boom-generation women return to their jobs within a year after having a child and nearly half were in the labor force by the time the child was two years old. Recently the increase in working married women with children has been *faster* than that of women without children. It is not clear whether they wanted to get back to their careers, to get away from their kids, or both. As of 1980, one-half of all school-age children had both working mothers and working fathers. The biggest increases, as we have seen, were among women with preschool children, previously the group most likely to be kept from working by the double bind of household duties and social pressures. Since 1965, the number of preschool children with working mothers

243

has leaped 65 percent, despite the absolute decrease in numbers of children that age. By the end of the seventies, one in every three children under the age of six— 7.5 million preschoolers—had a working mother. Nearly half of all mothers with preschool children now work (compared to 20 percent in 1965), and *one-third of those with a child under a year old are in the labor force.*

These baby-boom women have helped make nursery school one of the few growth areas in education today. In the 1970s, while elementary schools across the country were closing their doors, nursery-school enrollment more than doubled. The proportion of all 3–5-year-olds enrolled shot from 6 percent in 1965, before the boom generation's kids arrived, to 50 percent eleven years later. Not all of the increase can be laid to working mothers, either, since children whose mothers are in the labor force are only slightly more likely to be enrolled than those whose mothers do not work.

The job of combining working with mothering has never been easy, which is presumably one reason why working mothers have so few children. Moreover, children are affected at two times by a mother's work— when she is on the job and when she is at home—and both can be stressful.

Back in their parents' generation, when the Procreation Ethic was in its heyday, the idea that a mother would ever voluntarily leave her children to work was practically unthinkable. Mothers gave constant care to their toddlers if only out of fear that one mistake would scar their children for life. However, the theory of cognitive dissonance teaches that if a person's behavior conflicts with his or her views, the person will soon change the views to "fit" the behavior. A working mother today finds it increasingly difficult to believe that her activity hurts her marriage or her children—even if she once felt that way. Thus, the polls show that the enormous increase in working mothers during the sixties and seventies was accompanied by a reversal in the proportion of women believing that a mother's work is harmful to children. When the Daniel Yankelovich firm asked a sample of all parents if small children are worse off if the mother works instead of staying home, 69 percent said yes. When the same question was put to a group of *working* mothers, however, they were split about fifty-fifty. And when the question was asked of a group of baby-boom mothers, fully two out of three thought that children of working mothers were just as well raised as anyone else (though a majority preferred that mother work only from "economic necessity"). In time, as the proportion of working mothers continues to grow, we may eventually expect society to go full route and pressure women to work and to give their children the nonmaternal "freedom" to boost their independence and self-confidence.

Despite the remarkable change in the number of working mothers, there has been relatively little public support of caring for their children. Only about 5 percent of the children of working mothers are enrolled in day-care centers. Instead, the great majority—75 percent—are cared for in their own homes, most often by a relative. One survey found that 30 percent of all such children under thirteen come home either alone or with their brothers and sisters to an empty house after school. Understandably, working baby-boom mothers have campaigned vigorously for more public commitment to day care. Their support has come after a revision in child-care views similar to those that followed the entry of women into the labor force. In the 1950s, organized group care for very young children was considered a social evil rivaled only by godless Communism. Richard Nixon reflected this outlook when he rejected government-sponsored day care as a sinister force that would somehow undermine the sanctity of the American family. Defenders of day care have argued that the alternative—millions of children shuttled by harried mothers between baby-sitters or even left unattended at home—hardly strengthens the foundation of the family.

Today it is an unpopular and unacceptable notion to suggest that day care is anything but wonderful for young children. But some child psychologists lately have become worried about the lack of information about the effects of the removal of children under the age of two from their mothers. One prominent child psychoanalyst, Selma Fraiberg, now believes that mothers should stay with their children during their first eighteen months. Day-care centers, she says, teach only "survival values" to small children often overwhelmed by the situation around them. Unable to cope, they retreat into themselves, miniature zombies desperately fending off a confusing world. Even if licensing standards raise the overall quality of a day-care centers, baby-boom mothers still face the problem of being cut off from their small children. Ultimately, they may find the most workable and humane solution will not be in changing the day-care situation but in changing their working situation. Innovations like flexible working-hours and shortened work weeks may do more for the parents of the baby boom—and their children—than millions of dollars spent building corrals for four-year-olds.

Divorce is the other wall between baby boomers and their children. The divorce boom came with the baby boom and has left a residue of lonely children. In the first half of this century, one out of every four school-age children suffered the loss of a parent through either death or divorce. Today almost every other child will feel that loss, and the reason will almost always be divorce. Each year since 1960, the total number of children affected by divorce in the United States has gone up. The most acute rises have come after the baby boom's coming of age. In 1972, more than one million children were involved in divorces. By 1976, three times as many children were caught up in divorce as had been twenty years earlier. And almost all of them were feeling the pain, turmoil, and guilt that accompany the rendering of any family. The nuclear family of *Leave It to Beaver* or *Father Knows Best* was losing a war of attrition.

Millions of young parents were divorcing not only their spouses but their children as well. The idea of keeping the marriage together "for the kids" was discredited. The result was that the emerging baby-boom life-style of the seventies and eighties, as it turned out, was not to be communes or cults. It was single parenthood. The burgeoning divorce rate has created nuclear-family fission: the explosion yielded energy and a proliferating number of single-parent families. *Esquire* and *Cosmopolitan,* always quick to sniff out trends, were running articles on the anguish of dating single parents ("What do you say to her/his kids at breakfast?") And in Marin County, California, young single parents were solving the inevitable child-care problems by banding together, six or seven families to a house, to share babysitting and household chores. (All of which were considerably lightened in the summers, when the children were shipped en masse to their estranged fathers or mothers.)

In shows like *Bachelor Father* television long ago gave

us the stereotype of the endearingly clumsy single father struggling to cope with housework. It was sometimes funny but almost always false. The number of single fathers has multiplied threefold since 1960, all right, but so has the number of single mothers. In 1978, there were 1 million children living with single fathers, but there were 11 million living with single mothers. Since 1960, the number of female-headed households with children has risen by 150 percent. These, moreover, were not middle-class matriarchies. Nearly half of all female-headed families currently live below the government-defined "poverty level" (in contrast to less than 10 percent of families headed by men).

All of these figures conceal a staggering racial difference. Fewer than half of black preschool children were living with both natural parents in 1977, compared to 87 percent of white preschoolers. Even assuming that there is an undercount of "invisible" black men, the situation is appalling. Two out of every three black children in a female-headed family lives in poverty. The result is that more than one-half of all children of black baby-boom mothers are growing up in disrupted families who are living in poverty. Little wonder that blacks are concerned about finding their roots: only these children are not looking, like Alex Haley, for their African forebears; they are looking for their grandparents.

It is difficult to say what all the effects are for the children growing up in single-parent families. Those who survive divorce typically absorb a frightening burden of guilt and tension and anxiety. Their parents are likely to be working. The children of single parents are the group most likely to attend day-care centers. Some, reduced to two hours of parental contact a day, are frequently victims of loneliness and isolation and depression. Unable to observe a marriage firthand, they miss the lessons of compromise and give-and-take and sharing that most human relations require. The baby-boom parents themselves, raising their children unaided, vacillate between too little communication and too much guilt. Fathers wind up like Santa Clauses, burying their ambivalence toward their children in presents. In a recent survey of the American family, Daniel Yankelovich found that single parents are distinguished by their greater sense of inadequacy. Unable to enjoy the freedom of the child-

247

less or the security of a nuclear family, they are left helplessly stranded between two worlds.

One of the reasons why many baby boomers have a negative view of childhood is that the memory of their own tumultuous childhood is still fresh. It was, for them, a difficult time for parents and children both. The disadvantage of crowding has now been replaced by cost. At the end of the seventies, a family with an annual income of $10,000 would have to spend $50,000 to raise a child to 18—and that's not counting the costs of higher education or a mother's forfeited wages. Moreover, contrary to their parents, the baby boomers are unsure about the rewards of parenting. The Good Times Generation never doubted its priorities: first family, then marriage, and finally self. But the baby boomers turned it upside down: their first priority was the self. Then came marriage, if it worked. And finally family, if that worked, too.

In a time when just having children places stress on a family, the penalties can be severe. Child abuse—a classic sign that a family cannot cope—became most visible in the United States when the baby boom came to parenthood. The homicide rate for children aged 1–4 tripled between 1950 and 1975 and is now a greater cause of childhood mortality than any disease. In the late 1970s, the age group that felt the largest percent increase in homicide was, sadly, 1–4. An estimated two million children are abused physically each year. Granted that some of the increase is a reporting phenomenon—doctors, for example, are better able to identify child abuse cases now—the incidence of child abuse is still high enough that experts deliberately use the word "epidemic."

Parents under 30 are much more likely to beat children than those over 30. But is there any reason to think that the boom generation is more prone to child abuse than any previous generation? Perhaps. Parents don't cause child abuse; stress does. And the families of the baby boom have experienced more marital stresses than any generation in history. We also know that single parents—of which the baby-boom generation has produced millions—are more vulnerable to child abuse than anyone else. A young, lonely, single mother may find herself chronically depressed by poverty and her inability to deal with both a job and her children. So, in her frustration, she abuses her children. The child is a victim, and so is the mother.

There is another aspect of child abuse that is unique to the baby boom. Teenage mothers are more likely to abuse their children than older women. And, even during the decade of the baby bust, the number of babies born to teenage women was *increasing*, virtually the only age group to do so. Some wanted babies for status, others were pathetically ill-informed about contraception. But the result is that 600,000 teenagers a year become mothers, most of them tragically ill-equipped for the job. Many are not married, thus adding another layer of stress to their lives. In 1960, before the boom women arrived, only 5 percent of all births were to unmarried mothers; in 1976, the number had tripled to 15 percent. Most of them were less able to cope with the demands of parenting than far poorer women in developing countries, who at least benefit from an unwritten "curriculum" of motherhood passed down through the generations. Among older women, parents who could be the source of much on-the-job motherhood training are just as likely to live across the country as across the town. The education system does so little in this area that the first baby many women touch may be their own.

All of this may sound unduly harsh. Ask any baby-boom parents if they love their children and the answer is that of course they do. And there is every reason to suppose that, as individuals, they do. As the first generation to regulate its fertility effectively, the baby boomers have enjoyed a greater portion of "wanted" babies than in the past. But the most telling question, as Kenneth Keniston has pointed out, is not how parents feel about their children. It is how they feel about other people's children. And the record so far is that the baby boom has ushered in an era of public attitudes toward children that vary between benign neglect and outward hostility.

The child-oriented society, once so prevalent that it seemed a permanent fixture of American life, peaked in 1967 when the number of children of "dependent" age (under 18) reached 70 million. Then two things happened: first, the youngest baby boomers began to leave the ages of childhood, and second, the oldest baby boomers did not have enough babies to replace them. In the seventies the number of children under the age of 5 dropped by 1 million and the number aged 5–13 dropped by 5 million. The number of children in husband-wife families, meanwhile, was dropping even faster—by 9 million in the seventies. Today only 39 percent of all households have any children at all, and the nuclear families of married couples with children amount to less than one-third of all households.

A society that was older and more frequently childless had less use for the messy ways of children. "Adults Only" apartment houses and entire communities began springing up to keep the youngsters away. Families in some such adult ghettos were evicted for the "crime" of childbearing. The Supreme Court decreed that teachers could spank the little brats in school. The state of Oregon drew up a law prohibiting the sale of disposable diapers, an act that in the fifties could have touched off an uprising of harried mothers, the environment notwithstanding. Hollywood, which had given us Shirley Temple, was presenting an increasingly sinister side of kids in movies like *Rosemary's Baby, The Exorcist, It's Alive,* and *The Omen.*

By this time, birthrates were tumbling and Momism was in full rout. Instead of devoting every moment of their lives to their children, parents were increasingly turning the job over to the schools and experts. Mothers were hectoring their children to brush their teeth and wash behind their ears, all right, but some parents were unsure if even that was their role. Yankelovich has found that one in four modern fathers believes that the primary responsibility for teaching children good health and nutrition habits lies not with families but with the schools. The contrast to the overprotective generation of grandparents could not be more striking. Isolated from their parents, besieged by experts, and unsure of their own roles, these baby-boom parents had lost the inner maps that were supposed to guide them through parenthood. "Child rearing is one of the biggest casualties of the modern age that is being ushered in by this generation," says sociologist James Coleman. "We are becoming the first species in the history of the world which is unable to care for its young."

No one knows anymore who is responsible for the children. A society that has to ask parents, "Did You Hug Your Child Today?" or "It's ten o'clock. Do you know where your children are?" is not expressing full confidence in parents. But society has not been eager to assume responsibility either. The children growing up as offspring of the baby boomers are not unlike children growing up in one of the sixties' communes: in a group where everyone is responsible, the net result is that no one is responsible. We have been particularly slow about confronting the problems of working mothers. Most European countries routinely give mothers such benefits as long maternity leaves, family allowances, housing allowances for additional children, health care for children, and child-care grants. But the extraordinary persistence of the idealized nuclear-family stereotype in the United States has effectively blocked any such assistance. Legislators are particularly reluctant to admit that the traditional breadwinner-housewife family could be in anything but apple-cheeked good health. To do otherwise, as Yale's Keniston has remarked, would "force us to take more seriously the need to publicly support these adults involved in the difficult business of child-rearing." (Fortunately, there is at least one area in which baby-boom mothers have been luckier than their predecessors. Infant mortality, one index of how well a society cares for its young, dropped by 25 percent in the seventies and is half the level of the fifties. But it remains scandalously high compared to other industrialized countries and, among blacks, is still almost twice as high as among whites.)

The disadvantages of children in this kind of a world are clear. And with the advent of effective fertility, the baby-boom generation was the first to make childbearing a choice. But when parenthood became an option, it was trivialized to the point of becoming just another life-style. As Betty Rollin put it, "The notion that the maternal wish and instinct is biologically predestined is baloney." Once Americans began asking themselves not how they could help their children, but how their kids could help them, the answer became obvious. Of 50,000 parents who replied to a question from Ann Landers, 70 percent said they would not have children again. And when the University of Michigan's Survey Research Center asked female college graduates how they felt about having children, the result was similar: in two decades the percent feeling positive about children dropped from 50 percent to 28 percent. What they were saying, in effect, was that motherhood was devalued and that children were a burden.

If parenthood was no longer the preeminent value, then what was? Plato had said that the root of man's love for his children was his yearning for immortality. This yearning still remained, but now the baby boomers seemed to want to fulfill it not through their children but through themselves. Christopher Lasch has argued that this attitude originated with the original break between generations. The baby boom grew up without strong identification with its parents which, according to strict Freudian theory, is necessary to the construction of the superego. Lacking an internalized sense of duty, the baby boomers fell back on the group. They turned to their cohort for guidance and approval. This corresponds to the stage in the individual's life cycle Erik Erikson identified as generativity, "the concern for establishing and guiding the next generation." If an individual fails to enrich himself or herself through identification with the next generation, Erikson said, "regression to an obsessive need for pseudointimacy takes place, often with a pervading sense of stagnation and personal impoverishment. Individuals, then, often begin to indulge themselves as if they were their own—or one another's—one and only child."

Erikson could just as easily have been describing a generation that was singularly reluctant to undertake what had previously been considered the major responsibility of adulthood: the care of the next generation. Instead, they preferred to operate independently like the TV free spirits they so admired—Kojak and Rockford and even Mary Tyler Moore. Interestingly, in *Passages*, her study of the "Predictable Crises of Adult Life," Gail Sheehy discusses the idea of *generativity* almost entirely in the careerist context, saying little about parenthood. The possible reason why was indirectly touched on in Lisa Alther's *Kinflicks*, when a young man explains why he doesn't want children:

> I always saw the world as a stage. . . . And any child of mine would be a ballsy young actor wanting to run me off stage altogether, watching and waiting to bury me, so that *he* could assume center stage.

Joe Klein, writing in *Rolling Stone*, similarly wondered if "it is possible that by not experiencing the sacrifices of parenthood, we are stunting our growth, condemning ourselves to a permanent adolescence." By avoiding responsibility for the next generation, the boom generation could continue to pursue the interests of its own.

In his polls, Daniel Yankelovich has isolated a group of parents, almost entirely baby boomers, who are less child-oriented and more self-oriented. They are the educated elite, the wealthy New Breed which regards children not as an obligation but as one of many options. This is no insignificant minority view, Yankelovich says, but is held by 43 percent of all fathers and mothers who have children under the age of thirteen.

> New Breed parents tend to be better educated and more affluent. They represent the "Haves" rather than the "Have Nots." New Breed parents have rejected many of the traditional values by which they were raised: marriage as an institution, the importance of religion, saving and thrift, patriotism and hard work for its own sake. And they have adopted a new set of attitudes toward being parents and the relationships of parents to children. New Breed parents question the idea of sacrificing in order to give their children the best of everything and are firm believers in the equal rights of children and parents.

The New Breed, says Yankelovich, has rewritten the traditional contract parents made with their children. Parents used to devote themselves to their children with the assumption that, in their old age, their children would in turn take care of them. But the New Breed (read baby boom) parents see it differently. They are saying to their children, "We have a right to our own lives and we aren't going to kill ourselves for you. On the other hand, we won't expect you to take care of us when we're older, either."

Specifically, nearly one-half of the New Breed agreed with this statement—"Parents should *not* sacrifice in order to give their children the best"—while only 16 percent of the Traditionalists did. Asked if "children have no obligation to their parents regardless of what parents have done for them," three out of four of the New Breed agreed. More than two out of three New Breeders think that "it's important for parents to have their own lives and interests—even if it means spending less time with their children." At the same time, paradoxically, the New Breed parents are not so secure in their own attitudes that they are willing to pass them along. Instead, Yankelovich has found that they continue steadfastly to transmit to their children the traditional values they have rejected themselves. Thus, ironically, the same people who called their parents hypocrites for preaching one thing while practicing another were themselves guilty of a similar transgression.

In the space of a decade, the boom generation had demolished many of our oldest ideas about marriage and family. In doing so, it had come close to balkanizing the institution of the family itself. It had broken down many of the links between husbands and wives, between parents and children, between grandchildren and grandparents. Parenthood had been devalued. America was no longer a society dominated by children or even by families. As families continued to break down, more and more children were caught up in divorce and grew up with a different idea—if any idea at all—of how the traditional family operated. Many of these children are emotionally and psychologically wounded. A decade earlier, the psychiatric field of childhood depression did not exist. Now it is a growth industry. Children as young as six and seven are trying to kill themselves in numbers previously unthinkable. Yet these are the same people who will carry us through the twenty-first century. Three out of every four children born in 1980 can expect to live to the year 2045; one-half will reach 2055, and one out of every four will reach 2056. They will be the real legacy of the boom generation.

Chapter 17

THE NEW CONSUMER

Sometime in the last decade, the iconography of advertising began to change. The kids in the Coke ads started looking older. The women in the Geritol ads were getting younger. Clairol's Loving Care hair color was telling women reassuringly, "You're not getting older. You're getting better!" Club Med, which had prospered for years on its blend of sun, sea, and sex, began to talk about men taking their *wives*, of all people, to the tropics. One such Club Med ad even posed the most delicate question of all—"Should you bring your children on a Club Med Vacation?" The answer was (surprise!) yes, but the ad campaign depicting a father and his child, a daughter, discreetly skirted one aspect of the baby boom's life-style. Where was the mother? Was this father a single parent? Was his daughter an only child? Was Club Med saying that a grown-up, divorced baby boomer could take his only child on a vacation and *still* have a chance to score a chick?

As the baby boom entered young adulthood, the message was becoming increasingly clear. It was our dominant generation in childhood, it was our dominant generation in adolescence, and it will be our dominant generation in adulthood. In its lifetime, it would *always* be our dominant generation, compelling public attention through the magnetic pull of its numbers and its vast buying power. What mattered now was not population growth as a whole but population change within age groups and all it implied for household size, lifestyles, and consumption patterns.

Where were the changes? In the 1970s, the single fastest-growing age group was 25–34, the family-building years beloved by merchandisers for their heavy-spending habits. In the decade, this group ballooned from 25 million to 36 million, an increase of more than 1 million a year, almost all of them baby boomers. Compared to the under-25 group, the 25–34-year-olds spend 50 percent more on such household items as major appliances, furniture, curtains, rugs, and housewares. They also have more disposable income to spend on travel and luxury items. Experts who saw these figures coming at them were clicking their heels with excitement. In 1970, the Census Bureau director George Hay Brown declared, "We are heading into a society with an affluent majority." Real income, he said, would double by 1985 as millions of baby boomers married and started buying for their families. Fabian Linden, the Conference Board's guru, announced that the new Era of the Young Parent would give us 4.3 million babies annually by 1980 and children in the homes of three out of every five families.

We know from experience that a trend is not necessarily a law. Thanks to outside factors like the energy crunch, inflation, and two recessions, real family income barely budged in the 1970s. Furthermore, there was no reason to expect the baby boom to buy the same things in the same way in the same time as had previous generations. They were a New Breed of consumer that would best reward those who best understood them. Let me mention here just a few of the changes the baby-boom carried with it into its twenties and thirties:

EDUCATION. Just thirty years ago, the 25–34 age group was practically uneducated by today's standards. Only one person in five then had *any* college experience and only one in ten had a degree. But the entry of the baby boom has, in effect, given us a new class of educated adult consumers. Now almost one-half of all 25–34-year-olds have been to college and one-quarter have degrees. Trained in rational decision-making—to compare, question, and analyze—baby boomers as a group are far less likely to obey blind brand loyalties. Goods must prove themselves. On the other hand, baby boomers are more likely to appreciate the differences that quality can make. They do not buy any stereo set; they buy the best stereo set. They do not buy any tennis racquet, they buy the best tennis racquet. The transformation of the 25–34 age group into an educated class powered the cultural boom of the seventies. More people went to museums and ballets and theaters in that decade simply because there were far more people who had been exposed to the arts by college (and, it should not be forgotten, television).

WORKING COUPLES. In this country, fashions and markets are determined by whichever socioeconomic group has the most disposable income at any given time. In 1976, the number of two-income families surpassed those with only one provider for the first time and have since claimed the lion's share of the nation's purchasing power. At least one-half of the country's 25 million working couples are baby boomers. They have helped boost the discretionary income of all young couples higher than at any time in history. In 1978, the aggregate income of the 20–34 age group, roughly corresponding to the boom generation's older cohorts, was $335 billion, an amount one-third of the United States total for all ages and greater than the GNP of the United Kingdom.

What did they buy? An extra car, to begin with. In the seventies, the population of automobiles grew twice as fast as the human population in absolute numbers and nearly five times as fast in percentage, despite the energy crisis. Ford estimated that two-income couples brought 41 percent of its new cars in 1978. And that's not all. Working couples need more life and health insurance to protect their incomes. They want time-saving devices like frozen gourmet pizzas. The Cuisinart food processor is thus the consummate baby-boom product: it saves time and is used for the sophisticated meals favored by the educated and affluent. Working wives buy more shoes and cosmetics than housewives and, surprisingly, spend more on homecare products like floor waxes. Working couples eat out more, travel more, socialize more with friends than relatives, go to the theater more, and drink more liquor than other couples. Working wives have less brand loyalty than housewives.

CHANGING HOUSEHOLDS: The now-familiar litany of family change brought by the baby boom—later marriage, less marriage, more divorce, and fewer children—has also meant a dramatic change in the way all people live . . . and spend. Marketers had originally expected a "Parent Boom" in the seventies that would give us more parents than ever before. The total number of families with children under 18 did creep up from 28 million in 1968 to 30 million ten years later. But at the same time, the number of parents with children under 6 *declined*. Just one-half of all families had any children in them by the end of the decade. And, as a porportion of all households (that is, including people who live alone), married couples with children skidded from 44 percent in 1960 to 40 percent in 1970 to 32 percent in 1979.

Faced with the unexpected arrival of the baby bust, market forecasters hastily revised their judgments. No, the seventies would not be the decade of the Young Parent. Instead, it would be the decade of the Young Marrieds. But while the number of husband-wife families neared a record 50 million, as a proportion of all households they, too, dropped from 71 percent in 1970 to 62 percent in 1979. The Young Marrieds boom also turned out to be a bust.

We were left with a Young Adult boom. Most of the total increase in households took place not among families but among people living alone, many of them young. Their numbers increased from 11 million in 1970 to 17 million in 1979, a gain of 60 percent. Among all households, persons living alone rose from one in every six in 1965 to nearly one in every four by 1980. Many of them were baby boomers who, not burdened by the costs of children, were able to devote far bigger slices of their income pies to recreation, travel, restaurant meals, and the good life. Family-size packaging was out; single servings were in.

All of these qualities of the baby boom—its bigness, its education, its iconoclasm, its enormous disposable income —helped make it a new kind of consuming generation. This was the first wave of affluent, educated consumers who knew what it wanted. Indeed, all its life it had incessantly been told what it wanted by television. Now, for the first time, it had the money to buy it. In marketing terms, the interesting thing about the baby boom in the 1980s is not that it was the first generation of *children* raised on television. It is the first generation of *consuming adults* that had been raised on television.

As if in response to the lifelong lessons of TV commercials, the boomers in adulthood began to buy more and save less than any generation in history. The old Protestant Ethic values of saving and self-sacrifice amounted to little in a time when the operative question was not how much you owned but how much you could borrow. What their parents thought were luxuries—television, second cars, household help—the boom generation thought were necessities. Never had de Tocqueville's maxim that in the

United States what the few have today the many will demand tomorrow seemed more true.

Let's consider a question. At this point in its life, what was holding the baby boom together? Did it still have a generational identity? How could it even think of itself as a generation anymore? Rock and roll was no longer the uncommon denominator of the baby-boom generation. For that matter, the real underground press was dying out. Although many baby boomers were still in college, the leading edge of the generation had moved on and the campuses had quieted. If they were not physically together, as they had been during their years of schooling, what was left to coalesce the baby boomers now? Did their size really affect their attitudes anymore? Or was the idea of the baby boom as a "generation" merely a conceit, a convenient way of describing a group of individuals who had little in common other than age and a similar set of problems?

The answer, I think, is that even if the baby boomers were not inclined to think of themselves as a generation, they would anyway because *there is a large number of people who have the incentive to want to make them think that way*. They are the nation's consumer-goods corporations and particularly their allied market-research firms. Long before the baby boom arrived, they had concluded that it is easier to sell what the market wants than to get the market to buy what they want to sell. And the baby boom was, if nothing else, an enormous market of like-minded individuals. By creating and marketing products aimed directly at the boom generation, these entrepreneurs intensified the generation's self-awareness. And the greater the self-awareness, the easier it was to market products exclusively for it. Thus developed what is the hidden generation-based mechanism that will bind the baby boom for the rest of its days. The Media Generation's spending power and group consciousness are linked in an unending feedback loop. The baby boom did not name the Pepsi Generation; Pepsico did.

It did not take long to see that the commercial impact of the boom generation went beyond its numbers and included its values. Detroit may have expected that young adults would have made the seventies the heyday of the convertibles; instead, they helped kill off the canvas tops. The baby boomers wanted cars but did not see them as status symbols as their parents had. Gift boxes of candy, once a young man's fancy, were abandoned by youth. Hallmark could not sell greeting cards on traditional holidays, but kids were snapping up "affection" cards decorated with gauzy landscape photographs and pseudopoetry for the inarticulate. Unlike their thrift-minded parents, the baby boomers bought expensive items on the theory that they would need less repair.

Hence, the emergence in the 1970s of the independent market-research firm. For the manufacturers baffled by this puzzling generation, the market researchers were prepared to quantify both the boom generation's numbers and its attitudes as well. As New York's Citibank noted in its newsletter, "The race for new markets will go to the nimble rather than the swift—to those who can anticipate the changes in lifestyle implied by the demographics of the future." The researchers bought Census Bureau computer tapes and set about analyzing them, living in the kind of symbiotic relationship with the boom generation that pilot fish have with sharks or tiny birds with alligators' teeth. Wherever the boom generation went, the market researchers followed hard on its spoor, armed with flip charts and words like "psychographics" and "paradigms." Exploring the boom generation's topography, they created a mystique of the marketing safari that Livingston himself would have envied. Arnold Mitchell at the Stanford Research Institute talked about the austere "Simplicity" patterns emerging from the antimaterialist baby-boom consumers. The firm of Needham, Harper & Steers classified all products as exhibiting either "earth values" (simple, long-lasting, inexpensive) or "feather values" (showy, expensive, ephemeral, sensual, and indulgent). The baby boom, the firm said, wanted *both* "feather values" and "earth values."

The most refined studies have been undertaken by the research firm of Yankelovich, Skelly and White. Selling, it said, had evolved through different stages. The first approach was the sales approach, focusing on the product itself. Next companies learned the marketing approach, focusing on the consumer. Then, the consumer was segmented behaviorally as well. Once that was done, companies could find the psychological "hot button" they must push to make the consumers buy.

Yankelovich originally separated the population into five segments—Traditionalists, New Conformists, Forerunners, Autonomous, and Retreaters—and tried to spot the changing values, size, and consumption habits of each. But as the boom generation arrived, Yankelovich centered its attention on the New Breed of Americans whose age and New Values conincided strikingly with the baby boomers. Parenting was not the only area in which the New Breed were unlike other Americans. They did not believe that women should stay home. The men were not willing to put up with drawbacks in their jobs. They were not selflessly loyal to organizations. They did not blindly acquiesce to authority. They did not define their identities through their work. They thought there was more to life than slavishly earning money. They did not think conventional success was necessarily related to their self-fulfillment. They thought society "owed" them self-fulfillment, a good living, and medical care, and possibly even a college education for their children. The people who shared these views were most often under 30, but their attitudes were quickly spreading through other age groups and more than half of the people in the country agreed with them. They were, Yankelovich resoundingly concluded, "the advance signs of life in the 21st century, of the third millennium."

This kind of talk used to be enough to send many businessmen running for the bomb shelters. Instead, Yankelovich offered a service to help them come to grips with the warp speed of social change. It is the "Yankelovich Monitor," a thick volume sent out once a year to some 110 corporate clients who ante up $15,000 to see it. Based on annual interviews with 2500 people, the Monitor spots and tracks some thirty-five different social trends (for example, "Anti-Materialism," "New Romanticism," "Return to Nature," "Living for Today," "Anti-Hypocrisy") and sorts them into such broad categories as "Psychology of Affluence Trends" or "Trends Related to the Weakening of the 'Protestant Ethic.' "

The idea is that a company then fine-tunes its products and sales effort to strike these sensitive chords within the boom generation. If a cereal company stresses its "natural" ingredients, it is obeying Trend No. 14 in the gospel according to Yankelovich ("Return to Nature"). Or if it stresses the cereal's hearty flavors, it is following Trend No. 9 ("Sensuousness"). In all cases, the point is the same. Instead of resisting the baby boom, or trying to change its flow, the savvy corporate strategist will try to ride the baby boom's wave. In short, the values of the

Woodstock Generation had entered the marketplace and, amid enthusiasm all around, swept aside everything in their path. Instead of eroding the boom generation's self-image, the market economy was continuing to reinforce it and ultimately to exploit it.

Take blue jeans. The company founded in 1853 by a penniless Bavarian immigrant named Levi Strauss had made a modest success in its first century selling its model 501 Double X denim jeans to farmers and cowboys. Then, in the mid-1950s, James Dean wore jeans in *Rebel Without a Cause* and Marlon Brando wore them in *The Wild One* just as the first baby boomers were growing up. Suddenly, jeans were more than clothes: they were a symbol of a way of life that was anti-Establishment, anti-adult, antielitist, earthy, proletarian, democratic, and, more than anything, youthful. That mystique made blue jeans the worldwide uniform of the baby-boom generation. They were banned in American schoolrooms, bid up to extortionate prices in Paris, and smuggled behind the Iron Curtain. But Levi Strauss had caught a wave. Between 1962 and 1970, its sales and net profits grew fivefold and between 1970 and 1977 its sales again quintupled while profits almost septupled. It became the largest clothing manufacturer in the world, a $1 billion corporate behemoth that found itself in the unlikely position of being praised by Charles Reich in *The Greening of America* for making a product that was "a deliberate rejection of the neon colors and artificial, plastic-coated look for affluent society."

But that was the sixties ethos. By the mid-seventies, the older baby boomers required something different. They still wanted jeans, to be sure, but now they were skintight, slinky things with signatures like Gloria Vanderbilt, Pierre Cardin, and Diane Von Furstenberg stitched on the rear. Prices ran from $30 to $200 for jeans made of velour, silk, satin, and occasionally denim. Women in New York dieted down until their hipbones were sticking out like a sacred cow's but they still needed pliers to tug up the zippers on their Yves Saint Laurent tummy-tighteners. Calvin Klein was merchandising fashion jeans in toddler sizes, and Sasson came out with a special elastic backing to accommodate diapers in its jeans. Fortunes were made by men like the Nakash brothers, three Israelis who started Jordache in March 1978 and eighteen months later were ringing up $30 million a year in sales.

Once again, the baby boom had transformed the market just when it was least expected. Jeans had once been the cultural totem by which this generation measured its independence and its commitment to the sweaty democratic values of the frontier. These clothes, Charles Reich wrote, "deny the importance of hierarchy, status, authority, position, and they reject competition." But what values were jeans measuring now that they were huckstered at Bloomingdale's? If anything, it was sex appeal and status. It was the difference between *Rebel Without a Cause* and *Grease,* between James Dean and John Travolta, between passion and posing, and, for the boom generation, between its rites of adolescence and its rites of adulthood.

Someday, before it is too late, every marketer in the country should be required to inscribe in his or her soul this law: Those Who Live by the Baby Boom Shall Die by the Baby Boom. The pig that moves through the python will bring booms and busts wherever it goes. A good example of the perilous life to those who attach their fate to the baby boom is fast food. In the sixties, the fast-food industry surged to record profits by serving mountains of stringy French fries to the baby boom's ravenous teenagers. McDonald's grew to a franchising network of 5000 stores and John Y. Brown was able to turn an investment of $2 million in Kentucky Fried Chicken in 1963 to $280 million when he sold the company eight years later.

But then in the seventies, as the boom started to move on, fast food lost its sizzle. There were rising meat costs, rising minimum wages, and rising costs of gasoline to get customers to the stores. There was also the fear that there would soon be fewer customers altogether. In the 1980s, the number of Americans aged 5–17, the heart of the traditional fast-food market, would likely *decline* by more than half a million. Already older customers were showing their preferences for sitting down and eating instead of gobbling up their food in their cars. Kentucky Fried Chicken, with thousands of take-out windows and few seats, was almost fatally damaged. Ralston Purina lopped off 270 of its drive-in Jack-in-the-Box restaurants in one swift blow. Even mighty McDonald's saw the price of its stock halved during the fast-food crisis as investors worried about "market saturation."

If the $25-billion fast-food business survives the shake-out of the seventies it will be by keeping the customers who made it—the baby boomers. Stores once painted in garish pop-style reds and greens are redecorating in warm, earthy browns and yellows with an eye to pleasing the mature customer. McDonald's added its breakfast menu in 1976 to attract working people and is now turning to a dinner market with steak sandwiches and a Mc-Feast menu for the mellow diner who wants to linger for a while. Others have built mini-playgrounds outside to lure young families out of their homes.

If the new tactics work, the prognosis for the fast-food industry may not be so grim. Previously, the industry had prospered by feeding teenagers. The conventional wisdom was that the older people preferred to stay home. But we already know that the behavior of one generation at a particular age is no guide to what the baby boomers will do. What if the craving for fast food stays with the baby boom, becoming a characteristic of that generation as well as of youth? Certainly, its behavior so far points in that direction. The boom generation has fewer links with the home than previous generations. More baby boomers live alone and are, therefore, more inclined to eat out. Even in families, the new generation of 30–40-year-olds will have more working mothers with less time for at-home cooking. Americans now spend 40 percent of their food dollars eating outside the home. Fast-food restaurants command half of all meals eaten outside the home and are gaining as a proportion of all meals, whether inside or outside the home. The thought that fast-food franchises will someday be filled with elderly types eating prune-based dishes and soggy French fries may have more than a sesame seed of truth to it.

The Pepsi Generation—meaning the soft-drink market, not the associated state of mind—is also imperiled. The 13–24 age group will decline by an estimated 4 million between 1976 and 1985. This age group is the headwater of the soft-drink industry, with each individual guzzling an average of more than 800 cans of soda a year. A strictly demographic projection, then, would suggest that the industry faces a shortfall of 3.2 million unsold cans by 1985.

Marketers, armed with computer printouts of the boom generation's every quirk and preference, are already at work to make the soft-drink habit stick. Pepsi is not pushing the teenage market but has introduced citrus-flavored drinks like Aspen for older people. (The company's existing lemon-lime drink, Mountain Dew, is already a hot item.) Coca-Cola is adding a lemony drink called Mello Yello, presumably aimed at aging Woodstockers. But the fastest movers of all in the late seventies turned out to be carbonated mineral waters like Perrier, which bear roughly the same relationship to soda pop as Cacharel jeans do to Levi's (Yankelovich Social Trend No. 3, "Physical Fitness and Well-Being").

The other side of the coin is that as the baby boomers forsake one market, they prime the pump in another. So, as they began to put down their soft-drink cans with one hand, with the other they were raising beer bottles. As of 1979, beer consumption in the United States had increased every year for the previous twenty, reaching a total of 23 gallons per capita. Meanwhile, the generation that cared first about itself (Yankelovich Social Trend No. 2, "Physical Enhancement") was not about to get fat in its adulthood quaffing all those suds. Miller Brewing had only 4 percent of the market until an infusion of Philip Morris cash pushed its low-calorie Lite beer to phenomenal sales and the company to number two in the industry and a 20 percent market share.

Wine sales are also flowing like a river. It began with the boom in sugary "pop" wines in the sixties as every possible nut, berry, and fruit was turned into a wine or liquor. But as the boom generation continued to grow up, so did its tastes. Dry white wines now outsell all others, and old-line French liqueurs like Benedictine, once aimed almost exclusively at the silver-sideburn set, are aggressively pursuing the more refined younger drinkers. The growth in oenophilia may yet provide the best proof that this generation can get high on something other than marijuana.

Magazines and newspapers, with their insistence on tapping the prime 18–34 market (a category that, not coincidentally, exactly matched the baby-boom cohort in 1980), have also provided a sensitive sounding of underlying generational shifts. In the sixties, the then-rebellious baby boomers fostered dozens of underground papers crammed with political rhetoric, rock reviews, and usually lurid personals. Then, in the seventies, as their readers moved on, the papers were driven out of business more effectively than if the government had banned them. But the baby boom's need for unconventional reporting was still there. So in the place of "underground" newspapers, we now have "alternative" newspapers providing for readers who have outgrown record reviews and are interested in detailed reporting as well as where to buy a better begonia. Papers like the *Boston Phoenix, Maine Times,* and the *Pacific Sun* have pioneered the way to this over-21 readership by combining the kind of detailed political analysis not usually carried by the daily papers with shopping guides. Even the old *Berkeley Barb,* devasted by a circulation drop from 90,000 to 12,000, briefly survived by cutting out the most lurid personals and stressing reader service.

Other magazines have been left foundering once the prevailing wind of the baby boom shifted. *Parents* magazine saw its circulation tumble from 2.1 million in 1971 to 1.4 million in 1979. (Interestingly, the total number of actual parents in the United States did not decline in those years. What had declined, evidently, was their interest in parenting.) Rock magazines like *Crawdaddy* (later *Feature*) disappeared altogether as young people became more interested in reading about quiches in *Cuisine* than in counting Elton John's sunglasses. The ultimately age-specific magazine, *Seventeen,* revised its motto to "Today, she's really 18–34." And, after watching its circulation dive in the seventies, *Playboy* decided to catch up with one segment of its audience by risking its first over-30 centerfold.

When the baby boom's young adults were not thinking about decorating with hanging plants, they were evidently thinking about sports. At least that's what the numbers suggest. The cult of the young adult changed the place of sports in American life in a way that we are just beginning to understand.

First, organized sports became big business largely because of the influx of young spectators. Young adults buy most sports tickets and, in a decade, attendance at sporting events grew by more than 100 million. Introduced to baseball and football and basketball by television, the baby boomers flocked through the turnstiles in record numbers. Here, if nowhere else, they could relive the strong group emotions they had last felt in the demonstrations and rock concerts of the sixties. If the Indianapolis

500 is a redneck Woodstock, then Yankee Stadium is an urban Altamont.

The second change the baby boom brought was a new golden age of participant sports. The number of tennis players rose by 45 percent in 1973–76. Then racquetball and squash had their first flings. Later it was jogging, the perfect activity for a generation first confronting the emotional chasm of the thirtieth birthday. Even the whimsical campus pastime of Frisbee was captured by commercial interests who organized big-time competitions and $30,-000 endorsement contracts. What had happened, in short, was that the baby boomers were turning sports into a consumer industry. Here is *Sport* magazine describing its readers in a typically flamboyant piece of promotional literature:

> They're men under 30, active and affluent, whose sport-centered lifestyle influences the nation's buying habits and boosts discretionary income. They turned jeans into high style. They made the active sportswear market grow by leaps and bounds. They said "Da" to vodka, gin and white wine. They said "Okay" to the everyday use of toiletries and grooming aids. They made the hot comb a hot item. They're into golf, tennis, cycling, jogging. And the rest of us follow their lead.
>
> We call them Young Money.

When the baby boom was in its young adulthood, it made sports a fad. Miniature golf and croquet notwithstanding, it was something new in American life when Adidas could sell 13 million pairs of running shoes in a single year. And who is to say that, when millions of blistering joggers finally hang up their togs in middle age, croquet and miniature golf will not then seem the perfect candidates for a renaissance at the hands of the baby boom?

Entering its thirties, the baby boom seemed to be on the verge of paying off at least some of the glowing promise it had offered back in the maternity wards of the fifties. Television's consumer trainees were powering an overheated market economy, saving less and spending more than their parents ever had. Many economists believe that as much as one-fifth of the recent decline in the overall national savings rate, as well as the rise in total consumer debt, can be explained solely by the arrival of the baby boomers into their high-spending ages.

The country's first enclosed mall was built outside Minneapolis in 1956. Since then, malls have spread out over cornfields and asparagus patches, paved over with shoulder-to-shoulder lineups of Sears, Penneys, Magic Pans, Waldenbooks, Bath Trends, The Gaps, and Thom McAn shoe shops. Unlike old-style, linear shopping centers, which had transferred the dominant visual image of commercial life from the urban center to the highway, the new malls turned their backs to the highways, too, curling in on themselves like wagon trains on the prairie. Hermetically sealed from the vagaries of weather, they presented a curiously stable and timeless environment, reminiscent of Las Vegas gambling casinos where clocks had been removed from the walls. The malls are places where there is no sense of place. But for many baby boomers, they are the closest thing to what their parents would have called "Downtown." Americans now spend more time in shopping malls than in any other single place save the home and the job. Malls are among the few places in our country where people of all ages gather for a common purpose. Teenagers have made the malls their most popular hangouts. Indeed, according to a Rutgers University study, many suburban teenagers no longer identify their place of residence as a town or county but rather as "Three miles from the Oxford Valley Mall" or "near Quaker Bridge Mall." Elderly people, too, come to the malls, not to shop but, as they always have, to sit on benches and observe the young. Crime is relatively rare in the malls; the real terror is the anomie of their strangely airless ambiance.

Thus, the baby boom has transformed the marketplace. Its influence has been profound and will be lasting. At the same time, it is not the arsonist behind every fire. Polaroid, for instance, blamed the low birthrate for the poor debut of its instant home movies at the same time Kodak was attributing its own record sales to the influx of baby-boom parents photographing their children.

If the cult of the adult had brought any one message to the market economy, it was that the antimaterialism of the sixties was fast disappearing. The idealists of those days, assured *Playboy* magazine in its promotional copy, have become "the new materialists." The magazine continued reassuringly:

Sure they burned draft cards and tore up the campus and smoked funny cigarettes and never cut their hair and made us despair. . . . They haven't lost one iota of that intensity. They've just totally redirected it. They've traded the SDS for IBM and GM . . .

The sigh of relief was almost audible. The baby boom was no longer anti-Establishment. It *was* the Establishment.

Chapter 18

THE HOUSING BUBBLE

In the fifties, we worried about where the baby boomers would grow up. In the sixties, we worried about where they went to school. In the seventies, we worried about where they would live.

Suddenly, guests at dinner parties found something else to talk about besides crime. The new and more compelling topic of conversation was housing. Specifically, it was the extended and unparalleled rise in rental and house prices that lasted throughout the seventies and posed a far greater threat to middle-class stability than any number of purse snatchings or ripped-off TV sets. House prices were inflating beyond comprehension, buoyed by a soaring demand that seemed to be spurred by the home fever rather than deterred by it. It was America's version of the South Sea bubble of the early eighteenth century or the Dutch tulip mania of the seventeenth century. Like any panic, it fed on atrocity stories. There was the man who bought a Manhattan town house for $300,000 and sold it six months later for $600,000 (only to be offered $800,000 a week later). A condominium atop Nob Hill in San Francisco was bought for $500,000 in 1978 and sold for $1 million a year later. In just five years, the average selling price of a house in Washington, D.C., doubled to $100,-000.

Many Americans who had climbed on the real-estate merry-go-round in the sixties suddenly found themselves house-rich. But millions more, especially those in the baby-boom cohorts entering their family-forming years in the seventies and eighties, were devastated by rising prices, rising mortgage rates, prohibitive down-payment requirements, and extortionate maintenance and utility rates. The median price of a new house in America nearly quadrupled from $18,000 in 1963 to $64,000 in 1980. Family income, at the same time, trailed far behind, making the dream of home ownership even more difficult for young families. In 1970, according to an estimate by the Department of Housing and Urban Development, half of the people in the country could afford to buy the median-priced new house. Today only 13 percent can. In fact, nearly two-thirds of all American families in 1980 could not afford to purchase the homes in which they live.

Once again, the boom generation was its own undoing. The baby boom has always been most visible during its times of transition: from birth to the beginning of schooling to its entry into the labor force. As it encountered each new passage, the giant generation forced readjustments by society along the way. No sooner had one institution managed to swallow the bulk of the boom—as colleges had by the seventies—than the boom's leading edge was forging irresistibly ahead, causing still more indigestion.

What the baby boom needed next was a place of its own. We could have predicted it. Young people almost always move from home between the ages of 18 and 24. When the boom generation's turn came, it made the transition with a wallop. It was the difference between the country's adding half a million new households every year in the sixties, before the boom arrived, to adding 1.5 million new households every year in the seventies. The total number of households, which had grown from 53 million in 1960 to 63 million in 1970, then jumped to 77 million in 1979. The rate of increase was three times faster than the population as a whole.

The odd thing was that the rise in the number of households was even greater than might have been expected from the entry of a new generation into its family-forming years. In numbers alone, the addition of millions of baby boomers explains only about one-third of the numerical rise in households over the past fifteen years. The other two-thirds of the increase resulted largely from the way the baby boom behaved. By leaving home earlier, marrying later, marrying less often, and living alone more often, the baby boomers redoubled their impact on the housing market.

The best way to understand what happened is to look at the distinction the Census Bureau makes between two types of households: family and nonfamily. Family households are related people who live together: married couples, with or without children, single parents, or any combination of relatives. But nonfamily households comprise people living alone or with people not related to them (thereby including cohabiting couples). In the seventies, family households grew imperceptibly, just over 1 percent a year, and actually declined from four out of every five households to three out of four. So many baby boomers remained unmarried that, despite the large number of candidates, the portion of all households headed by married couples with children declined from 44 percent in 1960 to 32 percent in 1979.

The number of nonfamily households, on the other hand, has increased ten times as fast, growing 50 percent in the sixties and then a staggering 69 percent in the seventies. The overwhelming majority of nonfamily households consists of a single person living alone. Today 17 million Americans—more than one in every five households and twice the number in 1960—are living alone. Of them, six out of every ten are women and three out of ten are women over the age of 65. But the fastest-growing category of single people is not the old but the young: adults under the age of 35—baby boomers all—increased by 45 percent in the seventies and are now twice as likely to live alone as their predecessors. This enormous increase in single-person households, combined with the falling birthrate, has caused the households to shrink to their smallest sizes in history. The average American household fell below three persons for the first time in 1974 and by 1979 was down to 2.78. Today more than half of all households consist of only one or two people living together.

What caused the boom generation to want to be alone? One factor is a matter of timing. The baby boomers have typically made the break from their parents' homes at an earlier age than previous generations. Many of them left home to go to college and never came back. As college enrollments multiplied from 4.8 million in 1963 to 11.2 million in 1972, there was inevitable weakening of family ties. The affluence of those times also helped the baby boom to go out on its own. After World War II, for example, shortages in both housing and income forced 9 percent of married couples to live with someone else, usually their parents. Now that prosperity has reduced the appeal of coresidence, only 1 percent of married couples share the roof with someone else. (The domestic life of

All in the Family, where the Bunkers lived, however uneasily, with the Stivics, was more a figment of Norman Lear's imagination than anything esle. And even Gloria and the Meathead moved out when he got a better job.)

The changes the baby boom brought to family life further increased the number of single-person households in society. The rising age of marriage meant that more people in their early and mid-twenties were remaining single —two-thirds of all men 20–24 and nearly half of the women. (Some of these, to be sure, were consolidated in unmarried-couple households. But the 1.3 million cohabiting households is only a small fraction of the total.) The doubling of the divorce rate has also contributed to the rise in total households—but its long-run effect is harder to pin down because four out of five divorced people later remarry. If a divorce created one extra household, a remarriage eliminates another. Even so, the maintenance of a larger, rotating pool of divorced people added another growing group of new households to the total. The number of divorced women heading households doubled in the seventies and is now one-third of all female-headed households.

Though under-35 householders contributed by far the largest portion of new growth in households during the seventies, they by no means were the only ones. The shrinkage of families occurred at both ends of the age spectrum: if the baby boomers were leaving the extended family, well, so were their grandparents. All throughout the seventies, the proportion of older people living with their families decreased. Instead of living in an extra bedroom in the house of one of their children (most often a daughter), older Americans were increasingly going it alone in condominiums and apartments. In 1968, less than half of all widows over 65 lived alone, but by 1975, nearly two out of three of them did. Many of them, when widowed, were able to live alone thanks to generous retirement and pension plans. Indeed, most older people would rather not live *with* their children but *near* them— "intimacy at a distance," as gerontolotists call it.

The initial result of the baby boom's arrival, with its vast influx of prospective householders, was an explosion in demand for apartments. From Manhattan to Marina Del Ray, millions of new apartments were built to provide shelter for the baby-boom young. During the late sixties and early seventies, as the first baby boomers left college, the percentage of new housing starts accounted for by apartments rose from one-third to nearly half the total.

That was just the beginning. Between 1970 and 1971, as the baby boomers born in 1946 turned 25, more than 1.9 million new households were formed in America, a record that still has not been equaled. Many of them issued from the first wave of baby boomers joining the traditionally house-hungry 25–34-year-old group. As the baby boom poured into those ages, the percentage of all households headed by 25–34-year-olds shot up from 18.5 percent to 20.5 percent in just four years.

In the meantime, what was happening to supply? In a perfect market economy, supply rises to meet demand, thereby keeping prices stable. But housing starts were falling further and further behind. Restrictive land-use and zoning laws were depressing housing, as were inflationary building costs. Even in years like 1972, when the construction industry built a then-record 1.5 million single-family units, only one-quarter of them were bought by married couples. The balance went to the millions of single people and unmarried couples flooding into the market. Most of them lived in small houses or apartments, since the four- and five-bedroom houses of the fifties were already becoming obsolete in the low-fertility seventies. Whatever slim chances the housing supply might have had of catching up to demand were killed off once and for all by the recession of 1974–75, during which housing starts all but died on the vine, declining by 65 percent.

In other times, we might have expected a recession to tamp out the overheated housing market. The economic news was all bad: unemployment was up from 4.9 percent to 8.5 percent and stocks had slumped nearly 50 percent. But demand was still outracing supply. In the seventies, construction of new houses rose only 11 percent, while the total of outstanding mortagage loans increased nearly 200 percent. The difference was in inflated housing prices.

Even during the recession, the average sales price of a new home went from $30,500 in 1972 to $42,600 in 1975. By 1977, the median value of a typical single-family house had risen 53 percent over 1973. The mad momentum peaked in 1978, when 817,000 new houses and 3.9 million existing houses were sold, a 29 percent and a 65 percent increase, respectively, since 1973. In just one year, the average price of a single-family house had stepped up another 14½ percent, compared to an overall inflation rate of 8 percent. Incredibly, the total 1978 increase in house prices—$140 billion—was about the same as for the entire decade of the sixties.

In California, where more baby boomers live than anyplace else, the increases were astronomical. In the seventies, California led the nation in the number of new households and, not surprisingly, also posted the highest real-estate gains. In all the Western states, the median values of housing had risen 76 percent in four years. In cities like Los Angeles and San Francisco, where foreign investors and others were pumping up prices in a speculative frenzy, prices were tripling in a year and $100,000 became the standard price for the basic three-bedroom rancher. New home buyers were locked out, but people who had bought in years earlier were cashing in. Some were making hundreds of thousands of dollars simply by swapping houses every year. Beverly Hills types were making as much off their real estate as in show business. (The most successful house-traders epitomized what could be called the Law of Inverse Properties: namely, that the architectural style of the house is inversely proportional to the personal style of the entertainer. The *outré* Cher, for example, perfers staid Tudors, while the more reticent Robert Redford lives in a spectacular glass-and-steel aerie perched atop a Utah mountain.)

How could the baby boomers cope? The dream of home ownership had been the steady beacon ardently followed by their parents' generation. The boom generation had inherited this part of the American dream, at least, judging from the sustained demand. They, too, craved a plot of land to call their own. Only now the dream was receding. Inflation was growing faster than both. The baby boomers were discovering to their dismay that the competition of their own number had once again caught them in a bind: it had depressed their relative wages while at the same time raising housing costs.

Surprisingly, however, the baby boom not only managed to solve this problem of financing its housing but did it even more eagerly than its parents. The average age of home ownership dropped during the seventies as the baby boomers started moving in. Meanwhile, the proportion of householders owning their own dwelling increased from 64 percent to 70 percent. How did they achieve successful housebuying against such long odds? They became "house-poor," hiking their down payments from the usual one-quarter of income to a hefty 35 percent of income. Another reason is that many of them were financing houses on two incomes. If a couple could live on one spouse's salary, the other's could be stashed away to build up equity for that crucial first down payment. In California, where two incomes are practically a prerequisite for first-time house buyers, the number of mortgages taken out by two-salary families in recent years went from one out of every five mortgages to one out of two. Experts like Kenneth Rosen of Berkeley now speak of "three-income" families benefiting from monthly paychecks and a 1 percent monthly appreciation on their housing investments.

Finally, thanks to inflation, high housing prices actually fed on each other. With prices leaping 12 percent a year, many couples saw owning a house as the only port in the storm of inflation. Runaway prices thus became a self-fulfilling prophecy. People wanted to buy houses to beat inflation. The resulting demand made prices rise even higher, which spurred still more demand. Only the government and the banks could break the cycle by clamping down on mortgage money, which they finally did during the credit crunch of 1979–80.

As the baby boomers began feathering their hard-won nests, another category of magazines suddenly got hot. The "shelter books" like *House & Garden* were suddenly brimming with readers and advertisers trying to reach them. Here is how *House & Garden* ("The Magazine for the Eighties") happily described its new readership:

—They're exploding the number of single-person households.
—They're making the dual career, dual income family the norm.
—They're raising the median age for marriage.
—They're lowering the birth rate.
—They're populating our rural communities.
—They're peopling our hi-rises.
—They're homesteading our inner cities.
—They're the biggest market of young, affluent, home-motivated people in history. . . . They're the new

establishment that's shaping society and the home marketplace. They're ready for *us* . . . we're ready for them.

One side effect of the baby boom's housing crunch, as well as its decline in average family size, has been the rush to condominiums. Prompted both by rent-control laws which cut into their profit margins, as well as demand from baby-boom buyers seeking to build equity, landlords began converting apartments into condominiums all over the country. In 1977, 50,000 apartment units were converted into condominiums; in 1978, the number was 100,000; in 1979, it was 130,000. Prices were going up almost as fast, with the per-room selling price of Manhattan co-op units doubling in the late seventies. Condominiums, with half the floor space of a house, make abundant sense for single people and small families who would rather see their money go toward ski vacations in Aspen than real-estate taxes and crabgrass control. In Washington, a city where young, single people dominate now as much as they once did in Berkeley and Madison, entire apartment complexes are occupied by single people. And the entire Borough of Manhattan, where more than one-half the apartment units are occupied by single people, young and old, was practically a singles ghetto.

But what of the eighties? Will the number of households continue to rise at the explosive rates of the past decade? Or can we expect some easing of the pressure? The answer is not as available as we might think. There is a temptation to use the present age-specific rates of home ownership, for example, as a kind of barometer to predict the future. By applying the present rates of household formation against projected population changes that are already in the cards—all the people who will be buying houses in the eighties have already been born—we should be able to make some reasonable guesses about future home ownership.

The problem, though, is that predicting trends on the basis of population change sometimes has all the reliability of predicting the weather. We can make a reasonable guess that it is likely to rain but not when it will start or when it will end or how much will fall. Anyone in the 1960s predicting household formation in the seventies would have necessarily fallen short. The changes in age structure made inevitable by the baby boom would have been spotted, all right, but no one could have guessed just how those baby boomers would act. Who could have known that the divorce rate would triple in a decade? Or that birth rates would be halved? Or that the baby boomers would turn single people from a class of renters into a class of renters and owners? Or that the unprecedented rise in working women would provide a wholly unexpected source of buying power?

All this is true, but like the weathermen, demographers still must make do with what information they have. On the face of it, the current of housing demand should still be running high well into the 1980s. Population change alone should boost the number of households from 80 million today to over 90 million in the late 1980s and then to anywhere from 97 million to 107 million by 1995. (The Census Bureau, painfully aware of the variation changing tastes can bring, typically offers a range of household projections.) Those nmbers suggest that only an exceptional rise in the number of housing units could continue to meet the steady demand.

More important than the number of households is what kind of households will be needed and who will need them. We already know that in the 1980s the number of households under 25 will inevitably decrease as the boom moves past that age—good news, perhaps, for renters but bad news for landlords. The crucial 25–34 house-buying bracket will continue to be filled by younger baby boomers, growing from 36 million to 41 million. The massive 1957 cohort, the baby boom's largest, will produce more 25-year-olds in 1982 than ever before in American history. But the evidence of recent history is that most of the stresses produced by the baby boom come not with the children born during the 1957 peak but rather earlier when the cutting-edge babies of the late forties make their tumultuous arrival. By the time the 1957 babies arrive, we are usually ready for them. Thus, while the 25–34 age group will account for some two-thirds of the growth in house ownership through 1985, its impact will be considerably softened afterward.

It is quite possible that the housing boom could end much sooner than expected. If *all* house buyers are considered, the demographic pressure on housing should continue until around 1987. But more than half of *first-*

time house buyers are under 30. That group will start declining before 1985. A bad economy, plus even a slight ease in housing demand, could erode the confidence that has existed until now that a house is a safe investment. Some economists believe that in the early 1980s, housing prices could fall across the country for the first time since the Depression. The impact on the baby boomers, many of whom would be stuck with mortgages larger than the value of their homes, would be devastating. But, considering the generation's calamitous coming-of-age to date, it would not be surprising.

Chapter 19

THE NOSTALGIC STYLE

Think back to the '60s.

Did you worry about taxes back then? Car payments? Mortgages? The cavity-prone years of your kids? If you didn't then and you do now, something happened.

You grew up.

To celebrate the flowering of your adulthood, we put together a whole new sound for you. We play all the great songs from 1969 to 1976. But we play them beautifully—gently arranged for easy listening.

It's not the kind of music that screeches and thumps. It's the kind of music you use as an accompaniment for your life.

You've grown up.

> —Advertisement for Los Angeles radio
> station, 1979

Where were you in '62?

> —Advertisement for the movie,
> *American Graffiti*, 1973

Nostalgia is the arthritis of the baby boom. In fact, when the Swiss physician Johannes Hofer originally coined the word in the late seventeenth century, it was thought not to be an emotion at all, but a disease. Its symptoms, which included profound melancholy and loss of appetite, seemed particularly to affect Swiss mercenary soldiers away from home. Hofer and others searched determinedly for the exact physiological location of the "Swiss disease," which, they hypothesized, was possibly brought about by eardrum damage caused by the continuous clanging of cowbells in the thin Alpine air.

It is probably not true that the boom generation's nostalgia springs from neurological damage caused by listening to rock 'n' roll, but it is certain that, even in their youth, the boom babies became the most powerfully nostalgic generation in history. For most of the 1970s, the dominant cultural style was not forged from the new but from the old. There was Fonzie and the Sweathogs, *American Graffiti* and *The Buddy Holly Story. Grease* became the longest-running show in Broadway history and *Vanities,* another 1950s waxworks, became the longest-running play in off-Broadway history. Fifties' figureheads, like Buffalo Bob and Clayton (The Lone Ranger) Moore, and even the old Hit Paraders, like Dorothy Collins and Snooky Lanson, were touring again. Old Donald Duck comic books were selling for $1000 apiece and Carl Barks, who wrote and drew them, became the object of a pseudoscholarly cult. The first 1939 number of Marvel Comics brought $13,000 in 1979. Even Barbie dolls, all 110 million of them, were becoming collectors' items by the time Barbie turned 21 in 1980. In the absence of a powerful new youth culture to usurp it, the baby boom was continuing to impose its memories of its own *belle époque*—the 1950s—on society. Kids who were not even born until 1970 were growing up talking about cooties and hickies and nerds.

Why did the baby boomers, aging into their twenties and thirties, retreat to the images of their Paradise Lost? This ought to be a simple question to answer, but is not. The explanation is frequently put forth that the culture of the Rock & Protest Era, as we have come to think of it, was somehow more exciting and creative than our own and therefore more attractive. A reviewer writing in the *Atlantic Monthly* put it this way:

> To the students of the seventies with little more to nudge their political consciences than the Panama Canal, the passions of war protests must sound romantic indeed. . . . And adolescents tuned to the bland ballads of Donny and Marie Osmond, or Karen and Richard Carpenter, must find the joyful explosion wrought by the Beatles exhilarating.

Or, similarly, here is another writer in *New Times:*

> [For] a new generation of teens weaned on Nixon and glitter rock and without any positive satisfying youth

experience to cherish and stamp as their own . . . the Beach Boys' music transports them back to the early Sixties, when people did go to the prom and scamper on the beach.

This is generational chauvinism. In actuality, nostalgia has very little to do with the comparative merits of the pop music of the fifties versus the music of the seventies. Nostalgia tells us more about the conditions of the present than the past. And, in the case of the baby boom, I think, nostalgia speaks most clearly about the strains it has faced dealing with a troubling present and an uncertain future. Jeff Greenfield was closer to the real truth when he wrote of revivals of 1950s hits that

> out of the passions unleashed by the music of fifteen years ago has come, in part, a generation so embittered, that it retreats back into the blaring tenor saxophones and raucous rhythms of a music which our parents found subversive, but which suggests to them an Age of Innocence, a time before the war, on the other side of the Generational Fault.

Nostalgia, in short, reflects the discontinuities of the baby boom's turbulent coming of age. The giant generation, ill at ease with its place in a society that has yet to metabolize it, looks back to the last time it knew when its life was serene and its identity certain. Once they are lovingly recaptured and relived, even the smallest details of the earlier time can accumulate and help shore up identities threatened in the present. Columnist Russell Baker has pointed out that Asian villagers who have lived for generations in one place would be baffled by nostalgia. Why? Because nostalgia is the special affliction of people who have traveled so far or so rapidly in space, or time, that they are confused by the present and have no taste for the future. Nostalgia thrives on dislocations in the life cycle, whether in the life of an individual or the life of a generation.

Since nostalgia attempts to bridge gaps in our lives, between old selves and new selves, it follows that it is most likely to break out at times when disruptions are the sharpest. In the life of an individual, this typically happens after adolescence. When we enter our twenties, we are on the other bank of the river from adolescence.

As we attempt to deal with a whole new set of mature relationships, we begin to savor the ecstasies of adolescence and forget the agonies. There is nothing new about this in American generations. F. Scott Fitzgerald dwelled in the romanticism of youth most of his life. And Leslie Fiedler has argued that in America there is no emotional life after adolescence.

Consider now the individuals of the baby boom. They passed their puberty with the largest and most self-conscious generation ever. Further, their adolescence was prolonged and intensified by near-universal secondary education and an unprecedented increase in higher education. They were brought together by age segregation and rock 'n' roll into a youth culture that took center stage in American life. What psychologists call their "ego strength" was healthy, vigorous, and unchallenged. As Jack Heifner, who wrote *Vanities,* once observed, "The best years of their lives were, unfortunately, the first years of their lives."

What happened to them next was what Fred Davis, a sociologist at the University of California, accurately calls "perhaps the most wide-ranging, sustained and profound assault on native belief concerning the 'natural' and 'proper' that has ever been visited on a people over so short a span of time." The children of the baby boom then experienced the now-familiar blows—the Kennedy assassinations, riots in the cities, protests, the war in Vietnam, the counterculture, women's liberation, homosexual liberation, and the accelerating pace of technological change. Yeats's metaphor of the center that would not hold was becoming a cliché. Staggered and disturbed by change, questioning all its assumptions about society and the family, the baby boom was winding up with something close to a collective identity crisis. Moreover, these changes were striking the baby boom just at the time it was making its difficult transition out of adolescence.

Thus, as individuals and as a generation, the baby boom was groping to find itself in a remade world. In his study of the nostalgic impulse, Davis writes:

> Just as the phasing of the life cycle periodically entails status transitions that in their perceived discontinuity and attendant anxiety evoke nostalgic reactions from individuals, so do untoward major historic events and

283

abrupt social changes pose a similar threat and evoke a similar response from people in the aggregate.

The centripetal forces endangered in adolescence would have been enough to foster the baby boom's nostalgia even without the upheavals of the sixties. But the sixties snapped something else within the generation at large that intensified its need for nostalgia. "Do you know why my friends and I are reading all through Thackeray again?" a baby-boom woman asked Francine du Plessix Gray. "Because there's so little continuity in our lives. Women my age can't remember the names of half the men we've slept with since we were 17." Another woman told Davis about a friend who

> thought it had to do with the fact that we were all born around 1947 and 1948, that we're all about 25 and should be getting it together in some way. But lots of these people are going through a lot of turmoil right now which makes them very nostalgic for the past due to the transitional stage we're going through now and the age we're at.

Nostalgia, then, is a functional emotion which, by shoring up a sagging sense of identity, can help either a person or a generation cope with difficult times. In nostalgia, the baby boomers have found a haven from anxiety and a means of reaffirming stable identities badly shaken during the passage from adolescence. It bears the same relationship to anxiety that aspirin does to a headache: it offers temporary relief. For the baby boomers, it was not that the past was so wonderful, it was that the present is so troubling.

One place where we see this clearly is baseball. Strictly speaking, baseball is a sport of an earlier generation. But it has a strange fascination for those individuals on the cutting edge of the baby boom. Ted Gold, one of the young radicals killed in the 1970 bomb-factory explosion in a Manhattan town house, used to tell friends that he could never become a true revolutionary until Willie Mays retired. James Simon Kunen, one of the 1968 Columbia University demonstrators, described in *The Strawberry Statement* his ambivalence about reconciling his opposition to the system with his support of the Boston Red Sox. Only at baseball games, he felt, could he "talk to anybody at all and share something and be together and understand." Why baseball instead of football? The reason, I think, lies in the special character of baseball during the fifties and early sixties when the baby boom was growing up. In those days, before the time of expansion and free agents, all the events of baseball unfolded in a single summer's night in only eight ball parks. At the beginning of the 1950s, there were sixteen major-league teams; at the end of the 1950s, there still were sixteen major-league teams. Unlike the more volatile and technocratic professional football, baseball, in the fifties, offered a reassuring tintype of an unchanging world of small-town values. In baseball, the baby boom found the objective correlative of its childhood—stable, predictable, and timeless. The answer to Simon and Garfunkel's question—"Where have you gone, Joe DiMaggio?"—was not just that he was selling coffee makers.

This brings me to another aspect of the baby boom's nostalgia boom: mass production. Some types of nostalgia are felt exclusively by individuals. A person might remember a particular adolescent romance or a particular house. This kind of experience cannot be shared. But, just as so many of the disruptive events of their adolescence—the assassinations, the Vietnam War, to name only two—affected almost all baby boomers, so their nostalgia can be thought of as a deeply social emotion whose comforts lie primarily in sharing it. It tells us that we are not alone, that others went through the same things, that others take the same comforts. To this generation, knowing that Beaver Cleaver lived on the same street may be trivia, but it is not trivial. The mutual fund of shared experience—on TV or on records—reassures the baby boomer that he or she is not cut off from the past. Like every other passion of the baby boom, nostalgia has been reinforced by the generation's collective buying power. The media—television, movies, music—have delivered up nonstop images of old drive-ins, sock hops, and hit records which have both exploited the boom generation's nostalgia and whetted its appetite for more. Indeed, as Fred Davis observes, the media have become our prime source and supplier of nostalgia. We remember, not the old times, but rather the old *records,* old *television shows,* and old *movies.* "The media images," Davis writes, "tend toward a much greater uniformity of meaning and constriction of evocative association. Their possibility for subsequent recycling, manipulation, and symbolic control are, therefore, greatly enhanced." In other words, the baby boom had become the first generation to receive nostalgia standardized and freeze-dried. The result was to intensify the boom's sense of a commonly shared culture while, at the same time, to increase the sales potential of nostalgia to the mass audience.

Mucis, with its ability to distill the most complex emotions into a few brief minutes, is the most dependable carrier of nostalgia. Record stations began packaging "golden oldie" marathons narrated by the likes of Orson Welles. Any record that had left the charts was an instant "oldie," ready to be dusted off to supply an easy emotional jolt. It may have been cheap, but it was real. Proust had his Combray and *petites madeleines;* the baby boom, Detroit and the Supremes. *Grease* went from Broadway to movies and sold 22 million albums around the world. Another fifties act, Sha Na Na, devoted itself to preserving the sound and feel of the old hits in a stylized presentation straight out of Kabuki drama. The Boston Pops, the only orchestra more sensitive to the public's tastes than most disc jockeys, cranked out an album of Beatles songs. Young rock singers, like Shaun Cassidy and Leif Garret, began cutting songs that had been hits before they were born. Their motive, though, was at least partly practical. Most songwriters in the seventies were writing songs then for an older baby-boom market. To find material for their younger fans, singers like Cassidy and Garret had to rummage back into the fifties and sixties for lyrics aimed at the then teenage baby-boom audience.

As the baby boom grew up, it carried its singers along with it. In the earliest, preboom rock era, singers had all the longevity of fireflies. Carl Perkins wrote "Blue Suede Shoes" on a potato skin and faded. Groups like the Diamonds, the Elegants, the Silhouettes, and Tune Weavers did not last long either. But others, such as Bo Diddley, Chuck Berry, and the Drifters, became nostalgia acts, the Rudy Vallees of their day. In rock's Pleistocene era, a singer was over if he or she had crossed 25. But by the end of the seventies, the baby boom created a pop-music generation gap with as many singers over 30 as under. Even Johnny Mathis emerged in 1979 with his first hit in twenty years. "I don't want to be singing 'Satisfaction' when I'm 40," Mick Jagger once said. But he will, and his audience will still be there.

Then there were the Beach Boys. Led by Brian Wilson, the only American who has been described as a "genius" more often than Thomas Edison, the Beach Boys created a hedonistic myth of California life which, even if they didn't believe (Brian has never surfed!), we did. His cousin Mike Love was right when he said that "the Beach Boys are inseparable from the white, middle-class karma." As if to prove it, Patty Hearst, a baby boomer herself, had a Beach Boys album stashed among her possessions when she was finally arrested. But then, sadly, Brian's wonderfully inventive music dried up as he went on his own surfin' safari into chemicals and disease. Without him, the Beach Boys toured listlessly and without great success. "Brian Wilson is the Beach Boys," one of them said. "We are his messengers." So when the time came for the Beach Boys to make their mid-seventies "comeback," Brian was gussied up in the traditional white clothes and led pathetically onstage to perform again. Like Bob Dylan, the Beach Boys had become prisoners of their oldies and their attempts at creativity were inevitably booed down. Even the old heroes like Jimi and Janis and Elvis were brought back by impersonators in macabre revivifications. Captured by nostalgia, rock was no longer revolutionary; it was reactionary.

Hollywood discovered nostalgia not long after the era of the "youth" films ended. If rebelliousness no longer played in Peoria, the studio heads wondered, maybe nostalgia would. In fact, many production chiefs were baby boomers who had been brought in because of their presumed familiarity with the *Weltanschauung* of their peers. They had grown up on the "language" of films and were as serious about making the Great American Movie as previous generations used to be about writing the Great American Novel. So what did they make? *American Graffiti*.

From the moment the film opens with "Rock Around the Clock" throbbing from a car radio, *American Graffiti* goes straight to the emotional jugular. George Lucas, the director, had invested $80,000—10 percent of his budget—for the rights to forty-one old rock hits to sweeten his sound track. The investment paid off in grosses of $50 million as *American Graffiti* became the boom generation's *Roots* and one of the biggest money-makers of all time. Combining rock with the movies was the consummate baby-boom ploy. The wonder is not that Lucas did it, but why no one else had thought of it earlier.

American Graffiti milks the boom generation's nostalgia almost rapaciously. A decade of teenage experience—specifically, white, middle-class suburbanite teenage experience—is compressed into one night of cruising in California through the device of a radio station's "golden oldie" show. The nonstop music and eerie nighttime filming give *American Graffiti* a romanticism Lucas balanced with an almost obsessively scrupulous fidelity to period detail. Technically, the period of the film—1962—was only eleven years before its release, but it might as well have been Edwardian England on *Masterpiece Theatre* so great was the sense of antiquity.* It was precisely this quality of lost innocence that gave the movie its poignancy. "It was my life," Lucas once said. "I spent four years driving around the main street of Modesto, chasing girls. It was the mating ritual of my times, before it disappeared and everybody got into psychedelia and drugs."

Women have, with some justice, criticized *American Graffiti* and films like it (a later example was *Animal House*) as profoundly sexist. What few women do appear in *American Graffiti* are sterotypes at best. And, when an epilogue reveals the eventual fate of the protagonists, all of them are men. Interestingly, studies have shown that men are typically more susceptible to nostalgia and, in fact, have a greater need for it. For all the general notions that women are "emotional," men are far more likely to get weepy in their beer talking about the old gang. Why? Fred Davis believes it is because men in modern societies usually face severe discontinuities between youth and adulthood. They have to contend with

---

* The year of the movie's "Where Were You in '62?" slogan was carefully chosen to keep the period within the pre-Kennedy assassination idyll while still maximizing its potential audience. People aged 12–29 buy three-fourths of all movie tickets. The real high-school class of 1962 turned 29 in the year *American Graffiti* was released. Its target audience thus included them and everyone younger.

288

the strains of leaving home for college, or for the military, or for a job, or to move to another city. Women, on the other hand, traditionally stay home until marriage. (Presumably, though, we can now expect a surge in nostalgia from baby-boom women grappling with the fears and uncertainties brought by their new roles in the 1980s.) A movie like *Animal House,* where women are treated like the sex objects they once were, can help soften the blows feminism has delivered to the male ego. Moreover, the period setting frees nostalgia films to indulge in the kind of antediluvian male fantasies that would be unacceptable in a contemporary story.

The struggle to adapt to change is just as prominent in *American Graffiti.* Curt, the main character, must reconcile himself to the fact of leaving home for college. But he is not free to leave until he first confronts, and defeats, his old life in the incarnation of a local deejay. When Curt seeks him out in the dead of night, he could be Theseus entering the labyrinth to slay the Minotaur. What he finds, though, is not a terrible creature with a bull's head, but Wolfman Jack.

What the movies initiate, television imitates. As youth films like *Easy Rider* swept through Hollywood, television followed up with youth-audience shows like *Mod Squad.* The problem was that whether through timidity or lack of imagination, television was able to portray the countercultural life only by opposing it. Instead of embracing kids, TV turned against them, casting them as a criminal subclass who were dealing drugs at worst and were greedy hypocrites at best. On TV, Andy Hardy had become an acidhead. The Monkees and the Smothers Brothers were around, to be sure, but the real youth revolution was best seen in the commercials, where miniskirted models in boots were boogalooing for Goodyear.

In the early seventies, Fred Pierce of ABC realized that what the youth audience really wanted was not the spurious "relevance" of the lawyer and doctor shows, but nostalgia. So, while CBS was still programming rural comedies and playing off the older side of the generation gap with Archie Bunker in *All in the Family,* ABC flipped to the youth point of view. *Happy Days* may have been only a stepson of *American Graffiti,* but it made a star out of Henry Winkler and rose to number one in the ratings. Once it tapped the baby boom's premature nostalgia again with *Laverne & Shirley*, the network's critics began calling it the Acne Broadcasting Company.

It is easy enough to ridicule the nostalgia boom. There is, after all, something dishonest about it. *American Graffiti* gave us not the fifties anyone really lived, but the fifties they *wished* they had lived. It is adolescence without pain, confusion, loneliness, and insecurity. If the Broadway musical of *Hair* was once removed from anything approaching reality, then the movie version was twice removed. Milos Forman staged *Hair* as if it were *A Midsummer Night's Dream* with hippies instead of elves. Nostalgia makes bad art and worse history. It is a Disney version of the past, not unlike the turn-of-the-century town at Disneyland built at five-eighths scale to enhance its charm.

Nostalgia has another function besides softening the pain of the present. It is the means by which a generation can agree on the "official" version of its past. Once the baby boomers began to leave college, for example, they were no longer bound by mere proximity. What was left? The memories of all the things they had seen and done together. Nostalgia, then, became the crucible in which they could pour the raw material of experience and forge a collective biography. Because it is selective, filtering out discordant or unpleasant facts, nostalgia can help impose a sense of order upon what might otherwise be a confusing and featureless past. These selective, shared memories, according to Fred Davis, "bestow meaning and purpose on the otherwise accidental fact that contemporaries have seen, thought, and felt many of the same things at the same time." Nostalgia helps us see our fellow travelers on the river of time as persons with whom we do not merely coexist, but with whom we share what German social philosopher Alfred Shütz has called a "We-Relationship." In a group as strongly age-graded as the baby boom, the sibling relationship between its members, as reinforced by nostalgia, became a powerful tie. Little wonder then that, afflicted by a troubling present and crowded on all sides, the baby boomers sought refuge in the kinship bond provided by nostalgia. By binding them together, nostalgia helped the baby boomers define themselves and explain themselves to other generations as well. No one else grew up when they did and saw and did the things they did. The special thrill of hearing the first Beatles records, for instance, belongs almost exclusively to the baby boom. It is practically as useful as a birth date in distinguishing generations. No other generation felt quite the same way—that music would somehow make them free. The selling of the baby boom's nostalgia has also helped other generations understand it. The children of the baby boomers may be learning more about their parents' social histories from watching *Happy Days* than they could ever learn at the dinner table. (In 1978, the number one show among children aged 2–11 was *Happy Days*.)

Advertisers learned to use nostalgia as an easy way of reaching just the audience it wanted. When Mazda used Doris Troy's 1963 hit, "Just One Look," on its television commercials in 1980, it was unerringly defining its target audience of grown-up baby-boom car buyers. As Fred Davis and others have pointed out, the rise of mass education and mass media eroded individual differences and promoted "A certain homogeneity in the collective coffers of nostalgia memory." Nostalgia did not need to be sold to fragmented markets of Northerners or Southerners or city people or rural people or educated and uneducated. It could be sold to an entire generation, one whose shared experience overwhelmed the traditional distinctions of wealth, race, and region.

The baby boom's nostalgia almost exclusively involves the fifties and first few years of the sixties. But what about the rest of that difficult decade? Shouldn't it be a potential wellspring of nostalgia, too? After all, the largest number of baby boomers spent their formative years in the sixties. Feelings for those times seemingly ought to be more intense than for the fifties and ought to evoke an even lustier nostalgic boom.

It didn't happen. Attempts to merchandise the sixties in movies like *Sergeant Pepper's Lonely Hearts Club Band* and *I Want To Hold Your Hand* flopped. The television version of *Loose Change* failed, too. Yet the promoters persisted. In 1979, a group tried to cash in on what looked like a surefire success: a tenth anniversary concert at Woodstock. The name, as they pointed out, was practically a brand name. There would be a movie, and a sound-track album, and spin-off paperbacks, T-shirts, and maybe lunch-boxes. A computer would distribute tickets nationwide at $75 a pop. It was a perfect idea in every respect except one. Nobody cared. This is what one musician said to the *Washington Post* when he heard of the project.

> Look what the establishment did to the fifties. They took whatever was relevant to us and turned it into a million-dollar cliché. Everybody thinks it was like *Grease* and *Happy Days*. Now they're getting ready to sell us the Sixties. Those were great times. Why can't they let our dreams alone?

On the commercial level, sixties nostalgia does not work. This is not surprising. The sixties have an altogether different place in the life of the baby boom than the fifties. Nostalgia for the fifties can satisfy the baby boom's need for wholeness and reassurance. But the sixties were schizophrenic; things were flying apart. Nostalgia exists to shore up personalities troubled by change, but the sixties offered no such solace. Indeed, the sixties are more likely to remind people of the disharmonies in their lives. The sequel of *American Graffiti* was predictably a failure. By updating the characters into the disorienting and disjointed sixties—complete with flower children, protests, raucous rock, and Vietnam—the filmmakers lost the connection that had made the original film so effective. *More American Graffiti* was truer to its period, too, which is why it failed. It no longer fulfilled the emotional needs of the audience.

The decade of the sixties remains the great problem of the baby boomers. What little nostalgia is there is mixed in with wistfulness, feelings of unfulfilled promise, and some bitterness. Even at the end of the seventies, the baby boomers were still struggling with the meaning of the sixties. When the tenth anniversary of Woodstock finally did roll around, aging hippies emerged from the thickets like Japanese soldiers who walked out of the jungle on some Pacific island twenty-five years later to hear that the war was over. Rubbing their eyes in the sun, they talked about the sixties as if the seventies had never happened.

If the sixties left a predominant emotion, it was the feeling that the boom babies had a bright future behind them. In a way, they did. The exhilarations of the sixties had raised the hopes of the baby boom even more than the fifties had. In that decade, someone says in Sara Davidson's *Loose Change*.

we had thought life was free and would never run out. There were good people and bad people and we could tell them apart by a look or by words spoken in code. We were certain we belonged to a generation that was special. We did not need or care about history because we had sprung from nowhere.

But something went wrong. "We blew it," Peter Fonda said in *Easy Rider*. Sara Davidson thought so, too. "For four years I felt I had blown it, my generation had blown it, the Sixties had blown it, and we would never again see the heights." At one point in her *Loose Change* we come across this tableau:

> Joe lit a joint and passed it to Rob. "It's not just you, man. Everyone I know has this feeling that somehow, we made a mistake."
> "What went wrong?" I asked. "All these bright, idealistic, committed people—how could they have miscalculated so badly? Was it mass hallucination? Were our perceptions wrong?"

Some, like Ray in *Alice's Restaurant*, wanted another chance to recapture the ineffable spirit they felt slipping between their fingers. If only they'd had a farm, he said, "if we'd just had a real place, we'd still be together . . ."

Instead, they wound up with what John Updike called "a slum of a decade" in which all their hopes were dashed. Here is how Rona puts it in *Kennedy's Children:*

> The last big march was against the mining of the harbor and besides the old chant of "one-two-three-four, We don't want your fucking war," my friends were muttering, "Why are we here? We've been marching since we were babies and all we did was make Jane Fonda famous." Some people will tell you it ended when they murdered the students at Kent State, and everybody left the Village. Or when the papers played up the drug-cult murders and people got scared of each other. Or when the pot famine hit and all the kids got hooked on alcohol. Or when *Hair* opened and Abbie Hoffman became a guest-star. Or when Leary got brainburned and ran away. Or when the Beatles sued each other. And Donovan retired to his private island, and Dylan to his million-dollar farm. Or when Janis and Jimi

293

died—so young!—and those were our heroes, the models for our lives! The men don't understand Women's Lib and the women can't dig Gay Power. The blacks don't need us and the Indians don't want us. And the new kids are no use—my sister lives on downers. And my little brother is a nineteen-fifties fascist! He wrote me, "Fuck the Revolution! I don't want anything collapsing on me! I want fifty thousand a year, and when I lose my looks I'll overdose!" They're selling sixties nostaglia albums already.

Perhaps the most painful yearning the baby boom felt after the sixties was for the tribal unity fostered by the protests and rock concerts. Music in the sixties was the language of the cultural revolution. In 1975, the man from *The New York Times* suffered tangibly from *mal du pays*:

> Rambling outdoor concerts like this used to be occasions that far transcended the music played at them. They were symbolic clusterings of a new society, laboratories for the way people would get along in the future. They were charged with purpose of one sort or another—political, utopianism, hippie love vibes, religious release. But most everybody in high school looks like a hippie these days; the emblems of a counterculture have become the fashions of the mainstream.

Unlike the fifties, the sixties did not yield a sustaining mythology. The children of the baby boomers already know more about Hula-Hoops than they do about the black lights and be-ins of the sixties. Like the decimated British elite of World War I, many of the boom babies began to think of themselves as a lost generation after the sixties. "We are," said Lee Weiner, Chicago Seven defendant, "refugees from a future that never happened."

And what is the future of nostalgia? It will be a fixture of the baby boom's life. The size of the generation alone will guarantee the continuation of the disruptions and dislocations that precipitate the nostalgic response. As they continue to enter the labor market, baby-boom women should have a particularly acute need to seek nostalgic refuge from the growth pains of the present.

Nostalgia is the healing emotion the baby boom will need in the years ahead. The boom generation should pray, for instance, that the Beatles never have a reunion. The memory of the Beatles is far more important to this generation than any inevitably disappointing concert ever could be.

Chapter 20

THE CRISIS OF THE BABY BOOM

Whatever happened to the Class of '65? We asked that question in the seventies, but it was not until 1980, the fifteenth anniversary year of the first full high-school class of baby boomers, that we really found out. The answer was that they were in trouble.

Here is a typical list of articles advertised on the cover of a single issue of a magazine called *New Woman*:

"Is Your Marriage in Trouble?"
"How Reasonable is Your Guilt?"
" 'Tis the Season to be Jolly—So Why Are You So Depressed?"
"Foods That Make You Smarter, Healthier, Sexier"
"How to Build a Super Memory"
"A Way to Get Rid of Those Incredible Headaches'

This is not a parody. The editors who drew up that articles list are telling us as much about the mental health of the baby boom as any number of Ph.D. dissertations. Everywhere are the signs of depression, divorce, illness, and what *The New York Times* soberly called "a generational malaise of haunting frustrations, anxiety and depression." Approaching midlife, the baby boomers are floundering. They have rejected the value system of their parents, but have come up with nothing better to replace it. All they know is that life has failed to fulfill the great expectations they had established for themselves during the fifties and sixties.

Somewhere along the line the idealistic baby-boom generation turned into the jaded Me Generation. When *Chicago Magazine* sent a reporter to the tenth reunion of the Class of 1966 at New Trier High School, the alma mater of the likes of Rock Hudson and Ann-Margret, he found the joy of auld acquaintance but also ruined lives, deep depression, cynicism, and a widespread conviction that their generation had blown its chances. The old idea that the younger generation would bring the country a better future was dying off. Now Americans were saying something else. Watch out for number one. Spend it while you can. Life is a lemon. "The seventies are just the garbage of the sixties!" said Carla in *Kennedy's Children,* and most of her peers would agree. Psychiatrists now estimate that up to one-third of the people in their twenties and thirties are "very depressed and anxious" most of the time. The President's Commission on Mental Health thinks that 15 percent of all young people have observable symptoms of mental illness. They were growing up absurd. Even Ricky Nelson, of all people, has gone on the *Mike Douglas Show* to talk about his own breakdown.

Suddenly society seemed to have developed a case of the jitters. In addition to the clinical signs—the rises in suicide and alcoholism, for example—there were also the booms in charismatic religions, self-help organizations, and human-potential movements. Behind it all was an obsessive search for individual happiness. Unlike previous generations, which found happiness only as a by-product of doing something well, the baby boomers pursued it as an end in itself. The result was that the baby boom found itself in the middle of a generation-wide identity crisis. It had lost cultural contact with the older and younger generations and was on autopilot, spinning toward the ground. The traditional rites of passage that had bolstered other generations in their times of crisis were no longer operative. The decline of American confidence during the seventies was the basis of President Carter's "national malaise" speech of 1979. What is less well known is the degree to which the baby boom in particular was both a cause and a component of the country's failure of confidence. The baby boom was alienated, fragmented, shattered and disenchanted. George Orwell had said that at fifty every man had the face he deserved. The baby boom was getting the face it deserved at thirty—and it did not like what it saw.

These are hard judgments, but the unhappy evidence is there. If homicide provides an accurate index of the overall crime level in society, then suicide is a similarly grim measure of social despair. And the baby boomers, especially young baby boomers, have been taking their own lives more frequently than any generation in history. In the past two decades, suicide among teenagers has tripled. It is now the leading killer of young Americans after accidents. This would not be such a startling figure if the increase were matched in other age groups, suggesting that outside social forces, perhaps inflation or unemployment, might have affected everyone equally adversely. But the astonishing fact is that *the nation's overall suicide rate has remained level over the same period.* In other words, some force acting exclusively upon youth has made them more likely to die by their own hand. I think that it is the arrival of the baby-boom cohorts into its most vulnerable years.

It's possible to track through the suicide rate the aging of the boom generation into the different age groups. The suicide rate for 15–19-year-olds took its biggest leap between 1970 and 1971. Then 20–24 took its biggest jump a few years later, and 25–29 skipped up a few years after that. In a decade, the suicide rate for 20–24-year-olds tripled, meaning that those babies born at the height of the boom, in 1953–57, were three times as likely to kill themselves as those born in 1944–48. In the meantime, the suicide rate among their 40–44-year-old parents, members of the Good Times Generation, actually declined. In some affluent suburbs, like Chicago's North Shore and Ridgewood, New Jersey, suicide was a contagion, sweeping through high schools at the rate of one or two a month. Death rates from auto accidents and homicide were also increasing for young people at the same time, leaving the 15–24-year-old baby boomers as the *only* age group in this period to register an increase in mortality.

A less final, but equally suggestive reading of the baby boom's mood comes from identical surveys conducted by the University of Michigan in 1957 and again in 1976. The surveys found that over the two decades the general level of "worry" among all adults remained approximately the same. But a closer look showed a startling discrepancy: the level of worry among young men and women 21–39, the group just entered by the boom generation, rose from 30 percent in 1957 to 50 percent in 1976. Only the increased optimism of the older generation had prevented a measurable increase in overall public anxiousness. Further examining the causes of concern, the

Michigan researchers found that the younger people were having greater difficulty connecting to their roles and relationships in society. Where previous generations had relied on established roles to guide them, the baby boom had to find its own way. The price of its freedom was anxiety.

As early as 1966, Louis Harris noticed that lack of political trust was highest among the youngest cohorts, *among both liberals and conservatives.* In 1979, a *New York Times*/CBS poll found that the single group most pessimistic about the country's future was not the old, as had been previously the case, but the young. A 1978 Louis Harris poll conducted for *Playboy* found that the most alienated class in society was made up of baby boomers 18–22 who had not attended college. Fewer than one-half of them agreed with the statement that "the average man is probably better off today than he ever was." Harris further found a "distinct disaffection of young, blue-collar nonstudents, 18–22." They were, in short, "the most discontented, pessimistic, and alienated" group in society.

What went wrong? As the largest, most widely studied, and most publicized generation ever, the baby boomers gained from the start an acutely felt self-awareness and sense of their own destiny. This generation wanted everything: to be the best educated, to reform society, to integrate motherhood and career, to integrate a husband's job with a wife's job, and to have healthy, fulfilled lives on top of it all. Even when they saw the naïveté of their aspirations, they could not turn them off. "I live with a desire to excel or be productive," said one baby-boom woman to the *Los Angeles Times.* "But," she apologized, "I realize through it all that it is bourgeois."

Advertising, meanwhile, was continuing its never-ending effort to raise consumption aspirations to unrealistic and unattainable visions of the good life. According to a perceptive writer, psychiatrist Robert Coles:

> We model ourselves desperately after other people because we haven't really been taught to accept the limitations of life—not when advertising offers us the moon and when one or two of us actually gets there, whereupon we conclude that in no time at all the rest of us will be following suit. It is a grandiosity that serves the interests of those who have things to sell.

Coupled to the baby boomers' high aspirations was an unheard-of-new idea that neither their parents nor any of their forebears would have recognized. It was the idea that life is not difficult.

Ridiculous? It did not seem so impossible when the baby boom was growing up in the affluent fifties and sixties. For most of human history, people had thought that life was hard, brutal, and tragic. But the baby boom's early affluence developed in it what Daniel Yankelovich has called "the psychology of entitlement." What other generations have thought *privileges,* the baby boomers thought were *rights.* They believed, for instance, that they should have the right to send their children to college, no matter whether they could afford it or not, that they have the right to a secure retirement, and that they have the right to the best medical care, regardless of cost. All those kids at Woodstock could afford to be there because they knew, down deep, that they could always get jobs if they needed them.

Yet what they found instead was a lifetime of stress and competition that depressed them as much as any disease. Researchers at the University of Pennsylvania have studied diaries kept by college students and are convinced that "the baby boom two decades ago contributed to the heightened competition and increased academic stress among college students today" and that the overall effect of their numbers has "serious implications for the health of young adults in the United States." Because of its own size, among other things, the baby boom experienced the shock of the first decline in real income since World War II and faced the real possibility of becoming the first generation in American history that could not expect to equal the living standards of its parents. Add to that the effects of overwhelming personal problems: parental divorce, illegitimate pregnancies, alcohol and drug abuse, and the social isolation brought on by the generation's own reduced marriage rate and increased childlessness. (In one Los Angeles study, one-half of adolescent suicide attempts were found to be children whose parents had divorced within the previous five years—not an encouraing prospect for the children of the much-divorced baby-boom parents.) This generation was as discombobulated as if it had been thrown into the Peloponnesian War, where, as Aristophanes said, "Whirl is King, having driven out Zeus."

The short of it is that the baby boomers encountered a disastrously large gap between their aspirations and their opportunities. They had set for themselves idealistic goals that their own size made self-defeating. Worse, their failure to meet their aspirations—and the sinking realization that they might never achieve what they had set out to do—had the effect of discouraging their willingness to try. The generation wound up with a classic anxiety syndrome: high aspirations, low motivation. They were still dreamers, but were unable to take the risks necessary to achieve their dreams.

When the world did not deliver on its promises, the generation felt betrayed. "We were raised in the Fifties and Sixties and never seemed to want for anything," a 29-year-old chemist told *The New York Times* in 1979. "We learned how to spend money. Now we've got to learn how not to." The fact that they are the best-educated generation ever has only compounded their frustration. *The New York Times* ran an article in 1979 by a 30-year-old baby boomer complaining about his inability to make ends meet on his salary. It was $30,000 a year. A recent poll of graduates of Smith College found that 40 percent of the Class of '49 considered themselves optimistic; only 20 percent of the star-crossed Class of '69 felt the same way. In *Loose Change* we learn of a 16-year-old girl

> who had organized a moratorium in her school when she was twelve, who had taken acid at fourteen and slept with her boyfriend when she was fifteen and now, in the fall of 1971, she was telling me that she was fed up. "I tried for two years to change things and saw it was impossible. I have other things to worry about, like getting into college."

Previous generations had enjoyed the heady feeling that, as F. Scott Fitzgerald put it, "It was bracing to be an American." But, as one baby-boom woman appraised her times, "Sometimes you get the feeling nothing has gone right since John Kennedy died. We've had the Vietnam War, all the rioting and the energy crisis. Before then you were used to America winning everything, but now you sometimes think our day may be over."

The leadership that might have helped the baby boomers deal with their frustrations was conspicuously absent.

They had already rejected the adult role models provided by their parents who, they found, were just as confused by the social turmoil as they were. Their political heroes were dying off at a frightening rate. John Kennedy was first, but there were also Martin Luther King and Robert Kennedy and Malcom X. And rock? The necrology of wasted rock stars was rising every year. The Beatles were gone and Dylan might as well have been. The most prominent politican the boom generation had produced was Cleveland's unfortunate mayor, Dennis Kucinich. When the members of the Class of 1969 at Princeton were asked at their tenth reunion which people in public life they most admired, the leading choice, by an overwhelming margin, was "Nobody."

So many baby boomers live alone that, in the future, they will be particularly susceptible to stress. In his book, *The Broken Heart: The Medical Consequences of Loneliness,* Dr. James J. Lynch found that unmarried persons visit physicians more often and stay in hospitals longer than married people with similar illnesses. Without a person to care for them, evidently, they must rely on the institutions. People who have never married are seven times more likely to be admitted to mental hospitals. In some big cities, many people are so desperate for a level of human contact above that of TV game-show confessionals that telephone services have started with the sole objective of cheering up the depressed and lonely.

What was left? Little other than freedom. The baby boomers were free to go it alone, to find their own way among a myriad of choices. But what in the sixties was exhilarating turned out in the seventies to be something different. Uprooted from the past, the baby boomers were left weightless. "Man cannot live unbounded in an empty sea of free choice . . . without an increase of inner conflict," said the psychologist and writer Rollo May. The baby boomers needed boundaries in their world to define their own identities. But wherever they pushed, there was no resistance. "Uncertainty was the legacy of our generation," a 32-year-old told the *Boston Globe* in a revealing use of the past tense. "Our parents' generation was sure of certain values. We weren't. We had freedom, but the flip side of freedom is instability."

Born into an affluent society, the young baby boomers never had a chance to test their character. Then, in the seventies, they were overwhelmed by a world that seemed to offer limitless choice. What they felt, ultimately, was anomie, a term Emile Durkheim borrowed from medical literature to describe the condition of people who have lost their traditional moorings and are disoriented in a normless world. The sociologist Robert Merton later expanded the concept of anomie to include the disparity between what people want and what they have. In the sixties, the baby boom solved the anomie problem with its commitment to a youth culture. "You remember the early Sixties?" asks someone in *Loose Change*. "Sure, I remember," comes the reply. "I thought I'd never grow old. Life was one big joke. We knew what politics was then. It was marches, elections. Now politics means who you fuck, what you eat, how you cure a cold."

In the seventies, the baby boomers were left with plenty of choice, but nothing to commit to. Life was an open classroom, but the teacher was absent. They were unsure about what it meant to grow up, to become a parent, even what it means to be a man or a woman. All they had to go on were the unrealistically high expectations nurtured by the youth culture. "*Time* had been right about our wide-ranging possibilities," wrote the authors of *What Really Happened to the Class of '65*, "but it had not foreseen the fact that we might be paralyzed by them." In the stories and novels of Ann Beattie, a writer who has sensitively captured the *moeurs* of her generation, the characters almost universally suffer from indecision and lack of commitment. *Loose Ends* likewise records the inability of a likable baby-boom couple to commit to anything other than ego. They are unable to decide about careers, about children, or each other. In the end, they are left apart, each with halfhearted new attachments, which they carelessly compromise for a weekend together.

Disappointed by the failure of their high expectations, the baby boomers were pulling back, withdrawing their forces within a safe perimeter. Why risk their emotions in a free-fire zone? The idea was growing that it was pointless to have faith in anything but the self. The columnist Ellen Goodman reflected on the generation after a depressing Harvard Square encounter with a jaded "Sixties kids" she called Jack:

> Others, like Jack, had lost the conviction that "it" made any difference; that "they" could make a difference. The distinctions between friends, ideals, politics, jobs,

seemed no more important to them at this point than the choice of drinking black coffee or regular. . . . They embraced their lack of purpose as if it were a benign response to a harsh world. They regarded struggle as foolish, difference as illusions.

Many baby boomers, especially the youngest ones, found it difficult to live in an ambiguous world devoid of meaning and purpose. They craved the certainty that their parents, schools, and religions had been unable to give them. So they joined cults.

The latest wave of cults in the United States began in the late sixties, when the first baby boomers were making the transition from adolescence. Since then, an estimated three million people have, at one time or another, been at least briefly involved with such groups as the Unification Church (Moonies), Church of God, Scientology, Hare Krishna, and Synanon, and Americans have become used to the spectacle of parents suing to regain control of their children. Demographically, however, the increase in cult membership is not particularly surprising. People are most vulnerable to the appeal of cults when they leave adolescence. The baby boom brought to cults more potential recruits, just as it had earlier done the same for the Boy Scouts. The problem was compounded, however, because families were losing their control over children at the same time. To the children, parents seemed to have nothing useful to tell them about life. Indeed, parents themselves often seemed unable to cope. With society giving families little support, and with divorce easier and easier, the children had to look elsewhere for guidance. Some found it in the solipsistic youth culture. Others found it in the cults, which presented themselves as a source of authority. To a generation raised by experts, the gurus were experts in life. And they could provide all the love and happiness and self-worth usually offered by families. Moreover, by making decisions for them, the cults would liberate the baby boomers from the imprisoning freedom they had grown up with.

People who join cults usually do so when their support systems have failed. One study of the Moonies found that the majority of them had recently experienced a personal crisis; one-fourth of them had had drug problems in the past. California, a thriving petri dish of cult groups, is also the state where many baby boomers live and a refuge of the rootless. Recruiters from cult groups usually hit colleges at exam time, when students are under stress and therefore most susceptible. Where members of previous generations might have turned to a psychiatrist, the baby boomers turned to cults. It is typical of this multitude that it would try to find a group solution to the kind of problems previous generations have attempted to solve only as individuals.

Chapter 21

TURNING THIRTY

We think of you as a person who is always reaching out for more . . . We think of you as a person who wants it all and who wants it now.
—Playboy Book Club advertisement

You deserve a break today.
—McDonald's television commercial

Advertisers have always responded quickest to any sub-surface tremors and quiverings within the psyche of the boom generation. And what they were telling us as the boom babies began to cross into the landscape of their thirties was that this generation was frightened. It had learned the tough lessons of its upbringing. It was worried about the future. It would not sacrifice itself to the old verities of family, community, church, and state. Instead, it was withdrawing its attention to the closest thing at hand: itself.

Instead of improving society, the baby boomers were improving themselves. They were jogging, climbing mountains, painting, and playing racquetball. Faces that once sweated on picket lines were now sweating in health spas. They were concerned about the inner person, too. They were reading books with titles like *I'm OK—You're OK*, *Looking Out for No. 1*, *Power!*, and *How to Be Your Own Best Friend*. This now-familiar crusade at self-improvement might have been a lonely task in an earlier era, but the baby boomers were no Benjamin Franklins working alone at their task. Like everything else, they did it together. The baby boomers provided the manpower for a human-potential movement that was spinning off profits faster than McDonald's could sign up franchises. (In both cases, the market was the same.) People paid hundreds of dollars a weekend to hear Werner Erhard, or someone paid by him, call them "assholes." In Washington, government workers anted up $300 to sit through 60-hour "Lifespring" sessions at Ramada Inns. Life was just not meeting their expectations. And if est or Lifespring did not work, well, there was always rolfing, gestalt therapy, yoga, Fischer-Hoffman psychic therapy, acupuncture, Reichian therapy, bioenergetics, health foods, tai chi, Esalen, Arica, Silva Mind Control, and transcendental meditation.

De Tocqueville had remarked on the American belief in "indefinite perfectibility," and now the baby boomers were ardently in pursuit of it. The relevant question was "Am I happy?" and if you were not, you changed (pick one) your job, your spouse, your city, or your clothes. "Don't you love being a woman?" Max Factor asked. Of course, replied Miss Clairol, "This I do for me." And Charles of the Ritz chimed in with the rationale: "Because you'd rather be yourself than anyone else." The flower-child fashions of the sixties were dumped in favor of the do-it-yourself eclecticism of Diane Keaton. People were lining up to have themselves baked by ultraviolet lights at "tanning" salons. It sounded like excess, but the *Cosmopolitan* woman was reassuring: "My favorite magazine says don't worry about 'too much' as long as the 'too much' makes you feel utterly fulfilled, utterly utilized, and usually, utterly happy." And utterly exploited. "It's a very selfish decade," Tom Hayden complained. "It's all me. People who experienced profound disappointment trying to change the system are jogging and growing vegetables and concentrating on brightening their corner of the world."

There was a point to the seventies' orgy of self-gratification. The concentration on self was the baby boom's way of adapting to its reduced circumstances. This seemingly sybaritic life-style was often associated with California, but it really was the property of the generation. When the Eagleton Poll at Rutgers University asked one thousand New Jerseyans which was more important, (a) working hard and doing what is expected of oneself, or (b) doing the things that give you personal satisfaction and pleasure, hard work nosed out pleasure in all age groups by 43 percent versus 41 percent. But, among the all-baby-boom group under 30 years old, two out of three voted for the pleasure principle over the work ethic.

The new cult of the self even produced a language all of its own, which was often satirized but was particularly well suited for talking about emotions. Laid back. I know where you're coming from. Go with the flow. No question. I hear you. Get over. This laconic argot was commonly heard in Marin Country, California, the birthplace of mellow. What is mellow? "Mellow," said *Doonesbury*, "teaches us that it's okay to flash on a power trip as long as you're upfront about it." Mellowspeak also provided the necessary vocabulary to rationalize behavior that the baby boomers themselves would have once rejected as a counterproductive and depressing self-indulgence in their earlier years.

The mellow generation was also laid back politically. Look at the voter participation rates in recent elections. Voter participation has been steadily declining in presidential elections, dropping from 60 percent in 1968 to 54 percent in 1976. In the off-year election of 1978, the national turnout of 38 percent was the lowest since 1942; for the first time, more than 100 million Americans did not vote.

We might have expected the opposite. As early as 1968, the baby boomers had demonstrated their political clout when Eugene McCarthy's "children's crusade" helped drive Lyndon Johnson from the presidency. Then, in response to the boom's youthful presence, the voting age for presidential elections was lowered to 18 for the first time in 1972. But for all their greater education and supposed involvement, the young voters did not amount to much. Between 1972 and 1976, reported voter turnout decreased more sharply for young voters than for older persons. Only 15 percent of the 18–24-year-olds voted in 1976, and 50 percent of all nonvoters in that year were under 30. Astonishingly, despite the enfranchisement of 18–20-year-olds, the median age of the voting public has not declined. Why? Because the younger people go to the polls so much less often than older people. In the off-year election of 1978, persons 65 and over were three times as likely to vote as those 18–20.

Did the baby boomers run out of conviction or just out of adrenaline? How could the generation that had promised so much deliver so little? The two most popular theoreticians of the Me Decade are Tom Wolfe and Christopher Lasch. Wolfe, the reporter, actually coined the term in a well-known article in *New York* magazine. Lasch, a

308

historian at the University of Rochester, filled in its psychological basis in his book, *The Culture of Narcissism*. While both of these studies are insightful and richly detailed, neither deals with what I believe is the crux of the matter: the baby boom did it. We cannot understand how narcissism had come to roost in America unless we first see how it was carried by the maturing cohorts of the boom generation.

Both Wolfe and Lasch finger the unprecedented affluence of the fifties and sixties as a prime malefactor. Prosperity, says Wolfe, meant that we had given birth to "the new man, the first common man in the history of the world with the much-dreamed-of combination of money, free time and personal freedom." But what did he want with his wealth? Appallingly, to those who had believed so long in his nobility, he did not want to wear woodsy lumberjack shirts and chop wood and take his kids camping. Instead, he wanted to realize his potential as a human being. "If I've only one life to live," Clairol told women, "let me live it as a blonde!"

Lasch sees the glitter of narcissism not merely in self-actualization movements, but in society's worship of youth and athletics, fascination with celebrity, fear of competition, and acceptance of impersonal human relations. Just as the Narcissus of myth could not consummate his self-love, so society is engulfed in "a desperate concern for personal survival, sometimes disguised as hedonism." Everywhere are sadness, emptiness, loss, repressed rage, and unsatisfied craving. Narcissism originates, Lasch says, "as a defense against feelings of helpless dependency in early life, which he tries to counter with 'blind optimism' and grandoise illusions of personal self-sufficiency." He could be describing the baby boom at large when he then adds,

Since modern society prolongs the experience of dependence into adult life, it encourages milder forms of narcissism in people who might otherwise come to terms with the inescapable limits on their personal freedom and power—limits inherent in the human condition—by developing competence as workers and parents. But at the same time our society makes it more and more difficult to find satisfaction in love and work, it surrounds the individual with manufactured fantasies of total gratification.

What Lasch regards as the spiritual sickness of our times is aided and abetted by advertising. Throughout its life, the baby boom has had more advertising aimed at it than any group of people in history. The way to the generation's pocketbook, it seemed, was through its ego. It was surrounded by so many images of itself fashioned by the media that it began to believe them. As the generation entered the high-spending years of its twenties and thirties, the media began to focus on it with increasing intensity. Academics might worry about narcissism, but not advertisers. One magazine assured its customers that its typical male reader was a

> maturing male adult of the 1970's. . . . elbowing his way in, saying, I want it all, all of it that's good in all aspects of life. . . . He doesn't worry about the future because that's tomorrow and it's not worth a cent today. He's very much focused into today and what he can do for himself today.

By telling people to "live their dreams today, not tomorrow," the media were transforming the old ideal of success. You would be judged not by what you saved, but what you spent. You would be respected not for sacrifice, but for self-assertion. If the emphasis in advertising in the fifties was on selling to families, the emphasis in the seventies was selling to individuals. In the society at large, a historical transformation was under way as we moved from an economy based on production to one based on consumption.

As I have indicated, the baby-boom generation was the primary agent of this transformation. But a question remains. Why did it happen when it did? In the rebellious sixties, to the contrary, baby boomers sounded more like an idealistic army who were explicitly rejecting the materialism of their parents. What made them suddenly withdraw their concern from reforming society to reforming themselves? The most frequent answer is that it had something to do with the end of the Vietnam War, or the stagnant economy of the 1970s. But there is an additional explanation that, I think, tells us most about the continuing role of the baby boom in our national life. It is that the boom generation was entering a critical point in its life cycle. It was turning 30.

We have already seen how, as the baby boom negotiated each of its lifetime transitions, the aftershocks have rippled through the entire society. When the baby boom began its schooling, the attention of the entire nation turned to education. When the baby boom entered its adolescence, the country became obsessed with the youth culture. When the baby boom entered its twenties, we became a country dominated by the needs and concerns of young adults—from sex to marriage, to finding jobs, to buying houses.

It was no different as the baby boomers approached 30. Suddenly, for the first time in their lives, they could see the sand running out of their hourglass. They were running out of time, the time they needed to achieve all they had hoped. The anxiety brought by a sense of closing options can be overwhelming. Writing about "the formidable stroke of 30" in *The Great Gatsby,* F. Scott Fitzgerald worried about "the portentous, menacing road of a new decade." It meant for him "the promise of a decade of loneliness, a thinning list of single men to know, a thinning briefcase of enthusiasm, thinning hair."* The celebrated football player Fran Tarkenton viewed his own thirtieth birthday as the time when "you know the trouble spots. You know what you can do and what you can't do." (He retired not long afterward.) In his study of adult development, *The Seasons of a Man's Life,* Daniel Levinson paid considerable attention to the "severe and stressful" period he called the Age Thirty Transition. "The provisional, exploratory quality of the twenties is ending and a man has a sense of greater urgency," Levinson wrote. "Life is becoming more serious, more restrictive, more 'for real.'" The feeling is growing among the baby boomers that if they are to make something out of their lives, if they are to realize their goals, if they are to do everything they intend, they must do it *now.*

In the decade of the seventies, some 32 million Americans had their thirtieth birthdays, an increase of 39 percent over the sixties. In the eighties, another 42 million baby boomers will cross 30. This means that every individual stress signal and effect we associate with turning 30 is being repeated more than ever. The overall effect of the baby boom on the country's age structure was now revers-

---

* In his original draft of the novel, Fitzgerald had written of a "thinning assortment of illusions" before he found his more graphic metaphor.

ing. In the sixties, the baby-boom children had pushed the median age of the country down until it reached a low of 27.9 in 1971. (Never, incidentally, were half the people in the country under 25, despite the assertion then commonly made.) But then, as the baby boomers began turning 30, the median age began a steady rise that is still continuing. In 1979, the median age crossed 30.0, meaning that half of us are on one side of the once-dreaded generational Rubicon, half of us on the other. That, in its own way, was as significant a demographic milestone as 1920, when for the first time, more Americans lived in the cities than on the farms.

The generation that had placed so much faith and energy in youth could now feel the cold breath of age at its back. Biologists date the decline of the organism from the age of 30, a fact not lost on most people. "On my next birthday I'll be 30," lamented one baby-boom woman in a magazine article, "and already I notice that here and there is the beginning of a line where smooth skin used to be. I now listen to music on 5 rather than 10 on the volume control, and a muscle I hurt last week hurts a little more and little longer than it did just two years ago."

When Americans went on a fitness kick, it was because the baby boomers were beginning to feel flabby. Kids who, in the sixties, had all the confidence of youthful health were suddenly showing up in health spas to be steamed, sweated, washed, rubbed, and slapped with eucalyptus fronds. Tennis boomed, but it was the jogging craze that brought out the generation in the greatest numbers. Millions of them were out on the road, fighting off the inevitable. For them, the enemy was not fat and sloth; it was aging and death.

The anxieties were contagious. Levinson writes of the Age Thirty Transition as a time when a man "urgently seeks personal gratification of various kinds, but he is burdened by the residues of childhood conflicts regarding such gratification." In his short story, "The Death of the Russian Novel," George Blecher put it this way:

Sometimes I sit down with myself and say, "Look, you're thirty now. At best, you've got fifty years more. But what are you doing with it? You drag yourself from day to day, you spend most of your time wanting, wanting, but what you have is never any good and what you don't have is marvelous."

312

Other writers who might have previously regarded the end of adolescence as the most poignant of life's crossroads were looking beyond it. The climactic scene of *Vanities* takes place as the characters approach their thirtieth birthdays. Ralph Pape's play, *Say Goodnight, Gracie,* deals with the problems of three men approaching 30 at the time of a high-school reunion. In many of these works the characters complain that they had peaked too soon, that they are going downhill from here, that they had already lived the best years of their lives. Levinson, himself, says that the Age Thirty Transition was particularly difficult for those people born in the 1940s "who entered adulthood during the 'protest' decade of the 1960s and turned 30 during the 1970s." The success of a book like Gail Sheehy's *Passages* owed directly to the need of many baby boomers to find reassurance that they were not alone as they confronted, for the first time, the vicissitudes of age and change.

Another way to describe this crisis is in terms of the future. As it approached and crossed 30, the collective baby boom, like many individuals, developed a fear of the future. Ahead lay the possibility of more chaos, more disillusionment, more dissolution. If the past was a failure, then the future was unthinkable. Unlike the earlier Good Times Generation, which had seen all its dreams come true and remained resolutely optimistic about the future, the baby boom was becoming less ambitious, and more doubtful and more pessimistic. It sometimes seemed almost pointless to ask. John Kerry, a onetime antiwar activist turned district attorney, gave the typical answer: "So help me, God, I don't have a sense where I will be in five years. I don't know where I'll be in six months." Ironically, the loss of confidence in the future was strongest among those former activists and reformers who had once placed so much hope in a better world. Their attitude had spread until, by the end of the 1970s, more than three out of every four Americans agreed with President Carter's assertion that "the erosion of our confidence in the future is threatening to destroy the social and political fabric of America."

In a culture devoted almost exclusively to the present, time is foreshortened and life is shorn of meaning. The faster the rate of change, the more difficult it becomes for people to maintain their relationship with the past and future—or, in human terms, with the generations older

313

and younger than they are. Social change, Kenneth Keniston writes, "increasingly entails a psychological distancing of the past, a sense of unknowability of the future, and a new emphasis on the present." The baby boom long ago cut itself off emotionally from the generation of its parents. The baby boom's lack of interest in sacrificing for children, or even having them, tells us something different. It is that the old idea that the dreams of the parents would be carried out by the children was leaving the world.

Toward the end of the 1970s, we began to hear a new adjective used about our culture. We were told that it was "decadent." This, too, says something about our view of the future. Decadence implies that a society is not merely ill, but terminally ill. Decadence is, as Lance Morrow wrote in *Time*, "the one word that will do to point toward something moribund in a culture, the metastasis of despair that occurs when a society loses faith in its own future, when its energy wanes and dies." To look a little closer at the idea of decadence, I want to examine the rise and fall of the dominant musical style of the late seventies. It is also the one most clearly associated with the *Zeitgeist* of decadence. It is disco.

We have seen that rock lost much of its dynamism in the seventies, as the baby boom aged. We were left with oldies and, on radio, the rise of the "mellow" sound. Heavy mellow replaced heavy metal when program managers began to notice that the baby boom—and its associated purchasing power—was getting older. Why should they program Kiss and Led Zeppelin for teenyboppers and sell Clearasil ads, when they could program Crosby, Stills and Nash for the baby boomers and sell everything from stereos to sports cars? Mellow began on FM radio in San Francisco (where else?) and the new trend, emphasizing a strongly harmonic sound, spread to Los Angeles and New York. Ratings soared, and the typical price of a 60-second spot shot from $10 in 1967 to $76 in 1976. Performers like Barry Manilow and Neil Diamond owed their careers to the mellow sound. Laid-back musical styles, like country rock, folk rock, and Nashville, flourished as well.

The mellow sound might have sustained itself as a musical form, but it had problems. For one thing, you couldn't dance to it. The endlessly repeated tribute to a song on *American Bandstand*, after all, was that it "has a good beat and you can dance to it." But rock had become danceless. The performers had taken over and turned the fans into spectators. Then in the mid-seventies, the largely black and Hispanic audiences began dancing to a different drummer: disco. It played down electric guitars (the essential instruments in old-time rock 'n' roll) and featured a numbingly repetitive throbbing beat and a dominant rhythm section—"rhythm without the blues," as its critics charged.

This slick, high-energy, musical fusion—there was some rhythm and blues, some Motown, some Latin, and some African—caught on at first with the baby boomers who were too old for Kiss and too young to stop dancing. And once they wanted disco, then the nation wanted disco. It took off almost as fast as rock had in the fifties. More than 20,000 discos sprang up overnight in shopping centers and cities. Mike O'Harro, the singles bar King, returned from a European self-exile, started the capital's leading disco, Tramps, and offered his advice to other disco entrepreneurs at $500 a day. Others began to offer disco franchises, the inevitable marketing mechanism to attract the fast-food generation.

By 1978, one-half of all the singles on the record charts were disco tracks. Former rockers like the Rolling Stones, Rod Stewart, the Beach Boys, and the omnipresent Cher recorded disco songs. Disney released a *Disco Mickey Mouse* album with disco versions of "Chim Chim Cher-ee" and "Zip-a-Dee-Doo-Dah." Record companies started all-disco labels. New York radio station WKTU, which was languishing with its "mellow" sound, switched to a wall-to-wall disco format and leaped past WABC to become the nation's most listened-to radio station. The disco sound-track album from the movie *Saturday Night Fever* became the industry's all-time best seller with 15 million copies sold in the United States and 25 million around the world. Braniff International airline added disco-flavored sound tracks to its gate areas to speed up the pace of boarding. Bill Graham's rock temple of the sixties, the Fillmore East, was being turned into a disco. By the end of the decade, the disco industry, not counting Spandex pants, was doing an estimated $8 billion a year. It was the biggest baby-boom fad ever. But while the rock revolution had been started by young teenagers, disco barely touched them at all. Now the music market that mattered was the 18–34 age group, which, at the end of the seventies, corresponded almost exactly to the baby-boom cohorts. These were the same people who had discovered the Beatles, only they were out of school and were bringing their musical values to adult life. Disco, moreover, was the consummate modern style. It was taut, sinewy, and hard. Demographic studies showed it was most favored by single and divorced people living in the coldly urban world of strangers. Their jobs were depressing and their prospects worse. The lyrics spoke not of teenage passions and high school, as songs had during the fifties and sixties, but rather of boring jobs and adult lust. The common lyrical theme, from Gloria Gaynor to the Bee Gees, was *survival*. In a deteriorating world in which all institutions were crumbling, disco offered a way out. Rick Sklar of ABC Radio even found something encouraging about the anomie of the boom generation. "Is disco a surrogate family?" he wondered. "If we really do live in the age of the alienated, lonely individual, seeking solace in the rhythm of disco, and the trend continues, then disco could become even stronger."

Disco glistened with a kind of desperate amorality. Inside the shimmering dance palaces, the celebrants snorted cocaine and sucked on towels soaked in ethyl chloride. The acrid fumes of "poppers"—amyl nitrate—hung in the air. Yet there was a compelling allure to it. The movie *Saturday Night Fever* preached the need to flee the destructive disco ambiance for the larger horizons of Manhattan and a career. Yet the cameras celebrated the energy of the disco itself, dwelling lovingly on its narcissism in a kind of cinematic *Schadenfreude*.

Disco spoke with the sensibility of the times. Unlike rock, which was so strongly related to the cultural tides of its day that it served as an ersatz language, telling baby boomers about each other, disco cut people loose from other people. If there was something to say, the baby boom did not want to hear it. It was hard to imagine the idea of disco stars getting behind political candidates the way rock stars once did. The motive of rock was involvement; the motive of disco was escape. Whether or not disco offered the necessary emotional validity to help a musical form survive is another question. The music itself was not the problem. (The same people who put down disco as formula-ridden are likely to romanticize the honesty of country & western, which is just as clichéd.) The real question was whether the boom generation would remain so depressed that it sought its release in a life-style devoted to surfaces and emptiness. Ultimately, beset by inflation and recession, disco lost its allure.

What were the lessons of the seventies for the baby boomers? One was the discovery that, despite it all, they could be self-centered, ambitious, and hungry for wealth as everybody else. If their former theme was opposition, now it was acquisition. Harvard's Class of 1969, which had seized buildings during its turbulent tenure on campus, came back for its tenth reunion in 1979 and found that it was not all that different from other Harvard classes. Nearly two out of three were doctors, bankers, or lawyers. In an introduction to its reunion book, a class writer took note of the changes almost wistfully: "Our biographies of five years ago stressed alternative life styles in alternative places. This report seems to show new occupations and interests which are far closer to the 'mainstream' leadership roles we had previously and often strenuously rejected."

On the surface, at least, it did look as if the Woodstock mentality had somehow merged with the Bloomingdale's mentality. The generation that had once marched against Vietnam was now marching for Proposition 13. Patty Hearst was a movie-of-the-week. Abbie Hoffman, even as a fugitive, sold the film rights to his letters to his wife. This is the generation that saw convicted Watergate defendants making more money than the prosecutors who jailed them. "Watergate was when I started becoming cynical," one baby boomer explained. "I just could not believe it. They were making all this money. I said to myself, Jesus, if you can get rich on that, then what are the values that mean anything? I learned then that the real bottom line is money."

Not that this generation sold out the first time it had the right price. Yankelovich has detected what he believes is a crucial difference: the boom generation wants money not as a symbol of success, but as a means to excitement and adventure. They care more for the internal symbols of success—the ability to enjoy a good vacation—than such external symbols as a Cadillac. They want careers, but careers that will provide not just money but *fulfillment*. "To my father, I think a job was a job and no more," said one baby-boom wife. "But I guess I'm looking for more, for some satisfaction in work."

317

The baby boomers were caught in a closing cage. Their own vast number had severely reduced their fortunes throughout life. Now, as they approached and crossed 30, the gap between their expectations and their circumstances was painfully evident. They tried to compensate for disappointment, or at least avoid it, by the withdrawal into self. But that did not work. They had spent a decade trying to get closer to one another, to learn intimacy, to get rid of their hang-ups, to let it all hang out . . . and they were still frightened.

Many baby boomers, to be sure, had not given up. They were still asking questions and still wanted to play by the old, hard rules they had devised when they were younger. Here is one such writer in *Mother Jones* magazine:

> There is a lost generation out there—I am part of it— submerged like Atlantis. But we are beginning to surface. We were born too late to buy the American dream straight off the Ozzie and Harriet car lot. We were born too early to render everything in terms of disco, though we sometimes clumsily try. What we bought, instead, from the '60's was some kind of idea of our own historical importance, a feeling that our actions should be weighted with responsibilities.

The baby boom's Age Thirty crisis brought disillusionment and the cult of the self. But there is contained within it a prophecy of a better day. It is simply that, as the boom generation continues to age its way through the population python, the troubles associated with any particular age-group will inevitably diminish. This has already begun to take place, though most people have not recognized it. When most of us are asked about the critical changes that affected the country during the 1970s, we talk about gasoline shortages and rising prices. Some mention the entry of millions of young mothers into the labor force. But the seventies also saw a change that was glacial enough not to be observable in any one year, but can only be seen over the decade. It was the last hurrah of the youth culture.

The median age of the population increased two full years in the 1970s until, as we have seen, more than one-half of us are over 30. This means that all the emotional investment we have made in the potential of youth is decreasing. We no longer idealize youth. We make fewer and fewer movies about youth. We are becoming an aging, middle-aged society. Slowly, incrementally, the idea is growing that it is not youth who will save us, but the middle-aged.

One baby boomer I talked to realized this in an unlikely place. "I had just turned 30 on a business trip," he said, "and I was feeling pretty sorry for myself. I went into a hotel bar and was sitting there looking around. The funny thing I noticed was that everyone else there looked as old as I felt. I remembered that five or ten years earlier, the place would have been full of kids. I was wondering what happened to the kids . . . when suddenly I had this incredible realization. Those old guys in there with me were the kids! They had grown up, just like me. It didn't matter that I was 30. Thirty was old in a young world, but young in an old world. I was 30, but I was still young! I haven't felt sad since."

That is the hope of the baby boom. Unlike Lord Byron, who felt in his thirties that "My days are in the yellow leaf," the boom generation has the prospect of another flowering. Just as it had previously made childhood and adolescence and young adulthood the centers of national attention, it was preparing to introduce the country to middle age.

PART IV

The Baby Boom
in the Future

A generation is fashion: but there is more
to history than costume and jargon. The
people of an era must either carry the burden of change assigned to their time or die
under its weight in the wilderness.
—Harold Rosenberg

Chapter 22

THE EMERGING SUPERCLASS

So far, what we have seen of the baby boom's life seems dishearteningly bleak. Oppressed by its numbers, the boom generation watched its great expectations yield to diminishing expectations as its troubles piled up. By the end of the seventies, *Fortune* estimated, the baby boomers had effectively lost ten years' income relative to the cohort just ahead of them and hardly seemed to have reason to look forward to the future. But that's not the case. In the next decade the baby boom will be moving into its Golden Era. The smoking frictions associated with its size will, for once, be minimized. Instead, the boom generation will attain its peak earnings and economic power and be in a position to carry out its dreams. Within the cohort itself, moreover, there is arising an extraordinarily privileged group which will come to dominate the generation.

This is the Superclass. It is composed almost entirely of the young, educated adults of the baby boom. They are most visible on the two coasts—in New York and Boston and San Francisco and Los Angeles—and their capital is Washington, D.C. They are growing in power because they are socioeconomically distinct from most other Americans. They are the professional-managerial working couples who command more discretionary income than any other group. They dress differently from most people, entertain themselves differently, eat differently, travel to different places, buy different things, and have different values. They have far fewer children.

The origins of the Superclass are in the demographic changes that will continue to affect the country in the 1980s and 1990s. Youth, which had dominated the country for so long that it almost seemed a natural force, like gravity, will no longer be a decisive factor in the future.

The number of 18-year-olds reached its all-time high in 1980. For the next two decades, the once-volatile 18–24-year-old group will decline in numbers and influence. The older age groups will likewise be losing ground: the 45–54 group will grow less than 3 million in the eighties (after plunging 700,000 in the seventies), and the 55–64 group will drop 400,000 in the eighties.

Where will the power be? The 25–44-year-old segment will virtually swallow the entire baby boom in a single gulp. In the next decade the older 35–44 bracket will grow fastest, gaining a million a year through the decade. Four out of every nine additional households will be headed by someone between 35 and 44. (Bob Dylan, the lyricist of "Forever Young," will turn 40 in 1981.) By 1990, the 35–44 group will be 40 percent larger than in 1980. The younger 24–34 group will also continue to grow as it digests the entire group of 4 million-plus birth cohorts born in the fifties.

What this means is that the baby boom will move en masse into its peak earning years and will have the wealth and the power to bend America to its will. By 1990, the baby boomers will head every other household in America and will mobilize the greatest concentration of buying power ever assembled. *Fortune* has estimated that median family income will grow 20 percent in the eighties, largely because of the influx of baby-boom couples. Much of the gain will go to the emerging Superclass. Nearly one-third of the nation's 67 million families, according to *Fortune*, will be earning from $25,000 to $50,000 (in 1977 dollars) and 4 million families will earn over $50,000 annually.

There are two sides to the growth of the Superclass. The first is simply the increase in numbers of young people entering the high-income years. The second and related trend is that so many of these young people have added the second income of a working wife. These Superclass working women do not have to work for economic reasons. The Census Bureau has shown that nearly 60 percent of the wives who took jobs between 1960 and 1977 were married to husbands with *above-average* incomes. These second paychecks have propelled many young baby boomers into the Superclass. These are the government couples who have the money to afford $150,-000 houses in Washington, D.C. suburbs, or microwave ovens, or vacations in the Caribbean. It is no coincidence that families with annual incomes of $25,000 or more in 1977 had a higher proportion of working wives than any other income class. The two out of every three wives in the 25–34 age group who are working have helped certify their families in the Superclass and kept them ahead of inflation, recession, and many of the disadvantages sufered by their cohort.

Over the next ten years, the 35–45 portion of the Superclass will explode in size as the first baby-boom cohorts enter it. It will grow by 11 million new consumers and increase its buying power 50 percent faster than that of the rest of the population. Little wonder that, to many marketers, the demographic map of the United States is beginning to look like the Steinberg map of the United States as seen from New York: instead of a landscape dominated by Manhattan, however, they see one dominated by a single generation. The Superclass will make Madison Avenue change its idea of the prime target market. Despite all the attention historically given to 18–34-year-olds, for example, *The single biggest spending age group in the country is the 35–44-year-olds.* They spend 34 percent more than average for food away from home, 30 percent more for alcoholic beverages, 37 percent more on household furnishings, 45 percent more on furniture, 44 percent more on clothing, and 56 percent more on boats and recreational vehicles. The Conference Board estimates that the number of households in the 35–44 bracket will increase from 13 million in 1980 to 20 million in 1990. Their combined spending power will rise 70 percent until they will command one-third of the country's discretionary income.

What will the Superclass baby boomers buy? In 1990, they will be 75 million strong, an Everest of demand. The temptation is to extrapolate from present trends: if the 35–44-year-olds of today like gin more than bourbon, then the increase in their number presumably promises a robust market for Beefeater's. The problem is that the increase in 35–44-year-olds will not be made up of *today's* 35–44-year-olds, none of whom are baby boomers. Rather, the 35–44-year-olds of the future are today's 25–34-year-olds, all of whom are baby boomers and are as different from other generations as one individual is from another. The real question is whether tastes and preferences are based in certain ages or in certain generations.

We already know that 35–44-year-olds buy many of

the durables that bolster the economy. Detroit sells more new cars to 35–44-year-olds than to any other age group. That potential will increase 37 percent in 1975–85, a fact that may help autombile manufacturers compensate for the energy crisis. Likewise, the middle-aged baby boomers promise to build boom markets in furniture, rugs, housewares, financial services, life insurance, and power tools—all products and services that traditionally draw on their age group. (So it is that New York Life buys commercial time during televised National Football League games in order to reach the sport's prime audience of family-building 35–44-year-old men.)

Bowling, a sport that was almost killed off by the baby boom during the Youth Society (the average bowler is 30.6), is making its comeback as the boom generation grows into it. Tennis, on the other hand, boomed as baby-boom adults discovered the sport and then collapsed as the market became saturated. (Sales of tennis rackets peaked at 9.2 million in 1975 and fell to 5 million just three years later.) Another sport, cross-country skiing, is favored by Superclass adults in their thirties and grew 30 percent a year as baby boomers presumably swapped their tennis racquets for ski poles. The preoccupation of the new Superclass with health and fitness will boost demand for expensive frills like health clubs, exercise classes, and 10-speed bicycles. The ritual of the Superclass will not be hanging out at the soda shoppe but rather signing up for aerobic dancing and yoga.

The travel industry likewise sees prosperous times ahead. People aged 35–44 are already 45 percent more likely to travel than the average American. Moreover, the 35–44-year-olds of the future—educated, single, childless —will have more of the time, income, and inclination to travel than their predecessors.

Television, the medium through which advertising is mainlined into the boom generation, is unerringly reflecting the tastes and values of the Superclass. Back during the heyday of the Procreation Ethic, the idea of a show that did not punish a divorced person was unthinkable. So the John Forsythe of *Bachelor Father* (1957–62) had to be a single man who adopted his orphaned niece—a nicety that seems quaint today. In the seventies, ABC programmed its way to the top with *Happy Days* and *Charlie's Angels*. But by 1980, ABC had lost its audience and its lead to CBS, which was programming Superclass series like *60 Minutes* and *Dallas*, which assumed maturity if not always intelligence. (One of the reasons that soap-style dramas like *Dallas* worked in prime time may be that Superclass women who might have previously watched daytime serials now were limited by their work schedules to evening viewing.) In 1979, the country's radio stations reported that the category of demographics most often requested by advertisers was for 18 and over —a remarkable change for a medium once geared almost exclusively to young teenagers. Even Lawrence Welk, it's worth remembering, lost his network show not because of lack of popularity (his ratings were high) but because advertisers considered his audience too old. In the future, they might see that as an advantage.

Another way television caters to the economic power of the emerging Superclass is by confirming its prejudices. For all its wealth, the Superclass is essentially antiauthoritarian. Many of its members are in the professoriate or in the college-educated group trained to doubt absolute authority. As the baby boomers enter the Superclass, their own disillusioning experiences are reinforcing this tendency. Thus, in the fifties and early sixties, television's authority figures—the Matt Dillons, the Sergeant Fridays, and the Perry Masons—were aloof, secure, and unchallenging. Parents were wise; kids were charmingly wrong. But by the end of the seventies, after Vietnam and Watergate, authority figures were no longer benign Marcus Welbys or Ozzie Nelsons. They were instead cynical hypocrites—corrupt businessmen, corrupt police, even corrupt teachers—who were doomed to derision or arrest. It was as if, having denied the wish fulfillment of the boom generation for so long, television suddenly caved in. The only authority figure the baby boom would trust on television, it seemed, was Walter Cronkite (and he, too, had a nostalgia quotient after having hosted *You Are There* two decades earlier).

New magazines are sprouting up every day as advertisers attempt to track the Superclass. *Vogue* published a kind of Me Generation handbook called *Self*. The entry of women into the workplace spawned an entire new genre of magazines like *Savvy, Working Woman, Enterprising Women, Working Mothers,* and *New Woman.* The old *Esquire* was purchased and retooled by two baby-boom tycoons, Christopher Whittle and Phillip Moffit, who noted that "We always publish something about the times in which we live." Indeed, they have progressed from campus guides (Nutshell) to a list of titles that could be a generational biography: 18 Almanac, Graduate, On Your Own, New Marriage, and Successful Business. A new group of science magazines that might never have found a readership ten years ago are now published for educated baby boomers who, ever since Sputnik and the bomb, have appreciated the impact of science in their lives. Publisher Matty Simmons, whose National Lampoon prospered from the young, iconoclastic baby boom in the seventies, may find the same generation in the eighties more supportive of his first magazine property, Weight Watchers.

One of the questions the next decade will answer is whether many products are, in fact, youth products or baby-boom products. What will be the fate of Cokes in an unyoung society? Or rock records? Or Big Macs? Will they stay with the generation or will they stay with the age group? Denims found new life as fashion jeans and Levis Strauss has lately introduced a line of broad-bottom jeans for baby-boom bodies sagging from the cumulative pull of roast beef and gravity. The company first tested them as "Gentlemen's Jeans" and then tried "Mr. Levi's" and finally "Levi's for Men" for the denims "cut to fit a man's build. With a little more room in the seat and thigh." (The company's ad campaign, meanwhile, was switched from Top 40 radio to the Superclass's preferred all-news stations.)

As recently as 1975, pop music looked like a doomed business. The overwhelming majority of records then were bought by 14–24-year-olds. Those were the kids whose first musical memories were of Elvis, who had brought the Beatles to America, and who had made music a bigger and more lucrative segment of the entertainment industry than even movies. The problem was that record buying stopped dead after the age of 30—and in 1976 the first baby-boom kids began to turn 30. In the 1980s, eventually, the crucial 14–24 group would *decline* by more than 7 million potential buyers. The nonstop party that had meant twenty-five years of uninterrupted growth for the music business seemed to be over.

What happened? For the three years from 1975 through 1978, overall record sales roared up nearly 20 percent each year. Two records, the *Saturday Night Fever* and *Grease* sound tracks, sold more than 27 million copies in 1978, more than the sum of *all* classical records. Record sales may never again achieve that high—and, in fact, slumped in 1979—but the point was clear. The baby boomers were taking their musical habit past the once-unbreakable barrier of 30. Since 1972, the average age of people buying records has increased every year and, according to a market survey by Warner Records, the 25–49 age group now accounts for nearly 44 percent of all purchases. That same age group will increase by one-fourth in the next ten years, a fact that offers a glittering promise even to country music, which is particularly well adapted to older listeners with its lyrical themes of loneliness, adultery, heartbreak, and alcohol. Warner Communications was able to conclude in its 1979 annual report that:

> The relationship today between music and people in their teens, twenties, thirties, and even forties, exemplifies the changing role of entertainment. Whether at home, at a concert, or at a disco, music is a constant presence, a matter of intense involvement, and a means of self-expression for an increasingly large percentage of the population.

The buying power of the boom may be enough to keep it forever young—or at least feeling that way. There is already a new market for over-30 models and movie stars. A recent *Harper's Bazaar* list of the ten most beautiful women in the world included none under 30. Older actresses, with their serenity and worldly wisdom, now inspire more consumer confidence than do vacuous-looking young blondes. Lauren Hutton wonders in magazine ads how to treat her skin now that she's over 30. A cosmetic called Oil of Olay runs TV spots claiming it can make "every age the best you've ever looked."

Movies that had once explored the problems of youth were now digging into midlife. If *The Graduate* was the archetypal sixties' film, with its mixture of adolescent rebellion and romanticism, then *Kramer vs. Kramer* brought the same actor, Dustin Hoffman, up-to-date with an older and more troubled generation a decade later. As the career-driven advertising man Ted Kramer, Hoffman watches his life fall apart as his wife walks out and later tries to gain custody of their son. So many other movies of the time echoed this theme of family disintegration that it

328

has become a cliché. There were also *An Unmarried Woman, Starting Over, The Goodbye Girl,* and *Manhattan,* all of which were filmed in New York (the world capital of angst) and all of which reflected the problems of a generation seeking clues from Hollywood about how to behave during divorce. The answers, in true Lotusland fashion, were reassuring: the single parent will be rewarded, the faithless will be punished, divorce is temporary, new romance will be found. Along the way a now-familiar stock character has been created—the single father who, cast aside by a feminist wife, learns painfully how to cope with his life and his children.

What all of these movies reflect most accurately is the self-absorption of the baby boom in its thirties. The women in *The Turning Point* grapple with the midlife crisis of roads not taken, whether motherhood or career. The Dudley Moore character in *10* is typically whiplashed by male menopause. Joan Didion has noticed in Woody Allen's commercial films "the notion of oneself as a kind of continuing career" with "an hour a day of emotional Nautilus training." Perhaps the single most devastating moment in any of these films comes when Meryl Streep's Joanna character in *Kramer vs. Kramer* writes her son a letter to explain her absence. "I have gone away because I must find some interesting things to do for myself in the world," she tells the bewildered boy. "Everybody has to and so do I. Being your Mommy was one thing but there are other things . . ."

A movie like *Kramer vs. Kramer* could never have succeeded in the year of *The Graduate,* nor could The *Graduate* have worked in 1980. Yet both films lived off the same audience, bookending a dozen years of the baby boom's life. Historically, more than one-half of all filmgoers have been under 25 and three-fourths under 30. After 30, though, as parents traditionally build families and stay home, moviegoing falls off abruptly. As long as the youth audience was there, Hollywood could profitably and safely gear its product to the adolescents. But as the baby boomers leave the prime moviegoing years and enter their thirties and forties, the moviemakers, like everyone else who makes youth products, face a simple choice. Should they continue to pursue their traditional market, even as it shrinks in numbers? Or should they reposition their products for an older, larger market?

There may not be a choice. The 16–20 age group by

itself accounts for one-quarter of all movie tickets sold. In the 1970s, as the crest of the baby boom passed through those ages, yearly attendance at the movies in the United States increased by 37 percent. But in the 1980s, the same 16–20 age group will *decline* by 20 percent. The baby boomers entering their thirties, on the other hand, are different from previous generations. If 30-year-old parents in the 1950s were devoted to hearth and home, the 30-year-old baby boomers might not be parents at all. Or, if they are, they are media children who expect movies to address their problems the same way their parents expected novels to address theirs. Little wonder that Disney has stopped filming its Don Knotts and Fred MacMurray family comedies. In the next decade, the movie market that matters will be middle-aged.

THE SUPERCLASS AT WORK

In the 1980s, as the baby boom completes its migration from the home and campus to the office and factory, it will bring some of the sharpest changes in the labor force since the generation first began looking for jobs in 1965. No longer, for example, will the labor force face the problem of absorbing huge numbers of new workers every year. Instead of labor surplus, we will be contending in the future with labor scarcity.

Let me be specific. In the seventies, as millions of baby boomers left the schools and looked for jobs, the labor force grew by 20 million (24.4 percent)—compared to only 7.5 million during the fifties (an 11½ percent increase) and 13 million during the sixties (18 percent). But during the 1980s, the growth rate will decline to around 1.3 percent annually and then to less than 1 percent annually in the 1990s. Companies may start recruiting and offering training programs and special benefit packages—perhaps including child-care programs and maternity leaves—to draw more younger workers and women into the labor force. Pressures should grow to relax immigration restrictions to provide the manpower needed for blue-collar and agricultural jobs.

Technically, at least, labor shortages should help minority groups get ahead as well. The problem, though, is that we may have already missed our chance to upgrade the skills of millions of disadvantaged minority teenagers enough to help them take care of improved demand. In the eighties the youth employment problem (which will never go away entirely) will increasingly become a black youth employment problem. Only 10 percent of all adults are black, but because their fertility is higher, 15 percent of all children are black. Black teenagers will go from 11 percent of the youth labor force in 1970 to 20 percent in the 1990s. As long as they are displaced in the marketplace by white teenagers and woman, they will constitute a permanently unemployable group that will carry its disadvantage to the grave. (College-educated black men and women of the baby boom, on the other hand, are fully participating members of the Superclass. By 1977, the average income of black college graduates under 35 was virtually the same as that of whites. Between 1969 and 1977, the average income of *all* blacks 24–34 rose from 79 percent to 95 percent of that of whites of the same age.)

An expanding labor force is just one way the economy guarantees growth. The other is improving productivity. For most of two hundred years, labor-force productivity —roughly defined as national income divided by the number of employed persons—had steadily improved in America. It ran as high as an average increase of 2.7 percent from 1948 through 1969. But then it dipped to 2.1 percent from 1969 to 1973, and all but collapsed altogether after that. Productivity ground down to 1.1 in 1973–78 and fell 0.9 percent in 1979, only the second such decrease for a full year since 1947.

This is of more than statistical interest. As the essential cushion between wages and prices, productivity growth is the key to increasing living standards and controlling inflation. The reason is that increases in man-hour output allow employers to increase wages without increasing prices. But if productivity is not increasing, an employer cannot afford to raise wages without raising prices as well. The result is inflation.

The entry of the baby boom into the labor force depressed productivity in two ways. First, the labor force was flooded with inexperienced young workers who were less productive than older workers already on the job. The younger workers at the bottom could not substitute for their older colleagues unless they were trained—and that took time and investment. Second, business investment did not match the growth of the labor force. With an influx of young workers, employers were able to maintain

331

production without investing in labor-saving equipment. Thus, as the baby-boom cohorts flooded the job market, the amount of investment per worker slowed down and depressed productivity. The arrival of baby-boom women in the labor market particularly cut into productivity. Many of them were inexperienced and began working at entry-level jobs. In 1978, 12 percent of working women had started on the job for the first time within the previous year and the average tenure of *all* women at work was only 2.6 years.

In the eighties, however, as the boom generation gains in age and maturity, the population pressures that had hurt productivity earlier will reverse. Economists estimate that the age-structure changes brought by the baby boom depressed productivity by around 0.3 percent annually in 1966–73 and 0.2 percent in 1973–78. In the future, however, capital that was previously diverted into training and recruitment will be invested in labor-savings equipment. And, if unskilled labor shortages do develop around 1990, business will have a further incentive to spend on capital investment and research. All of these forces could act as a brake on the debilitating inflation that so depressed the boom generation in the past decade.

THE PROMOTION SQUEEZE

For all its unparalleled wealth, the Superclass will face some problems ahead. One of them is that the working men and working women of the baby boom will find that, just as there once was not enough room for all of them to climb onto the occupational ladder, there later will not be enough room at the top. As each person tries to climb up the business and professional hierarchies, he or she will find other baby-boom competitors blocking the way. Millions of them crowded on the first steps of management will be forced to stay right there. A generation that had expected to be Chiefs will have to be Braves. In effect, the entire generation will be like a large group of people being moved from a big room into a smaller room. Some will shove their way in, picking up bruises in the process; others will try to get in and fall; still more will not try at all.

For many baby boomers, particularly educated women accustomed to a fast track, the frustration will be acute. Presumably they will not trash the corporate suites or employment offices as freely as they did the equally crowded college campuses of the sixties. But there will be changes in the business world. In some corporations, power struggles could erupt between Young Turks, eager for their chance to take over, and the older generation of executives clinging to their seniority. White-collar unionization, previously successful only in government, could come into its own in the eighties as the baby boomers railroad through early retirement packages and sabbatical plans designed to ease the older generation out of the way. The old idea that a person spent a lifetime climbing the ladder within one company is on the way out, too. The midcareer switch could become a way of life as baby boomers seek to improve their odds in the corporate game of musical chairs. Books like *What Color Is Your Parachute?* (about job-switching tactics) and *How to Get Your Promotion* have started popping up on the best-seller lists. In 1978, the number of workers changing occupations increased by one-third over the number five years earlier, and, if the trend continues, the eighties could be the golden age of executive recruiting "headhunters." By the time the baby boomer reaches 38, the average age of a midcareer change, the headhunters will be enjoying a boom market of their own.

Other concepts will have to change. As promotions become harder to find, baby boomers will have to reconcile themselves to longer climbs to the top. Instead of proceeding straight up, emphasis will be placed on job rotations, lateral transfers, and what some companies call "psychic benefits." Continuing education will help some advance. The part-time work force will continue its rapid expansion, as a means of working two people into one job. (Fifteen years ago there was one part-timer for every ten full-time workers; now there is one part-timer for every five.)

People born at the tail end of the baby boom in the late fifties will be particularly disadvantaged. Ahead of them, every base will be taken by their older brothers and sisters. The first baby boomers, by contrast, were the risk takers who barged into an exciting new world they were remaking. But the last baby boomers will grow up into a world already too crowded for them. Throughout their lives they will face the prospect of salaries that were not quite as large as they hoped, devalued education, and difficult promotions. What makes their plight particularly

333

painful is that it comes at a time when the baby boom's values are joining the mainstream and forging an altogether new definition of what work means in America.

THE NEW WORK ETHIC

When the baseball player Jim Bouton briefly tried an over-40 comeback as a relief pitcher in the minor leagues, he was appalled at the new generation of players. "These kids believed someone owed them a chance," he said. "I grew up thinking you had to earn it." Even worse to Bouton, he saw batters leaving their bats on their shoulders: "Why, back when I played, boys and girls, hitters swung that bat. *Nobody* got called out on strikes."

Bouton's fulminations are typical of the parents of the boom generation who ardently believed in the work ethic that, in their experience, had made America great. It meant hard work and delayed gratification. It meant loyalty. It meant providing for family. It meant sacrifice. But, as the boom generation came of age, each of these ideas began to be whittled away. According to Yankelovich's surveys, the number of workers who look on their jobs as their primary source of personal fulfillment has been halved since the late sixties. The number who think "hard work always pays off" has dropped from 58 percent to 43 percent. Among the highly educated, or those whose fathers went to college, the percentage who believe hard work leads to success was even smaller. Instead, a strange resentment seemed to be building up, perhaps as a legacy of Watergate, that those who worked hard and played by the rules wound up with the short end of the stick. And those who flouted the rules would get away with it. Then why try at all? Conventional jobs could hardly be fulfilling to a generation of students which, in one 1970 Louis Harris poll, listed its third most-favored career ambition as, poignantly, "explorer." The baby boomers were moving freely in and out of jobs at a rate that dismayed employers used to more dependable workers. One typical restaurant in Boulder, Colorado, which has a staff of 70 persons, went through 192 employees in a single year.

Daniel Yankelovich believes that the nineteenth-century work ethic died out because of "a growing mismatch between incentives and motivations." Previous generations worked hard because they had to. They had witnessed the Depression and knew what it meant not to work. But now society has added "floors" in the form of unemployment payments and food stamps to relieve some of the worst penalties of poverty. Then, too, the boom babies have had fewer family responsibilities to bind them to jobs. In the fifties, 70 percent of all households were composed of a working man, a nonworking wife, and one or more children under 18. Today those families amount to just 14 percent of all households. Each worker, therefore, has fewer mouths to feed.

Many of the noncollege baby boomers have rejected the self-sacrificing style of conventional careers and have withdrawn instead into Cyreniac fantasies of power boats, suburban homes, and ski vacations. But Yankelovich's New Breed are those members of the Superclass who feel differently. They are educated, white collar, and achievement-oriented. But they are restless with their jobs and find the present incentive system unappealing. They seem to want something from their jobs they are not getting.

What do they want from work? To understand it best, we might consider the experience of previous generations. As Yankelovich points out, many of the parents of the baby boomers made a "bargain" with society that meant dividing their lives in two. During the week, they worked obediently on the job, performing as society demanded. But then they retreated to a private world of their own, walled off by weekends and suburbs. There they could shed their gray flannel suits and "be themselves" with their families and hobbies. But this system depended on compartmentalizing their lives in order to satisfy both the demands of society and their personal desires.

The boom generation will have nothing of this. They do not see a dichotomy between private and social values and have no intention of denying their "real selves" on the job. In their minds, self-fulfillment and successful careers should not be incompatible. The purpose of a job, they argue, is not to satisfy their material needs but to satisfy their emotional needs. In Yankelovich's words, they are

trying to achieve a synthesis of the old and new values by assuming that it is possible to seek and find self-fulfillment and personal satisfaction in a conventional career, while simultaneously enjoying the kind of financial rewards that will enable them to live full, rich lives outside of their work.

An employer thus owes employees not just a living but security and self-fulfillment as well. The baby boomers take affluence for granted and are acutely attuned to such issues as vacation time, sabbaticals, flexible schedules, maternity leaves. They think they have the "right" to participate in decisions that affect their work. They want personal recognition, a chance to be heard, a chance to learn and grow. Their work must be meaningful and provide an outlet for self-expression.

In a way, they want to be students again. Where else were they allowed to take their dreams so seriously? Thus the baby boomers do not see themselves as lawyers or doctors or accountants—roles defined by society—but instead see themselves as joggers or tennis players or movie buffs, which are roles defined by their emotional needs. This, Yankelovich notes, is a dramatic reversal from the time when European visitors used to marvel at Americans habitually identifying themselves as "a car dealer" or "a veterinarian." Now that only 20 percent of people say that work means more to them than pleasure, the answer to the old question, What do you do? is not as interesting as asking, How do you play?

The Promotion Squeeze poses a problem for these values. There will be crushing disappointments ahead for the 68 percent of the generation who want jobs in which they can "express themselves" or for the 77 percent who want to be "challenged at work." On the other hand, these same frustrations will reinforce some of the New Values that emphasize "fulfillment" rather than the old Sammy Glick models of success. Unable to get ahead at work, they are self-protectively turning away from the external symbols of success and necessarily emphasizing the internal ones.

The Promotion Squeeze will also weigh heavily on those baby boomers who may not be members of the Superclass but who will have absorbed Superclass values. One reason that the 18–24-year-olds who did not go to college are the most alienated group in the country is that they have the same Superclass expectations of the college graduates but lack the means to achieve them. They, too, now endorse such issues as increased sexual freedom, premarital sex, tolerance of homosexuality, acceptance of abortion, and deemphasis of religion and patriotism. And they, too, believe that "interesting work" is just as important a job attribute as salary—only they are far less likely to find those interesting jobs. The bad "fit" between aspirations and reality is particularly painful for noncollege women, who have grown up in an atmosphere thick with feminism and frustration but have little hope of improving their own circumstances.

> That the majority of noncollege youth [says Yankelovich] face the prospect of growing difficulties with their jobs must be regarded as a matter of serious concern to the society. These young people, after all, represent the great bulk of the new labor force. The problem they face is compounded by the multiplier effect of higher expectations with lower opportunities: their New Values inevitably clash with the built-in rigidities and limited responses of the traditional work place.

THE POLITICS OF THE BABY BOOM

Not so long ago many of us thought that the boom generation would not even need to exert its influence indirectly through, say, its buying power, in order to take over. It would simply do it at the polling place. Was not this generation the world's largest interest group? What politician could dare stand in its way?

The Twenty-sixth Amendment consolidated the baby boom's power early on by giving millions of 18-year-olds the right to vote for the first time in the 1972 election. The young people who voted seemed to prefer younger candidates. The average age of the United States Congress dipped from 53 in 1970 to 49.5 for the Congress elected in 1978. The number of congressmen under the age of 40 doubled from 40 in 1971 to 81 in 1978, including James Shannon of Massachusetts, the first baby-boom congressman born after 1950. These baby-boom voters did not follow their parents' lead at the polls. The partisan correspondence between parent and child, historically as much a political truism as exists in America, *declined* for the *first* time in 1972. With their numbers, their mass identity, their special needs, and their independence from other generations, the boom generation seemed to have all the makings of a political tyranny.

It didn't happen. The boom generation turned out to be

a paper tiger, at least politically. This was clear as early as 1970, when antiwar college students founded the Movement for a New Congress, with the ambition of using the shoe leather of thousands of students to elect peace candidates that fall. Many colleges rejiggered their academic calendars to give students two weeks off in the fall to assist their electioneering. As Richard Nixon and Spiro Agnew answered with a law-and-order strategy of their own, the election was seen as nothing short of a referendum on youth.

The results were inconclusive. The Nixon-Agnew backlash did not carry the day, but neither did the students. Though the MNC had predicted as many as a million student workers, the *Congressional Quarterly* guessed that only 75,000 actually campaigned. The percentage of students campaigning was not appreciably higher than the percentage of nonstudents who campaigned. Some peace candidates won. Others lost. In fact, even the moral victories disheartened the students who had expected too much.

This experience was repeated in the 1972 presidential election. George McGovern was depending on 11.5 million newly enfranchised voters, among others, to make the difference for him. For the first time since the early 1900s, more than one-fifth of the eligible voters were under 26—and many of them were highly educated, articulate, and visible baby boomers thought to be against the war. Yet one of the strangest ironies in electoral politics resulted after McGovern announced a massive registration campaign designed to bring young voters to the polls. As it turned out, the registrations benefited not McGovern but Nixon. The reason is that most pro-McGovern voters were *already* registered. By registering additional young people, the McGovern forces were inadvertently pulling in more Nixon votes.

In the end, just 12 percent of the eligible under-26 voters went to the polls anyway. The only lesson seemed to be that young voters were unpredictable and nonpartisan. The traditional relationship between economic class and party leaning was steadily being eroded. Part of the reason, undoubtedly, was the fact that college-educated young have always been disproportionately independent. In 1978, as we have seen, nearly one-quarter of the baby-boom cohort then aged 25–29 had graduated from college. That compared to only 10 percent of their parents between the ages of 45 and 54. The educated baby boomers, therefore, were that much less likely to identify themselves along traditional party lines. The important thing to remember here is that education, not youth, is the dominant factor. When election analysts studied the 1972 results, they found that the biggest differences in behavior were not between young and old but between college-educated voters and noncollege voters. In fact, the most "abnormal" group in society—that is, the one voting most against the norm—consisted not of blacks or some alienated minority but rather the privileged group of white college graduates born between 1948 and 1954—in short, the battered, bruised leading edge of the boom generation.

What will the boom babies do in the next decade? One certain thing will be to continue to abandon the youth lobby. During the 1970s, 18-year-olds had managed to win the vote, lower the drinking age, and get rid of the draft. Now two out of three of those changes are being reversed (and the voting age presumably would be if not protected by constitutional amendment). So far, though, the baby boomers have not followed the traditional pattern of embracing political parties as they grow older. Unlike their parents, this generation has remained independent. The reason is that, as Mannheim argued, the crucial question to ask regarding a person's politics or a generation's—is not how old the person is but when the person was young. The baby boom was young during the most explosive growth of higher education in the nation's history. It was also young during Vietnam and Watergate and learned then its continuing distrust of the political system. (The success of the Prosposition 13 referenda around the country in the late seventies is typical of baby-boom politics: their support was nonpartisan and anti-government.) By gaining their political consciousness during the late sixties and early seventies, the baby boomers developed an iconoclastic frame of reference that can tell us more about the future behavior of this generation than, as Aristotle had supposed, the mellowing influence of aging. We see this tendency everywhere in the politics of the eighties. The fact that the political parties cannot effectively organize the opinion of the baby boom has contributed to the decline of the parties themselves and, indirectly, to the decline of voter participation. We can expect more third-party movements to base themselves on the unaffililated millions of baby boomers. We will have "event" and "issue" politics based less on political ideology than on a kind of "What does it do for me?" ideology.

This leads to a somewhat unsettling thought. It is that the baby boom may still be uniquely vulnerable to a mass political movement. We know that older voters vote more often than younger voters. We also know that educated voters vote more often than uneducated voters. As the boom generation crosses its fourth decade in the next ten years, and as it deepens its taxpaying stake in society, the political potential of those educated baby boomers will expand enormously. We also know that those same people will be growing up disaffected. Even the members of the Superclass will be working below their educational level and will be crowded out of advancement. Many of them will feel powerlessness, isolation, and meaninglessness—all the components of modern anomie. All of this approaches the psychological state of an ungrounded person particularly vulnerable to a charismatic religious leader—only it will be happening to an entire generation.

We know further that the most effective means of reaching the boom generation—television—is already set up and functioning. Indeed, the baby boomers are so used to being exploited commercially it is worth wondering if they would even know if they were being exploited politically. Many of the generation's past leaders have either failed it or died. But the need for heroes is still there, waiting to be filled.

Chapter 23

THE BABY BOOM AND CATCH-35

In 1966, the Communist leaders of Rumania were surveying their country's birthrates with mounting despair. For nine straight years the fertility of Rumanian women had plunged until it was well below the replacement level. The cause, the government concluded, was a state decree in 1957 that had legalized abortion and made it readily available on request. With a fee of less than $2 and only slight danger, abortion had become for Rumanian women a procedure as routine as having a tooth filled. Consequently, they had given up most other methods of contraception and depended almost entirely on abortion as their leading method of birth control. By 1965, four out of every five conceptions were ended in abortion.

What could be done? One way out of their quandary, the nation's leaders concluded, would be to make abortion more difficult. But instead of consulting demographers about the possible consequences, the Rumanian government took immediate action. In State Decree Number 770 on November 1, 1966, the government severely restricted abortions, outlawed contraceptives, and enacted a package of other pronatalist measures such as birth premimums and reduced taxes for couples with children. Nine months later, Rumania's reluctant mother heroines, as they've been called, responded in an extraordinary burst of proletarian fervor. In September 1967, the number of births *tripled* over the previous December. For the year of 1967, both the crude birthrate and the number of births was twice that of 1966. Newspapers reported instances of three new mothers sharing a single hospital bed. Doctors urged women to stay at home to have their babies to save space. There was even a shortage of nurses, since most of them were pregnant, too. The Rumanian government had succeeded far beyond its wildest hopes. It had unleashed what is believed to be the sharpest increase in the fertility of a large population in the history of the human species.

Immediately after 1967, Rumanian fertility rates dropped by 50 percent as women began to find other means of contraception. (A further reason for the drop is that, in contrast to 1967 when almost every eligible woman in the country became pregnant at the sound of the government's whistle, now most had just given birth and were removed from the running for at least a few months.) But over the next decade, Rumania doubled its rate of population increase and produced an estimated 39 percent more babies than might otherwise have been expected (compared to an "excess" of 34 percent during America's baby boom). The Rumanian baby boomlet, which on a graph looks less like a pig in a python than a giraffe in a python, is also producing predictable dislocations as it pushes through the age cycle. In 1972, Rumania abruptly had twice as many children in kindergarten as the year earlier. In the late 1980s it will have twice as many people entering the labor force and marrying (and thereby producing an "echo" boom of their own). Around the year 2040, Rumania can expect even a tomb boom.

An extreme case? Perhaps, but the pressures to promote fertility are growing every year in the developed countries. Already five nations—Austria, Britain, Luxembourg, and East and West Germany—have more annual deaths than births. Many others—including Belgium, Denmark, Czechoslovakia, Hungary, Norway, and Sweden—are facing imminent population decline. None of these countries is taking it lightly. The prime minister of Luxembourg has complained of a "suicidal attitude" among his citizens. And as early as 1976 France's President Giscard d'Estaing warned that no country with a middle-sized population could realistically aspire to grandeur. (At the time of Napoleon, France was one-fifth of Europe's population; it is now one-twentieth.) The West Germans were running a TV show with titles like, *Are the Germans Dying Out?* and in Australia, where the boom had been strongest, words like "madness" were used to describe the drop in fertility. One demographer, Charles Westoff, believes that European fertility could drop as low as 1.5 children per mother (the lowest rate ever recorded for an actual cohort of women was 1.8 for those born in 1907 in England and Wales), and that the real question for the year 2000 is not whether we shall have to reward women to have children but how much the reward will have to be.

The question America's baby-boom mothers are posing for the future is whether or not their lowered fertility will prevail. At a time when women are having only half as many children as their mothers, the family is increasingly being described as "obsolete" or "extinct." The place of women in the family has certainly changed: they marry later, go to work before having their first child, and return to work after having their children. So many of them have left the home, whether through working or divorce, that the traditional American family is more likely to be found in the pages of the *Saturday Evening Post* than on Main Street.

Today the old-style nuclear family of a breadwinner husband, housewife mother, and one child is only 16 percent of all households. Add another child and the percentage falls to less than 10 percent. Most Americans spend *some* part of their lives in a nuclear family, to be sure, but the questions remain: Has the baby boom pulled the pins from underneath the family? Has it lost the will to reproduce itself? Or is what we are seeing a helathy adaptation to change? Will future generations, like salmon thrashing upriver to spawn, continue to obey the primordial impulse to procreate?

Demographers, still feeling the embarrassments of the baby boom and the baby bust, are understandably cautious. Few of them think, for example, that the current total birth rate of around 1.8 children per mother could hold up for the lifetime of the cohort . . . but it *might*. The problem is that there are too many unknowns. Half the births of 1980 were to women who were not yet married in 1975. In the next five years, 10 million women now aged 15–19, about whose fertility habits little is known, will enter their prime reproductive years. All our assumptions about fertility could be changed by what they do. Or even by technological change. Back in 1900, people thought New York City could never grow to one million because there would be no room to stall all the horses. A significant victory by the Right to Life organization, for example, could have a similar impact on fertility (but presumably not as severe) as Rumania's State Decree Number 770. The previous low fertility mark for a group of American women was set by the 1906–10 cohort. Every 1000 women born then—the grandmothers of the baby boom—produced 2286 children (or 2.286 per mother). The baby-boom women born in 1946–50 are presently running well below their grandmothers' fertility at comparable ages. If the 1946–50 women continue to complete their childbearing at an average rate similar to previous generations, they will end up with a record low of only 2200 babies per 1000. Younger baby-boom women are having even fewer children at the same ages.

There is, unfortunately, a problem with projecting future births like this. It is that no one can say for certain whether women are merely delaying births or not having them at all. The 1946–50 cohort, for example, is at least biologically capable of producing babies until the year 2000, when its youngest members turn 50. That leaves plenty of years for these women to change their minds about having children or to make up for lost time. The 1946–50 women might well follow the pattern of their mothers born in 1910–25, whose childbearing was curtailed in their younger years by the Depression, but who caught up with a vengeance immediately after World War II. But as each year goes by, it will become harder and harder for the baby-boom women to catch up with the widening fertility gap between them and their mothers. Every 1000 women born in 1936–40 had produced 525 births when they were 20–24 in 1960. But those women born in 1951–55 had given birth to only 325 babies—38 percent fewer—at the same age in 1975.

One way demographers have tried to solve this problem is by asking women how many children they *expect* to have over the rest of their lives. The baby boomers plainly expect fewer. Between 1967 (the first year the Census Bureau collected such data) and 1978, the average number of births expected by 18–34-year-old wives dropped from 3.1 to 2.3. The decline was most drastic among white college graduates, who in 1978 expected to have only 1.9 children apiece. Yet, even these guesses may be high. Women contemplating children do not anticipate the interruption of a divorce, for example, or difficulty in conception. One government demographer, Arthur Campbell, has shown that if women now really have as many babies as they say they will, their fertility would have to rise by as much as 20 percent in their later years. And as they grow older, women are often forced to reduce their expectations. When they were teenagers in 1967, baby-boom women born in the late 1940s said they expected to have 2.719 babies apiece. Just five years later in 1972, these same women scaled back their expected families to 2.282 children each. As always, the polls had "anticipated" the fertility practices of the present, not the future.

Perhaps the biggest mystery in the minds of baby-boom women is the question of how many *ever* will have children. When asked in 1978, only 11 percent of the baby boom's women said they expected to remain childless all their lives. Since that figure compares with what happened during the boom itself, when 8 percent of the women born in the 1930s had no children, the *idea* of motherhood would seem to be alive and well. But there are some conflicting trends emerging among the youngest and most educated baby boomers. Fully 15 percent of the boom's college-educated women say they expect to remain childless—and seem to mean it. In recent years, the proportion of childless women in their twenties has doubled (to 41 percent for those 20–24) and now 18 percent of *all* women born in the peak baby-boom cohorts of 1954–60 say they never expect to have children. Ultimately, their childbearing may come to resemble not their mothers but their grandmothers in the 1908 cohort who achieved the all-time record low fertility largely because 22 percent of them had no children at all.

As for those women who say they will have children, the time is fast approaching for them to fish or cut bait. However improbable, no less than 22 percent of all childless women 30–35 claim that they will eventually have *two* babies. So far, these women have been able to reconcile their acceptance of the motherhood ideal with the fact of their childlessness by telling themselves that they will catch up later. Their decision could be delayed along with their babies. But time must eventually force a reckoning. In 1981, a half-million more women will cross 35—often seen as the last chance for childbearing—than in the previous year. By the end of the decade, 18 million women will face the catch-35 dilemma. There is already anguished pillow talk in baby-boom households as the decision is faced. Will a child hurt my career? What will our parents think? For some women, this will be the time of *Torschlusspanik* (literally, "closing-time panic") in which they see their last chance to fulfill their fantasies about motherhood and feminity. Some will grab for it all—husband, baby, and career—and try to bear up under the inevitable strains. Other women will perhaps reluctantly recognize that, for them, fertility delayed was fertility denied. Later was never.

No one should underestimate the pull of parenthood. Betty Rollin, who had opened the seventies with her assault on mandatory motherhood, admitted at the end of the decade that she "feels like I've missed something." According to novelist Anne Roiphe, "There's a difference between what one says at 20 and what one says at 38. We're seeing a whole rash of people having babies just in the nick of time." And here is Paula Cizmar, a baby-boom feminist, wrestling with her decision in a magazine article:

> On my next birthday I will be 30 and I don't want to be a casualty of the war between my politics and my biological clock.

Cizmar questions her motives . . .

> Why do I want to have a baby? Am I simply afraid I'll miss something if I don't?

. . . and, like the baby boomer she is, worries that she will somehow fail to live up to her own high expectations:

> Combining motherhood with work presents me with a horrible possibility—two opportunities to succeed or fail. And suppose I fail at both?

Older women have already begun to squeeze in their first births before it's too late. The uptick in births at the end of the 1970s was due in part to postponed births finally arriving. We can see this in the age-specific birth-rate for older women. In 1970, the birthrate for women 30–34 having their *first* child was 7.3 per thousand. In 1977, as the first baby boomers entered the 30–34 group, the rate jumped 36 percent to 9.9. Well-known women like Erica Jong and Paula Prentiss and Nora Ephron were issuing their first children in their mid-thirties. "Just once in my life I would like to do something that everyone else isn't doing," complained Ephron, "but that seems not to be my destiny." Nor will it be for 37 million baby-boom women who will face a similar moment of decision. (A hidden catch-35 is that many older women who have postponed pregnancy will find that, when they want to, they may not be able to because of the physiological changes brought on by age and use of birth control. Three decades ago, one of ten couples was believed to have difficulties conceiving children; today, the figure may be as high as one out of six.)

As each year passes, the possibility that the boom women will be able to "catch up" on the babies they did not have in the seventies diminishes. There are only two ways left for them to have as many babies as they say they'd like to have. One would require a dramatic reversal of their present level of childlessness. Even given the recent increase in fertility among older women, a widespread turnabout seems unlikely. Princeton's Westoff has predicted that as many as one of every four baby-boom women will wind up childless. The other way for the boom generation to make up for "lost" fertility would be if families with two children suddenly added a third. But the popularity of contraception among the boom parents—not to mention the increase in women working —seems to reduce that possibility. During the boom years, up to one-third of all births after the second were reported as "unwanted." As of 1973, only one-sixth of third and higher births were said to be unwanted. Regardless of what future generations do, it seems more than possible that the cohorts of the baby boom will enter midlife as the least fertile generation in our history.

I have been talking of the baby-boomers as if they were solely responsible for the baby bust. So far, they have been. But future fertility deals with the next generation. Will it be the same or different? To put it another way, has the baby boom introduced new ideas and habits of family and fertility that the succeeding generation will inherit and carry forward? Or are the changes carried by the baby-boom generation exclusive to it? Will a new, smaller generation act differently and reverse all the changes the boom babies brought to the family in the seventies and eighties?

This takes us back to the "relative income" hypothesis of Richard Easterlin. Once again, Easterlin sees a self-generating mechanism in which fertility operates like a metronome, rocking back and forth from boom to bust to boom again. Large cohorts will be relatively disadvantaged and produce small cohorts which, in turn, will be relatively advantaged and produce large cohorts. The fate of a cohort is therefore inextricably bound to its size.

Now the post-baby-boom generation is growing up. Their cohorts are averaging one million persons fewer than at the height of the baby boom. They will find their labor relatively scarce and, Easterlin says, will have it easier in the job market and everywhere else. Crime and unemployment will be down. With less competition, they will enjoy better entry-level jobs, higher relative income, and faster promotions. The institution of the family, freed from the batterings inflicted by the young baby boomers, will stabilize as that generation ages. Even the former "marriage squeeze" will reverse. In the mid-1980s, the smaller cohorts of women born after the baby boom will be able to look for marriage partners among the last, large cohorts of baby-boom men. These men of the "bachelor bulge," in turn, will face a shortage of available younger women and may turn to older baby-boom women as a suitable new supply of potential mates. (The bachelor boom has already begun in Britain, where there are five percent more Englishmen at 20–24 than younger women.)

Easterlin is convinced that this generation will perceive its improved affluence and raise its fertility over the next two decades. Beginning in 1980, the ratio of young workers to old workers will begin to favor the young again, thus enhancing their opportunities and promoting their fertility. Easterlin believes that a new baby boom will result that could see 2.7 births per woman in the 1980s. And if that sounds high, some demographers in his camp have projected the rise to "a plausible high figure of 4.15" around the turn of the century. What this would mean, then, is that the baby-boom generation would be unique: its family practices would *not* be passed on to future generations.

Other demographers, most notably Charles Westoff of Princeton, take the opposite view: namely, that the social and economic trends which contribute to low fertility are here to stay. The movement from traditional, agrarian society to modern, industrial society has been accompanied for two hundred years by a decline in fertility. As children have been transformed from an economic asset to a liability, and as infant mortality has declined, the rationale for having more children has accordingly diminished. Furthermore, the most recent decline in fertility has not been exclusive to countries which had baby booms but has been felt by most developed countries in the world. Some of the sharpest declines have been in countries which did *not* see age dislocations brought by baby booms. Now that the long-term historical trend has reasserted itself, the boom looks more and more like an aberration.

Westoff also argues that the Easterlin hypothesis ignores the sweeping changes in women's status and expectations. These include:

THE DEVALUATION OF MARRIAGE. Thanks in part to the baby boomers, marriage is no longer defined as the only legitimate status for a woman. Married couples with children as a percentage of all households dropped from 44 percent in 1960 to 32 percent in 1979. If countries like Sweden and Denmark are reliable lead indicators, the attrition will continue. Marriages declined in Sweden by 30 percent between 1966 and 1975. In Denmark, the proportion of unmarried 20–24-year-olds rose to more than 60 percent in 1975. According to an annual poll of American college freshmen, the percentage who feel that raising a family is an important goal in life fell from 71 percent in 1969 to 57 percent in 1979.

COHABITATION. The doubling of the number of unmarried couples in the United States in less than a decade means that most of one million women have been effectively removed from childbearing. Many of them are experimenting with "trial marriages" and will someday marry and have children. But cohabitation delays it. And, as Westoff has pointed out, cohabitation is increasingly regarded as a *permanent* life-style. In Denmark, one-quarter of all women 18–25 live with a man to whom they are not married. And one out of every four of them rejects the idea of *ever* marrying.

DIVORCE. The men and women of the baby boom have all but killed off the traditional marital idea of one partner forever. It is hard to imagine that any future generation will be able to revive it. One Wall Street firm has estimated that by 1985 there will be more divorces in the United States than first marriages. The high incidence of remarriage used to be regarded as proof of disillusionment in spouses, not in marriage, but that, too, is changing. The remarriage rate is dropping in the United States and has sunk by 50 percent in Sweden since 1965. And historically, the longer women stay out of marriage, the fewer children they have.

WORKING WOMEN. Of all the changes brought to women's lives, this clearly would be the hardest to roll back. Current estimates are that two out of three women in their prime childbearing ages will be working in the 1980s. If their wages continue to rise, as Butz and Ward have pointed out, that fact alone will continue to change the economics of childbearing. Babies will not be worth the cost of forfeited salaries. Only a massive increase in day care, they say, could weaken the link between market wages and the price of children and thereby allow increased fertility. As time goes on, and women become increasingly integrated into the labor market, it becomes harder and harder to believe that massive numbers of them would sacrifice their careers and wages to prolonged motherhood.

Easterlin's answer to the problem posed by changed women's career and family values is essentially that they focus attention on the wrong thing. He maintains that the Procreation Ethic of the 1950s has not been rejected but rationalized out of sight by baby-boom women who have been forced into the job market by their husbands' deteriorating economic situation. They could easily embrace the Procreation Ethic again—as they did in the forties and fifties. Indeed, he points out that many of the same arguments now made against another boom—for example, the increase in education, women's work, contraceptive knowledge, and so on—seemed just as valid then.

Westoff's reply is that women's roles have changed so radically since the mid-forties that they cannot be compared. Easterlin, for example, holds that, as young men's opportunities improve in the 1980s and 1990s, women will marry them quicker and have children earlier, as they did in the fifties. But Westoff counters that such an argument is sexist at heart:

Why enlarged economic opportunity will not be exploited by women as well as by men is not explained. The notion that women are all anxious to quit their jobs and to return to the kitchen and nursery as soon as economic conditions permit misses what I believe are quite permanent changes among increasing propor-

350

tions of young women in their perceptions of what life is all about in the late 20th century.

Westoff then goes on to an interesting speculation. As independent as women have become, what if the present trends were to lead to full economic equality? There would be just as many female bankers as male bankers. Both sexes would receive the same wages. What, then, would be the consequences for marriage and fertility? The institution of marriage, he says, would lose one of its few remaining sociological rationales. If traditional marriage were described in strictly contractural terms, it might sound like this: women offer their sexual, companionate, and maternal services in return for the security and status of a man's income. Westoff admits this is "hardly a romantic view of the relationship" but one that does help explain why the institution has lasted.

Under a full-equality system, however, women would be economically independent of marriage. They would be free to enter into relationships on other grounds. But what motivation would they have? Sexual and emotional companionship are increasingly available outside of marriage, as witness the popularity of cohabitation. Childbearing is the other prime function of marriage. But that, as we have seen, is in full retreat. Childlessness both inside and outside of marriage is increasing. And, Westoff adds, if the large increase in out-of-wedlock births in Sweden is any guide, then marriage is losing its monopoly on children as well.

His conclusion is inevitable. Women will not make the choice to return to the Procreation Ethic. In fact, good times will only cement them more firmly into the work force and result in further atrophy of marriage and the family. The downward trend in fertility will continue into the next century until the American population reaches a peak of about 253 million in the year 2015, when it will begin to decline. (Population will continue to grow before then, despite below-replacement fertility, as long as the large bulge of baby-boom mothers has more babies than the smaller numbers dying off at the end of the age cycle.) Eventually, Westoff argues, "it is not hard to visualize a society in which a third of the women remain childless, which would mean that the remaining two-thirds of the women would have to average slightly more than three births each to replace the generation." The most intriguing question then will be not what makes fertility go down but what will make it stop. Demographers have no theoretical basis yet to explain why women who are economically free to give up the maternal way of life would ever want to return to it. As in the thirties, the survival of the species is once again under discussion; the debate has come full circle.

Chapter 24

SHRINKING PAINS

Schools sit abandoned. Frozen peas are packaged for two. College students turn materialistic. The number of bassinets in use falls 8 percent in a decade. Boy Scout membership plunges from 1.9 million to 1.1 million. There are fewer four-door cars. And the pig moves on through the python.

By having fewer children, the baby boomers have left us with a problem that, like its own tumultuous presence, will stay with us for a lifetime. It is the baby-bust generation, yin to the baby boom's yang, which is now growing up behind it. Just as we had to loosen our belts to make room for the baby boom, now we have to tighten our belts a notch as the baby-bust generation comes through. It is not comfortable in either position.

The immediate problem is that a country built on the ideology of expansion now must make the difficult transition to managing decline. So far there is little reason to think we shall succeed. Just as we did pitifully little in the fifties and sixties to anticipate and prepare for the boom generation's passage through the schools, we myopically continued to train hundreds of thousands of teachers in the sixties and seventies despite overwhelming evidence that they would not be needed. This lack of institutional flexibility is not altogether surprising. Administrators trained as expansionists are ill-prepared to change gears and think small. Our previous experiences at managing decline—the railroads and agriculture—are hardly inspiring.

Companies dependent on the baby boom discovered that, with the arrival of the baby bust, they had to change or else. In the 1960s, for instance, a prosperous Gerber Foods controlled 65 percent of the baby-food market and its stock sold at 32 times earnings. Eighty-eight percent of its sales and most of its profits came from its 160-odd flavors of baby foods. As a company more indebted than most to the baby boom, it proudly advertised its cherubic trademark and slogan, "Babies are our business . . . our only business."

But then those baby-boom kids grew up and stopped having babies. Gerber's sales abruptly stopped growing, and its profits and stock plummeted. To recover, which it finally did, the company diversified into vaporizers, shampoos, clothing, day-care centers, and even life insurance. It quietly deleted the word "only" from the slogan and then dropped the old motto altogether. Instead, it began pitching its easily digestible foods to the market that is sure to grow for the rest of the country. As a new slogan put it, "The Baby People Are Now Babying People Over Fifty."

Johnson & Johnson is another company hard on the trail of the boom generation. It sold its shampoos and oils to mothers in the 1950s and, after the children grew up, increasingly pitched its baby products to adults with ads showing hardhat workers using baby powder ("Best for Baby, Best for You"). In the seventies, the company got out of products like rubber pants and teething rings on the simple logic that they cannot be marketed to adults. Instead, Johnson & Johnson is now working both sides of the street, offering an Ortho Diagnostics line of diaphragms and contraceptive creams.

We might think that the toy industry would be devastated by the passing of the boom generation. But toy manufacturers know that they do not sell toys to just any children; they sell most toys to *first* children. The reason is that parents tend to act as if they have a finite amount of money to spend on children *no matter how many children they have*. That is, they set aside more or less the same number of dollars every year to spend on children, no matter whether they have one, two, or three. The real difference the bust makes is not to toy manufacturers but to children: those with only one sibling divide the loot in half, those with two or three are left with thirds or fourths. More than one-half of Fisher-Price's toys, for instance, are bought for first children. Accordingly, the company is less concerned with the overall number of children than with the proportion of first children. The good news for

Fisher-Price in the 1980s is that there are more parents and more first children than ever before.

Mattel is another toy company that has survived its bumpy ride with the boom generation. Kids once grew up with Mattel's Barbie dolls and its incessantly repeated slogan, "If it's Mattel, it's swell." But in 1974, stunned by the decline in births as well as executive-suite scandals and lawsuits, Mattel lost $6 million. Since then, Mattel has completed an astonishing turnaround; by 1979 it was reporting net earnings of $30 million. How did it do it? What saved the company was astute diversification—it now owns the Ringling Brothers circus and Golden Books and is producing movies—and, more importantly, it developed the cheap microprocessing chips that are implanted into computer toys. For a lonely group of kids growing up with fewer siblings to play with, and often working parents or just one parent, the new electronic games became instant playmates and the biggest toy innovation since plastic. Spurred by a line of toys that beeped, buzzed, and whizzed, Mattel regained leadership of the $5 billion toy industry. Overall, sales of electronic games multiplied from $21 million to $375 million in 1978–80, and one gadget, Mattel's Electronic Football, was so successful with adults in 1979 that it became the biggest-selling toy ever.

THE EDUCATION BUST

Private enterprise has been able to hang on and even profit from the boom generation's wild roller-coaster ride through the life cycle, but education—both public and private—is not so flexible. The public school system, for example, can be thought of as the ultimately age-dependent industry. The size of the public school system is defined almost exactly by the size of the eligible age group. Changes in the age structure are felt immediately and directly in the public schools, where enrollment rates run at very nearly 100 percent and are backed up by law. College and nursery-school enrollments also reflect the size of the eligible age group—though they can fluctuate depending upon how many of the potential students actually do enroll. In fact, particularly in college, the overall size of the relevant age group can have a feedback effect influencing how many students choose to go.

The departure of the baby boom showed up first in elementary schools. In 1965, there were fewer kindergarteners than graduating seniors for the first time in years, but President Lyndon Johnson still saw the need for "more classrooms, more books, more teachers, and more schools on a scale undreamt of even a decade ago." He was wrong. In the 1970s, enrollment in elementary schools dropped by more than 6 million. In 1978, five years after annual births had dropped to 3,137,000, the lowest total since 1945, kindergarten enrollment tumbled by 300,000 and elementary schools by nearly a million. Suddenly schools were closing by the hundreds. Between 1967 and 1975, the number of public elementary schools in the country dropped from 70,879 to 63,242. Suburbanites who had once campaigned for new schools were now angrily debating which to close. The buildings—many of them erected twenty-five years earlier for the first babyboomers—were being converted into hotels, museums, day-care centers, and senior-citizen centers.

Some regions were hit harder than others. During the baby-boom years, high birthrates effectively concealed the effects of national migration. Both farmers and residents of central cities, for example, were able to use high birthrates to make up for losses to migration. But now that those babies are grown up and are not being replaced, we can see more clearly how migration has been changing us all along. Like drifting snow, to use demographer Peter Morrison's simile, migration has created new features, covered up old ones, and in some places exposed what lies beneath.

The immediate effect of migration is on age structure. High-mobility people, for instance, are likely to be young. One-third are in their twenties, which also are the peak childbearing years. So many of them take young children with them that one-tenth of all migrants are children under four. Thus, when they move, they make the places they move to younger and the places they leave older. Migrants are also likely to be better educated than average and have higher IQs. The net result is that migration is a self-selecting process: it removes the youngest and smartest people, who have the greatest potential for further population growth, and leaves the old behind.

Unlike natural increase, migration is a zero-sum game: if someone wins, someone else loses. As a result of the migration from the farms, the number of children under 14 in the overall farm population has already declined 40 percent and some rural school districts have declined 50–60 percent. The same is true of inner-city schools, where the lower grades might be 60 percent smaller than the upper grades in the same school. New York City has closed sixty schools since 1975, and the prospects are hardly better in the other "Slush Belt" cities. Since 1970, ten of the twenty-five largest American cities have failed to grow significantly—that is, they have reached ZPG. Moreover, there has been no growth in *every* Northeastern or North Central city with a population of more than a half million.

The winners of the migration game are the "Sun Belt" and Mountain states. There, the baby boom might be thought of as continuing, thanks to the continuing flow of new, young, fertile citizens. Thus, though the North Central and Northeast states lost 20 percent of their under-5 population in 1970–77, eight of the twenty-nine states of the South and West *gained* children under 5. (In Utah, the increase was a boom-sized 36 percent.)

High school will feel the pinch next. In the twenty-three years from 1954 until 1977, the number of 9–12 graders doubled from 7.2 million to 15.8 million. In 1978, the biggest high-school senior class ever—3.16 million—left the nation's schools. That, in retrospect, was the high-water mark of the youth society. Afterwards, the high schools finally began to feel the result of the decline in births during the sixties. The number of students in high school will drop 15 percent by 1984 and as much as 25 percent by 1990, when the grades 9–12 will be filled by the small birth cohorts of 1973–76. Because of the uneven effects of migration, the change in high-school graduates will range from a loss of 59 percent in the District of Columbia to a gain of 58 percent in Utah. In the next decade, thirty-nine Eastern and Midwestern states will lose high-school graduates while eleven states—mostly in the West—will gain. (Two states will remain unchanged.)

In most of the country, the high school will lose the grip it has held on the American imagination for three decades. Adolescence will remain important to those students passing through high school, of course, but they will be from smaller, less visible generations. Their culture will lack the magnetism of the baby boom's. Their slang will not be picked up on the *Tonight Show*. Their music will not dominate the radio. Social scientists will be less interested in what they have to say. Advertisers will care less about producing magazines or television shows that appeal to them. In short, the high-school student of the future will not count as much.

Yet, there is at least one area in which youth will remain a valued commodity: the military. The government was able to end the draft in the early seventies and rely on an all-volunteer force primarily because the number of draft-age men remained so high. In a typical year, the armed forces could recruit only 20 percent of that year's cohort of 18-year-olds and still maintain their requirements. The problem is that the number of 18-year-old men topped out in 1979 and will decline 15 percent by 1985 and 20 percent by 1990. Military speakers, noting this decline, have already begun talking of the United States as a second-rate power and dropping ominous analogies to the fall in fertility of the Roman Empire. So desperate were the services to maintain manpower that some 12,000 soldiers illegally passed recruiting tests on little other basis than that they had measurable pulse rates. The revival of Selective Service—something unthinkable a few years earlier—beecame inevitable.

America's colleges and universities were last to feel the morning-after hangover of the baby bust. This was the generation that had built higher education in America. Higher education's share of the gross national product quadrupled from 2 percent during World War II to roughly 8 percent today. Between 1960 and 1980, the number of college students had swelled from 3 million to 11.5 million, an increase of 250 percent. Even during the 1970s, when the nation's attention (and the first baby-boom cohorts) began to leave college, attendance grew by one-third. The baby boom had created an entire new segment of higher education—community colleges—which grew from 400 in 1958 to 1100 in 1970.

Then the college boom stopped almost as suddenly as it had started. In 1975, the year the record cohort of 1957 began its freshman year, college attendance leapfrogged ahead by one million, the biggest jump ever. But in the next year, enrollment unexpectedly dropped by 1.5 percent, the first such decline since the GI Bill students left college in 1951. Ever since, attendance has wavered—up slightly in 1977, down in 1978, and up again in 1979.

Educators do not need a demographer to tell them that worse news is ahead. The traditional college-age 18–24 group will decline by 6 percent in 1980–85, drop 10 percent in 1985–90, and finally another 8 percent in 1990–

95. The number of 18-year-old college candidates will plummet by 25 percent by 1992. Overall, the 18–24 age group will lose 6.3 million people in fifteen years. Already twice as many colleges are closing as are opening. As many as 200–300 of the nation's 450 small, private liberal arts colleges may close in the 1980s and dozens more will be threatened. California, which enrolls one-sixth of the nation's college students, lost 93,000 students in the single year 1978–79. New York State will lose at least 30 percent of its college students in the next fifteen years. The final report of the Carnegie Council on Policy Studies spoke darkly of a "demographic depression" in higher education. "Excellence was the theme," said its chairman, Clark Kerr. "Now it is survival." Ironically, the generation that had once shouted about "shutting down the campuses" in the sixties was finally succeeding twenty years later.

Most of the shrinking strains I have mentioned so far were caused by the declining pool of potential students. But there is another, even more serious force weighing on the colleges. It is that the enrollment rate—that is, the portion of high-school graduates who actually enter college—is declining as well. It is clear that as the eligible age group shrinks, the only way colleges can maintain enrollment is to increase the percentage of those attending. But in the seventies, for the first time in our history, the proportion of young people in college *declined*. If it continues to fall, the actual number of students could decline twice as fast as the size of the age group itself. Indeed, one demographic consultant, Stephen Dresch, believes that the combination of a declining pool and declining enrollment rates could reduce college size by as much as 50 percent in the next ten years.

Who is not going to college? America's young men. The enrollment rate of 18–19-year-old white males began skidding as the boom generation made its way through college, dropping from 47 percent in 1969 to 39 percent in 1972. The proportion of 20–21-year-old men enrolled dropped from 41 percent in 1970 to 32 percent five years later. Within the entire 18–24 male age group, the percentage in college ebbed from 27 percent in 1966 to 26 percent ten years later. By 1978, the *absolute* number of men enrolled as full-time students dropped 3.4 percent.

The only thing that kept the education depression from being worse was the startling arrival of baby-boom women in higher education. Traditionally, college had been largely a male obligation. As recently as 1970, 40 percent of 18–19-year-old men entered college compared to 35 percent of the women. But for the rest of the decade women steadily gained in college enrollment as men drifted away. By 1976, women aged 18–21 were enrolling at higher rates than their male counterparts (36.2 percent versus 35.3 percent). Over the decade, the total growth in college enrollment consisted almost entirely of women; men increased by 723,000, but women had added 1.7 million new students after 1970. Finally, women passed another milestone of equality in the fall of 1979. For the first time ever, there were more women—50.7 percent—than men enrolled in college. The typical college student was no longer Joe College but Jane College.

What happened to these men, most of them born in the second half of the baby boom, to turn them away from college? One certain influence we have already seen was the devaluation of the college degree, brought on in large part by the oversupply of graduates. If Harvard economist Richard Freeman is right, the rate of return on investment in higher education declined from 11–12 percent in 1969 to 7–8 percent in 1974. That is precisely the same period during which the first baby boomers began graduating from college and during which the percentage of students entering college began to drop off. For baby-boom women, on the other hand, employment and income opportunities were mounting, providing added demand for female graduates and hence the incentive for more and more women to attend college.

There are other reasons contributing to the decline of male enrollment. One is that college rolls were artificially inflated during the sixties by men avoiding the draft; once the draft was ended in the seventies, they no longer needed that college deferment. Moreover, the number of Vietnam veterans attending college under the GI Bill began falling in 1978.

Then there is the "Sibling Squeeze," an ingenious theory developed by two University of Michigan scholars, David Goldberg and Albert Anderson. They pointed out that, during the baby boom, babies were born closer together than ever before, especially after 1950. Thus, when these closely spaced babies grew up, the chances were greater that, in the aggregate, more parents would have more of their children in college at the same time.

If a family had three children born in 1955, 1957, and 1959, for instance, the children would overlap in college and the parents would eventually have to pay twelve years' worth of college costs compressed into just eight years. In fact, the Michigan analysts noted that in 1967, 12 percent of all families with children 18–24 had more than one child in college, but by 1976, the proportion had risen to 16 percent. Is it not reasonable to conclude, they proposed, that parents sandbagged by rising college costs would encourage "marginal" students either to delay their college entry or not to go at all? In either case, the enrollment rate would then drop. The Sibling Squeeze theory also contains within it a prediction. It is that, since births were timed further apart after 1964, the pressure on parents will ease when those children begin entering college after 1981 and enrollment rates could rise once again.

David Riesman once commented that the free market works poorly in higher education, a principle that is being proven by many colleges in their haste to avoid the demographic disasters ahead. The buyer's market has now become a seller's market as college recruiters fan out across the world to bolster their sagging enrollments. There are "bounty hunters" who receive a bonus of 15 percent of the tuition for producing "body counts." Professional recruiters lure nontraditional and foreign students with promises that cannot always be realized. Some colleges are turning their admissions office entirely over to professionals, who are bringing the techniques of Madison Avenue—nothing new to the baby boom—to the process. It smacks of academic hucksterism. American University hired an ad agency to distribute T-shirts with the slogan, "Jog Your Mind." Another college distributed monogrammed Frisbees in Fort Lauderdale during the springtime student migration. Others opened booths at state fairs wth raffles for 10-speed bicycles. The mailboxes of sought-after high-school seniors are jammed with glossy brochures promoting "The Adrian Approach" or "The Kalamazoo Plan" or "The Olivet Experience." Sometimes college comes off less like education than summer camp. Here is Fort Lewis College in Colorado glowingly describing "the blueness of the big sky, the drama of the mountains . . . the clean air . . . the pungency of the cedar and piñyon trees on the campus and the sweetness of the summer flowers and new-mown grass . . . the exuberance of deep new snow under a blue sky and bright sun."

The other, more pernicious way that colleges are trying to compete is by making their own programs more attractive—which can mean lowering standards. The signs are there: the easing of admission requirements, the new emphasis on retaining students in academic difficulty, grade inflation, the abolishment of required courses, the stress placed on vocational and professional studies, pass-fail, the promoting of "popular" courses within departments to protect faculty staffing, and so on. In the future, wrote the Carnegie Council, "Students will be recruited more actively, admitted more readily, retained more assiduously, counseled more attentively, graded more considerately, financed more adequately, taught more conscientiously, placed in jobs more insistently . . . This may well become their Golden Age." Whether they are served as well by this kind of education is another matter. (Unlike high schools, colleges do not have an equivalent to the SAT tests to appraise the relative ability of their graduates.)

Nowhere is this idea of student-as-consumer clearer than in the now-burgeoning field of adult education. In recent years, colleges have shored up enrollments by enthusiastically adding more and more courses for older and part-time students. Between 1957 and 1975, the number of adults in continuing education doubled from 8.2 million to 17.1 million. The Census Bureau now estimates that, if the trend continues, adults over 24 could reach 40 percent of all college students. It's not surprising that colleges began to look to older students to bail them out. That's where the baby boomers were. Like blue jeans manufacturers who made their timely switch to fashion jeans, higher education also had to keep on the trail of its biggest market.

The change started in the 25–34 age group, now entirely occupied by baby boomers. In the 1970s, the number of male students 25–34 rose by 48 percent. But the number of women students in the same age group shot up 187 percent. Overall, the new 25–34-year-olds accounted for more than one-half of the total increase in college enrollment during the seventies. Slowly but surely, a system that was originally set up to serve youth of a certain age is now stretching to accommodate the baby boom as it proceeds through each age group.

Why are these older students going to college? For many of them, the training will provide the added credentials they need to widen their career options in the face of overwhelming competition. What better way to beat the "promotion squeeze" than by adding another degree? But the real point may be that, despite devaluation of a college education and despite the problems their generation has had in the system, many baby boomers still believe in education. They always have. It is as if they have lost faith in everything but their own potential and the power of education to liberate it.

The interest of these older students in their education is not without its dangers. On the one hand, the number of women in graduate schools doubled in the seventies—a welcome influx that may help those programs survive the demographic depression of the eighties. But some adult education programs are run more like fast-food franchises. Spurious "colleges" offer shopping-center branches and gimmicky courses in subjects like roller-coaster riding, marriage and divorce, and woodcrafts. It takes as many as six part-time students to bring in the cash flow of a single full-time student, a fact that presents many colleges with more problems than it solves. Someday we may yet achieve a variation of Karl Marx's old hope—to make students fishermen in the morning, carpenters in the afternoon, and critics in the evening—but that is a day the baby boom is not destined to see.

The teaching profession—once the largest single source of employment in the country—has been so decimated by the departure of the baby boom that it offers practically a laboratory study of the effects of declining population. Back in 1970, the baby boom added an all-time record number of new teachers to the labor market. They were joined by many older teachers who had earlier withdrawn from their jobs to have the boom babies. Together they produced tens of thousands of new teachers who, according to demographic forecasts, should have been adequate to instruct the army of new babies that was expected. What happened? In that same year, the combined enrollment of grades K–12 in this country declined for the first time since World War II.

We spent the rest of the decade trying to recover from that blow. Many of the teachers had made their career decisions and begun their training when fertility was high. Now it was too late. Millions of them were laid off or redirected into new fields. Since 1973, the annual production of new teachers dropped an estimated 42 percent. Yet the surplus continues and teachers colleges still turn out two teachers for every opening.

College teachers were hit just as hard. Hirings were restricted, promotions frozen, faculties were aging, and tenure was rarely granted. Hollywood saw something funny about it and did a comedy, *Lost and Found,* with George Segal and Glenda Jackson, but no one on the campuses was laughing. According to the Bureau of Labor Statistics, we are still churning out 11,000 doctorates annually, eight times the number of available jobs. The Mellon Foundation has estimated that by 1990 the United States will have to deal with a surplus of 60,000 Ph. D.s in the humanities alone.

Plainly, anyone who decided on a teaching career now would have better luck training to be an elevator operator. But nothing in demography is as simple as it seems. The paradoxical fact is that by the end of the 1980s, the United States may well have a teacher *shortage.* The argument, as developed by the Rand Corporation's Peter Morrison, works like this:

1. The supply is decreasing since students are less inclined to go into teaching than ever before. The percentage of female college students wishing careers as high-school teachers dropped from 17 percent in 1969 to 3 percent in 1979. Among men aspiring to teach, the drop was from 10 percent to 2 percent.

2. The smaller college classes of the future will mean a smaller overall pool of possible teachers.

3. In the mid-1980s, the large cohort of teachers trained in the fifties will begin to retire. For example, more than one-fifth of all teachers active in 1971 were 50 or older and are certain to retire in the 1980s.

4. At the same time, demand for teachers will rise— first in those Sun Belt states gaining children through internal migration and, eventually, in the entire country by the 1990s.

5. The combination of sinking supply with rising demand late in that decade will, therefore, cause a teacher shortage.

What kinds of students will be in the colleges in the 1980s? Are they the spiritual kid brothers and sisters of the first baby boomers? Or are they the beginning of a new generation? These are not unimportant questions. If the students following the boom generation are no different from it, then the attitudes of the baby boomers cannot be separated from the social changes shaping the nation. But if the succeeding generation is bringing with it a different set of values—as I think it is—then the tail end of the baby boom is marked off as sharply in character as it is in size.

What we see now is a generation coming to college that is as different from the baby boom as night from day. Today's students are passive, conformist, materialistic. They care about jobs while the first baby boomers cared about "life." Every year Alexander Astin of UCLA mails nearly 200,000 questionnaires to incoming freshmen in colleges around the country. His results map the topography of change as clearly as a generational geodesic survey. The freshmen of 1979, for example, were a different species from freshmen ten years earlier. Twice as many of them cared about being "well-off financially." They had less interest in public affairs and personal development. They cared more about business careers. They cared less about teaching. If they had liberal views, they thought of themselves as middle-of-the roaders. They were against preferential treatment for minorities. They were less idealistic and increasingly cynical. The objective of influencing their society—paramount to the sixties generation—was endorsed by only 30 percent of the 1979 students. But if the men were discouraged, the women were forceful and ambitious—the number planning professional careers tripled in a decade and the number planning business careers quadrupled.

"College students today have seen the people from my generation going nowhere," one member of Columbia's Class of 1971 told *The New York Times*. "They don't want that. They know what they want to do." His view was shared by John Aristotle Philipps, a Princeton student who designed an A-bomb and lived to write about it:

> My generation is different. We have no war to protest against. We share no common passions. We share no common music. We share no common drugs. We are a fragmented group of individuals. There is no sense of common crisis among college students in the seven-

ties. We have no collective itch, so we no longer scratch each other's backs.

In the sixties, students studied sociology so they could change the world; in the seventies they studied psychology so they could change themselves; in the eighties they will study business administration so they can survive. If the baby-boom cohorts came into college fighting war and racism, they left throwing toga parties and, in the case of Yale, rioting to keep graham crackers served in the dining halls. The University of Wisconsin at Madison, once a caldron of antiwar ferment, recently elected a Monty Python–styled Pail and Shovel party to head the student government. Drugs used to make a political statement on campus; now drugs are a cocktail-party recreation and one that is declining. (In 1979, student support for the legalization of marijuana *declined* for the first time.) Harvard has replaced its relevance-oriented "General Curriculum" with a toughened-up "Core Curriculum" loaded with rigorous required courses. It sounds for all the world like the Sputnik panic of the fifties. And that, once again, is where the baby boom came in.

Let me now turn to one final point about the plight in which the baby boom is leaving our colleges. What if hundreds of colleges really do close their doors in the 1980s? What if more and more of our 18-year-olds conclude that going on to college is just not worth it? Is that so bad? Some might argue that such a shake-out might even be desirable, a necessary corrective to the meritocratic excesses of the baby-boom years. How could we have hoped to raise *all* of our young to an educational level once enjoyed by only the very few?

The point is that the inevitable decline of higher education in the next decade will bring to an end one of our most ambitious dreams: the attempt to convert higher education from an elitist enterprise to a democratic one. As recently as 1950, only 40 percent of our high-school graduates went on to college. But by 1974, 60 percent of the baby boom's high-school graduates entered college. Of all the baby boomers born in 1946–60, more than 44 percent—or 25 million—have had at least four years of college. This, as we have said so often, was the best-educated generation in history. Moreover, if enrollment rates continue to fall, the baby boom may well remain our *only* such generation. Already the likelihood is strong

366

that, for the first time in American history, the next cohort of young Americans will receive *less* higher education than the cohort before it.

As higher education becomes less available, we will have removed one of the primary mechanisms by which generations seek to improve their lot in life. Previously, rising generations have counted on education as their means to the good life. But the result of restricting higher education to the rich is a reduction in social mobility. If either parent attends college, for example, the probability that their children will also attend increases 7 percent. This favors groups like Jews, who have a 52 percent ratio of college graduates among men in their thirties. Among Spanish-speaking Americans, however, the ratio of college graduates is only 5.3 percent. For them, opportunities will not be improving but receding.

Adult education, surprisingly, is no help because it is not used by the people who need it most. People with less than a high-school education constitute 40 percent of the adult population but make up only 13 percent of the participation in adult education. Thus, the vast majority of continuing education students are not those seeking basic degrees but rather college graduates seeking additional credentials. The ultimate result of adult education, then, is not to close the gap between the educated and uneducated but to drive them further apart.

We are now left with the disturbing possibility of creating two distinctly different and antagonistic castes. On one side will be the educational aristocracy, the new Superclass controlling all the shibboleths of power and privilege; on the other will be an underclass that is uneducated and resentful. The potential for conflict should not be underestimated. Stephen Dresch has already described his fears that any future cutoff of traditional avenues of social and economic development means that "fundamental and socially traumatic disruptions and dislocations can be anticipated to characterize late 20th century America." The baby boom will again be fighting its lonely battle, isolated from all other generations by its experience, its education, and its great expectations.

Chapter 25

THE FORTIETH WINTER

> *Begin the preparation for your death*
> *And from the fortieth winter by that*
> *thought*
> *Test every work of intellect or faith*
> —W. B. Yeats

There is a revolution coming. It is not the revolution of the young prophesied by Charles Reich nor is it a revolution of a class. It is a revolution that is still in its early stages but which will inexorably and inevitably succeed in changing the way we think and act. It is a revolution that was not started by the baby boom but which, in its most dramatic hour, will be entirely made by the baby boom. It is the revolution of the old.

Of the three great population shifts since World War II —the baby boom, the baby bust, and the aging of the population—two are complete. Only the third—the massive and continuing aging of the population—is continuing and building. Each day in America the army of the old increases its ranks by an average of 1400 as 5000 people pass 65 and 3600 die. In the next fifty years, the baby-boom cohorts will march on into old age, bringing extraordinary change to that period of life while leaving the detritus of the baby bust swirling in its tail wind.

This is a population revolution that can be compared to the other great upheavals of the American social order: the opening of the frontier, the Industrial Revolution, the wave of European immigration after the Civil War, and the internal migration from the farms to the cities. When this century began, there were perhaps 3 million people in this country over 65, or about 4 percent of the population. When the century closes, there will be 31 million people over 65, comprising more than 12 percent of the population. And before the baby boom is finished there will be 55 million people over 65 and they will amount to 18 percent of the population.

In that time, we shall rethink everything we know about what it means to be old in America. The baby boomers will be unlike any previous generation of elderly. They will change what has heretofore been the principal stereotype of old people—namely, that they are poor, uneducated, and unemployed. The baby boomers will challenge and strain every existing program and institution concerned with the welfare of older persons. They may well force the rethinking of one of humanity's oldest social contracts: the idea that the working generations will support the old and infirm. They will make old age a period increasingly dominated by women. Through their numbers they will continue to reshape our collective values and goals. Historians who look back on these times may fairly conclude that the most salient difference between the late twentieth century and the world inherited by our grandchildren will be this simple fact of the aging of the population.

Today there are 24 million elderly Americans and their number is growing twice as fast as the rest of the population. Since 1950, the over-65 age group has doubled; in the seventies alone it grew by one-fourth. Yet the most sweeping changes are still to come.

POPULATION 65 YEARS AND OVER

Year	Number (millions)	Percent Change	Percent of Pop.	Median Age
1980	24.9	—	11.2	30.2
1990	29.8	+ 20	12.2	32.8
2000	31.8	+ 7	12.2	35.5
2010	34.8	+ 9	12.7	36.6
2020	45.1	+ 30	15.5	37.0
2030	55.0	+ 22	18.3	38.0
2040	54.9	— 1	17.8	37.8

SOURCE: U.S. Bureau of the Census, "Estimates and Projections of the Population: 1977–2050," *Current Population Reports,* Series P-25, No.704, July 1977. Figures for Percent of Population and Median Age are based on Series II projections.

As the chart shows, between 1980 and 2040 the number of Americans over 65 will more than double from 25 million to 55 million. We can make this forecast with reasonable certainty because *all the people who will be over 65 in 2040 have already been born*. This growth, however, will not come smoothly and gradually but in bumps and jolts. The future growth of the aged is in effect the continuing record of past fertility. The over-65 group will grow quickly by 5 million in the 1980s as the cohorts of the 1920s begin to retire. After 1990, the first baby boomers will begin turning 45 and, for the first time ever, there will be more Americans over 55 than in elementary and secondary schools. But then, as the small Depression-era cohorts arrive, growth of the over-65 group will slow sharply, adding only 5 million over the twenty years 1990–2010. Even so, unless fertility increases drastically, the retired group could be the only age group left still growing in numbers and proportion.

Beginning in 2011 when the 1946 cohort turns 65, America will see the most sweeping population changes since the 1950s. It will not be a baby boom but a sexagenarian boom. In the twenty years from 2010 to 2030, the numbers of elderly in the country will explode by a million a year. The overall increase of 20 million—or 59 percent—amounts to virtually a whole new generation of old Americans. And if these seem faraway events, they are not. The changes beginning in the triphammer year of 2011 will take place within the lifetime of more than half the Americans living today.

Barring another baby boom, the relative influence of the aged will grow along with their numbers. Today only one in every nine Americans is over 65. In 2030, more than one in every six people will be 65 or over. This change, due primarily to the *small* generation after the baby boom, means that the old bar graph showing the age structure of the population as a pyramid with a large base in the younger age groups tapering to few numbers in the older ages will be stood on its head. The shrinking age groups at the bottom will be carrying the burden of supporting an increasingly top-heavy load of older citizens.

As we shall soon come to find out, the over-65 age group is hardly homogeneous and contains its own distinct subgroups. The fastest-growing age groups of all, for example, are those over 75. Since 1900, the over-75 group has grown tenfold, from 900,000 to 9 million. Its proportion of the overall over-65 group will go from 38 percent today to 47 percent by 2035. The expansion of the over-85 age group is even more precipitous. It has grown seventeen times since 1900, tripled in the last twenty-five years, and will quadruple again by 2050, when the last baby boomers have passed into it.

Because more people are living longer than ever before, the baby-boom generation should proceed into old age more intact than any previous generation (barring the disasters of famine, pestilence, and war that have too often been the human misfortune). Even if present life expectancy does not improve, seven out of every ten baby-boom men will live to 65 and eight out of ten women will make it to that age. And those who live that long can then expect to live another fourteen years (for men) or eighteen years (for women).

There is no reason to think that the baby boomers will be any more docile or malleable in old age than they have been in youth and adulthood. They will carry their special energy and character beyond 65 and alter all of our expectations for that period of life. Many of us habitually identify old age as the most reactionary stage of life. The aged are often seen as the intransigent, cautious, fearful defenders of the old order. They are not risk takers. They are unwilling to change. But how many of these qualities are qualities of age itself and how many are the result of the educational experience of the aged? In America, a person's age also tells you something about the time he was educated. Persons born in the first five years of this century, for example, were educated in the early twenties, when education was the privilege of the few. They completed an average of only 8.6 years of *any* schooling. Of the entire generation of Americans over 65 today, one-half have not completed a single year of high school. (Three out of five blacks over 65 never completed elementary school.) Only one-third of the current generation of elderly graduated from high school, only one in six had a single year in college and only one in ten holds a college degree. Higher education, moreover, was almost exclusive to men. Is it surprising that many of the elderly act the way they do not because they are old but because they were born before the education revolution?

Consider now the baby-boom cohorts who will be replacing them. Ninety percent of them have graduated from high school. Of the men, 27 percent have at least a college degree; of the women, 20 percent have college degrees. The differences in education between the generations have enormous implications for attitudes toward government, acceptance of authority, openness to change, voter participation, willingness to articulate complaints, and so on. The baby-boom generation will carry into its old age the social and political effects of its education. If the generations *after* the baby boom continue the present trend of receiving *less* education, then the boom generation may someday have the unique distinction of turning old age into the last bastion of culture and sophistication.

Around the time the first baby boomers have their fortieth birthday—Yeats's time of reckoning—in the late 1980s, they will be hit by two blows. The first is that the generation of their parents will begin to die. This was one of the most remarkable generations in American history. It was the Good Times Generation that survived the Depression, fought and won World War II, and went on to build the most sustained prosperity the world has ever seen. When the boom's parents die, they will take with them the living memories of all those events as well as the powerful optimism that created the baby boom itself. America may never again be quite so hopeful. The death of the parents will also give the baby boomers a delayed authenticity crisis. For years they had defined themselves *against* the values of their parents. Now they will be pushing and there will be nothing to push against. The fact of their own mortality will loom for the first time. This is the real identity crisis of midlife and the one that the baby boom has yet to confront and resolve.

At approximately the same time the baby boomers will lose a generational connection on the other end. As parents, the baby boomers will see their children leave them with a longer "empty nest" period than any previous generation. This is because children are leaving home sooner than ever before and because parents are living longer after their children leave. Over the long run, the period of childbearing has been shortened about three years, on the average, and the period after the children leave has been increased by eleven years, thanks to the improvement in survival rates. Thus, as Paul Glick of the Census Bureau has shown, baby-boom couples can expect to live without children about fourteen years longer than their parents, with most of the increase in their later years. Today couples can anticipate spending about one-third of their total married life together after the launching of their children.

Many of the Superclass couples will find this a period of happiness: often both spouses will be working and they will have the income to return to the affluence of their days as young childless couples. They will go to the movies, travel, and otherwise enjoy the good life. Yet others will feel cut off from both the past and the future. They had earlier turned their children over to day-care centers and schools and simultaneously turned their elders over to their apartments or to that omnipresent companion of old age, television. But now, after 40, the baby-boom generation will be abandoned by both. Its parents will be gone, and its children will be gone, carried off by divorce, time, or even choice. Indeed, the contract that the baby boomers had made earlier with their children was just that: they would limit their responsibility to the children and expected their children to do the same to them. The problem with this contract is that it does not equip people to deal with old age. The baby boomers, better than anyone, will know that those folksy Coke and Pepsi commercials showing enormous family reunions have nothing to do with their America, or perhaps any America that ever existed. The Ted and Joanna of *Kramer vs. Kramer* may remain as independent as ever, but they will make the loneliest journey into old age.

The baby boomers will have a different relationship to other cultures than today's elderly. The grandparents of the boom generation have more foreign-born members—roughly one in six—than any other group. As recently as 1970, one-third of all foreign-born persons in the United States were 65 or over, a fact that reflects past immigration policies. (First-generation European immigrants are concentrated in the upper age groups because their entry was considerably curtailed after World War I.) All the characteristics we associate with European-born grandparents—from their staunch patriotism to their lasagna—are now dying out with their generation. The coming generation of elderly, instead, will have stronger bonds to Latin America, as a result of the legal (and illegal) immigration of the sixties and seventies.

The baby boom has always attracted investment, and there is no reason to think that the Gray Market, thought of today as stagnant, will not have a boom of its own. This means not just hospitals, nursing homes, and trusses but a whole range of products and services that cater to the leisure-time spending habits of the elderly. Travel, drugs, and personal care will find expanding markets. Clairol already has its Silk & Silver hair coloring with an ad promising a life "Free, Gray, and 51." Wilson has marketed a "Squire" golf club with a weighted bottom (for added muscle). Aspirin will increasingly be promoted not for headaches but for arthritis pain. Campbell's, which had earlier switched from its kiddie alphabet soups to middle-aged "Manhandlers," has introduced a "Soup for One" line for solitary senior citizens. Garden products will take off. (Burpee doubled its seed sales in just five years in the seventies.) Another familiar boom-generation supplier, Wrigley, now has "stick-proof Freedent for the denture set." Wrigley's shift is not far from that of street food vendors in Atlantic City, who slice crisp, "thin-cut" French fries in the summer for a youthful clientele, then switch to chewable "thick-cut" slices in the winter for the old folks.*

New Magazines like *Prime Time* started announcing "The Joys of the Empty Nest" for what will someday surely be called The New Old. *Modern Maturity* began selling ads for the first time and *Retirement Living* changed its name to the more spritely *50 Plus*. Television also stands to gain from the wave of elderly people, who currently watch more than anyone else. Daytime television is in the process of switching its attention from younger women (presumably off working) to older, retired people. Not that TV will program for the older baby boom the way it has in the past for older people. Television viewing is positively related to age but negatively related to education and income. The dreary cycle of game shows and soaps that suited one generation of elderly may not wash in the future. The elderly have hitherto been thought of as immune to fads, but the baby boom might change that, too. It is not too hard to imagine the next generation, sitting moist-eyed in a media room as wired up and specialized as a kitchen, watching a twenty-first century version of Lawrence Welk reprising the rock hits of the fifties and sixties for those who still remember.

* * *

* Denture manufacturers may not altogether prosper, however, despite the enormous increase in the aged. As the first generation to grow up with fluoridated water, the baby boomers have the healthiest teeth in the nation's history.

The opportunities offered by the baby-boom aged may be overshadowed in the long run, however, by the formidable burden this same generation will dump on the nation's social services. A quantum increase in retired people will mean millions more in hospitals, millions more in nursing homes, and millions more dollars in taxes. Social Security is the economic backbone of the aged, but, even with 100 million workers presently contributing, the system cannot hope to bear up under the enormous pressures that will be generated by the baby-boom elderly.

The boom generation has already been in dependency once before, in childhood, but aside from education, the costs of childhood are assumed largely by the government. Our best estimates now show that the costs of supporting an elderly dependent is three times that of supporting a child. Even with the existing increase in elderly, charges are mounting astronomically. At the beginning of the seventies, federal programs providing retirement and health benefits to the elderly amounted to $46 billion, or 23 percent of the total budget. The same costs now total more than $200 billion, or nearly 40 percent of the budget. The entry of the baby-boom generation will swell those costs —as well as the resulting tax burden. Under present rates, and disregarding inflation, the Social Security tax could theoretically rise from about 10 percent of today's taxable payroll to 15 percent by the year 2025, an increase of 50 percent caused by aging alone. The impact would be just as formidable on the overall tax burden borne by each citizen. Today the total federal, state, and local tax bill amounts to about 33 percent of the gross national product —11 percent for social insurance programs like Medicare, and 22 percent for other services. As President Carter's 1979 budget message pointed out, if the 22 percent for "other" services remains the same, and if the ratio of retirement benefits to wages remains the same, the total tax burden fifty years from now would have to grow 50 percent just to provide for the elderly baby boomers.

When Social Security was first adopted in 1935, the pay-as-you-go system seemed to work. Then there were ten workers for every person over 65. Life expectancy was below 63, two years under the retirement age. As long as the population grew larger, Social Security's Ponzi scheme could work: it would always be taking in more than it was paying out. Today, however, the ratio of workers to beneficiaries has fallen drastically, while our expectations for the system have increased. Social Security is no longer seen exclusively as an income floor but as a complex system of retirement cash benefits (Old Age and Survivors Insurance), disability insurance, and health insurance (Medicare and Medicaid were added in 1965 to assist those elderly with low incomes), all designed to ensure the good life for retired people. (Like everyone else, the Social Security Administration failed to see the baby boom coming. A 1946 projection predicted a range of 147–191 million for the United States in 1975. The actual total was 213 million.)

Who will pay the bills in the future? For the next twenty-five years or so, the baby boomers will. And, thanks in part to the 1977 revisions of the Social Security law, the system will be easily floated by the boom-generation workers. In the 1980s, the older 55–64 age group will *decline* by 400,000 as the smaller, Depression generation grows into it. The tax burden of supporting the elderly will then rest on the younger baby-boom cohort. Thanks to it, we shall be well equipped for the rest of the century to pay Social Security, as the moneyed 35–54-year-old segment of the working force rises from 38 percent in 1980 to 51 percent in the year 2000. Overall, the 16–64 working-age group will amount to two-thirds of the population in 2005–10, its largest share in history. But then, as the legion of elderly begins to gain 30 million new recruits after 2010, the roof will fall in. The ratio of workers to beneficiaries will fall from today's six to one to three to one and conceivably two to one in 2050. With only two workers supporting every retired person, it is easy to see why the pump will run dry around 2025. Then there will be real potential for intergenerational strife—the retired baby boomers struggling with overtaxed workers for a slice of the shrinking pie.

There are at least some ways to soften, if not avoid, the economic blows ahead. One possible reform is to end the social reliance on payroll taxes for social insurance and draw upon general revenues. Another would be to make corporate pension plans transferable if an employee leaves. Most desirable of all, perhaps, would be to keep more older workers in the labor market. But the problem is that the trend is running in the other direction: more and more workers, especially men, are retiring earlier and adding to the dependency burden. Because of a 1961 liberalization of retirement provisions, one-half of all men now go on Social Security at 62 instead of 65. Eighty-nine percent of Ford and General Motors auto workers take early retirement, and blue-collar workers are not the only ones with job fatigue. At General Foods, 70 percent of the work force retires early. Since 1970, the labor force participation for men 55–64 has dropped from 83 percent to 73 percent. The decline is even more rapid for men over 65: in 1957, nearly half of them worked; today only one in five is still in the labor market.

What makes them stop working? For many, it is a matter of health. Others are just tired of their jobs or are freed from the financial obligations of dependents. Then there are the promises of the leisure society and a package of Social Security benefits large enough to help them enjoy it. (Yet older 55–64 women, conversely, are working more than ever: 24 percent did in 1948 and 42 percent do now.) Ironically, it works at least partly to the baby boom's benefit in the short run that so many workers are retiring early. By opening up the jobs at the top of the ladder, they are clearing routes for the baby boomers to escape the squeeze of their own mass.

The reforms passed by Congress in 1979 may help keep some workers on the job. Most workers cannot be forced to retire now until the age of 70—though the real problem is persuading them not to. One incentive is the recent Social Security reform offering 3 percent benefit bonuses for every year worked after 65. A more Draconian step would be simply to raise the age of eligibility for Social Security benefits from 65 to, say, 68 or 70. That, combined with elimination of the early retirement option at 62, may well be in store for the boom generation. The generation may yet spend the end of its days in unwilling labor because we do not know what to do with it otherwise.

Once they do retire, what will life be like for the baby boomers? How will they be cared for? Where will they live? Will they command political power? How will it be used? These are difficult questions and, as we have seen, none of them can necessarily be answered by extrapolating from the behavior of present elderly Americans.

At least one thing, though, seems certain. The boom generation will be increasingly female and increasingly alone. This is because a strange flip-flop of sex ratios has taken place within the space of the last generation. As with all previous generations, there were slightly more boy babies born during the boom years than girl babies. (This is believed to be a result of natural selection caused by the slightly higher infant mortality rate among boys than girls.) But because of the higher death rate of men throughout their lives—presumably a consequence of their life-styles—the proportion of women in each baby-boom cohort has increased each year. The last census in which men outnumbered women in America was 1940. In 1980, men still outnumbered women at every age up to 23. But 23 was the turning point. At every age older than 25, women were in progressively larger majorities. The absence in the boom's history of heavy immigration, which traditionally adds men to a population, has further tilted the balance. What demographers call "differential mortality" shows up vividly after 65. In 1960, a 65-year-old white women expected to outlive her male counterpart by 2.9 years. In 1973, the gap had grown to 4.1 years. The result is that the number of women over 65 is now growing twice as fast as men. By the year 2000, there will be half again more women than men over 65. The female majority is even larger after 85, an age that one of every three baby-boom women can hope to reach but fewer than one of every six men will see. What this means is that in the future, we shall increasingly think of old age as a province of elderly women.

The fate awaiting these elderly women is quite different from that in store for elderly men. Most men 65 and over are married and live with their wives. But most women over 65 are widowed and live alone. The reason is that men are less likely to outlive their wives, both because of their higher mortality and because they usually marry younger women. The figures are revealing:

—Seventy-five percent of men over 65 are married and live with their wives, but only 37 percent of the women are married and living with a husband.

—More than one-half of all women over 65 live alone, but only 16 percent of the men live alone.

—Of all American women, 20 percent are widowed by the age of 60, then 60 percent by 65, and 70 percent by 75. But only 14 percent of men are widowers by 65 and 23 percent by 75.

The fact is that, barring a sudden shift in life expectancy, the common experience of most baby-boom women will be the eventual loss of their husbands. Many of them already know this. I spoke with one woman who described a discussion she had had with some female friends:

> We were talking about what it would be like when we were old—how we'd have to use Duraflame logs in the fireplace or how we'd eventually move into a small apartment in the city. Then, all at once, we realized that we'd all made the same assumption. Our husbands would not be there.

What prospects do solitary older women have? Women outnumber men in nursing homes two to one but, contrary to popular belief, relatively few actually live there. Only 6 percent of the elderly live in nursing homes in any one year and only 20 percent ever live in nursing homes. Instead, 80 percent of all health care given older persons is provided by adult daughters. Older women have traditionally shopped around among their children to find a place to live. But this job will be harder for the baby-boom elderly. Many of them will be childless, or have no daughters, or will be estranged from their children by divorce, or will have children unable to care for them because of their own jobs. Their situation will not be unlike that of present-day grandmothers who, born in 1906–10, averaged only 2.3 children apiece and have their own problems finding care. At least there are two consolations for the baby-boom women: they have more siblings to turn to for help, and they are more likely to have surviving children because of increased life expectancy. (There is a 90 percent likelihood that a daughter born to a 1970s mother will be alive by the mother's seventieth birthday.)

The inevitable conclusion is that, in one form or another, the government will have to provide assistance for the baby boom's elderly, whether it be medical, financial, social, or legal. That would not be surprising. One of the leitmotifs of this generation is that its size has increasingly forced families to abdicate responsibility to the government. These burgeoning older groups have the heaviest medical bills and are least able to live alone. Of the very elderly, moreover, the fastest-growing segments are nonwhites and women, who traditionally suffer most acutely from poor health, loneliness, and poverty. The final irony may be that the iconoclastic baby-boom women, who had so ambitiously reshaped our schools and jobs, will ultimately find that their last revolution was to make an entire generation the ward of the state.

In addition to affecting the age distribution of the population, the aging baby boom will also affect the geographical distribution in a way that is not often understood. Let me explain what I mean. Nearly 40 percent of all people in their early twenties move each year. Theirs is the age group most directly affected by the forces that cause migration—the end of schooling, the first job, marriage, and military service. But as America ages, the rate of migration will slow. There will be more two-paycheck families. The older the country gets, the more people will be frozen in place. To some, this might suggest a country of millions of aged clustered in central cities or in retirement communities in the Southwest.

I think something quite different will happen. Most people age "in place"—that is, they stay where they've put down roots. For all the popular image of gray-haired lemmings marching to places like Phoenix and Sun City, the fact is that only 5–15 percent of all elderly persons move after retirement. In the decade of the sixties, for example, the states of Florida, Arizona, and California showed a net gain of only a half-million migrating older persons—far less than one might think. Why are old people congregated so heavily in a few urban locations such as New York City's Upper West Side? They did not move there. They stayed there. They were the same people who moved to the cities in the twenties and thirties. When their children moved out to the suburbs to have the baby boom, the grandparents were left in increasing concentrations in the cities, where they had always been.

The baby boomers, however, did not settle in the cities. They settled in the outer suburbs. If they stay there, the aging communities of the future will not be the St. Petersburgs and Tampas but rather the Boulders and San Joses and Fort Lauderdales. Many of the original suburbs built by the baby boom's parents, such as Shaker Heights, Ohio, and Evanston, Illinois, have already started to age in place. Between now and the turn of the century, in fact, there will be a burst of new school construction as many of the baby boom's original schools, built all at once in the fifties and sixties, yield at the same time to the wrecking ball.

How terribly strange
To be seventy
       —Simon and Garfunkel

We take it for granted that more and more people will
live to see 70 in every generation. More people are living
longer now because of the combined effects of better
medicine, better hygiene, and better diet. In Colonial
America, with its high infant and maternal mortality, life
expectancy at birth was barely 30 years. It had risen to
49 years by 1900. Then, over the next half-century, life
expectancy rose steeply.

Year	Life Expectancy at Birth
1920	54.1
1930	59.7
1940	62.9
1950	68.2
1960	69.7
1970	70.9
1980 (est.)	73.2

In the first half of this century, life expectancy gained
nineteen years. Since 1950, however, progress has slowed
to only five years. For a man of 45, moreover, life expectancy is now less than five years greater than it was in
1900.

What is happening is that life expectancy is approaching life-span. This is an important distinction. Life expectancy is a statistic that is useful to demographers but
confusing to most people. It is an estimate of the *average*
number of additional years a person can expect to live,
based on *all* age-specific death rates for a given year. It
reflects infant mortality as well as adult mortality. Over
the years, by eliminating many of the infectious diseases
that have plagued children, we have greatly improved
life expectancy at the younger years. But we have made
less progress on the ailments that afflict the elderly: heart
disease, strokes, and cancer. Thus, while an individual's
chances of living from birth to 65 have been greatly improved, the chances of living beyond them have not improved so appreciably.

Life-span, on the other hand, is the biological limit of

the species. It has not changed measurably in human history. In Biblical times, a lucky few lived to around 100 and died. In Colonial times, a few more lived to 100 and died. And today even more live to 100 and die. What has changed is not life span but the larger number of people approaching that limit.* (Most demographers place little credence in reports from places like Soviet Georgia of supercentenarians living to remarkably advanced ages.)

To improve the baby boom's life expectancy now, we would have to attack the degenerative diseases that afflict the old. Of them, heart disease is by far the most serious. A 65-year-old person today has a fifty-fifty chance of dying from heart disease, which accounts for as many deaths in that age group as all other causes combined. If heart disease were to be miraculously eliminated as a cause of death, life expectancy at 65 would instantly leap ahead another eleven years. (By comparison, if cancer were eliminated, the gain in life expectancy would be only two and a half years.) Other chronic conditions like senile dementia (Alzheimer's disease) will receive increasing attention. So, too, will the battle against the depressions of old age. More and more books of the future will bear titles like *The Myth of Senility* and *Sex After Sixty*.

The other way to increase life expectancy in the future will be to focus not on the disease-associated causes of death but to tinker with the underlying biological clock that causes aging. The generations that kept pediatricians busy in the fifties and sixties and psychiatrists busy in the seventies and eighties will eventually do the same for gerontologists. It is not inconceivable that their investigation of the underlying genetic and cellular mechanisms of old age could conceivably produce the same sort of breakthrough for the baby-boom elderly that Jonas Salk did for the baby-boom children.

There's one catch to any talk about life expectancy in the future. It's women. We know that women live longer than men and that, until recently, the gap was growing

* There is a widespread misunderstanding about this point. People frequently think that the aging of the U.S. population is due to the fact that we've conquered disease. That's only partly true. The population is getting older, on the average, because the baby bust has given us so few young people. Indeed, medical advances in infant mortality will actually make a population younger by keeping more children alive, thereby bringing down the average age.

larger every year. In the past three decades, for example, life expectancy has increased three years for men but six years for women. This inequality has usually been laid to the difference in male life-styles: they smoke more, they drive cars more, they suffer the stresses of working, they have more accidents, and generally live closer to the edge. What will the changing sex roles today mean for female life expectancy? If baby-boom women take the financial benefits of living and working like men, will they not get the financial benefits of living and working like men, will they not get the liabilities as well? Though it is too early yet to tell if the life expectancies of men and women are converging along with their working and living habits, some evidence is there that they will. For example, federal health officials have reported that one in three Americans with a drinking problem is a woman, compared to one in six a decade ago. Heart disease death rates are now falling faster for men than women. The suicide gap between men and women, usually blamed on the female habit of choosing less-lethal sleeping pills instead of guns, is narrowing. In 1963, men were four times as likely to be involved in automobile accidents; in 1977, after the number of women drivers had doubled, the ratio had dropped in half.

Perhaps the most ominous threat to baby-boom women is the precipitous increase in lung cancer blamed on cigarette smoking. The death rate of women from lung cancer has tripled since 1960 and will be up fivefold by 1983 when, according to the U.S. surgeon general, it will pass breast cancer as the leading killer of women. There is no telling how high it may go. Smoking is rare in the current generation of 80-year-old women. But by the time the baby-boom women reach old age, the cumulative effects of their smoking could be devastating.

Within the baby-boom generation, cigarette smoking has varied considerably, depending upon how old each cohort was when it was exposed to such factors as the surgeon general's reports, antismoking commercials on television, and new tobacco company ad campaigns aimed at women. Among the baby boomers born in 1950–56, for example, one-half of the men and one-third of the women were regular smokers by the time they entered their twenties. The next group of baby boomers, born in 1956–62, smoked even more; two-thirds were smoking ten or more cigarettes a day as teenagers. This last group of baby-boom women, in fact, has become the first age cohort in which the women smoke *more* than the men. Since then, smoking has generally dropped in all younger age groups (though women still smoke more than men), suggesting that the baby-boom women will remain on record as the heaviest smoking women ever. (A factor not unrelated is that these same baby boomers were the last adolescents to be exposed to television cigarette advertising, which went off the air for good January 2, 1970. As they look toward their old age, these women who had been told so insistently, "You've Come a Long Way, Baby," have good reason to wonder what the destination would be.)

Between now and the end of the century, the baby boom will be preparing us for the reign of the old. With it will come what in many ways will be a restoration of the power and position of the elderly in society. Through most of history, the aged have controlled the family and the land. It took modernization to destroy their power. The aged lost control of the land when the agrarian economics coverted to industrialization. They lost their authority when mass education ended their monopoly on wisdom. They lost their utility when technological change made their skills obsolete. It was not until the coming of the baby boom that we adopted the philosophy, if not the literal practice, of ancient Sardinians who pushed their elders off cliffs when they were no longer useful. We did not destroy the elderly but just ignored them. Instead of following the aged as guides to the future, we followed the young as guides to the future. Television has presented a particularly gloomy picture of old age, habitually portraying the aged as eccentric, stubborn, nonsexual, silly, and little worthy of respect. How ready can the baby boomers be for the descent of life, considering the grim picture portrayed on television since childhood? As a study conducted at the University of Pennsylvania pointed out, "The best and possibly only time to learn about growing old with decency and grace is youth. . . . Images of old age we absorb throughout life cultivate our concept of aging."

Inevitably, the hubris of youth is destined to decline. We will gain an elderly class that promises to be relatively healthier, better educated, and more certain of its desires. We will almost certainly learn that all old people do not always live in nursing homes, are not all disabled, are not mentally defective, and can lead full and satisfying lives. As we learn not to devalue age, we will no longer clothe it in dread. For the baby boomers, to be old may someday have all the possibilities of youth.

This is not a frivolous comparison. The subculture of the aged has much in common with adolescence. Both are age-segregated groups whose unity derives from that fact. Both are largely unemployed and are dependents. Both are experiencing biological changes in their bodies. Both are heavy users of drugs. Both face social inhibitions against their sexuality. Both are obsessed with the feeling of their own morality. Both have high rates of depression and suicide. Both are ready to bend the world to their liking.

If the baby-boom generation continues to produce and promote innovation throughout its life cycle, if only to find solutions to the problems caused by its mass, we may wind up with an entirely different notion of what life is like after 65. The distinction between "work" and "leisure" could break down as older people necessarily drift between part-time work and part-time retirement. Old age itself will become less clear an indicator of a person's status. Our ideas about seniority will have to change if we expect to keep many older people in the labor market while still providing opportunities for the younger generation. The sexuality of the elderly, sometimes seen now as embarrassing or even threatening, will be increasingly accepted. Youth will lose its monopoly on education: the idea that one's educational life precedes one's working life is already yielding as increasing numbers of older students mix school and job. Retirement will be seen not as an end of life but simply another life stage, one requiring retirement consultants (already a growing field) for both employer and employee.

Bernice Neugarten of the University of Chicago has proposed that the old age bench mark of 65 will have to be scrapped. Instead, we might better think of a new and underutilized life stage called "Young Old," roughly the ages of 55 to 75. These will be relatively healthy baby boomers whose vigor, labor participation, and education will continue to entitle them to play an active role in society. Only past 75 will we meet the "Old Old," the retired or relatively infirm whose role will conform more to our present-day stereotype of the elderly. In the early twenty-first century, Neugarten has written, we are likely to become "not a society oriented toward youth but one oriented toward the young-old."

To some, of course, the prospect of the baby-boom gerontocracy is no more inviting than the baby-boom youthquake was. The fear is that an ice cap of older people will stifle new ideas and cause economic stagnation in its ceaseless defense of the status quo. The French demographer Alfred Sauvy thought that a society dominated by the old would lose its creative pressure in its "slide towards inevitable decadence, like a tree with too much foliage for there to be any young growth."

By the year 2000, for instance, the median age of the *voting* population will be around 42 or 43. We already know that older people vote far more often than the young, thus multiplying their impact. In Florida, an estimated one-third of all ballots cast are by the elderly and in the state's Broward County, half the voters are believed to be over 65. In the 1976 presidential election, two-thirds of the entire over-65 population went to the polls, compared to less than half of the 18–34 group. In the 1978 congressional elections, voters over the age of 75 were more likely to get to the polls than voters under 35.

While we know that older voters vote more often, we have surprisingly few clues as to *how* they will vote. In 1972, George McGovern ran better among voters over 40 than among those 20–39. In the past, older voters have been less willing to change their views—but that could be as much a result of their education as their ages. What is clear is that people often carry the politics of their youth into old age. The voters of the future will remember not the Depression or the postwar recovery but will remember Vietnam and Watergate. An increasingly large share of the older voting population will be educated women who have worked and contributed to Social Security all their lives. (Unions are already starting to bargain as hard on pension issues as they used to on payroll issues.)

Such will be the destiny of the boom generation. It will age into the biggest and most powerful interest group ever assembled. Its needs will put back on the front pages the kinds of crepuscular issues that used to be buried in the senior citizen columns. It will make interesting demands on our ability to care for it. It will turn our youth priorities into elderly priorities. It will be at the center of the national debate. It will link the fertility of our past with its future, and ours. And it will never go gently into that good night.

Chapter 26

CONCLUSION: THE LEGACY OF THE BABY BOOM

> The fateful act of living in and with one's generation completes the drama of human existence.
> —Martin Heidegger

The assertion that its generation is somehow *special* has defined the baby boom from the beginning. It is not the first generation to make this claim, but none has ever said it more forcefully or more convincingly. The baby boomers believe it because they were told to believe it. Their parents arrived on the far side of the Depression and World War II with the exhilarating prospect of raising the biggest and most privileged generation the world has ever seen. And even if the baby boomers had not originally thought of themselves as a community of interest, there were people with the incentive to make them feel that way. Their combination of education and affluence has made them a Superclass with an economic power that outstrips the GNP of most countries. The baby boom is consumer society's R&D division—testing new products, new fads, new drugs, new morality, even new ideas about marriage and children.

We promoted their solidarity by the way we raised them. Ours is an age-segregated society and the baby boom is the most age-segregated group within it. They were a critical mass, generating their own chain reactions without the benefit of leaders. What few they had—the Ricky Nelsons and Abbie Hoffmans and even Elvis Presleys—were from an older generation. They needed no Scott Fitzgerald, no Ortega, no Nietzsche to show them the way. They assembled their identity out of the mass, like those one-celled creatures who congregate to form a larger organism by specializing their biological functions. The qualities that united them were more important than the things that divided them. Thus, the counter-cultural values of the white, upper-middle-class, educated elite filtered more quickly to the blue-collar uneducated of the baby boom than they did to the larger population. The Superclass incarnated the prevailing spirit of its times, and people of other ages had no choice but to join it. This generation, to use Francois Mentré's metaphor, was like an army that recruited into its ranks all those individuals capable of bearing arms.

Of the ideas that bind the baby boom, none is stronger than the belief that this generation has a mission in life, what Ortega called a *quehacer*. Their overachieving parents had excelled the dreams of the grandparents, now it was the task of the baby boom to make, if not the perfect society, then the perfect person. Rapid technological change was the fact of their lives, and their role was to oversee it. Indeed, they originally saw themselves as the beneficiaries of progress. To prepare for it, they had been educated like no other generation. With their education came high mobility and high aspirations. These baby boomers will be satisfied not simply with an affluent society but only with one that will fulfill the expectations that their self-confidence and sophistication have fostered. Women want both careers and families. Men want to equal the incredible achievements of their parents. They would be strong of body and fulfilled of mind.

Now, as it washes up in the 1980s, the baby-boom generation is experiencing a shift in the way it thinks about itself and its future. Optimism is yielding to pessimism. Altruism is yielding to narcissism. The generation that grew up convinced of its special place in society is not finding it. The maternity wards were too crowded; there were too few pediatricians; the schools were crowded; they were sent to Vietnam; they couldn't find jobs; they couldn't get promoted. Instead, they found themselves causing booms in crime, in suicide, in divorce, in childlessness, in venereal disease, in housing prices, and in property taxes.

Edmund Wilson once remarked of Hemingway's *A Farewell to Arms* that the force of disillusionment derives from the strength of the original hope and belief. Here,

388

too, was the Achilles' heel of the boom generation. It was betrayed by its own illusions. But some of them do not realize it yet, like polar bears in southern zoos who prepare for a winter that never comes.

The young baby boomers grew up with unrealistic and unachievable expectations. They did not experience the corrective lessons of the past. Isolated by age and education, abetted by television, they were whipsawed between high aspirations and low motivation. They wanted, but were kept (by their own numbers) from reaching. They had little appreciation for the role of sacrifice and commitment in life. The hope of the sixties, when the generation thought that it just might change the world, turned into a generational malaise of frustration and anxiety. And the worst of it was that they were not sure what their aspirations were *supposed* to be. The affluence of their fathers proved impossible to sustain. But they had been looking for something beyond affluence. They had expected to be the masters of change, but now change had mastered them. Other generations had mapped their experience by such signposts as wars, revolutions, plagues, famines, and economic crisis. The plague of the baby boom was uncertainty. It bore the terrible inner scars of the Kennedy and King assassinations. The idea of the assassin continues to dwell in the baby boom's mind. Vietnam was an assassin. The bomb is an assassin. All that is good or hopeful or promising could be blotted out forever by an assassin. That fatalism is now part of the life of the baby-boom generation. Not unlike Californians who build houses on top of the San Andreas Fault, they await disaster. The baby boom's massive size is its own Palmdale Bulge, a demographic abnormality, heaving and buckling as massive, invisible forces grind just below the surface.

The faith in the future that powered the boom generation through the sixties is shattered. The entire generation has instead fallen back on premature nostalgia, as if to prove Fitzgerald's maxim that there are no second acts in American lives. "Camelot," muses Wanda in *Kennedy's Children*. "I think maybe we all had a glimpse of Camelot —once—just once—in our own lifetime—before it crumbled." Already reunions of the Port Huron Statement SDS people or the Columbia 1968 radicals are being faithfully reported in the press like reunions of the D-day invasion divisions of their parents' generation. Both groups share a *nostalgie du front,* though for the boom generation the front wasn't Normandy but the no-man's-land of youth.

In physics, the Heisenberg Uncertainty Principle tells us that there is a built-in limitation to our understanding of nature. When we deal with certain subatomic particles, the very act of looking at them changes them. A particle struck by as much as a single photon will be altered. Thus, we cannot pin down the location of a particle with infinite precision by any procedure whatsoever and still hope to know anything about its future momentum.

We have the same problem with the baby boom. It is moving up through our age structure and changing each group as it goes. Every day it changes us, yet we have been slow to recognize the changes as they occur and slower still to predict them. The baby boom bombards us daily with photons that are changing our institutions and values. In the past, we have identified the passage of the baby boom at such stress points as entry into schooling and entry into the labor force. Only recently have we begun to scan the full shoreline of the baby boom, mapping its various inlets and harbors, depths and shallows, and islands and beaches. Research firms like Yankelovich, Skelly and White are busily drawing up their profiles of a generation that will be making and breaking markets for the next half-century. Now the federal government is making its own belated effort to keep track of at least part of the boom generation. The National Longitudinal Surveys at Ohio State University have studied the labor force experience of three different groups of young men and women, most of them baby boomers. Another National Longitudinal Study of the High School Class of 1972 has tracked 22,000 adolescents into and out of college and their first job experiences. These studies can help us see the baby boom at moments of transition, but their long-range value is limited. None of them will pursue the same group throughout its life, and none of them involves the birth cohorts of 1952 to 1956, the crucial years when annual births first topped four million and which, therefore, were most affected by their own numbers.

These studies can help us understand and even predict some of the quantitative changes the baby boom will bring as it proceeds through its life cycle. But what of the qualitative changes carried by the generation? How have they changed us? Are the boom generation's characteristics particular to it? Or does the generation carry what Australian aborigines call *arungquiltha*—the magical power that an arrow will acquire if it is rubbed against a certain stone? Even if the arrow falls in its flight, the *arungquiltha* will follow and strike down the enemy. Its power is transmitted without the help of a carrier.

The boom generation's *arungquiltha* is all around us. One sign is the increased tolerance everywhere for different life-styles. An unmarried couple living together would have been a scandal in the generation of the baby boom's parents. Now it is ordinary, a stage in the courtship process conventional enough to be a staple of prime-time television. The baby boom has also brought more tolerance, if not wholehearted enthusiasm, for homosexuals, communes, *ménages à trois,* and a whole range of nontraditional life-styles.

The boom generation is the first one to grow up with widespread integration. This has meant increased opportunities for blacks and more than a glimmering hope for racial progress in the country. In the decade after 1966, black students doubled their share of the total college population from less than 5 percent to more than 10. Unemployment remains high among black teenagers, but even that should improve as the baby boom finally moves on and turns the oversupply of unskilled labor into a shortage. In future generations, in fact, the Hispanic minorities will command proportionately more attention. In the 18–24 group, for instance, the proportion of Spanish-speaking people will grow from 6.5 percent in 1980 to 21.7 percent by 1990. The baby boom may be remembered someday as the last American generation to grow up *without* a sizable and influential Spanish minority.

The boom generation has seen its skepticism challenge all of our institutions and values. The government, the church, the military, the professions, and the schools have all been reformed in one way or another by the baby boomers. The work ethic itself was examined by this generation and found wanting. Authority everywhere remains in decline. The experience of trying to start their families amid the raging inflation of the late seventies has made the baby boomers all the more pessimistic about the ability of leadership anywhere to intervene successfully in their lives. (In one recent poll, two-thirds of the baby-boom group said they thought inflation would *never* be

391

brought under control. Less than half of the Good Times Generation was that pessimistic.)

The working women of the baby boom have redefined the family norm in America. They have broken the Procreation Ethic and let a thousand life-styles flower. A working mother no longer apologizes for her decision. Childless couples no longer have to defend their decisions, either. Women are free to pursue education and careers on an equal basis with men. There is far less hypocrisy about sex (though just as much obsession). Trial marriages and tentative sexual relationships are accepted. Divorce is so commonly accepted that the continuing pool of divorced adults—filled at one end by divorce and emptied at the other by remarriage—now amounts to 10 percent of all people between the ages of 24 and 54. Ultimately, this feat—the breakdown of the monopoly of the family—may prove to be one of the most enduring and irreversible acts of the boom generation.

For all its frustrations and failures as a mass, the baby boom has produced some superb individuals through a kind of social Darwinism. These are the people, many of them women, who were toughened by their battles and climbed out of the crowd. They are the ones who will lead their generation across the second millennium. And if the future brings difficulties, the strength of the baby boom remains its ability to adapt. If it has not yet fully worked out the problem of male-female sex roles in a world where most women work, it will. If it has not worked out the problem of wanting children but not the responsibility, it will. Transformed by technology and social upheavals, the boom generation has absorbed the lessons of the postindustrial world and showed its willingness to adapt to it. Along the way it has converted us to its causes.

The final adaptation ahead of the baby boomers is to accept the idea that their invincible cohort, like all others, will pass. Already the baby-boom experience is not exclusive. There is a new generation growing up of 54 million Americans, nearly one-quarter of the total population. Not a single one of them was alive when John Kennedy was killed. Few remember Woodstock. The Beatles are the Glenn Miller of this generation. They have never shared the hopes and expectations of the postwar generation.

Generations of the future are in the grip of the past,

demographically, just as the secret of the oak is folded within the acorn. But the baby boom will not find it easy to yield to the new generation. It has held the center stage of American life too long and will be reluctant to give it up. The unique historical experience that cut the baby boomers off from their parents and grandparents will do the same with their children. Unlike previous generations, the baby boomers do not necessarily seek the solace of knowing that their children will carry on the job they began. What other generation, indeed, has set for itself such ambition or had such a capacity to achieve it.

Hardest of all to give up will be the generational idea itself. It feeds on the idea of discontinuity between peoples. Communication across generational borders is difficult at best, and the chauvinism of the baby boom could make it almost impossible. What is needed is the generational equivalent of *ego-integrity,* the quality Erik Erikson identified with the last stage of life. It means, he said, "the acceptance of one's one and only life cycle as something that had to be and that, by necessity, permitted of no substitutions." Only then can a person—or a generation—accept fate as the frame of life and death as its boundary.

The last members of the brigade of the baby boom will live well into the second half of the next century. Some of them may end up like the last survivors of Napoleon's Grand Army, custodians of a dead dream. Or perhaps a better analogy will be to Ishi, the last "wild" Indian in the American West, who was captured in 1911 after the massacre of his tribe and spent the last days of his life in a San Francisco museum. Like Ishi, the last baby boomer will be the survivor of a tribe that once roamed the land and ruled all that it saw. And like Ishi, the tribe of the baby boom will live and die believing more than anything else in itself.

Acknowledgments

I began this book with the idea of putting between two covers the story of the largest and most influential generation America has ever produced. That I was able to undertake this formidable and, at times, daunting task owes primarily to two people who believed in it from the start. One is a gifted editor, Joseph Kanon, who nourished this book from the beginning with enthusiasm and intelligence and whose discerning judgment is evident throughout. The other is my literary agent, Maxine Groffsky, who has given me not only sound advice and encouragement but also an expert editorial eye. I count myself luckier than most writers to have worked with them both.

That I have been able to finish this adventure owes to more people than I can possibly mention here. I am deeply indebted to Herbert S. Bailey, Jr., the director of Princeton University Press, and Richard B. Stolley, managing editor of *People* magazine, who granted me, respectively, the space and the time to write this book. I have also benefited from the resources of the Office of Population Research at Princeton University. I am particularly grateful to two of its senior faculty members, Charles F. Westoff and Norman B. Ryder, who have freely given me their time and patience. Other demographers whom I have interviewed or who have been otherwise helpful include Ansley Coale and Bryan Boulier of Princeton University, William P. Butz and Peter Morrison of the Rand Corporation, and Michael S. Teitelbaum of the Ford Foundation. My intellectual debt to Richard Easterlin of the University of Pennsylvania is also considerable. Among the scholars in other disciplines I have consulted are Marvin Bressler, Suzanne Keller, Kenneth Rosen, and Nancy Weiss. While much of the argument presented in this book owes to their insights, let me add that any errors of fact or interpretation are entirely of my own making.

My understanding of the baby-boom generation has gained as well from interviewing dozens of other people who have necessarily lived with and observed it. Among those most helpful were Allen Freeman of Warner Brothers, Willet Klausner of Universal Pictures, Michael Linden of the Motion Picture Association of America, James MacGregor of ABC, David Park of the Boy Scouts of America, Joseph Peritz of Yankelovich, Skelly & White, Jerry Schulman of CBS Records, Kenneth Silver of the UCLA Medical Center, and Leon Ullensvang of Pet, Inc.

Other friends and literary people who have helped me with their collective advice, suggestions, and support are Charles Creesy, John D. Davies, John Friedman, Margaret Keenan, Ralph Keyes, John McPhee, John I. Merritt, James W. Seymore, Patricia Taylor, Edward Tenner, Edward R. Weidlein and Joseph Wisnovsky. I have been assisted in the actual writing and research by many people, but I am especially indebted to Emily Buchanan, Eva Martinez, Mary Lou McKenzie, Tracy Pogue, Lee Powell, Mary Solak, Loralee Strauss, and Jim Wageman.

Those who know most about the baby-boom experience, of course, are those who lived it. I have interviewed or queried a great number of boom babies in these years. Among those who were particularly helpful more than once were John Dippel, Claudia Dowling, Cutler Durkee, Jim Jerome, Byron W. Jones, Charles E. Jones, Margarietha B. Jones, Louise Lague, Cheryl McCall, Richard K. Rein, and Martha Smilgis.

I owe more than I can adequately say to my wife Sarah, to whom this book is rightfully dedicated. She has not only unfailingly given her faith and support to the writing but also has improved it immeasurably with the critical intelligence and good taste of a born editor. Finally, it is with her I share the hope that the generation of our own children—Rebecca, Landon, and Catherine—will see a less arduous coming-of-age and will have the good fortune to achieve at least a small measure of its own great expectations.

Year	Births	Year	Births
1940	2,570,000	1960	4,307,000
1941	2,716,000	1961	4,317,000
1942	3,002,000	1962	4,213,000
1943	3,118,000	1963	4,142,000
1944	2,954,000	1964	4,070,000
1945	2,873,000	1965	3,801,000
1946	3,426,000	1966	3,642,000
1947	3,834,000	1967	3,555,000
1948	3,655,000	1968	3,535,000
1949	3,667,000	1969	3,630,000
1950	3,645,000	1970	3,739,000
1951	3,845,000	1971	3,556,000
1952	3,933,000	1972	3,258,000
1953	3,989,000	1973	3,137,000
1954	4,102,000	1974	3,160,000
1955	4,128,000	1975	3,144,000
1956	4,244,000	1976	3,168,000
1957	4,332,000	1977	3,313,000
1958	4,279,000	1978	3,328,000
1959	4,313,000	1979	3,473,000

SOURCE: U.S. Bureau of the Census, *Current Population Reports*, Series P-25, No. 802, "Estimates of the Population of the United States and Components of Change: 1940 to 1978," U.S. Government Printing Office, Washington, D.C., 1979.

THE LIFE OF THE BABY-BOOM GENERATION
(numbers in millions)

Year	Under 5	5-17	18-24	25-34	35-44	45-54	55-64	65+
1940	10.6	29.8	16.6	21.4	18.4	15.6	10.6	9.1
1950	16.4	30.9	16.1	24.0	21.6	17.5	13.4	12.4
1960	20.3	44.2	16.1	22.9	24.2	20.6	15.6	16.7
1970	17.1	52.5	24.7	25.3	23.1	23.3	18.7	20.0
1980	16.0	46.0	29.5	36.2	25.7	22.7	21.2	24.9
1990	19.4	45.3	25.2	41.1	36.6	25.3	20.8	29.8
2000	17.9	51.1	24.7	34.5	41.3	35.6	23.2	31.8
2010	19.2	48.5	28.4	36.3	34.7	40.6	32.9	34.8
2020	19.8	51.6	26.3	39.6	36.4	34.1	37.2	45.1
2030	19.6	52.9	28.6	37.4	36.7	35.9	31.4	55.0

SOURCE: *Current Population Reports*, Series P-25, No. 704, "Projections of the Population of the United States: 1977 to 2050," U.S. Government Printing Office, Washington, D.C., 1977.

NOTE: The projections used in this table assume an average level of completed childbearing of 2.1 children per mother.

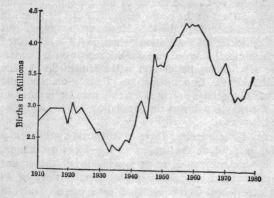

ANNUAL BIRTHS   1910-1980

CHART BY: Loralee Strauss

397

Notes on Sources

Originality, as John Kenneth Galbraith has remarked, is a virtue easily exaggerated, especially by authors contemplating their own work. My own debt to the scholars and writers who have explored various aspects of the baby boom's experience before me is extensive. Wherever possible, I have attempted to cite the sources of my research in the text itself. Any reader interested in pursuing a particular subject will, I hope, be able to find a trail blazed in the Bibliography. In the following chapter notes, I will set forth in greater detail the remaining sources I have cited directly. Additionally, there are some general comments that may be of use to anyone who wishes to investigate further the life and hard times of this generation.

Perhaps the best single source of information about the continuing impact of the boom generation can be found in the published records of the U.S. House of Representatives Select Committee on Population, which in 1978 conducted public hearings and issued an excellent report on the consequences of changing population in the United States. The 1972 President's Commission on Population and the American Future also prepared a richly detailed report and series of research volumes on population issues facing the country.

Beyond those reports, there is surprisingly little else available in print on the subject of the boom generation. There is no demographic study specifically of the origins of the baby boom, nor is there any social history of its special experience. Consequently, I have prepared here a bouillabaisse, blended not from spices and seafoods but rather from Census Bureau reports, scholarly articles, fiction, and journalism. Most of the newspaper accounts are from *The New York Times, Washington Post* and *The*

Wall Street Journal. Of the magazines, I have used *Time* and *Newsweek* and particularly *Fortune,* which followed population changes carefully in the fifties and sixties. Useful scholarly journals include *Demography* and *Population and Development Review.* A recent addition is *American Demographics,* a lively monthly of interest to market researchers. Most of the statistics in this book are drawn from the Census Bureau's annual *Statistical Abstract of the United States* and its *Current Population Reports* series. The U.S. Department of Labor's *Monthly Labor Review* contains well-researched articles about employment trends as well as a complete set of statistics. My own interviews with demographers and others caught up in the thrall of the boom generation—including scores of baby boomers themselves—are cited here anonymously. Finally, I have not listed in these chapter notes those references that can be readily located in the Bibliography.

Introduction: The Pig and the Python

The necessary introduction to generational theory remains Karl Mannheim's 1929 essay, "The Problem of Generations," which first introduced the subject to modern sociology. Bruno Bettelheim has elaborated further in his own similarly titled essay. S. N. Eisenstadt's *From Generation to Generation* is an excellent anthropological study of generational transmission in different cultures, ranging from the African Nyakyusa to the German *Wandervögel.* In 1965, Norman B. Ryder published his seminal essay, "The Cohort as a Concept in the Study of Social Change," which for the first time linked the size of a generation to its experience and its social impact. Herbert Moller's paper, "Youth as a Force in the Modern World," also explores the role of generations in carrying out social change in recent history. Lewis S. Feuer based his exhaustive 1969 study, *The Conflict of Generations,* entirely on the assumption that generational differences matter. In his underrated *Youth and Change in American Politics,* Louis M. Seagull cogently demonstrates how generational change has affected American politics, though he does not identify the baby boom as such. The fall 1978 issue of *Daedalus,* the journal of the American Academy of Arts and Sciences, is devoted exclusively to a series of essays on the generational question. Finally, Robert Wohl's erudite book, *The Generation of 1914,* is ostensibly about the World War I period but contains a brilliant summary of generational thought in Western Europe in the first two decades of this century.

As for direct citation, the prefatory passage is from the sixth book of the *Iliad*, in which the Trojan Glaucus is battling Diomedes, the strongest of the Greeks. The F. Scott Fitzgerald observation about generations is' reprinted in *Esquire*, October 1968. Kurt Vonnegut's definition of a *"granfalloon"* can be found in his novel, *Cat's Cradle* (New York: Delacorte Press, 1963). The de Tocqueville observation that "each generation is a new people" appears in his *Democracy in America*. The concluding quotation is attributed to Bergen Evans by Peter A. Morrison in his paper, "Dimensions of the Population Problem in the United States," reprinted in *Population, Distribution, and Policy*, vol. V of research reports prepared by the 1972 President's Commission on Population and the American Future.

Chapter 1—The Birth of the Boom

A full discussion of the Theory of Demographic Transition can be found in William Petersen's college-level textbook, *Population*. It is also discussed in detail in the September 1974 issue of *Scientific American*, which was devoted entirely to the subject of population and contains relevant articles by Ansley J. Coale ("The History of the Human Population"), Charles F. Westoff ("The Populations of the Developed Countries"), Norman B. Ryder ("The Family in Developed Countries"), and Judith Blake ("The Changing Status of Women in Developed Countries"). I have drawn much of my information about the American demography from Irene B. Taeuber and Conrad Taeuber's definitive study, *The People of the United States in the 20th Century*. A review of the demographic debacle of the 1930s can be found in Joseph J. Spengler's *Facing Zero Population Growth* as well as in *The Economic Consequences of Slowing Population Growth*, edited by Thomas J. Espenshade and William J. Serow.

The *Life* article about Soviet pronatalism appears in the issue dated September 3, 1945. Talcott Parsons's comments attributing the fertility decline to male-female competition are in his "Certain Primary Sources and Patterns of Aggression in the Social Structure of the Western World," in *Essays in Sociological Theory, Pure and Applied* (New

York: Free Press, 1949). The *Fortune* article about experts wanting the "best" people to reproduce appears in the issue dated March 1943. Gunnar Myrdal expressed his concern about population decline in a Godkin Lecture delivered at Harvard in 1938. The predictions of Spengler, Lorimer, and Dublin are summarized in John E. Knodel's "Demographic Components of the Recent Recovery of Fertility in Selected Industrialized Countries." The *Life* account of the "Birth Rate War with Hitler" is dated December 1, 1941. Frank W. Notestein's *Atlantic Monthly* article appears in the issue of June 1946.

Chapter 2—The Procreation Ethic

A thorough analysis of the various socioeconomic components of the baby boom appears in *Postwar Fertility Trends and Differentials in the United States* by Ronald R. Rindfuss and James A. Sweet. Likewise, *Trends and Variations in Fertility in the United States* by Clyde V. Kiser et al. analyzes the different sources of fertility increase during the baby-boom period. An outstanding scholarly contribution has been made by Norman B. Ryder's "Components of Temporal Variations in American Fertility," which seeks to sort out the varying effects of changed timing and real increases in births during the boom and bust periods. I have also benefited from a series of lectures given by Ryder on this subject and others at Princeton University in the fall and winter of 1979–80.

The *Population Index* article concluding that "no one anticipates the restoration of levels of fertility that could be regarded as high" is cited by Richard A. Easterlin in his 1978 presidential address to the Population Association of America. The *Population Index* article casting doubt on our understanding of fertility behavior is dated April 1949 (15: 114–28) and was written by Ryder and George J. Stolnitz. Joseph Davis's critique of demographic theory appears in the Spring 1950 issue of *Foreign Affairs* as well as in "The Population Upsurge in the United States" (War-Peace Pamphlet No. 12, Stanford, Calif., 1949). The Population Reference Bureau's examination of collegiate fertility is reported in *Time,* June 29, 1949. *Fortune*'s assertion that prophecies about fewer babies "can be thrown out of the window" appears in January 1954. The thunderstruck British visitor is observed by William E. Leuchtenburg in his *A Troubled Feast.* The *Fortune* account of lines for nylon stockings appeared originally in June 1946, and is reprinted in the issue of February 11, 1980.

Fred Vinson's expectation that Americans would have "to learn to live fifty percent better" is cited in Eric F. Goldman's *The Crucial Decade—and After*. The ideas about "erasing old class lines" and viewing babies as "a consumer durable goods" is from the *Fortune* of August 1953. The Harvard senior's "minimum production goal" is cited in Leuchtenburg's *A Troubled Feast*. The *Look* paean to America's "wondrous" mothers is cited in Peter Lewis's *The Fifties*. Rona Jaffe's novel, *Class Reunion*, was published in 1979 by Delacorte Press. Betty Friedan's admission of the rewards of motherhood is cited in Lewis's *The Fifties*. David Riesman quotes the Princeton senior in his introduction to Roy Heath's *The Reasonable Adventurer*. Riesman defines the "Found Generation" in his essay in *American Scholar* XXV, no. 4 (Autumn 1956), reprinted in *Abundance for What? and Other Essays*. (Garden City, N.Y.: Doubleday, 1964). A full report of the twenty-fifth reunion of Harvard's Class of 1954 appears in *The New York Times*, June 6, 1979.

Chapter 3—The Big Barbecue

American life in the 1950s is so misted over with nostalgia that it is becoming difficult to see the period as it really was. Fortunately, there are several relatively clear-eyed social histories: Goldman's *The Crucial Decade*, Leuchtenburg's *A Trouble Feast*, and Lewis's somewhat romanticized *The Fifties*. William H. Whyte's *The Organization Man* remains the best single summary of the prevailing *Zeitgeist*. The romance of the suburb is lightly but revealingly treated in a *Time* cover ("The Roots of Home") of June 20, 1960.

The names given to the children of the fifties are discussed in George R. Stewart's *American Given Names* and in Christopher P. Andersen's *The Name Game*. General Electric's snafu with its fertile employees is described in *Fortune*, January 1954. *Time* pronounced the new babies "consumers" in its October 18, 1954, issue; *Fortune*'s exultation over the boom is dated April 1951. *Time*'s worry about our having "enough people to consume the goods" is in the issue dated January 10, 1955. *Life*'s cover story on the baby boom is in its issue dated June 16, 1958. The

Fortune article on "the New Suburbia" is dated November 1953. *Time*'s joke about the housewife's right foot appears in its cover story of June 20, 1960. E. B. White's prescient observation about television is from his "One Man's Meat" column in *Harper's Magazine,* collected and published by Harper & Bros. under the same title in 1942. Joyce Maynard's comment about her generation being trained as consumers appears in her autobiography, *Looking Back,* which, for all its precociousness, holds up as a surprisingly perceptive appraisal of her times. Dwight Macdonald's observation about the generation organized as consumers is cited by Reuel Denney in his essay, "American Youth Today: A Bigger Cast, a Wider Screen," in Altbach and Laufer's *The New Pilgrims.* (The association between consumption aspirations and television is not, however, exclusive to the boom generation; it was just first. A 1980 study by Scott Ward of the University of Pennsylvania's Annenberg School found that children who watch television ask their parents for an average of thirteen products a week—all items they have seen advertised on television.) Finally, Steven Spielberg's memories of the Davy Crockett craze appear in an interview by Chris Hodenfield in the January 24, 1980, issue of *Rolling Stone.*

Chapter 4—From Spock to Sputnik

The John Updike story, "Separating," originally appeared in *The New Yorker* and is collected in *Problems and Other Stories.* Richard Hofstadter's label of America as the land of the "overvalued child" appears in *The Cult of Youth in Middle-Class America,* edited by Richard L. Rapson. Jeff Greenfield's recollections of atomic anxiety appear in his affecting memoir, *No Peace, No Place: Excavations Along the Generational Fault.* The *Washington Post* article about nuclear nightmares is by Richard Preston (May 27, 1979). Charles Hansen is the antinuclear activist who in 1979 sent letters to several publications with instructions on how to build a hydrogen bomb. He is quoted in *The New York Times,* September 18, 1979. The *Life* article about "The Crisis in Education" is cited in Goldman's *The Crucial Decade—and After.* Frances Fitz-Gerald's articles about American schoolbooks appeared in *The New Yorker* in 1979 and are published under the title, *America Revised: History Schoolbooks in the Twentieth*

Century. The Californian who found that "the kids are the only ones who are really organized here" is quoted in *Fortune,* November 1953. The statistics I have cited about fifties diseases are gathered from the Public Health Service and from the Center for Disease Control in Atlanta, Georgia.

Chapter 5—The Tyranny of Teen

The history of rock and roll is another dangerously overchronicled subject. Yet for all the attention lavished on the subject, the best single source remains the first: Lillian Roxon's *Rock Encyclopedia.* The *Rolling Stone Illustrated History of Rock & Roll* also contains several evocative essays on some of the genre's formative figures. The growth of the youth culture is particularly well described in *The Adolescent Society* by James S. Coleman, one of the few observers of those times who actually went into high schools to find out what was going on.

Jeff Greenfield's comments about the role of rock in forming generational consciousness appear in his *No Peace, No Place.* Dick Clark's early days are described in his as-told-to autobiography, *Rock, Roll & Remember.* Sigmund Neumann's definition of a generation appears in "The Conflict of Generations in Contemporary Europe," *Vital Speeches of the Day, V* (1939). Jerry Garcia remembers the Kennedy assassination in Peter Joseph's useful book, *Good Times: An Oral History of America in the Nineteen Sixties.* The nostalgic van-owner is quoted in the *Washington Post,* September 4, 1978. The dramatist Carl Zuckmayer's feeling of generational chauvinism appears in his *A Part of Myself* and is cited by Wohl in his *Generation of 1914. Time*'s euphoria over the "amazing U.S. economy" appeared in its issue of February 5, 1965. The Purdue study of 2000 teenagers is cited by William Manchester in his *The Glory and the Dream.* The president of Thom McAn, Francis C. Rooney, Jr., is quoted in *Fortune,* December 1969. Rudi Gernreich's remark that "fashion starts in the streets" apears in Joseph's *Good Times.* Kenneth Keniston's prematurely optimistic opinion about young people "fitting in" appears in *Time*'s Man-of-the-Year cover ("The Under-25 Generation") of January 2, 1965. David Riesman's more jaundiced view is quoted in *Fortune,* February 1959.

The idea of youth as a "barbarian" generation was first voiced by Daniel Boorstin in his essay, "The New Barbarians," in *The Decline of Radicalism* (New York: Random House, 1969). But it was Norman Ryder who showed how the leviathan generation disrupted society in his study, "The Demography of Youth," published in *Youth: Transition to Adulthood,* the Report of the Panel on Youth of the President's Science Advisory Committee. In that same volume, James S. Coleman's paper on "Youth Culture" relates the generation's self-awareness to its large number, its age segregation, and its affluence. *The New Pilgrims,* edited by Altbach and Laufer, contains many insights into the problem of youth, as does Margaret Mead's 1970 study of the generation gap, *Culture and Commitment.* Additionally, John Lofland published an instructive analysis of "The Youth Ghetto" in the *Journal of Higher Education,* March 1968.

The opening Samuel Johnson quotation is from *The Rambler* (1750–52), 50. The rock critic who compares *Sgt. Pepper* to the Congress of Vienna is Langdon Winner, cited by Griel Marcus in his essay on "The Beatles" in the *Rolling Stone Illustrated History of Rock & Roll.* Tom Wolfe's *The Pump House Gang* was published by Farrar, Straus & Giroux in 1968. Clark Kerr's prediction that the new generation would be "easy to handle" is cited in Manchester *(The Glory and the Dream)* and in Time-Life Books' *This Fabulous Century, 1960–1970.* The Westchester father worried about his children disappearing "into some strange offbeat life" is cited by Robert C. Albrook in his essay, "Parenthood Today Is No Bore," in *Fortune*'s collection, *Youth in Turmoil.* Jacob Brackman defines the generation that "doesn't take the news straight" in "The Put-On," published in *The New Yorker,* June 24, 1967. Norman Mailer's idea of "a time that's divorced from the past" is cited in Leuchtenburg's *A Troubled Feast.* Bruno Bettelheim developed his argument about the necessity of fairy tales in *The Uses of Enchantment* (New York: Alfred A. Knopf, 1976).

Chapter 7—The Vietnam Generation

I have benefited greatly in this chapter from the statistics and insights assembled in Lawrence M. Baskir and William A. Strauss's excellent study, *Chance and Circumstance:*

The Draft, the War, and the Vietnam Generation. Also, Samuel Lubell's *The Hidden Crisis in American Politics* convincingly demonstrates how the failure of draft reform in the 1960s sustained the antiwar movement.

Pierre Drieu la Rochelle's thoughts about the 1914 soldiers are cited in Wohl's *Generation of 1914.* James Fallows describes his ordeal by preinduction physical in "What Did You Do During the Class War, Daddy?" in *The Washington Monthly,* October 1975. Leslie Fiedler's comment about Vietnam casualties, cited in Baskir and Strauss, appears in "Who Really Died in Vietnam," *Saturday Review,* November 18, 1972. The Rhodes scholar's observation about his caste appears in *Chance and Circumstance,* and the *Harvard Crimson* editorial is cited in Fallows's *Washington Monthly* article. The World War I casualty statistics are from Wohl's *Generation of 1914.* Leon Botstein is quoted in Mary Alice Kellogg's book, *Fast Track.* The concluding quotation from the bereaved mother is from Baskir and Strauss's *Chance and Circumstance.*

Chapter 8—The Road to Woodstock

Kenneth Keniston's reputation as a sort of Boswell to the younger generation rests largely on the two substantive books he published about the sixties, *Young Radicals* and *Youth and Dissent.* He, along with Theodore Roszak *(The Making of a Counter Culture)* and Charles Reich *(The Greening of America),* have done the most to explain the ways of the younger generation to the older. But Reich, in particular, has since fallen out of favor, largely because of a few of his most hyperbolic statements. All of their writings offer an easy target in the less utopian eighties, an unfortunate fact that tends to obscure the real contribution each of them made. I have also benefited from Morris Dickstein's examination of the cultural life of the sixties, *Gates of Eden.*

The Abbie Hoffman exchange is from the transcript of the trial of the Chicago Seven, as edited and published by Bantam Books in 1970 under the title of *The Tales of Hoffman.* The Lillian Hellman judgment that the hippies comprise "a better generation than we were" is in *This Fabulous Century, 1960–1970.* The college student-turned-newsboy is quoted in Joseph's *Good Times.* Daniel Yankelovich's "Forerunners" are defined in his quite underrated study, *The New Morality: A Profile of American Youth in the 70s.* An interesting account of the Hermann Hesse phenomenon written by his biographer, Theodore Ziolkowski, is in *University: A Princeton Quarterly* 70 (June 6, 1970): 31–37. Kenneth Keniston's criticism of Reich appears in *Youth and Dissent,* and the entire question is aired in *The Con III Controversy: The Critics Look at the Greening of America,* edited by Philip Nobile (New York: Pocket Books, 1971). James S. Kunen's reflection on "the best years of our lives" appears in *The Strawberry Statement.* Roger Simon's detective novel, *The Big Fix,* was published by Straight Arrow Books in 1972. Peter Townshend's rather outré comment about his parents "screwing until they were blue in the face" is in *The Sixties,* edited by Lynda Rosen Obst. The *Newsweek* epitaph on Woodstock is from its issue dated July 16, 1979. Jerry Garcia's Woodstock quotation and Bill Graham's valediction to the Fillmore ballrooms are both from Joseph's *Good Times.* Daniel Yankelovich's appraisal of the spread of the New Values during the sixties and seventies appears in *The New Morality.*

Chapter 9—Children of the Media

The rise of the youth movie is discussed perceptively in Robert Sklar's *Movie-Made America* and colorfully in James Monaco's *American Film Now,* which also contains a useful summary of Hollywood marketing practices. My discussion of television owes much to Erik Barnouw's definitive history of broadcasting in the United States, especially vol. III, *The Image Empire* (New York: Oxford University Press, 1970). Barnouw's *The Sponsor* also describes the influence on us of what he calls "a modern potentate." A sweeping case against television is made in Marie Winn's *The Plug-In Drug* and also in Jerry Mander's *Four Arguments for the Elimination of Television.* Jeff Greenfield's *Television: The First Fifty Years* is an amiable and insightful history of the medium.

The opening quotation from René Dubos appears in "The Despairing Optimist," *American Scholar,* Winter 1975–76. Those readers interested in *The Graduate* as a kind of cultural icon should see the lengthy analysis written by Jacob Brackman in the July 27, 1968, issue of *The New Yorker.* The role that television plays in teaching premature sophistication and other lessons of adult life was originally pointed out by Jeff Greenfield. William Belson's CBS-sponsored study is described in his *Television Violence and the Adolescent Boy* (Lexington, Mass.: Lexington Books, 1979). Leonard Eron's University of Illinois study is described in *Time*, May 28, 1979. William Paley's opinion that young people "don't want a good beginning, middle, and an end" is quoted in *Newsweek*, March 5, 1979. The Roper Reports study is based on a survey of 2002 women interviewed September 23–30, 1978, described in *Public Opinion*, August/September 1979. (Interestingly, while money and sex previously led the list of causes in marital discord, in this study the choice of TV stations ranks first for the first time.) The coming of television to Essex, California, is described by Charlie Haas in "Invasion of the Mind Snatchers," *New Times*, July 24, 1978.

Chapter 10—The Mystery of the Disappearing Scores

I have drawn extensively in this chapter on the detailed and well-written Report of the Advisory Panel on the Scholastic Aptitude Test Score Decline, published under the title of *On Further Examination*. I have also used the voluminous appendix to the report, which contains 27 scholarly papers on the subject of the decline. Also, Robert Zajonc's article relating the SAT score decline to birth order in the family appears in *Science*, April 16, 1976.

The incident of the valedictorian refused admission by George Washington University is described by Paul Copperman in his *The Literacy Hoax*. A. Bartlett Giamatti's nicely formed architectural metaphor about the "soaring spans" of language is from a speech he gave at the December 28, 1978, annual meeting of the Modern Language Association. The Harvard man who says, "We weren't a television generation," is quoted in *The New York Times*, June 6, 1979.

Chapter 11—The Crime Boom

Charles E. Silberman's book, *Criminal Violence, Criminal Justice* contains a good introduction to the relationship between the age structure of the population and the crime rates in the fifties and sixties. James Fox's article, "Generations and the Generation of Crime," treats the same subject in further detail. The University of Pennsylvania's Marvin E. Wolfgang similarly traces the age-specific patterns of crime in "Real and Perceived Changes of Crime and Punishment," *Daedalus* 107 (Winter 1978): 143–57. Many of the homicide statistics in this chapter are from "Homicide Trends in the United States, 1900–74," by A. Joan Klebba. The full-page advertisement placed by The Campaign to Check the Population Explosion appeared in *The New York Times*, February 23, 1969.

Chapter 12—Why Johnny Can't Earn

Many of the statistics in this chapter are drawn from articles in the Department of Labor's *Monthly Labor Review*. I have also used a number of reports prepared by the National Commission for Manpower Policy, most notably Special Report No. 24 (June 1978), "Discouraged Workers, Potential Workers, and National Employment Policy." A similarly useful document is "Youth Unemployment: The Outlook and Some Policy Strategies," a budget issue paper for fiscal year 1979 prepared by the Congressional Budget Office. The results of the National Longitudinal Study of the High School Class of 1972 are described in periodic reports from the National Center for Educational Statistics. The definitive scholarly examination of the oversupply of college graduates is Richard B. Freeman's *The Overeducated American*. Richard Easterlin developed his theory in his 1968 book, *Population, Labor Force, and Long Swings in Economic Growth*. The example given in this chapter of the widget manufacturer's labor problem comes from Easterlin's article, "Here Comes Another Baby Boom," coauthored with Michael L. Wachter and Susan M. Wachter.

Chapter 13—Rosie's Daughters

A primary source for this chapter is *Women's Changing Roles at Home and on the Job*, Special Report No. 26 (September 1978) of the National Commission for Manpower Policy. It gathers some two dozen papers presented at the Secretary of Labor's Invitational Conference on the National Longitudinal Surveys of Mature Women, held on January 26, 1978. Other useful sources include William H. Chafe's book, *The American Woman*, Judith Blake's article in the September 1974 *Scientific American* ("The Changing Status of Women in Developed Countries"), and a series of eight articles on "Women at Work" published by *The Wall Street Journal* in August and September of 1978.

As with the previous chapter, the *Monthly Labor Review* has been invaluable.

The quotation opening part 3 of this book is from an article titled, "From Baby Boom to Buying Boom," in the May 1979 issue of *BBDO Magazine*, published by the advertising agency of Batten, Barton, Durstine & Osborn, Inc. The quotation heading chapter 13 is from Robin Cook's *Sphinx* (New York: G. P. Putnam's Sons, 1979). Valerie Kincade Oppenheimer's discussion of the "Pink Ghetto" appears in her powerfully argued book, *The Female Labor Force in the United States*. Adlai Stevenson's graduation speech at Smith College, "Women, Husbands, and History," was delivered June 6, 1955. Stevenson's message to the Smith women was that "there is much you can do . . . in the humble role of housewife—which, statistically, is what most of you are going to be whether you like the idea or not just now—and you'll like it!" Interestingly, Stevenson urged these future mothers of baby-boom children not to raise just "well-adjusted, well balanced" personalities but strive to produce "more idiosyncratic, unpredictable characters." Judging from the results, they more than succeeded. Stevenson's speech is reprinted in full in *The Papers of Adlai E. Stevenson*, vol. IV (*Let's Talk Sense to the American People, 1952–55*), edited by Walter Johnson (Boston: Little, Brown, 1974).

Chapter 14—The Marriage Squeeze

This chapter is grounded statistically in two different numbers of the Census Bureau's *Current Population Reports:* "Marital Status and Living Arrangements: March 1979" (Series P-20, No. 349, issued February 1980), and "Divorce, Child Custody, and Child Support" (Series P-23, No. 84, issued June 1979).

The article by "Mrs. X" appears on the Op-Ed page of *The New York Times* ("Teetering Near Divorce") on August 23, 1979. Gay Talese's postmortem on his visit to a New York massage parlor is from *Esquire*, November 1979. Paula L. Cizmar's somewhat condescending comment about the marriages of her parents' generation is from *Mother Jones* ("Aunt Mary Said There'd Be Days Like This"), February/March 1979. Erik Erikson's discussion of intimacy appears in his essay, "The Life Cycle: Epigenesis of Identity," in *Identity: Youth and Crisis*. Biff's speech is from Act 1 of Arthur Miller's *Death of a Salesman* (New York: Viking Press, 1949).

Chapter 15—The Baby Bust

Many of the figures used in this chapter come from the Census Bureau's "Fertility of American Women: June 1978," *Current Population Reports,* Series P-20, No. 341, issued October 1979. Charles Westoff's article in the December 1978 *Scientific American,* "Marriage and Fertility in the Developed Countries," is a concise and tightly reasoned summary of the recent decline in fertility in the industrialized countries. Norman Ryder's article, "The Future of American Fertility," in *Social Problems* (February 1979) also discusses the fertility decline in detail. A popular discussion of the birth dearth, as well as many other population issues, can be found in Ben J. Wattenberg's *In Search of the Real America.*

The opening quotation of Dr. John S. Billings is cited by Peter A. Morrison in "Emerging Public Concerns Over U.S. Population Movements in an Era of Slowing Growth," in Espenshade and Serow's *The Economic Consequences of Slowing Population Growth. Fortune*'s erroneous speculation that annual births would hit five million in 1970 appears in its February 1959 issue. James Neville Land's speech warning of overpopulation is reported in *Time,* August 26, 1957. *Fortune*'s concern over the "squalling millions" is in its issue of February 1959. David Lilienthal's fears about overpopulation ("300,000,000 Americans Would Be Wrong") are in *The New York Times Magazine,* January 9, 1966.

The economist who advocated issuing "marketable licenses to have children" is Kenneth E. Bouldin. In *The Meaning of the 20th Century* (New York: Harper & Row, 1964), Boulding concedes that the idea seems "absurd at the moment" but that fact merely reflects "the total unwillingness of mankind to face up to what is perhaps its most serious long-run problem." Fabian Linden's prediction of "a new birth boom" in the seventies appears in the Conference Board *Record,* June, 1969. *Fortune*'s prediction of a rise in births is in its June 1970 issue, and Philip M. Hauser's "tidal wave of births" is reported in *The New York Times,* February 25, 1971.

Betty Rollin's article ran in the September 22, 1970, issue of *Look* and is reprinted in *Pronatalism: The Myth of Mom and Apple Pie,* edited by Ellen Peck and Judith Senderowitz. Joann Lublin's column is from the January 2, 1976, *Wall Street Journal.* (A footnote to Lublin's article is that in the summer of 1979 she decided to risk combining motherhood and career and had a baby boy.) The Japanese experience during the Year of the Fire and Horse is described in Michael S. Teitelbaum's "International Experience with Fertility at or Near Replacement Level," in *Demographic and Social Aspects of Population Growth,* vol. I of research reports prepared for the U.S. Commission on Population Growth and the American Future. The West German demographer worried about his "dying people" is cited by Westoff in *Scientific American,* December 1978.

Chapter 16—The Baby Boom as Parents

The evolving nature of parenting in this country has been faithfully chronicled by Mary Cable in her *The Little Darlings: A History of Child Rearing in America.* It has remained for the Daniel Yankelovich organization to chart the attitudes baby-boom parents have toward their children, most notably in "Raising Children in a Changing Society," the General Mills *American Family Report, 1976–77.* Leslie A. Fiedler discusses "the cult of the child" in his essay, "The Eye of Innocence," in *No! in Thunder: Essays on Myth and Literature.* The dramatic break the baby-boom parents made in choosing children's names is commented on by George Stewart in his excellent social history, *American Given Names.* James Coleman's observation about our becoming "the first species in the history of the world which is unable to care for its young" is in his interview in *U.S. News & World Report,* March 27, 1978. The Daniel Yankelovich quotation about the New Breed is from his General Mills *American Family Report, 1976–77.*

Chapter 17—The New Consumer

George Hay Brown's conviction that "We are heading into a society with an affluent majority" appears in the November 1970 issue of *PRB,* the bulletin of the Population Reference Bureau. Fabian Linden's prediction of 4.3 million annual births by 1980 is in the Conference Board *Record,* June 1972. The promotional copy for *Sport* magazine ("They made the hot comb a hot item . . .") is in

The New York Times, September 17, 1979. The *Playboy* ad is cited by Mary Alice Kellogg in her book, *Fast Track.*

Chapter 18—The Housing Bubble

Much of the information in this chapter comes from a single number of *Current Population Reports:* "Household and Family Characteristics: March 1978," Series P-20, No. 340, issued July 1979. I have also drawn on a Census Bureau report released in August 1979, entitled *Financial Characteristics of the Housing Inventory for the United States and Regions: 1977,* Series H-150-77, as well as on "Projections of the Number of Households and Families: 1979 to 1995," *Current Population Reports,* Series P-25, No. 805, issued May 1979. A *Wall Street Journal* article (July 27, 1978) discusses in detail the influence of the baby-boom generation on housing prices. The *House & Garden* advertisement appears in *The New York Times,* November 15, 1978.

Chapter 19—The Nostalgic Style

An excellent theoretical treatment of the basis of nostalgia can be found in Fred Davis's *Yearning for Yesterday: A Sociology of Nostalgia,* which seeks to explain nostalgia more in terms of the crises of the present than in the allure of the past. The radio station ad copy is for Los Angeles station KPOL (now KZLA)/FM 94. The *Atlantic Monthly* reviewer turned off by the Osmonds and the Carpenters is Betsy Carter (August 1978). The similarly disposed *New Times* writer is Neal Gabler (April 2, 1976). Jeff Greenfield's tribute to 1950s music appears in his *No Peace, No Place.* Jack Heifner's comments about "the best years of their lives" are in *The New York Times,* September 9, 1979. Francine du Plessix Gray's reference to the woman who could not "remember the names of half the men we've slept with" is from *The New York Times Book Review,* October 2, 1977. George Lucas's memories of "driving around the main street of Modesto" are in *The Movie Brats* by Michael Pye and Lynda Myles. The rock musician dismayed by plans to revive Woodstock is quoted in the *Washington Post,* April 3, 1979. The *New York Times* man feeling homesick at outdoor concerts is John Rockwell, writing on May 13, 1975. Lee Weiner's observation about being "refugees from a future that never happened" appears in *People,* September 12, 1977.

Chapter 20—The Crisis of the Baby Boom

The issue of *New Woman* with the symptomatic cover type is dated December 1979. *The New York Times* article about the "generational malaise" appears February 29, 1976. The *Chicago Magazine* article appeared in the September 1976 issue. The woman who feels that her ambitions are "bourgeois" is cited in the *Los Angeles Times*, May 1, 1973. The Robert Coles observation about advertising is cited by Coles in a personal letter to the author. The woman who felt that "nothing has gone right since John Kennedy died" is quoted in *The New York Times*, August 26, 1979. The interview with the uncertain 32-year-old is in the March 18, 1979, edition of the *Boston Globe*. Ellen Goodman's encounter with "Jack" is described in her book, *Close to Home* (New York: Simon and Schuster, 1979).

Chapter 21—Turning Thirty

This might well be judged the "Me Decade" chapter, though I hope it is more than that. Neither Christopher Lasch, in his *The Culture of Narcissism,* nor Tom Wolfe in his christening of the "Me Decade" in *New York* magazine (August 23, 1976), specifically associated the indulgences of these times with the baby-boom generation. An earlier writer who, in fact, came closer to what I believe is the central point is Henry Malcolm, whose unappreciated and prescient *Generation of Narcissus* was published back in 1971. I have also gained from my reading of Daniel Levinson's excellent study, *The Seasons of a Man's Life.*

Tom Hayden's despairing view that "It's all me" appears in *Newsweek,* September 5, 1977. The sybaritic magazine reader "very much focused into today" is claimed by *Playboy.* The use of age 30 as a reference point for deriving age curves of biological decline is discussed by Robert R. Kohn in *Principles of Mammalian Aging* (Englewood Cliffs, N.J.: Prentice Hall, 1971), cited by Levinson in *The Seasons of a Man's Life.* The baby-boom woman noticing "the beginning of a line where smooth skin used to be" is Paula Cizmar, writing in *Mother Jones.* George Blecher's story, "The Death of the Russian Novel," is cited in Gail Sheehy's *Passages.* John Kerry is quoted about his uncertain future in the *Washington Post,* October 22, 1978. Lance Morrow's *Time* essay on decadence appears in the September 10, 1979, issue. Rick Sklar's speech about the relationship of disco to the family was given before the Washington Ad Club, May 3, 1979. The wistful writer in the Harvard '69 ten-year reunion book is quoted in *The New York Times,* June 9, 1979. The *Mother Jones* writer feeling "submerged like Atlantis" is Paula Cizmar.

Chapter 22—The Emerging Superclass

My concept of the Superclass owes in part to the earlier idea of the "New Class" mentioned by John Kenneth Galbraith in *The Affluent Society* and more extensively developed by Alvin W. Gouldner in his *The Future of Intellectuals and the Rise of the New Class* (New York: Seabury Press, 1979). But while they have dealt largely with the academic and professional elite, I am discussing here the rise of a generational elite, composed largely of the two-income families of the baby boom. The outlines of this group and its enormous spending power have been sharply drawn by Walter Kiechel III in "Two-Income Families Will Reshape the Consumer Markets," published in *Fortune,* March 10, 1980. Another *Fortune* article of similar interest is Walter Guzzardi, Jr.'s, "Demography's Good News for the Eighties," in the issue of November 5, 1979. My discussion of the work habits of the baby boom has been aided by Daniel Yankelovich's studies, particularly his *Work, Productivity, and Job Satisfaction* (with Raymond A. Katzell) and his paper, "Work, Values, and the New Breed." The population projections in this chapter, and in the remainder of this book's concluding section, are all from "Projections of the Population of the United States: 1977 to 2050," *Current Population Reports,* Series P-25, No. 704, issued July 1977.

The Harold Rosenberg citation opening Part IV is from his *The Tradition of the New.* Joan Didion's criticism of Woody Allen is from *The New York Review of Books,* August 16, 1979. Jim Bouton's disparaging comments on the new generation of baseball players are from *Sports Illustrated,* April 9, 1979. Yankelovich's observations about the new work ethic and the "psychology of entitlement" are from his "Work, Values, and the New Breed." The voting behavior of the baby boom, and all other generations, is described in "Voting and Registration in the Election of November 1978," *Current Population Reports,* Series P-20, No. 344, issued September 1979.

Chapter 23—The Baby Boom and Catch-35

The definitive account of the fertility fiasco in Rumania is Michael S. Teitelbaum's article in *Population Studies* of November 1972. The Paula Cizmar article is, once again, from *Mother Jones*. Nora Ephron's complaint about having a child in her mid-thirties appears in *The New York Times Magazine*, November 11, 1978. Britain's bachelor bulge is discussed in *Time*, August 28, 1978. Easterlin's prediction of a new baby boom is laid out in its briefest form in "The Coming Upswing in Fertility" (coauthored with Michael L. Wachter and Susan M. Wachter) in the February 1979 issue of *American Demographics*. Westoff's counterargument appears in the December 1978 *Scientific American* ("Marriage and Fertility in the Developed Countries"). His point about the "permanent changes among increasing proportions of young women in their perceptions of what life is all about in the late 20th century" is from his Fall 1979 letter to *The Wharton Magazine*. Finally, his hypothetical vision of a society in which "a third of the women remain childless" is from his March/April 1978 article in *Family Planning Perspectives* ("Some Speculations on the Future of Marriage and Fertility").

Chapter 24—Shrinking Pains

A useful general source of information about the effects of the baby bust is Espenshade and Serow's *The Economic Consequences of Slowing Population Growth*. I also have benefited in this chapter from the works of Stephen P. Dresch, who has extensively analyzed the effects of the birth decline on college enrollments. Most of the figures in this chapter have been supplied by the National Center for Educational Statistics. Also, the *Chronicle of Higher Education* is a well-edited journal of record of all matters involving the enrollment decline. Goldberg and Anderson's theory of the "sibling squeeze" is discussed by Peter A. Morrison in his "The Demographic Context of Educational Policy Planning." The prose in the Fort Lewis College brochure is quoted in *The Chronicle of Higher Education*, May 13, 1974. The member of Columbia's Class of 1971 is quoted in *The New York Times*, September 26, 1979.

Chapter 25—The Fortieth Winter

The demographic assumptions underlying much of this chapter can be found in "Social and Economic Characteristics of the Older Population: 1978," *Current Population Reports,* Series P-23, No. 85, issued August 1979. I have also found much aid in the writings of Bernice L. Neugarten and in Alicia H. Munnell's *The Future of Social Security.* The W. B. Yeats lines are from his poem, "Vacillation," collected in *Selected Poems and Two Plays of William Butler Yeats,* edited by M. L. Rosenthal (New York: Macmillan, 1962). The figures about incidence of lung cancer are from the various Reports of the Surgeon General. The University of Pennsylvania study of the image of the elderly on television was carried out by the Annenberg School of Communications in 1979. Alfred Sauvy's analogy of a society dominated by the old to "a tree with too much foliage" is cited in *The New York Times,* February 6, 1977.

Chapter 26—Conclusion: The Legacy of the Baby Boom
The Martin Heidegger quotation is from his *Sein und Zeit* (Halle, 1928), as cited in Robert Wohl's *The Generation of 1914.* Erik Erikson's idea of *ego-integrity* is explained in his *Childhood and Society.*

Bibliography

Abramson, Paul R. *Generational Change in American Politics.* Lexington, Mass.: Lexington Books, 1975.

A. C. Nielsen Company. *1979 Nielsen Report on Television.* Northbrook, Ill.

Advisory Panel on the Scholastic Aptitude Test Score Decline. *On Further Examination.* New York: College Entrance Examination Board, 1977.

——. *Appendixes to 'On Further Examination.'* New York: College Entrance Examination Board, 1977.

Aging in America's Future: A Symposium. Somerville, N. J.: Hoechst-Roussel Pharmaceuticals, 1975.

Allen, Frederick Lewis. *The Big Change: America Transforms Itself, 1900-1950.* New York: Bantam Books, 1961.

Altbach, Philip G., and Robert S. Laufer, eds. *The New Pilgrims: Youth Protest in Transition.* New York: David McKay Co., 1972.

Alther, Lisa. *Kinflicks.* New York: Alfred A. Knopf, 1976.

The American Assembly, Columbia University. *The Population Dilemma.* New York: Prentice-Hall, 1971.

Andersen, Christopher P. *The Name Game.* New York: Jove Publications, 1979.

Anderson, Mark W. "Toward a Sharper Definition of the 'Baby Boom.'" *World Future Society Bulletin,* July/August 1978, pp. 17-22.

Bane, Mary Jo. *Here to Stay: American Families in the Twentieth Century.* New York: Basic Books, 1976.

Barnouw, Erik. *The Sponsor.* New York: Oxford University Press, 1978.

Baskir, Lawrence M., and William A. Strauss. *Chance and Circumstance: The Draft, the War, and the Vietnam Generation.* New York: Alfred A. Knopf, 1978.

Batten, Barston, Durstine & Osborn, Inc. "From Baby Boom to Buying Boom." *BBDO Magazine,* May 1979.

Becker, G. S. "An Economic Analysis of Fertility." In *Demographic and Economic Change in Developed Countries.*

Universities National Bureau Conference Series 11. Princeton, N.J.: Princeton U. P., 1960, pp. 209-31.

Behrman, S. J., M.D.: Leslie Corsa, Jr., M.D.; and Ronald Freedman, eds. *Fertility and Family Planning.* Ann Arbor: U. of Michigan Press, 1969.

Bell, Oliver. *America's Changing Population.* The reference Shelf, vol. 46, no. 2. New York: H. W. Wilson Co., 1974.

Berelson, B. "Romania's 1966 Anti-Abortion Decree: The Demographic Experience of the First Decade." *Population Studies,* vol. 33, no. 2:209-33.

Bernard, Jessie. *The Future of Marriage.* New York: Bantam Paperback/World Publishing Co., 1973.

Billings, John S. "The Dimished Birth-Rate in the United States." *Forum* (now *Current History*), June 1893. Cited in Peter A. Morrison, "Emerging Public Concerns Over U.S. Population Movements." In *The Economic Consequences of Slowing Population Growth,* edited by Thomas J. Espenshade and William J. Serow. New York: Academic Press, 1978.

Blake, Judith. "The Changing Status of Women in Developed Countries." *Scientific American,* September 1974, pp. 136-47.
———, and Prithwis Das Gupta. "Reproductive Motivation Versus Contraceptive Technology: Is Recent American Experience an Exception?" *Population and Development* 1 (December 1975): pp. 229-49.

Boorstein, Daniel J. *The Americans: The Democratic Experience.* New York: Random House, 1973.

Bower, Robert T. *Television and the Public.* New York: Holt, Rinehart and Winston, 1973.

Bowers, Norman. "Young and Marginal: An Overview of Youth Employment." *Monthly Labor Review,* October 1979, pp. 4-16.

Brackman, Jacob. "My Generation." *Esquire,* October 1968, pp. 127-29.

Brooks, John. "Annals of Business: A Friendly Product." *The New Yorker,* November 12, 1979, pp. 58-94.

Brown, George H. "1985." *Population Reference Bureau.* Selection No. 34, November 1970.

Brown, Harrison, and Edward Hutchings, Jr., eds. *Are Our Descendants Doomed? Technological Change and Population Growth.* New York: Viking Press, 1972.

Bumpass, Larry L., and Charles F. Westoff. *The Later Years of Childbearing.* Princeton, N.J.: Princeton University Press, 1970.

Butz, William P., and Michael P. Ward. "Baby Boom and Baby Bust: A New View." *American Demographics,* September 1979, pp. 11-17.

——. *Countercyclical U. S. Fertility and Its Implications.* The Rand Paper Series-P-6263. Santa Monica, Calif.: The Rand Corporation, 1978.

——. "The Emergence of Countercyclical U. S. Fertility." Report No. R-1605-NIH. Santa Monica, Calif.: The Rand Corporation, June 1977.

Cable, Mary. *The Little Darlings: A History of Child Rearing in America.* New York: Charles Scribner's Sons, 1975.

Calhoun, John B. "Population Density and Social Pathology." In *The Urban Condition: People and Policy in the Metropolis,* edited by Leonard J. Duhl, M.D. New York and London: Basic Books, 1963.

Campbell, Arthur A. "Baby Boom to Birth Dearth and Beyond." *Annals of the American Academy of Political and Social Science* 435 (January 1978): 40-60.

Carr, Gwen B., ed. *Marriage and Family in a Decade of Change.* Reading, Mass.: Addison-Wesley Publishing Co., 1972.

Cavalli-Sforza, L. L. "The Genetics of Human Populations." *Scientific American,* September 1974, pp. 80-89.

Chafe, William H. *The American Woman: Her Changing Social, Economic and Political Roles, 1920-1970.* New York: Oxford University Press, 1972.

Chase, Alston. "Skipping Through College." *Atlantic Monthly,* September 1978, pp. 33-40.

Cizmar, Paula L. "Aunt Mary Said There'd Be Days Like This." *Mother Jones.* February/March 1979, pp. 21-30.

Clark, Dick, and Richard Robinson. *Rock, Roll & Remember.* New York: Thomas Y. Crowell Co., 1976.

Coale, Ansley J. "The History of the Human Population." *Scientific American,* September 1974, pp. 41-51.

——, and Melvin Zelnik. *New Estimates of Fertility and Population in the United States.* Princeton, N.J.: Princeton University Press, 1963.

Cohen, Wilbur J., and Charles F. Westoff. *Demographic Dynamics in America.* New York: Free Press, 1977.

Coleman, James S. *The Adolescent Society: The Social Life of the Teenager and its Impact on Education.* New York: Free Press, 1961.

——. "Role of Young Adults in the Years Ahead." Interviewed in *U.S. News & World Report,* March 27, 1978, pp. 61-62.

College Entrance Examination Board. *National Report: College-Bound Seniors, 1979.* New York.

Collins, Glenn. "The Good News About 1984." *Psychology Today,* January 1979, pp. 34-48.

Copperman, Paul. *The Literary Hoax: The Decline of Reading, Writing, and Learning in the Public Schools and What We*

Can Do About It. New York: William Morrow and Co., 1978.

Cottle, Thomas J. *Time's Children: Impressions of Youth.* Boston and Toronto: Little, Brown and Co., 1971.

Cramer, James C. "Employment Trends of Young Mothers and the Opportunity Cost of Babies in the United States." *Demography* 16 (May 1979): 177-97.

Cray, Ed. *Levi's.* Boston: Houghton Mifflin, 1978.

Cutright, Phillips. "The Teenage Sexual Revolution and the Myth of an Abstinent Past." *Family Planning Perspectives* 4 (January 1972): 24-31.

Davidson, Sara. *Loose Change.* New York: Pocket Books, 1977.

Davis, Fred. *Yearning for Yesterday: A Sociology of Nostalgia.* New York: Free Press, 1979.

Davis, Kingsley. "The Migrations of Human Populations." *Scientific American,* September 1974, pp. 92-104.

Dawkins, Richard. *The Selfish Gene.* New York and Oxford: Oxford University Press, 1976.

Day, Lincoln H., and Alice Taylor Day. *Too Many Americans.* Boston: Houghton Mifflin, 1964.

Demeny, Paul. "The Populations of the Underdeveloped Countries." *Scientific American,* September 1974, pp. 148-59.

Detray, Dennis N. "Child Quality and the Demand for Children." In *Economics of the Family,* edited by T. W. Schulz, pp. 91-116. Chicago: University of Chicago Press, 1974.

Dickstein, Morris. *Gates of Eden: American Culture in the Sixties.* New York: Basic Books, 1977.

Dippel, John V. H. "Growing Old Absurd." Unpublished article, 1979.

Dorn, Harold F. "Pitfalls in Population Forecasts and Projections." *Journal of the American Statistical Association* 45 (1950): 311-34

Douvan, Elizabeth. "Changes in the Family and Later Life Stages." Mimeographed. Ann Arbor, Mich.: University of Michigan, 1978.

Dresch, Stephen P. "A Demographic-Economic Perspective on the Future of Higher Education." Testimony for Presentation to Hearings on The Workplace and Higher Education: Perspective for the Coming Decade before the U.S. Senate Committee on Labor and Human Resources, 1979. Mimeographed. New Haven, Conn.: Institute for Demographic and Economic Studies, 1979.

———. "Demography, Technology, and Higher Education: Toward a Formal Model of Educational Adaptation." *Journal of Political Economy* 83 (June 1975): 535-69.

———. "Human Capital and Economic Growth. Retrospect and Prospect." In *U.S. Economic Growth from 1976-1986:*

Prospects, Problems and Patterns. Studies prepared for the use of the Joint Economic Committee, Congress of the United States. Ninety-fifth Congress, 1st Sess., 1977.

Drucker, Peter F. *America's Next Twenty Years.* New York: Harper and Bros., 1957.

——. *Men, Ideas and Politics.* New York: Harper and Row, 1971.

Durkheim, Emile. *Suicide: A Study in Sociology.* Translated by John A. Spaulding and George Simpson. New York: Free Press, 1951.

Dyer, Colin. *Population and Society in Twentieth Century France.* Suffolk, England: Holmer and Meier, 1978.

Easterlin, Richard A. *Population, Labor Force, and Long Swings in Economic Growth: The American Experience.* New York: Columbia University Press (for National Bureau of Economic Research), 1968.

——. "Relative Economic Status and the American Fertility Swing." In *Social Structure, Family Life Styles, and Economic Behavior,* edited by Eleanor B. Sheldon. Philadelphia: J. B. Lippincott, 1973.

——. "What Will 1984 Be Like? Socioeconomic Implications of Recent Twists in Age Structure." Presidential Address to the Population Association of America at its Annual Meeting in Atlanta, Ga., April 1978. Mimeographed.

——; Michael L. Wachter; and Susan M. Wachter. "The Coming Upswing in Fertility." *American Demographics,* February 1979, pp. 12-15.

——. "Demographic Influences on Economic Stability: The United States Experience." *Population and Development Review* 4 (March, 1978): 1-22.

——. "Here Comes Another Baby Boom." *The Wharton Magazine,* Summer 1979, pp. 29-33.

Editors of *Fortune. The Exploring Metropolis.* Garden City, N. Y.: Doubleday and Co., 1958.

Ehrbar, A. F. "The Upbeat Outlook for Family Incomes." *Fortune,* February 25, 1980, pp. 122-30.

Eisenstadt, S. N. *From Generation to Generation: Age Groups and Social Structure.* New York: Free Press, 1964.

Erikson, Erik H., ed. *The Challenge of Youth.* Garden, City, N. Y.: Doubleday Anchor Books, 1965.

——. *Childhood and Society.* New York: W. W. Norton and Co., 1950.

——. *Identity: Youth and Crisis.* New York: W. W. Norton and Co., 1968.

Espenshade, Thomas J., and William J. Serow, eds. *The Economic Consequences of Slowing Population Growth.* New York: Academic Press, 1978.

Feuer, Lewis S. *The Conflict of Generations: The Character and Significance of Student Movements.* New York: Basic Books, 1969.

Fiedler, Leslie A. *No! in Thunder: Essays on Myth and Literature.* Boston: Beacon Press, 1960.

Fischer, David Hackett. *Growing Old in America.* New York and Oxford: Oxford University Press, 1978.

FitzGerald, Frances. "Rewriting American History." *The New Yorker,* February 26, 1979, pp. 41-77; March 5, 1979, pp. 40-91; March 12, 1979, pp. 48-106.

Fitzgerald, F. Scott. "My Generation." *Esquire,* October 1968, pp. 119-21.

Foreman, Richard L. "Guiding Women and Minorities in a White, Male-Dominated Corporate Executive World." *Princeton Alumni Weekly,* June 5, 1978, p. 39.

Fox, James Alan. "Generations and the Generation of Crime." *Virginia Law Weekly,* March 31, 1978, pp. 1-5.

Francke, Linda Bird. "Advertising Grows Up." *Newsweek,* March 19, 1979, pp. 59-61.

———. "A Baby After 30." *Newsweek,* November 13, 1978, pp. 128-29.

Freedman, Deborah. "Fertility, Aspirations, and Resources: A Symposium on the Easterlin Hypothesis—Introduction." *Population and Development Review* (September/December 1976): 411-15.

Freedman, Ronald, and Bernard Berelson. "The Human Population." *Scientific American,* September 1974, pp. 30-39.

Freeman, Richard B. *The Overeducated American.* New York: Academic Press, 1976.

Galbraith, John Kenneth. *The Affluent Society.* New York: New American Library, 1969.

Galbraith, Virginia L., and Dorothy S. Thomas. "Birth Rates and the Inter-War Business Cycles." *Journal of the American Statistical Association* 36, no. 216 (December 1941): 465-76.

General Mills. *The American Family Report: 1976-77: Raising Children in a Changing Society.* Conducted by Yankelovich, Skelly and White. Minneapolis, 1977.

———. *The American Family Report, 1978-79: Family Health in an Era of Stress.* Conducted by Yankelovich, Skelly and White. Minneapolis, 1979.

Gerbner, George; Larry Gross; Nancy Signorielli; Michael Morgan; and Marilyn Jackson-Beeck. *Trends in Network Television Drama and Viewer Conceptions of Social Reality, 1967-1978.* Violence Profile No. 10. Philadelphia: The Annenberg School of Communications, University of Pennsylvania, April 1979.

Gerzon, Mark. *The Whole World Is Watching.* New York: Warner Paperback Library, 1970.

Ginsberg, Eli. "The Job Problem." *Scientific American*, November 1977, pp. 43-51.

——, ed. *The Nation's Children*. White House Conference on Children and Youth: The Family and Social Change, vol. 1. New York: Columbia University Press, 1960.

Goldman, Eric F. *The Crucial Decade—and After: America, 1945-1960*. New York: Vintage Books, 1960.

Goldman, Paul. *Growing Up Absurd*. New York: Random House, 1960.

Greenfield, Jeff. *No Peace, No Place: Excavations Along the Generational Fault*. Garden City, N. Y.: Doubleday and Co., 1973.

——. *Television: The First Fifty Years*. New York: Harry N. Abrams, 1977.

Grier, George. *The Baby Bust*. Washington, D.C.: The Washington Center for Metropolitan Studies, 1971.

Gustaitis, Rasa. "Old vs. Young in Florida." *Saturday Review*, February 16, 1980, pp. 10-14.

Guzzardi, Walter, Jr. "Demography's Good News for the Eighties." *Fortune*, November 5, 1979, pp. 92-106.

Hadley, Arthur T. *The Empty Polling Booth*. Englewood Cliffs, N.J.: Prentice-Hall, 1978.

Hall, Edward T. *The Hidden Dimension*. Garden City, N.Y.: Anchor Books, 1969.

Handlin, Oscar, and Mary F. Handlin. *Facing Life: Youth in the Family in American History*. Boston: Little, Brown & Co., 1971.

Hardin, Garret, ed. *Population, Evolution and Birth Control*. San Francisco: W. H. Freeman and Co., 1969.

Harter, Carl L. "The 'Good Times' Cohort of the 1930's: Sometimes Less Means More (and More Means Less)." *PRB Report* 3 (April 1973): 1-4.

Heath, Roy. *The Reasonable Adventurer*. Pittsburgh: U. of Pittsburgh Press, 1964.

Henderson, Cathy, and Janet C. Plummer. *Adapting to Changes in the Characteristics of College-Age Youth*. Washington, D.C.: American Council on Education, 1978.

Herbers, John. "Changes in Society Holding Black Youth in Jobless Web." *The New York Times*, Mar. 11, 1979, p. 1.

Herman, Melvin; Stanley Sadofsky; and Bernard Rosenbert, eds. *Work, Youth, and Unemployment*. New York: Thomas Y. Crowell Co., 1968.

Hertzberg, Hazel W. "The Now Culture: Some Implications for Teacher Training Programs." *Social Education* 34 (1970): 271-79.

Hoogan, Jim. *Decadence: Radical Nostalgia, Narcissism, and Decline in the Seventies*. New York: William Morrow and Co., 1975.

House, James S., and William M. Mason. "Political Alienation in America." *American Sociological Review* 40 (1975): 123-47.

Human, Sidney. *Youth in Politics: Expectations and Realities.* New York and London: Basic Books, 1972.

Insel, Paul M., and Henry Clay Lindgren. *Too Close for Comfort: The Psychology of Crowding.* Englewood Cliffs, N.J.: Prentice-Hall, 1978.

Jaffe, Frederick S. "Low-Income Families: Fertility in 1971-1972." *Family Planning Perspectives* 6 (Spring 1974): 108-10.

Jarvik, Lissy F., ed. *Aging into the 21st Century: Middle-Agers Today.* New York: Gardner Press, 1978.

Johnson, Thomas A. "Cost of Black Joblessness Measured in Crime, Fear and Urban Decay." *The New York Times,* March 12, 1979, p. 1.

Johnston, Denis F. "The Aging of the Baby Boom Cohorts." *Statistical Reporter,* March 1976, pp. 161-65.

Joseph, Peter. *Good Times: An Oral History of America in the Nineteen Sixties.* New York: Charterhouse, 1973.

Kahn, Herman; William Brown; and Leon Martel. *The Next 200 Years: A Scenario for America and the World.* New York: William Morrow and Co., 1976.

Katzell, Raymond A., and Daniel Yankelovich. *Work, Productivity, and Job Satisfaction.* New York: Harcourt, Brace and Jovanovich, 1975.

Kellogg, Mary Alice. *Fast Track: The Super Achievers and How They Make It to Early Success, Status and Power.* New York: McGraw-Hill, 1978.

Keniston, Kenneth. *The Uncommitted: Alienated Youth in American Society.* New York: Harcourt, Brace, 1965.

——. *Young Radicals: Notes on Committed Youth.* New York: Harcourt, Brace and World, 1968.

——. *Youth and Dissent: The Rise of a New Opposition.* New York: Harcourt Brace Jovanovich, 1971.

——, and the Carnegie Council on Children. *All Our Children.* New York and London: Harcourt Brace Jovanovich, 1977.

Kenney, Carol Brock. "After Housing What? The Market for the 'At Home' Lifestyle." *Consumer Capsule* (Loeb Rhoades, Hornblower and Co.) 4, no. 1 (April 1978): 1-17.

——. "Demographic Model of Consumer Markets in the 1980's." *Consumer Capsule* (Loeb Rhoades, Hornblower and Co.) 4, no. 3 (October 1978): 1-52.

Keyfitz, Nathan. "Population Waves." In *Population Dynamics,* edited by T. N. E. Greville. New York and London: Academic Press, 1972.

Keynes, John M. "Some Economic Consequences of a Declining Population." *Eugenics Review* 29 (March 1937): 13-17.

Kiechel, Walter, III. "Two-Income Families Will Reshape the Consumer Markets." *Fortune,* March 10, 1980, pp. 110-20.

Kiser, C. V.; Wilson H. Grabill; and Arthur A. Campbell. *Trends and Variations in Fertility in the United States.* Cambridge, Mass.: Harvard University Press, 1968.

Klebba, A. Joan. "Homicide Trends in the United States, 1900-74." *Public Health Reports* 90 (May-June 1975): 195-204.

Klein, Joe. "Growing Old Absurd." *Rolling Stone,* June 30, 1977.

Knodel, John E. "Demographic Components of the Recent Recovery of Fertility in Selected Industrialized Countries." Ph.D. dissertation, Princeton University, 1965.

Kokinski, William Severini. "The Malling of America." New Times, May 1, 1978, pp. 30-50.

Kunen, James Simon. *The Strawberry Statement: Notes of a College Revolutionary.* New York: Random House, 1969.

Ladd, Everett Carll, Jr. "New Divisions in U.S. Politics." *Fortune,* March 26, 1979, pp. 88-96.

Lasch, Christopher. *The Culture of Narcissism: American Life in an Age of Diminishing Expectations.* New York: W. W. Norton and Co., 1978.

Lecht, Leonard. "The Labor Force Bulge Is Temporary." *Across the Board,* December 1977, pp. 15-28.

Lee, Ronald Demos. "Demographic Forecasting and the Easterlin Hypothesis." *Population and Development Review* 2 (September/December 1976): 459-68.

———. "The Formal Dynamics of Controlled Populations and the Echo, the Boom and the Bust." *Demography* 11 (November 1974): 563-85.

Leuchtenburg, William E. *A Troubled Feast: American Society Since 1945.* Boston: Little, Brown and Co., 1973.

Levinson, Daniel J. *The Seasons of a Man's Life.* New York: Alfred A. Knopf, 1978.

Lewis, Peter. *The Fifties.* New York: J. B. Lippincott, 1978.

Linden, Fabian. "From Here to 1985." *Across the Board,* June 1977, pp. 21-25.

———. "The Great Reshuffle of Spending Power." Part 1. *Across the Board,* November 1978, pp. 61-64.

———. "The Great Reshuffle of Spending Power." Part 2. *Across the Board,* December 1978, pp. 61-65.

Lindert, Peter H. "American Fertility Patterns Since the Civil War." Center for Demography and Ecology, University of Wisconsin, Madison, Working Paper 7-4-27, September 1974.

Lingeman, Richard T. *Don't You Know There's a War On?*

The American Home Front, 1941-1945. New York: G. P. Putnam's Sons, 1970.

Link, Arthur S., and William B. Catton. *American Epoch: A History of the United States Since the 1890's.* New York: Alfred A. Knopf, 1963.

Lofland, John. "The Youth Ghetto: A Perspective on the 'Cities of Youth' Around Our Large Universities." *Journal of Higher Education* 39 (1968): 126-39.

Lubell, Samuel. *The Hidden Crisis in American Politics.* New York: W. W. Norton and Co., 1970.

Lunde, Donald T. *Murder and Madness.* Stanford, Calif.: The Portable Stanford, 1975.

Lurie, Alison. *The War Between the Tates.* New York: Random House, 1974.

"The Lush Suburban Market." *Fortune,* November 1953, pp. 128-31, 230-37.

Mackey, Mary. *McCarthy's List.* Garden City, N.Y.: Doubleday and Co., 1979.

McPherson, Michael S. "The Demand for Higher Education." In *Public Policy and Higher Education,* edited by David W. Breneman and Chester E. Finn, Jr., pp. 143-93. Washington, D.C.: Brookings Institution, 1978.

Malcolm, Henry. *Generation of Narcissus.* Boston and Toronto: Little, Brown and Co., 1971.

Malthus, Thomas Robert. *Malthus: Population: The First Essay.* Ann Arbor: University of Michigan Press, Ann Arbor Paperbacks, 1959.

Manchester, William. *The Glory and the Dream: A Narrative History of America, 1932-1972.* Boston and Toronto: Little, Brown and Co., 1974.

Mander, Jerry. *Four Arguments for the Elimination of Television.* New York: William Morrow and Co., 1978.

Mannheim, Karl. "The Problem of Generations." In *The New Pilgrims: Youth Protest in Transition,* edited by Philip G. Altbach and Robert S. Laufer. New York: David McKay Co., pp. 99-138.

Masnick, George S., and Joseph A. McFalls, Jr. "Those Perplexing U.S. Fertility Swings: A New Perspective on a 20th Century Puzzle." *PRB Report,* November 1978. pp. 1-10.

Mason, Karen Oppenheim; John L. Czajka; and Sara Arber. "Changes in U.S. Women's Sex-Role Attitudes, 1964-1974." *American Sociological Review* 41 (August 1965): 573-96.

Mayer, Lawrence A. "It's a Bear Market for Babies, Too." *Fortune,* December 1974, pp. 134-37, 206-12.

———. "New Questions About the U.S. Population." *Fortune,* February 1971, pp. 80-85, 121-25.

———. "U.S. Population Growth: Would Slower Be Better?" *Fortune*, June 1970, pp. 80-83, 164-68.

———. "Why the U.S. Population Isn't Exploding." *Fortune*, April 1967, pp. 162-66, 186-92.

Maynard, Joyce. *Looking Back: A Chronicle of Growing Up Old in the Sixties*. Garden City, N.Y.: Doubleday and Co., 1973.

Mead, Margaret. *Culture and Commitment*. Garden City, N.Y.: Doubleday and Co./Natural History Press, 1970.

Medved, Michael, and David Wallechinsky. *What Really Happened to the Class of '65*. New York: Random House, 1976.

Michael, Robert T. "The Rise in Divorce Rates, 1960-1974: Age-Specific Components." *Demography* 15 (May 1978): 177-82.

Miles, Rufus E., Jr. *Awakening from the American Dream: The Social and Political Limits to Growth*. New York: Universe Books, 1976.

Miller, Jim, ed. *The Rolling Stone Illustrated History of Rock & Roll*. New York: Random House/Rolling Stone Press, 1976.

Moller, Herbert: "Youth as a Force in the Modern World." *Comparative Studies in Society and History* 10 (April 1968): pp. 237-60.

Monaco, James. *American Film Now*. New York: Oxford University Press, 1979.

———. *Media Culture*. New York: Dell Publishing Co., 1978.

Morrison, Peter A. "The Demographic Context of Educational Policy Planning." The Rand Paper Series P-5592. Santa Monica, Calif.: The Rand Corporation, 1976.

———. *Demographic Trends That Will Shape Future Housing Demand*. The Rand Paper Series P-5596. Santa Monica, Calif.: The Rand Corporation, 1978.

———. "Emerging Public Concerns Over U.S. Population Movements in an Era of Slowing Growth." In *The Economic Consequences of Slowing Population Growth*, edited by Thomas J. Espenshade and William J. Serow, pp. 225-46. New York: Academic Press, 1978.

———. *The Future Demographic Context of the Health Care Delivery System*. The Rand Publication Series: N-1347-NICHD. Santa Monica, Calif.: The Rand Corporation, 1979.

———. "Overview of Demographic Trends Shaping the Nation's Future." Testimony before the Joint Economic Committee, U.S. Congress, May 31, 1978. Santa Monica, Calif.: The Rand Corporation, 1978.

Morrow, Lance. "Wondering If Children Are Necessary." *4Time*, March 5, 1979, pp. 42-47.

Moskos, Charles C., Jr. *The American Enlisted Man: The*

Rank and File in Today's Military. New York: Russell Sage Foundation, 1970.

Munnell, Alicia H. *The Future of Social Security*. Washington, D.C.: The Brookings Institution, 1977.

Myrdal, Gunnar. "The Transfer of Technology to Underdeveloped Countries." *Scientific American*, September 1974, pp. 172-82.

National Academy of Sciences. *Rapid Population Growth: Consequences and Policy Implications*. Baltimore: Johns Hopkins Press, 1971.

Neugarten, Bernice L. "The Future and the Young-Old." *The Gerontologist*, February 1975 (Supplement), pp. 4-9.

Newspaper Advertising Bureau. *Movie-Going in the Metropolis*. New York: June 1978.

Nie, Norman H.; Sidney Verba; and John R. Petrocik. *The Changing American Voter*. Cambridge, Mass., and London: Harvard University Press, 1976.

Nordberg, Olivia Schieffelin. "Reproductive Behavior of the American Birth Cohort of 1911-20." Ph.D. dissertation, Princeton University, 1975.

Norton, Arthur J. "Forecasting Households." *American Demographics*, March 1979, p. 23.

———, and Paul C. Glick. "What's Happening to Households." *American Demographics*, March 1979, pp. 19-22.

Notestein, Frank W. "The Facts of Life." *Atlantic Monthly*, June 1946, pp. 75-83.

———. "The Population in the World in the Year 2000." *Journal of the American Statistical Association* 45 (1950): 335-49.

Obst, Lynda Rosen, ed. *The Sixties: The Decade Remembered Now, by the People Who Lived It Then*. New York: Random House/Rolling Stone Press, 1977.

Olson, Sidney. "The Boom." *Fortune*, June 1946; reprinted in *Fortune*, February 11, 1980, p. 109.

O'Neill, William L., ed. *American Society Since 1945*. Chicago: Quadrangle Books, 1969.

Oppenheimer, Valerie Kincade. "Demographic Influences on Female Employment and the Status of Women." *American Journal of Sociology* 78 (1973): 946-61.

———. "The Easterlin Hypothesis: Another Aspect of the Echo to Consider." *Population and Development Review* 2 (September/December 1976): 433-55.

———. *The Female Labor Force in the United States: Demographic and Economic Factors Governing Its Growth and Changing Composition*. Berkeley: University of California, 1969.

Ostfield, Adrian M., and Don C. Gibson, eds. *Epidemiology of Aging*. Bethesda, Md.: Public Health Service, 1975.

"The Over-the-Thrill Crowd." *Time*, May 28, 1979, p. 39.

Packard, Vance. *A Nation of Strangers*. New York: David McKay Co., 1972.

Parrington, Vernon Louis. *Main Currents in American Thought: An Interpretation of American Literature from the Beginnings to 1920*. New York: Harcourt, Brace, 1930.

Patrick, Robert. *Kennedy's Children*. New York: Samuel French, 1976.

Pauly, David. "Crime in the Suites: On the Rise." *Newsweek*, December 3, 1979, pp. 114-21.

Peck, Ellen, and Judith Senderowitz, eds. *Pronatalism: The Myth of Mom and Apple Pie*. New York: Thomas Y. Crowell Co., 1974.

"Perils of the Productivity Sag." *Time*, February 5, 1979, pp. 126-27.

Peterson, William. *The Politics of Population*. New York: Doubleday and Co., 1964.

———. *Population*. New York: Macmillan, 1975.

Phillips, John Aristotle, and David Michaelis. *Mushroom: The Story of the A-Bomb Kid*. New York: William Morrow and Co., 1978.

Playboy Enterprises. *The Playboy Report on American Men*. Poll conducted by Louis Harris and Associates. Chicago, 1979.

"Population Changes That Help for a While." *Business Week*, September 3, 1979, pp. 180-87.

"The Population Is Soaring." *Fortune*, August 1953, p. 100.

Preston, Samuel H., and John McDonald. "The Incidence of Divorce Within Cohorts of American Marriages Contracted Since the Civil War." *Demography* 16 (February 1979): 1-25.

"Preview of the Postwar Generation." *Fortune*, March 1943, p. 116.

Princeton University Class of 1969. *Tenth Reunion Book*. Princeton, N.J.: 1979.

Pye, Michael, and Lynda Myles. *The Movie Brats*. New York: Holt, Rinehart and Winston, 1979.

Quinn, Jane Bryant. "Baby-Boom Economics." *Newsweek*, June 18, 1979, p. 70.

Rapson, Richard L., ed. *The Cult of Youth in Middle-Class America*. Lexington, Mass., Toronto, and London: D.C. Heath and Co., 1971.

Reich, Charles A. *The Greening of America*. New York: Random House, 1970.

Revelle, Roger. "Food and Population." *Scientific American*, September 1974, pp. 160-70.

Richards, James J., Jr. "Some Psycho-Social Consequences

of a Change to a Replacement Birthrate in the U.S." *Journal of Applied Psychology* 59 (1974): 1-8.

Riesman, David, with Nathan Glazer and Reuel Denny. *The Lonely Crowd*. Abridged edition with a 1969 preface. New Haven, Conn., and London: Yale University Press, 1976.

Rindfuss, Ronald R., and James A. Sweet. *Postwar Fertility Trends and Differentials in the United States*. New York, San Francisco, and London: Academic Press, 1977.

Rollin, Betty. "Motherhood: Need or Myth?" In *Pronatalism: The Myth of Mom and Apple Pie*, edited by Ellen Peck and Judith Senderowitz. New York: Thomas Y. Crowell Co., 1974.

Rosenberg, Harold. *The Tradition of the New*. New York: Horizon Press, 1959.

Ross, Douglas N., ed. *Population Trends and Implications*. New York: The Conference Board, 1977.

Ross, Heather, and Isabel V. Sawhill. *Time of Transition: The Growth of Families Headed by Women*. Washington: The Urban Institute, 1975.

Roszak, Theodore. *The Making of a Counter Culture*. Garden City, N.Y.: Doubleday, 1969.

Roxon, Lillian, *Rock Encyclopedia*. New York: Grosset & Dunlap, Tempo Books, 1976.

Ryder, Norman B. "The Cohort as a Concept in the Study of Social Change." *American Sociological Review* 30 (1965): 843-61.

——. "Components of Temporal Variations in American Fertility." A paper prepared for the Symposium on Recent Changes in Demographic Patterns in Developed Societies, January 6, 1978, at the Society for the Study of Human Biology, in London. Mimeographed.

——. "The Emergence of a Modern Fertility Pattern: United States, 1917-66. In *Fertility and Family Planning: A World View*, edited by S. J. Behrman; L. Corsa, Jr.; and R. Freedman, pp. 99-123. Ann Arbor: University of Michigan Press, 1969.

——. "The Family in Developed Countries." *Scientific American*, September 1974, pp. 123-32.

——. "The Future of American Fertility." *Social Problems* 26 (February 1979): 359-69.

——, and Charles F. Westoff. *Reproduction in the United States, 1965*. Princeton, N.J.: Princeton University Press, 1971.

——. "The United States: The Pill and the Birth Rate, 1960-1965." *Studies in Family Planning*, no. 20, June 1967.

Samuelson, Robert J. "Baby Boom Talk." *National Journal*, February 3, 1979, p. 191.

Sann, Paul. *Fads, Follies and Delusions of the American*

People. New York: Crown Publishers, Bonanza Books, 1967.

Scammon, Richard M., and Ben J. Wattenberg. *The Real Majority: An Extraordinary Examination of the American Electorate.* New York: Coward-McCann, 1970.

Seagull, Louis M. *Youth and Change in American Politics.* New York and London: New Viewpoints, 1977.

Sekscenski, Edward S. "Job Tenure Declines as Work Force Changes." *Monthly Labor Review,* December 1979, pp. 48-49.

Seligman, Daniel, and Lawrence A. Mayer. "The Future Population 'Mix.' " *Fortune,* February 1959, p. 94.

Seton, Cynthia Propper. *A Glorious Third.* New York: W. W. Norton and Co., 1979.

Shapiro, David, and Frank L. Mott. "Labor Supply Behavior of Prospective and New Mothers." *Demography* 16 (May 1979): 199-200.

Sheehy, Gail. *Predictable Crises of Adult Life.* New York: Bantam Paperback, 1977.

Sheldon, Eleanor Bernert, ed. *Family Economic Behavior: Problems and Prospects.* Philadelphia and Toronto: J. B. Lippincott, 1972.

Silberman, Charles E. *Criminal Violence, Criminal Justice.* New York: Random House, 1978.

Silver, M. "Births, Marriages, and Business Cycles in the United States." *Journal of Political Economy* 73 (June 1965): 237-55.

"Sixty-Six Million More Americans." *Fortune,* January 1954, p. 94.

Sklar, June, and Beth Berkov. "The American Birth Rate: Evidence of a Coming Rise." *Science* 189 (August 29, 1975), pp. 693-700.

Sklar, Robert. *Movie-Made America: A Cultural History of American Movies.* New York: Random House, Vintage Books, 1976.

Skolnick, Peter L.; Laura Torber; and Nikki Smith. *Fads: America's Crazes, Fevers, and Fancies from the 1890's to the 1970's.* New York: Thomas Y. Crowell Co., 1978.

Spengler, Joseph J. *Facing Zero Population Growth.* Durham, N.C.: Duke University Press, 1978.

Spock, Benjamin. *Raising Children in a Difficult Time.* New York: W. W. Norton and Co., 1974.

Starr, Paul. *The Discarded Army: Veterans After Vietnam. The Nader Report on Vietnam Veterans and the Veterans Administration.* New York: Charterhouse, 1973.

Sternlieb, George, and James W. Hughes. *Current Population Trends in the United States.* New Brunswick, N.J.: Rutgers Center for Urban Policy Research, 1978.

Stewart, George R. *American Given Names.* New York:

Oxford University Press, 1979.

Stewart, Ian R., and Donald G. Dicason. "Higher Education Faces Hard Times Ahead." *American Demographics,* June 1979, pp. 12-23.

Stockwell, Edward G. *Population and People.* Chicago: Quadrangle Books, 1968..

Sweet, James A. "Differentials in the Rate of Fertility Decline: 1960-1970." *Family Planning Perspectives* 6 (Spring 1974): 103-107.

Sweetser, Frank L., and Paavo Piepponen. "Postwar Fertility Trends and Their Consequences in Finland and the United States." *Journal of Social History* 1 (Winter 1967): 101-18.

Taeuber, Conrad, and Irene B. Taeuber. *The Changing Population of the United States.* New York: John Wiley and Sons, 1958.

Taeuber, Karl E., and James A. Sweet. "Family and Work: The Social Life Cycle of Women." In *Women and the American Economy,* edited by Juanita M. Kreps. Englewood Cliffs, N.J.: Prentice-Hall, 1976.

Tax, Sol, ed. *The Draft: Handbook of Facts and Alternatives.* Chicago: University of Chicago Press, 1967.

Teitelbaum, Michael S. "Fertility Effects of the Abolition of Legal Abortion in Romania." *Population Studies* 27 (November 1972): 405-17.

This Fabulous Century, 1950-1960. New York: Time-Life Books, 1970.

This Fabulous Century, 1960-1970. New York: Time-Life Books, 1970.

Thornton, Arland. "Fertility and Income, Consumption Aspirations, and Child Quality Standards." *Demography* 16 (May 1979): 157-75.

"Those Missing Babies." *Time,* September 16, 1974, pp. 54-63.

Tiger, Lionel. *Optimism: The Biology of Hope.* New York: Simon and Schuster, 1979.

Tilly, Louise A., and Joan W. Scott. *Women, Work, and Family.* New York: Holt, Rinehart and Winston, 1978.

Toffler, Alvin. *Future Shock.* New York: Bantam Books, 1974.

U.S. Commission on Population Growth and the American Future. *Demographic and Social Aspects of Population Growth.* Edited by Charles F. Westoff and Robert Parke, Jr. Commission Research Reports, vol. 1. Washington, D.C.: Government Printing Office, 1972.

———. *Economic Aspects of Population Change.* Edited by Elliott R. Morse and Ritchie H. Reed. Commission Research Reports, vol. 2. Washington, D.C.: Government Printing Office, 1972.

———. *Population and the American Future.* Report of Commission. Washington, D.C.: Government Printing Office, 1972.

——. *Population Distribution and Policy.* Edited by Sara Mills Mazie. Commission Research Reports, vol. 5. Washington, D.C.: Government Printing Office, 1972.

U.S. Congress, Joint Economic Committee. 1979 Economic Report of the President, Together with the Annual Report of the Council of Economic Advisers. Washington, D.C.: U.S. Government Printing Office, 1979.

U.S. Congress, House, Joint Hearing before the Select Committee on Population and the Select Committee on Aging. *Consequences of Changing U.S. Population: Demographics of Aging.* Vol. 1 95th Congress, 2nd Sess., May 24, 1978. Washington, D.C.: Government Printing Office, 1978.

U.S. Congress, House, Hearings before the Select Committee on Population, *Consequences of Changing U.S. Population: Baby Boom and Bust.* Vol. 2. 95th Congress, 2nd Sess., May 23, 25, and June 1, 2, 1978. Washington, D.C.: Government Printing Office, 1978.

——. *Consequences of Changing U.S. Population: Population Movement and Planning.* Vol. 3. 95th Congress, 2nd Sess., June 6, 7, 8, 1978. Washington, D.C.: Government Printing Office, 1978.

——.Report prepared by the Select Committee on Population. *Domestic Consequences of U.S. Population Change.* 95th Congress, 2nd Sess., Washington D.C.: Government Printing Office, 1978.

U.S. Congressional Budget Office. *Youth Unemployment: The Outlook and Some Policy Strategies.* Washington, D.C.: Government Printing Office, 1978.

U.S. Department of Commerce, Bureau of the Census. "Divorce, Child Custody, and Child Support." *Current Population Reports,* Series P-23, No. 84, June 1979.

——. "Estimates of the Population of the United States by Age, Sex, and Race: 1970 to 1977." *Current Population Reports,* Series P-25, No. 721, April 1978.

——. "Estimates of the Population of the United States by Age, Sex, and Race: 1976 to 1979." *Current Population Reports,* Series P.25, No. 870, January 1980.

——. "Fertility of American Women: June 1978." *Current Population Reports,* Series P. 20, No. 341, October 1979.

——. "The Geographical Mobility of Americans: An International Comparison." *Current Population Reports,* Series P-23, No. 64, Updated, 1976.

——. "Household and Family Characteristics: March 1978." *Current Population Reports,* Series P-20, No. 340, July 1979.

——. "Households and Families by Type: March 1979 (Advance Report)." *Current Population Reports*, Series P-20, No. 345, October 1979.

——. "Illustrative Projections of State Populations by Age, Race, and Sex: 1975 to 2000." *Current Population Reports*, P-25, No. 796, March 1979.

——. "Marital Status and Living Arrangements: March 1979." *Current Population Reports*, Series P-20, No. 349, February 1980.

——. *People of the United States in the 20th Century*, by Irene B. Taeuber and Conrad Taeuber (a Census Monograph). Washington, D.C.: Government Printing Office, 1971.

——. "Population Profile of the United States: 1978." *Current Population Reports*, Series P-20, No. 336, April 1979.

——. "Projections of the Number of Households and Families: 1979 to 1995." *Current Population Reports*, Series P-25, No. 805, May 1979.

——. "Projections of the Population of the United States: 1977 to 2050." *Current Population Reports*, Series P-25, No. 704, July 1977.

——. "Reasons for Interstate Migration: Jobs, Retirement, Climate, and Other Influences." *Current Population Reports*, Series P-23, No. 81, March 1979.

——. "School Enrollment—Social and Economic Characteristics of Students: October 1978." *Current Population Reports*, Series P-20, No. 346, October 1979.

——. "Social and Economic Characteristics of the Older Population: 1978." *Current Population Reports*, P-23, No. 85, August 1979.

——. *Social Indicators*, 1976. Washington, D.C.: Government Printing Office, 1977.

——. *Statistical Abstract of the United States, 1978*. Washington, D.C.: Government Printing Office, 1978.

——. "Voting and Registration in the Election of November 1978." *Current Population Reports*, Series P-20, No. 344, September 1979.

U.S. Department of Health, Education, and Welfare. *Health, United States, 1978*. Washington, D.C.: Government Printing Office, 1978.

——. *Healthy People: The Surgeon General's Report on Health Promotion and Disease Prevention*. Washington: D.C.: Government Printing Office, 1979.

——. *Smoking and Health: A Report of the Surgeon General*. Washington, D.C.: Government Printing Office, 1979.

——. "What Research Shows About Birth Order, Personality, and IQ." *Science Reports* (National Institute of Mental Health). DHEW (PHS) Publication No. (ADM) 78-638.

——. National Academy of Education. *Prejudice and Pride:*

The 'Brown' Decision After Twenty-five Years. Washington, D.C.: 1979.

——. National Center for Educational Statistics. *Projections of Educational Statisics to 1986-87*. Washington, D.C.: Government Printing Office, 1978.

——. National Center for Health Statistics. *Facts of Life and Death*. Washington, D.C.: Government Printing Office, 1978.

——. *Fertility Tables for Birth Cohorts by Color: United States, 1917-73*. Washington, D.C.: Government Printing Office, 1976.

——. Public Health Service. *Vital Statistics Report: Final Mortality Statistics, 1977*. Washington, D.C.: Government Printing Office, 1979.

U.S. Executive Branch. *The Budget of the United States Government, Fiscal Year 1981*. Washington, D.C.: Government Printing Office, 1980.

——. "Population Change and Long-Range Effects on the Budget." In *The Budget for Fiscal Year 1980*, pp. 52-57. Washington, D.C.: Government Printing Office, 1979.

U.S. National Commission for Manpower Policy. *Women's Changing Roles at Home and on the Job*. Special Report No. 26, September 1978.

U.S. President's Commission on Mental Health. *Report of the President's Commission on Mental Health, 1978*. Washington, D.C.: Government Printing Office, 1978.

——. *Appendix, Task Force Reports*. Vol. 3. Washington, D.C.: Government Printing Office, 1978.

Updike, John. *Problems and Other Stories*. New York: Alfred A. Knopf, 1979.

Vaillant, George E. *Adaptation to Life*. Boston and Toronto: Little, Brown and Co., 1977.

Van Gennep, Arnold. *The Rites of Passage*. Chicago: University of Chicago Press, 1960.

Veblen, Thorstein. *Theory of the Leisure Class*. New York: Random House, Modern Library, 1934.

Waldron, Ingrid, and Joseph Eyer. "Socio-economic Causes of the Recent Rise in Death Rates for the 15-24-Year-Olds." *Social Science and Medicine* 9 (July 1975): 383-96.

Ward, Michael P., and William P. Butz. "Completed Fertility and Its Timing: An Economic Analysis of U.S. Experience Since World War II." Report No. R-2285-NICHD. Santa Monica, Calif.: The Rand Corporation, April 1978.

Warner Communications. *The Prerecorded Music Market: An Industry Survey*. New York: 1979.

Wattenberg, Ben J. *The Demography of the 1970s: The Birth Dearth and What It Means*. New York: Family Circle, 1971.

——. *In Search of the Real America: A Challenge to the*

Chaos of Failure and Guilt. New York: Doubleday and Co., 1976.

Welch, Finis. "Effects of Cohort Size on Earnings: The Baby Boom Babies' Financial Bust." *Journal of Political Economy* 87 (1979): S65-S95.

Weller, Michael. *Loose Ends*. Working script. New York: Howard Rosenstone & Co., 1979.

Moonchildren. New York: Samuel French, 1971.

Westoff, Charles F. "Baby Boom Critic: Theory a Bust." *The Wharton Magazine*, Fall 1979, p. 67.

——. "The Decline of Fertility." *American Demographics*, February 1979, pp. 16-19.

——. "The Decline of Unplanned Births in the United States." *Science* 191 (9 January 1976): 38-41.

——. "Marriage and Fertility in the Developed Countries." *Scientific American*, December 1978, pp. 35-41.

——. "The Populations of the Developed Countries." *Scientific American*, September 1974, pp. 109-120.

——. "Some Speculations on the Future of Marriage and Fertility." *Family Planning Perspectives* 10 (March/April 1978): 79-83.

——, and Elise F. Jones. "The End of 'Catholic' Fertility." *Demography* 16 (1979): p. 209+.

——, et al. *Toward the End of Growth: Population in America*. Englewood Cliffs, N.J.: Prentice-Hall, 1973.

Westoff, Leslie Aldridge. "Princeton's Career Women." *Princeton Alumni Weekly*, June 5, 1978, pp. 33-38.

——, and Charles F. Westoff. *From Now to Zero: Fertility, Contraception and Abortion in America*. Boston and Toronto: Little, Brown and Co., 1971.

Wheeler, Thomas C. "The American Way of Testing." *The New York Times Magazine*, September 2, 1979, pp. 40-42.

Whyte, William H., Jr. *The Organization Man*. Garden City and New York: Doubleday and Co., Anchor Books, 1957.

Williams, Gregory. "The Changing U.S. Labor Force and Occupational Differentiation by Sex." *Demography* 16 (February 1979): 73-87.

Winn, Marie. *The Plug-In Drug*. New York: Viking Press, 1971.

Wohl, Robert. *The Generation of 1914*. Cambridge, Mass.: Harvard University Press, 1979.

Wolfe, Tom. "The 'Me' Decade and the Third Great Awakening." *New York* magazine, August 23, 1976, pp. 26-40.

Wolfgang, Marvin E. "Real and Perceived Changes of Crime and Punishment." *Daedalus* 107 (Winter 1978): 143-57.

"Women at Work." Series in *The Wall Street Journal*: 28, 31 August 1978: 5, 8, 13, 15, 19, 22 September 1978.

Wynne, Edward A. "Why Do We Expect Too Much?" *The*

Wall Street Journal, October 4, 1979.

Yankelovich, Daniel. *The Changing Values on Campus: Political and Personal Attitudes of Today's College Students.* New York: Washington Square Press, 1972.

——. *The New Morality: A Profile of American Youth in the 70's.* New York: McGraw-Hill, 1974.

——. "Work, Values, and the New Breed." In *Work in America: The Decade Ahead,* edited by Clark Kerr and Jerome Rosow. New York: Van Nostrand Reinhold Company, 1979.

Youth in Turmoil. Adapted from a special issue of *Fortune.* New York: Time-Life Books, 1969.

Youth: Transition to Adulthood. Report of the Panel on Youth of the President's Science Advisory Committee. Chicago and London: University of Chicago Press, 1974.

Zajonc, R. B. "Family Configuration and Intelligence." *Science,* April 16, 1976, pp. 227-35.

Zalaznick, Sheldon. "The Youthquake in Pop Culture." *Fortune,* January 1969, p. 84.

INDEX

439

440

441

449

451

Learn to live with somebody... *yourself.*

16   G-10